DEMYSTIFYING MEANINGFUL COINCIDENCES (SYNCHRONICITIES)

DEMYSTIFYING MEANINGFUL COINCIDENCES (SYNCHRONICITIES)

The Evolving Self, the Personal Unconscious, and the Creative Process

Gibbs A. Williams, PhD

JASON ARONSON
Lanham • Boulder • New York • Toronto • Plymouth, UK

Published by Jason Aronson
An imprint of Rowman & Littlefield Publishers, Inc.
A wholly owned subsidiary of The Rowman & Littlefield Publishing Group, Inc.
4501 Forbes Boulevard, Suite 200, Lanham, Maryland 20706
http://www.rowmanlittlefield.com

Estover Road, Plymouth PL6 7PY, United Kingdom

British Library Cataloguing in Publication Information Available

Library of Congress Cataloging-in-Publication Data
Williams, Gibbs A., 1937–
Demystifying meaningful coincidences (synchronicities) : the evolving self, the personal unconscious, and the creative process / Gibbs A. Williams.
p. cm.
Includes bibliographical references and index.
ISBN 978-0-7657-0702-4 (cloth : alk. paper)—ISBN 978-0-7657-0704-8 (electronic)
1. Coincidence. I. Title.
BF1175.W55 2010
150.19'5—dc22

2009039860

∞™ The paper used in this publication meets the minimum requirements of American National Standard for Information Sciences—Permanence of Paper for Printed Library Materials, ANSI/NISO Z39.48-1992.

Printed in the United States of America

Contents

Acknowledgments and Credits

A very special thanks to my wife, Christine, my psychoanalyst Rudolf Wittenberg, Gertrude Schmeidler, Monty Ullman, Julie Eisenbud, Robert Langs Meryl Johnson, and Jerome Siller—all of whom challenged and encouraged me to take my ideas seriously. Gratitude to my children Caitlyn, Michael, and Brie who for decades have tolerated my obsession. Thank you to my mother-in-law who has been a constant encourager.

I wish to pay tribute to those good and wise souls who collectively make up the collective consciousness without whose recorded experience I could never have conceptualized this book. Included in this list are the great speculative philosophers such as Plato, Aristotle, Spinoza, and Schopenhauer; the pragmatists: John Dewey, C. I. Lewis, and William James; the pioneering psychologists such as Sigmund Freud, Paul Federn, Carl G. Jung, Andre Spitz, Helene Deutsch, Robert Waelder, Harry Guntrip, and Dionald Winnicott; life-defining authors including: George Devereux, Hermann Hesse, Colin Wilson, Philip Phenix, Will Durant; inspirational teachers from Miami Beach High School including: Thyra Reaben, Elvin Albaum, and Edna Luck; Professor Zito, Professor Lionel Trilling, Professor Sydney Morgenbesser, Professor Frankel from Columbia University; teachers and supervisors contributing to my training as a psychoanalyst: including Frank Lachmann, Dr. Benjamin Wolstein, and Helen Block Lewis; introducers into the world of the esoteric occult: Dr. Larry Helfer, Reverend Bias, Sophie, Diane, Mason, Don Conte, Carole and Ray Rochlin, and Agatha.

A special appreciation to Julie Kirsch, editorial director of Lexington Books, who liked my ideas well enough to offer me a contract. For their constant and most helpful attention to detail and unflagging support a special thanks to Dan Zukowski, Madelyn Lorber, along with, Rita, Harold Hegelen, Budd Hopkins, and my brother Herb. And finally I am indebted to C, D, and G and all my other patients who shared their meaningful coincidences enabling us to begin to scientifically study the nature and use of these fascinating and challenging occurrences.

Preface

Imagine you are attending a one trick magic show. As the performance ends you find yourself in a state of awe. "Now that you are dazzled," says the magician, "I'll either repeat the trick as often as you like, or I'll show you how it's done." The choice is yours.

IN RECENT YEARS there has been an exploding interest in the topic of meaningful coincidences, often referred to as synchronicities (a term coined by Jung). Since the publication of Jung and Pauli's seminal work on this topic: *The Interpretation of Nature and the Psyche (1955)*,[1] the Jungian perspective has had an almost complete monopoly with respect to the theoretical, interpretive, psychological, scientific, philosophical, occult, and spiritual implications concerning the nature and use of meaningful coincidences.

Synchronicities are associated with significant psychological change—transformation, transcendence, and an expansion of consciousness—occurring in sudden, unexpected, dramatically impactful ways. In this connection they involve the whole self both in terms of being and becoming. They are also associated with primary motivators including trust, hope, faith, intentionality, and persistence.

Jung and his followers emphasize the fact that most people initially experience meaningful coincidences in a state of awe, inducing a strong belief that they contain a coded message derived from some assumed mysterious "spiritual" source transcending ordinary reality. These "messages" are believed to contain valuable information for the purpose of guiding individuals as they evolve spiritually during each person's lifetime. Further, these messages are thought to be intuitively received—passively channeled—bypassing the conventional active process of generating meaningful cause and effect connections.

Whereas all synchronicities are different, at the same time they have a common structure. This structure consists of two halves: (1) a subjective inner reality event (A) and (2) an objective outer reality event A' apparently uncaused but clearly connected by a felt sense of meaningfulness. It is this issue of rationally accounting for the nature of the nexus—that is the principle utilized to explain the nature of the connection between A and A'—that has—up to now—challenged and stumped investigators of these odd occurrences.

Central in his formulation about the nature of synchronicities is Jung's elimination of conventional causality as an adequate explanatory principle. In so doing Jung is left with a two part "explanation" as to the process leading to the production of synchronistic events. This two part "explanation" is partly psychological and partly super or trans-natural. In so doing Jung challenges the primary assumption of conventional scientific causality, that is, that knowledge of external reality obeys knowable laws of cause and effect (psychic determinism). Convinced that synchronistic events are rationally inexplicable, Jung (1955) provocatively concludes: "I doubt whether an exclusively psychological approach can do justice to the phenomena in question."[2] His challenging conclusion is a direct attack on Freud's exclusively naturalistic theory of mind.

Jung's anti rational conclusion is particularly striking in view of the fact that until their dramatic break in 1912 he was Freud's heir apparent. Even more striking is the rarely discussed fact that their breakup had its beginnings in the context of a shared synchronicity in Freud's study in 1909.[3] Although initially deeply impressed by this mysterious event Freud later found a rational cause and effect explanation for that which Jung believed transcended reason. Alarmed by Jung's immersion in the occult, Freud warned him not to get caught in the tide of "the black mud of occultism."[4] Jung, on the other hand, offended by Freud's criticism, was convinced that the occult offered mankind a way to connect with transcendent spirituality, for him, a necessary task to experience a fulfilled life.

Adamantly convinced in their rightness of their respective positions, these two titans sparked a theoretical (and personal) impasse. While Freud judged that Jung was losing his ability to think clearly, Jung judged Freud to be hyper rational. Note the explicit war of ideas between Jung—the advocate of faith versus Freud—the advocate of reason. Their de-facto war of ideas concerning the nature of synchronicities resurrected a philosophical dispute of long standing beginning with the arguments and counter arguments between Plato and Aristotle debating their differences as to the nature of reality and how we best attain and sustain true knowledge of it.

Their seemingly unbridgeable impasse led to a permanent rupture. The break with Freud also initiated a break down in Jung expressed as a "creative illness"[5] resulting in the formulation of his original theory of "analytic therapy." Central in the construction of his new theory was his lifelong preoccupation with the nature and use of meaningful coincidences.

Emerging from his illness, Jung was certain that he was on "the right path"—a path strewn with experiences of remarkable coincidences. Freud too was highly interested in these perplexing events but differed with Jung as to how to best account for them. Whereas Jung insisted that there must be a "spiritual" component transcending pure reason, Freud equally insisted that psychodynamic understanding alone should ultimately provide a rational explanation. Counter attacking, Freud (1933) issued a simple but forceful, and, until now, unanswered question (undoubtedly directed towards Jung): Are the assertions of the occultists accurate?[6]

Taking up Freud's challenge, this book explores the nature of meaningful coincidences (synchronicities) and their practical use from an original, naturalistic, non supernatural, non Jungian perspective. My work is the outgrowth of forty years of research utilizing material derived from my thirty seven year journal and from the detailed session notes of some synchronicity prone patients in my psychoanalytic practice. My perspective gives these perplexing events—receiving relatively scant attention in the academic literature—fresh theoretical understanding and practical tools for decoding them for more effective self enhancement.

During this time I have gone through three distinct phases with respect to my experience of, reactions to, theories about, preoccupations with, and conclusions reached concerning synchronicities. Initially awed by what I refer to as my "*Lazarus Rising*" synchronicity I was unknowingly a de facto Jungian. If I had not changed so radically over my forty year study of this subject, remaining in the same state of "Jungian" consciousness as I was initially, I would never have written this book.

Before, and at the beginning of my psychoanalysis, I had a largely Jungian take on synchronicities, meaning I was preoccupied with thoughts, fantasies, and theories, concerning the possibility (wish?) that I was actually connected to a transcendent divinity receiving coded messages from an intelligent "spiritual source." I was consumed with issues having to do with what I call at- onement consciousness. Thus I was preoccupied with concepts and experiences associated with merging, a desire for unity, unconditional acceptance, peace, love, avoidance of conflict, questing for perfection, and actively searching for absolute answers to ultimate questions. These questions included: Who am I and what do I really want, what is my life's purpose and how do I access it. I compulsively looked to the outside for answers believing that this was the only location in which they might eventually be found. I actively sought out signs that divinity was real and concerned about my personal welfare. I entertained a partially conscious and partially unconscious wish to be saved.

Phase two coincided with the first few years of my psychoanalysis when I experienced a shift from an over reliance on passive intuition to active skepticism, a more Freudian approach in understanding myself. This shift occurred in the context of my developing an increasing capacity to think critically. Critical thinking enabled me to search for answers to my big questions by analyzing my psyche—returning to my developmental origins rather than seeking them via attempts to transcend my earthly experience reaching towards an assumed realm of absolute meaning. A significant attitudinal shift focused my search for the truth to realized knowledge gained from my personal struggles rather than passively waiting for revealed knowledge from some transcendent source of divinity characterized as "except ye see signs and wonders, ye will not believe."[7]

I would characterize the sweep of my changing consciousness from one that was initially "relatively reactive" to one which became "relatively reflective" as I made a slow but steady progression in growing a self-structure. In my attempts to objectify my own subjective experience, I found meaningful coincidences making seemingly important but mysterious contributions in my dedicated identity questing.

Bair (2003), quoting Jung, said: "synchronicity has been in existence since the beginning of time, but it has no unifying origin, only appears sporadically, and does not progress logically. In other words, nothing comes about because of any one thing; nor does one thing lead directly to any other."[8] My investigation of these challenging phenomena demonstrates that there is in fact a remarkable experiential logic totally responsible for at least the kinds of synchronicities referred to in this book.

In this connection, finding myself unwilling to accept Jung's dismissal of causality as "unthinkable" as an explanation of these events, I set out to study them scientifically. Aiding in this effort I was particularly impressed by Kuhn's (1962) ground breaking monograph: "*The Structure of Scientific Revolutions*" who states: "Discovery commences with the awareness of anomalies, that is, with the recognition that nature has somehow violated the paradigm—induced expectations that govern normal science."[9] Observing that synchronicities fit Kuhn's criteria to a tee, I have found it fruitful to classify a synchronicity as a scientific anomaly.

At this time I became interested in researching the psychodynamics of meaningful coincidences from a Freudian perspective. So, for example: I systematically began probing the primary assumptions and core organizing concepts associated with these odd occurrences hoping to find some hypothesized order associated with the production of these anomalous events. For example, while it is obvious that all synchronicities are different, it became clear that they all have a common structure. Further, as I had kept copious notes in my journal, I noted that when analyzed, synchronicities were seen to be embedded in specific situational and psychological contexts. In other words, knowing the contexts from which synchronicities spring, they could be studied scientifically—an impossible task according to Jung.

The third phase began near the end of my treatment which was associated with my discovery of the British School of Psychiatry namely, Guntrip and Winnicott.[10] These new concepts led to a major reorientation of my views about meaningful coincidences. Now, I thought of them as transitional experiences that signaled major markers in my attempts to gain (a) a solid identity, and (b) expanding consciousness. I became increasingly aware of the power of the creative possibilities of my own and others' personal unconscious as a much more grounded guide than the vaguer symbolic guide of the collective unconscious stimulating archetypal images. I began to investigate the possibilities of two different logics (linear and durational) as a normal process in all humans; and, when viewed as overlapping (experiential logic) becoming fertile territory for the birth of these odd experiences. Since that time (4th phase), I have continued to explore and expand my ideas.

An immersion in the synchronicity literature indicates that the Jungian perspective raises more complicated questions than provides straight forward answers. Among these challenging questions are: if eliminating conventional causality as inadequate to explain the nature of meaningful coincidences is there an alternative conceptualization of causality that does adequately explain these occurrences? Are synchronicities created or discovered? What is the meaning of meaning? What is the relationship between causality and meaning? What is the meaning of spirituality?

With the self appointed task of researching these and other questions, armed with my increasing capacity to think critically, I began to look anew at the core organizing concepts associated with the Jungian understanding of synchronicities. Among these core concepts are conventional causality, meaning, meaning making, the transcendent function, a-causality, archetypal knowledge, the collective unconscious, and the likes.

Anticipating that the Freudians would deride his psychological/mystical/magical perspective, Jung formulated three anti-causal arguments. These are (1) The problem of rare and spontaneous events (an issue about method) (2) The Problem of Necessity and Relativity (an issue about meaning) and (3) A Problem of Simultaneity (an issue about time).[11] My discovery of these seminal anti-causal arguments crystallized the focus of my research. Thus the core of my understanding of synchronicities is largely my refutation and the ensuing implications of these three anti-causal arguments.

As my own consciousness has changed (evolved?) so too has my perspective concerning my reactions to, explanations of, and conclusions about the nature and function of the core organizing concepts used by Jung to formulate his perspective of these perplexing events. In this connection, rather than attempting to offer a definitive explanation for how inner and outer events mysteriously conjoin resulting in a synchronicity, I focus exclusively on the psychology of the observer to adequately explain this process.

Utilizing a method I call contextual analysis, my personal synchronicities, and the synchronicities gathered in treatment sessions, are seen to be the exclusive outcome of a knowable complex psychodynamic process which is analyzable, thus scientifically explainable. In so doing, the nearly all prevailing Jungian part natural and part super natural interpretation of meaningful coincidences is demystified.

People, in general, are hungry for pertinent information that meaningfully connects with the complexity of their unique experience. My approach is a blue print for identifying, interpreting, and utilizing the coded information associated with synchronicities in ways that are both person specific and practically useful. It might aptly be said that this book is a map for aiding individuals to identify their life's essential meanings, plus marking significant changes along their unique life's journey. Additionally this perspective identifies an intimate connection with "spirituality" in the sense of making a felt connection with one's idiosyncratic creative process. This operational definition of spirituality is characterized by its being grounded and immanent rather than transcendent and mystical.

Because of the hunger for grounded good guidance this book may open up an appreciation for naturalistic creative possibilities equally as wondrous to human beings as are messages purportedly channeled from "the other side," supposedly transmitted by angels, master teachers, and invisible archetypal influences.

An important implication of my work is that there is nothing mystical or divine about the origins of these anomalous events. While my analysis robs the "magic" associated with reacting to only the awe inspiring surface, it nevertheless affirms a wondrous appreciation for the creative capacities of each person to order his own internal and external chaos, potentially choosing to beam it in any direction he or she wishes.

I agree with Jung that these events are intimately connected to the unfolding of the self, but the self he is referring to is assumed already preformed but forgotten at birth, whereas my conceptualization of the self is, agreeing with Jacobson, (1964) (and other self theorists) initially an "undifferentiated matrix"[12] that gradually evolves as the developing child learns to impose order on the random raw data of his or her internal and external reality. In this perspective, rather than viewing the "messages" associated with synchronicities as passively received (channeled) from some transcendent "spiritual" source of absolute meaning derived from the collective unconscious, I view them, instead, as self generated messages, the byproduct of a person's idiosyncratic creative process whose origin is the personal unconscious, needing to be actively interpreted so to be able to fully utilize the rich information "hidden" in them.

A further result of my work is an expansion in understanding as to how human beings generate meaningful connections out of the seemingly random raw data of their individual and collective experiences whether synchronistic or not. In this connection, conventional scientific linear causality, relying exclusively on a play of ideas (linear logic), is expanded to include "messy" feelings, as well as the contribution made of such important but difficult to pin down mysterious "forces" including those of luck, chance, destiny, fate, karma, serendipity, and the likes. I call this hybrid logic "experiential" (synthetic) logic.[13]

This book is for all those people who are fascinated in trying to rationally understand the nature of these strange experiences. If they agree with my formulations, they will be helped to more fully appreciate the remarkable powers they have in jointly utilizing their conscious and personal unconscious for expanding their realistic powers of awareness. This expanded awareness is particularly useful in resolving fundamental problems with in-cohesive identities.

Thus these events may aptly be considered potentially rich material for an in-depth and in-breadth exploration of many patients' core concerns, particularly those initially complaining of severe identity problems. It should be noted for those who have already attained a cohesive self these events are useful in accessing, freeing up, and directing their energies to goal oriented objectives. One does not need to be a psychoanalytic patient to greatly benefit from the findings of my work. However, being a patient does afford both the therapist and the patient a rich concentrated mine of compact experience with which to scientifically investigate the nature and use of meaningful coincidences.

This book will appeal to professionals (psychotherapists, counselors, scientists, artists), who may find the examination of the organizing concepts of: reality, knowing, meaning, process of meaning making, space, time, simultaneity, unconscious (personal and collective), consciousness, consciousness of consciousness, self, cohesive self, levels of psychological development, structural theory, cathexis, transitional space, transitional phenomena, logic and logics, overlapping logics, causality, a causality, principles of quantum physics, and variants of causality and their interrelationships, stimulating and thought provoking with respect to adding additional perspectives concerning the popular issue of a new paradigm for understanding the nature of ourselves and our relationship to the object world.

This book is also directed to those who find themselves mired in their psychological complexity having thus far failed in their attempts to find satisfying answers outside themselves. Thus, this book offers hope for those who yearn for change but lack the encouragement and psychological know how for doing so.

This work is divided into four main sections, following an introduction; part I looks at theoretical perspectives and consists of chapters 2–4; part II deals with theory construction (chapters 5–8); part III presents a new theory (chapter 9); and part IV looks at practical applications (chapter 10).

After providing in the preface a rationale for writing yet another book on the nature and use of synchronicities, in chapter 1 I discuss the emotional power and intellectual challenge these perplexing phenomena present. In so doing I describe the phenomena, the associated awe response, and the implications of both, resulting in the efficacy of proposing an alternative naturalistic theory.

Chapter 2 details Jung's personal and professional interest in meaningful coincidences. I describe a life-defining confrontation in Freud's study in which Jung and Freud experienced a shared synchronicity, and recount Jung's most significant coincidence, known as the Scarab synchronicity, along with some important implications of this event. I also explore Jung's three anti-causal arguments to bolster his anti-rational account of synchronicities along with his provocative conclusion. Chapter 2 ends with an assertion that Jung's understanding of the nature of synchronicities raises more questions than provides absolute answers.

In chapter 3 I summarize Jung's three anti-causal arguments: (1) The problem of rare and spontaneous events; (2) the problem of necessity and relativity (meaning); and (3) the problem of simultaneity (time). Successfully refuting each of these anti causal arguments opens a pathway to constructing one or more naturalistic theories of synchronicities.

In chapter 4 I describe M. D. Faber's naturalistic regressive synchronicity theories, identifying it as a good first attempt to demystify these perplexing anomalous events.

Chapters 5 through 8 detail my vicissitudes on the way to constructing my own naturalistic theory of synchronicities. Chapter 5 describes my initial fascination and curiosity about the phenomena and the challenges they present.

Chapter 6 describes my de facto Jungian position as I became immersed in studying various aspects of the esoteric occult.

Chapter 7 describes the influences of a marked shift towards a more Freudian perspective in my attempts to understand the nature and uses of synchronicities. In this connection I applied my new organizing concepts in understanding the nature of nineteen personal synchronicities I amassed over the course of eleven years noted in my journal.

In Chapter 8 I describe my growing conviction that my findings repeatedly confirm the validity of my new naturalistic progressive synchronicity theory.

Chapter 9 is a formal account of my work entitled "A Theory and Use of Meaningful Coincidences."

Chapter 10 is an application of my new synchronicity theory in understanding the nature and use of some synchronicity prone patients receiving psychotherapy in my private practice. Additionally I summarize my findings, list and discuss some relevant observations, suggest a guideline for others to decode their own and/or their patient's synchronicities, and discuss my conclusions.

1

The Emotional Power and Intellectual Challenge of Synchronicities

"Every branch of physical science must consist of three things: the series of facts which are the objects of science, the ideas which represent these facts, and the words by which these facts are expressed. . . . And, as ideas are preserved and communicated by means of words, it necessarily follows that we cannot improve the language of any science without at the time improving the science itself; neither can we, on the other hand, improve a science without improving the language or nomenclature which belongs to it."

—Antoine Lavoisier, *Elements of Chemistry*

MEANINGFUL COINCIDENCES (SYNCHRONICITIES) are normally experienced as extraordinary events in the flow of time, contrasted with the more ordinary occurrences of mundane daily living. They are commonly referred to as small miracles, God's gift to human beings, coded messages from a transcendent realm of divinity, and the likes. Because they are normally felt to be emotionally powerful, while at the same time seemingly intellectually inexplicable, it is a subject that is increasingly compelling to growing numbers of inquisitive individuals.

I am relatively certain that the great majority of readers of this book would respond affirmatively if I were to ask them if they ever had what they considered to be an especially meaningful coincidence. Results of multiple surveys asking this question in workshops given on this subject resulted in a finding of approximately 95 percent of those reporting having had one or more synchronicities in their lives. To make sure we are focusing on the same material, what follows is one of the most striking coincidences I have ever heard. I call it the "Freddy Green" synchronicity.

An attractive, articulate, sensitive, middle-aged woman was engaged to be married in New York City on New Year's Eve. Her fiance, a musician, was scheduled to meet her after playing a gig. She was of course shocked beyond belief when he failed to show up at the agreed upon time. She was later mortified to find out that he had had a heart attack and died. Years later, this woman, who was then living in California, was rushed to a hospital suffering from a life threatening asthmatic attack. Gasping for breath she panicked. Feeling as alone, frightened, and vulnerable as she had ever felt in her life, she wished that her beloved Freddy Green had been both alive and with her. At the very moment she had this unexpected memory of her deceased fiancé of many years she heard an announcement over a loud speaker on a wall in her hospital room requesting: "Freddy! Please go to the green room." The woman was so startled and amazed by the profoundly meaningful six words she had just heard that she attributed her subsequent excitement to enabling her to breathe normally probably saving her life.

There are a number of responses one might have either in experiencing this type of occurrence from the inside out, as the receiver of such a coincidence, or, from the outside in, as an observer of these coincidental happenings. These responses range from simply "bathing," so to speak in the feelings of awe typically associated with these fascinating events, to analyzing how they happen and assessing what they mean.

One need only type the key words: coincidence, synchronicities, Jung, and psychotherapy into a search engine of a computer (accessing the internet) to obtain thousands of associated references. These references fall into one or more of the following five classifications: (l) describing the phenomena; (2) focusing on the typical emotional responses of awe and the uncanny (referred to as numinosity by Jung); (3) exploring philosophical, psychological, occult, spiritual, and scientific implications evoked by this "numinous" emotional response; (4) proposing and exploring alternative theoretical explanations to account for the production of these anomalous events; and (5) providing concepts utilized in the service of determining how best to decode the apparent embedded "messages" in the service of enhancing the quality of being and doing of the receiver of a given synchronicity.

Given the near avalanche of material on this subject, why, the reader might ask, is there a need for yet another book on the nature and use of meaningful coincidences (synchronicities). One might reasonably think that with so much material, the subject matter has been thoroughly explored. My answer—based on my lengthy investigation of these fascinating events—is that this is quite simply not true.

A careful examination of the accumulated research investigating meaningful coincidences indicates that most of it has been conducted by Jung, and his followers. I would estimate that the percentage of a Jungian (psychodynamic/supernatural) perspective to all others is approximately ninety five percent to five percent. As the reader may have surmised, a major objective of this book is to both understand how this impressive tilt came about and to attempt to redress this notable imbalance by presenting and exploring the key ideas comprising the five percent minority (naturalistic) point of view.

Historical Highlights

Whereas Jung is given credit for coining the term synchronicity to give special prominence to especially meaningful coincidences observed in his psychotherapy practice the phenomenon has been noted and researched for many hundreds of years, by independent investigators who have had a keen personal interest in this fascinating subject. Among them are Goethe, Leibnitz, Schopenhauer, Krammerer, Koestler, Freud, and Jung.

Schopenhauer, for example, has a particularly elegant description that captures the essence of the mysterious "logic" associated with these awe-inspiring occurrences. Schopenhauer (1850) wrote:

> Coincidence is the simultaneous occurrence of causally unconnected events . . . . If we visualize each causal chain progressing in time as a meridian on the globe, then we may represent simultaneous events by the parallel circles of latitude. . . .All the events in a man's life would accordingly stand in two fundamentally different kinds of connection: firstly, in the objective, causal connection of the natural process; secondly, in a subjective connection which exists only in relation to the individual who experiences it, and which is thus as subjective as his own dreams, whose unfolding content is necessarily determined, but in the manner in which the scenes in a play are determined by the poet's plot. That both kinds of connection exist simultaneously, and the self-same event, although a link in two totally different chains, nevertheless, falls into place in both, so that the fate of one individual invariably fits the face of the other, and each is the hero of his own drama while simultaneously figuring in a drama foreign to him—this is something that surpasses our powers of comprehension, and can only be conceived as possible by virtue of the most wonderful pre-established harmony. . . . It is a great dream dreamt by that single entity, the Will to Life: but in such a way that all his personae must participate in it. Thus everything is interrelated and mutually attuned.[1]

Long before I was aware of any one else's work on this topic, I chanced upon my own discovery of synchronicities in the context of a dedicated but illusive identity quest. Despairing from the results of an unsuccessful four-year psychotherapy experience (with a therapist with whom I was essentially not attuned) I was drawn like a heat seeking missile into the arcane world of the occult. I plunged into the literature of the esoteric occult including astrology, Qabalah, tarot, numerology, the mystics, Steiner, Regardie, Uspensky, and and the likes. Its appeal was strikingly powerful. Additionally I discovered the off-beat (for me) world of spiritualism.

A large part of the lure of the occult was based on the implications of its primary holistic assumption about the nature of reality and how one obtains knowledge from this assumed reality. The assumption is that there is an invisible (occult) primary unitary realm that is transcendent, conscious, and spiritualized. Knowledge of this transcendent realm of "absolute meaning" is assumed to be accessible by attending to signs, symbols, intuitions, feelings, and a process of seeking and studying correspondences.

A commonly used mantra among occultists captures the essence of this metaphysical perspective: "As Above, So Below."[2] In esoteric occult circles this deceptively brief formula is equivalent in its potential power as is Einstein's $E = MC^2$ is in conventional physics. The expanded version of this esoteric occult law is: "That which is Below corresponds to that which is Above, and that which is Above corresponds to that which is Below, in the accomplishment of the Miracle of One Thing. And just as all things have come from One, through the Mediation of One, so all things follow from this One Thing in the same way."[3] This means that on the earth plane (microcosm) "divided" individuals are potentially made whole by gaining direct and indisputable knowledge of this presumed primary transcendent reality (macrocosm). The nature of this pathway by which this meaningful connection is made is collectively known as the "sacred teachings," ancient wisdom, perennial knowledge, and so forth.

Specific knowledge gained from a connection to this realm of absolute knowledge is thought to reveal significant information for strengthening a given individual's identity (being) as well as in helping to harness his or her powers in directing them towards purposeful pursuits (doing). The esoteric occult is apparently the precursor of modern day self psychology.

I found this occult logic to be emotionally appealing in its promise of personal, sensible, meaningful connectedness, wrapped in a cloak of mystery, like the feeling children have when first learning how to transmit information using a secret code. In short, my dismal failure to attain targeted guidance on the earth plane in the form of effective psychotherapy was transferred to the hoped for possibility of attaining it on some yet to be contacted transcendental realm of spiritual reality.

The Phenomena, Awe Response, and Implications

Attending the first meeting of a spiritual consciousness-raising group I had the first of what I consider to be a series of nineteen especially meaningful coincidences recorded in my journal over a thirteen-year period. A description of the "Lazarus Rising" synchronicity follows.

Lazarus Rising: Synchronicity #1

The Contex

In my mid-twenties I discovered the First Spiritualist Church of New York. Besides my fascination in watching the blindfolded medium of the week reach into a hat in which were placed small pieces of folded paper (billets) on which were written questions asked by the faithful, addressed to those in spirit—sending "messages" presumably from those who had "gone over to the other side," master teachers, spirit guides and the likes, I was in awe of a number of sophisticated adherents who appeared totally dedicated to teachings of spiritualism.

Among them was a strikingly handsome and intelligent psychiatrist—L—who went into trance states claiming that the poetry he spontaneously spoke was channeled from Freud and Jung. He thought I might be interested in a group that was forming to learn more about how "spirit" reveals itself.

Although skeptical I open-mindedly agreed to attend a suggested spiritual consciousness-raising group (séance). Sitting in a circle of ten with the lights out, the medium (Agatha—a sweet little old highly energetic lady in her eighties) instructed us to describe anything we might see. Although joking around, much to my amazement, I instantly visualized a yellow light in my mind's eye surrounding the image of a grandmotherly face with granny glasses. I intuitively felt this grandmother image belonged to D, a friendly woman sitting next to me. D validated my ascription saying that indeed the glasses were an objective indicator that my "vision" belonged to her dead grandmother. Furthermore she added, not only did her grandmother wear such glasses when she was alive but they were carefully preserved by D having placed them on her mantle-piece. She asked me if I would like to come to her apartment to see them for myself.

Excited but skeptical I consciously mulled the idea of the possible actuality of divinity as really real, and if so, that its personal intercession as evidenced by my unexpected remarkable experience during the séance, might be evidence of its presence. I reasoned, for such occult events to be valid would mean that the conventional laws of cause and effect would be notably violated in attempting to explain such miraculous occurrences.

This profound idea flew in the face of my scientific training at Columbia College. But at this point in my life I was wide open to new possibilities in my consideration of the big issues of knowing the nature of reality and accessing knowledge of reality particularly, in view of the fact, that conventional science in the form of psychotherapy had failed me, or, as I wondered at the time, had I failed it?

Later that night, alone in my apartment, I was reading the New Testament in the hopes of receiving spiritual guidance. During the séance, I had been instructed that spiritual guidance would be forthcoming if (1) I formulated a specific "spiritual" question followed by (2) opening a bible at random noting the first words impressing my consciousness considering them to be the answer to my question in the form of a message assumed to be of divine origin.

The Coincidence

While consciously asking myself the question if miracles might in fact be really real, I opened the Bible and randomly turned to the story of Lazarus being raised from the dead. I was struck by the story's implications, reasoning that if the bible is the revelation of divinity communicated to mankind so that events like the rising of Lazarus might be literally true, then such phenomena as contacting "dead" spirits and personal spiritual guides at a séance, such as I had attended (initially judged to be as preposterous as it was seductive), might in fact be valid.

Excited, I called D to share my experience. Responding to my apparent revelation, excitement, and reflections, she exclaimed: "How uncanny!" for that very afternoon on a walk with L, her (unconventional) psychiatrist, told her that in a previous lifetime he had been present at the raising of Lazarus.

Upon hearing this amazing coincidental reference to the raising of Lazarus, being connected as it was to L, the remarkable psychiatrist; to D the unusually friendly woman; and the vision I saw at the extraordinary séance, I experienced an unexpected rush of awe combined with a felt sense of being in touch with an indefinable but highly significant shockingly good experience. (Jung would likely have named the sense of awe associated with this event as a numinosity.) Later I described my experience as being in touch with mysterious forces that, at that time, verified the possibility that so-called occult energies were apparently real and this meant that virtually anyone could access them at will.

I then experienced a heightened split between a wide open-side of me that desperately wanted to believe in the actuality of a transcendent spiritual realm that was a source of and accessible to potentially vital information concerning myself; versus, a skeptical cynical side of me that scoffed at such activities as highly stimulating but patently "unscientific" indulgences in the realm of the supernatural. I wondered if I was dangerously playing around in what Freud (1910) was cautioning Jung to be wary of; namely, "the black tide of mud . . . occultism?"[4]

Thus the attempt to satisfy both sides of me (the occult/spiritual voice and the philosophical/psychological/scientific voice) at first appeared to cancel each other out as seemingly mutually exclusive. But somehow, on this particular occasion, instead of succumbing to experiential paralysis: the emotional power combined with the intellectual challenge of this impressive first meaningful coincidence, made room for both pathways to be explored, not as a war in which I had to take sides but as a complex total experience to be understood in depth and breadth.

Soon after this experience, additional coincidences, equal to the power of the Lazarus Rising synchronicity, stimulated and reinforced a growing interest in my ongoing attempts to answer the question that Freud had raised in his own studies of the occult; namely, is what the occultists telling us true or not? My growing need to penetrate to the truth of the matter propelled me to immerse myself in the literature of meaningful coincidences. Arthur Koestler's short but comprehensive book called *The Roots of Coincidence* is a concise introduction to this complex subject.

Koestler (1972) identified the crux of synchronicities as: "a modern [derivative] of the archetypal belief in the fundamental unity of all things, transcending mechanical causality experienced as a 'symbiotic consciousness' or what Freud refers to as 'oceanic feeling.'"[5]

Acquaintance with the literature quickly established the fact that Jung and his adherents, have had a near monopoly with respect to the formal investigation of meaningful coincidences.

Jung's Depth Psychological/Supernatural Explanation

Jung observed that in his psychoanalytic practice he began noting that many of his patients spontaneously described coincidences which they found to be highly meaningful. Jung (1925?) was particularly impressed by a shared experience of a meaningful coincidence commonly referred to as the "scarab" synchronicity.

A young woman I was treating had, at a critical moment, a dream in which she was given a golden scarab. While she was telling me this dream I sat with my back to the closed window. Suddenly I heard a noise behind me, like a gentle tapping. I turned round and saw a flying insect knocking against the window-pane from outside. I opened the window and caught the creature in the air as it flew in. It was the nearest analogy to the golden scarab that one finds in our latitudes, a scarabaeid beetle, the common rose-chafer (*Cetoaia urata*) which contrary to its usual habits had evidently felt an urge to get into a dark room at this particular moment.[6]

Whereas the scarab coincidence had an apparent transforming effect on his patient "facilitating significant change" it had an undeniably profound effect on Jung as well, as he committed much of the rest of his life attempting to understand the nature, implications, and uses of synchronistic events.

Initially, as a dedicated Freudian analyst, Jung attempted to account for the production of synchronicities from the perspective of a scientist utilizing the methodology of Freudian psychodynamic depth psychology (psychoanalysis). Jung (1955) defined a synchronicity (meaningful coincidence) as "the simultaneous occurrence of two meaningfully but not causally connected events [wherein] an unexpected (mental) content (A) which directly or indirectly connected with some objective external event (A') coincides with the ordinary psychic state."[7]

However, while clearly meaningfully significant, underscored by a typical reported rush of awe, such occurrences as the scarab coincidence, apparently defy all attempts to understand their nature utilizing conventional cause and effect explanations. For example, looking closely at the details of the scarab coincidence, surely the patient's dream of the previous night did not create the scarab beetle to appear at the window-pane in the therapy office just at the moment she was discussing her dream with Jung. Nor is it reasonable to conjecture that the scarab beetle somehow caused the patient to dream about itself the night before the patient's next therapy session. Yet, at the same time there was no denying the impressive fact (both for Jung and his patient) that there were especially meaningful connections (associations) between the dream of the patient being handed a scarab, the scarab beetle at the window-pane, and Jung actually handing the scarab beetle to his patient.

Subsequent attempts by Jung and his followers to make rational sense of what appeared to be an irrational occurrence resulted in the same conclusion—that science (in the form of psychodynamics obeying laws of psychic determinism, i.e., causal analysis), can only go so far in understanding the nature of these anomalous events. At such points some other principle other than causality is apparently needed to fully "explain" the process leading to the production of these puzzling events.

The failure to link the subjective event A with the objective event A' by means of causality, yet remaining linked by meaningful connectedness (experienced as awesome and uncanny) had momentous implications for Jung. Jung (1955) clearly at odds with conventional psychoanalytic thinking, asserted: "I doubt whether an exclusively psychological approach can ever do justice to the phenomena in question."[8]

Upon acknowledging the seeming inability of rationality to account for the mystery of the linking principle, Jung (1955) completely eliminated conventional causality as an explanatory principle replacing it with his invention of the a-causal principle of synchronicity. This meant that by eliminating conventional causality as a means of explaining these anomalous phenomena, we are left with only "an equivalence of meaning" and "simultaneity" in describing synchronicities."[9]

In this connection, this exceedingly meaningful but seemingly un-caused event (the Scarab coincidence) led Jung (1955) to assert his radical, seductive, provocative, and challenging conclusion that with occurrences like this: "their 'inexplicability' is not due to the fact that their cause is unknown, but to the fact that a cause is not even thinkable in intellectual terms."[10] Thus, in one sentence Jung openly declared war on the Freudian bedrock assumption of psychic determinism—that, as a given effect follows from a cause in the physical world so too the same is assumed to hold true in the world of the psyche.

If Jung is right then nothing more need be said or if it is attempted then according to him nothing of particular value would be expected to have much added worth. However, early on in my pondering these odd events I noted that whereas all synchronicities differ from one another, at the same time, they all have a common structure.

Jung's Primary Assumption of a Supernatural Transcendent Reality

Jung's conclusion was radical enough but more was to follow. If psychology alone was unable to account for the production of a meaningful coincidence to where else could one look for its origin? Jung believed that the solution to the puzzle lay in the accompanying feelings of awe and the uncanny that he refers to as numinosity described by Progoff (1973) as "an aura of great light and great warmth. . . Expression of great psychic intensity accompanied by a great emotional affect, [bringing] an awareness of a special light, a numinosity carrying a sense of transcendent validity, authenticity, and essential divinity."[11] Jung believed that this particular intense feeling of numinosity was nothing short of the mystics' experience of a felt connection with a transcendent realm of spirituality.

The net effect of Jung's substitution from a causal explanation to an a-causal explanation, as well as shifting from an exclusive reliance on rational scientific method (systematic critical thinking) as the means of acquiring knowledge, to one relying more on intuition and feelings (referred to by Jung, as direct or unmediated knowledge by-passing the five senses hence un-interpreted), shifted the locus of understanding the nature of these perplexing events from a naturalistic perspective to a supernatural perspective.

In this light, most of the research in this intellectually challenging field of study has been largely a theme and variation of Jung's psychodynamic/supernatural theory. In so doing Jung's conclusion emphasizes the Platonic conceptualization of a "spiritualized reality" out there that assumes that the nature of reality consists of a knowable "predetermined and pre-patterned harmony." Says Jung (1955), "Synchronicity postulates a meaning which is 'a priori' in relation to human consciousness and apparently exists outside man."[12] Assuming the existence of this transcendent spiritual pre-patterned reality to be true, it follows, synchronicities, experienced as if they were coded messages, originate from this transcendent location.

Representative of this commonly held point of view is that of Frank Joseph (1999) who, in his book *Synchronicity and You* says, "Accepting the fact of meaningful coincidence makes it possible for us to follow a line of implication that leads us towards its ultimate source; after all, a meaningful message implies a sender. Meaning implies purpose. Purpose implies organized intent. Organization implies an organizer with a design plan" (see Alice Bailey 1951).[13]

A plan implies a planner. A design implies a designer. Whether we refer to this cosmic designer as God, Logos, the Universal Mind, or any of the other assorted labels. . . it remains a personality force, a conscious will. . . . This is about as far as a rational understanding of the phenomenon can take us. A logical acceptance of meaningful coincidence grants that a cosmic intelligence not only exists but communicates through apparent reality shifts specifically directed toward us as individuals.[14]

It is interesting to note that Jung said that most of his patients were not true believers but had lost their faith still desperately wanting something of significance to replace it. Given his particular spiritual perspective, it is no coincidence that the Jungian key to therapeutic success for such patients is reestablishing a felt connection to the assumed transcendent realm of spirituality. This is accomplished in therapy by a process Jung describes as reconnecting the patient to their lost "transcendent function."

The transcendent function is the restoration of the divided self at birth to a state of wholeness.[15] Given the importance that Jung places on this task it is reasonable to state that Jung's partially supernatural theory of synchronicities provides the rationale for his variant of psychoanalysis to be thought of as nothing short of a valid spiritual psychology.

Jung's Three Anti-causal Arguments

Even though Jung goes out of his way to indicate that his challenging supernatural perspective is, by its nature, not all together scientific, he nevertheless asserted three anti-causal arguments he hoped would silence his anticipated critics thus garnering intellectual legitimacy for his radical anti-scientific conclusion.[16] These three arguments are:

- The problem of rare and spontaneous events (an issue of methodology)
- The problem of necessity and relativity (an issue about meaning)
- The problem of simultaneity (an issue about time)

These arguments will be thoroughly explored resulting in a naturalistic rebuttal of each in chapter 3.

It might be asked: of what importance is it to investigate the nature and use of synchronicities? Theoretical and practical issues follow.

Theoretical Issues

Appearing to defy conventional scientific explanation, synchronicities evoke sheer fascination reflected in the awe response, pointing to a realm of reality significantly different than the one most commonly identified with early twentieth century science.

As a scientific anomaly these events challenge the bed-rock assumption of psychic determinism underlying psychoanalytic theory and thus call into question the validity of mechanical or linear logical causality as the primary concept in making sense of reality.

(A) plus (B) represents a theoretical clash between Jung (et al.) and Freud (et al.) that calls for thorough exploration and potential resolution.

This implicit Freud/Jung debate may be viewed in the larger context of a continuing philosophical dialogue between the Platonists (Jung and his followers) and the Aristotelians (Freud and his followers).

Advances in science, philosophy, psychology and spirituality point to a new unified paradigm generating revised and/or new organizing concepts fruitful in casting additional light on the "mysteries" of synchronicities.

Increasing numbers of patients receiving some form of psychotherapy are reporting these events. As most non Jungian therapists are likely to be relatively unfamiliar with alternative approaches to this subject matter it seems altogether worthwhile to at least acquaint these professionals with an in-depth and in-breadth account of an additional naturalistic perspective for their consideration.

Two additional reasons for investigating the nature and use of synchronicities are put forward by Ira Progoff, a Jungian interpreter (1973) who states, "Synchronicity is significant to us on two levels. On a theoretical level, it opens an additional dimension of consciousness with respect to the nature of human experience in the unfolding universe. And on an empirical level, it provides avenues for the factual study for some of the most elusive aspects of human life and destiny."[17]

A Practical Application of the Findings

It will be demonstrated that alternative theories of synchronicities associated with different clusters of organizing concepts will lead to an alternative method of decoding the messages from that of Jung. This is so because alternative organizing concepts (filters of experience) focus our attention onto different areas of experience enabling us to highlight the data that are most central to one's direct experience of the moment. Since synchronicities are associated with psychological problem solving, different interpretations of decoded messages are likely to yield different problem solutions.

Areas of Experience That Alternative Conceptualizations of Synchronicities Are Most Likely to Effect

- The nature of the self—what it is, where it is located, whether it is preformed or develops over time, how it changes, what change is, how change comes about, how permanent or short lived are the changes, the implications of changes for a therapist and his patient reporting synchronicities.
- Viewing the self as a *continuum of being*—ranging from fragmented to cohesive; and, a *continuum of doing*—ranging from scattered to focused, and directed towards attaining chosen ends.
- Viewing the self on a *continuum of evolving consciousnesses of self* ranging from kaleidoscopic consciousness, symbiotic consciousness, transcendent consciousness, and transitional consciousness to transformative consciousness, ego consciousness, and unity (synthetic) consciousness.
- The context(s) out of which synchronicities spring and the implications they have for decoding.
- Issues of final authority ranging from projecting one's final authority to accepting final authority for one's self.
- Decoding will be seen to range from abstract to person specific information depending on the degree of associated contextual information available.

- Information derived from synchronicities will be colored by the location assumed to be its origin—ranging from a realm of transcendent absolute meaning to messages that are self generated although often experienced as if they originate outside oneself.
- Significant differences in the connection of synchronicities and spirituality will be shown to be ranging from viewing spirituality as either connecting to a transcendent realm of spirituality or connecting to some location in the self associated with the primary experience of a newborn in pre-oedipal consciousness.
- The information decoded in the messages will be colored with respect to viewing them as derived from a connection to the collective unconscious or as a combination of the personal unconscious attuned to the collective consciousness.

The central organizing question guiding the structure and contents of the remainder of this book is:

- With synchronicities such as the "Scarab" and "Lazarus Raising" coincidences has science (psychodynamics) truly reached its limits to understand these anomalies from a naturalistic perspective? That is, is Jung right when he implies that a science of this type of anomaly is impossible?
- A major task of this book is to reconcile the mysteries of these seemingly a-causal events utilizing an alternative causal linking principle, viewing the production of these occurrences as self-generated messages marking significant change as a byproduct of one's idiosyncratic creative process. In so doing synchronicities are demystified.

My Personal and Professional Involvement with Synchronicities

Initially each of the synchronicity prone patients and myself (the subjects of this book) felt as if synchronicities were coded messages sent from some invisible, transcendent, "occult" realm of reality. Additionally each subject believed that the origin of the coded messages were spiritual forces that might be guiding them. Yet even as they entertained the remarkable possibility of being in touch with transcendent spiritual forces, each like me, was also skeptical and ambivalent about uncritically accepting such patently strange implications flying in the face of our mutually shared value of rationality.

Identifying myself as a truth seeker, I felt an increasing responsibility to try to clear up the mystery as to the truth or falsity of the mystical implications of my own and my patient's "numinous" experiences. Responding to them was not the issue. Instead, the issue was how *best* to respond to them?

Three Seminal Experiences and Meaningful Coincidences

Experience with a Wide Range of Therapies

Over a span of twenty-five years I experienced three alternative psychotherapies: a Sullivanian interpersonal therapy, a Gestalt psychotherapy, and a classically trained Freudian psychoanalytic therapy, plus a seven-year once-a-week supervisory session with a classically trained self psychologist. Undoubtedly the major effect of this concentrated guidance was to afford me a wide-ranging exposure to alternative assumptions about reality and the acquisition of knowledge of reality, plus an exposure to a variety of stimulating organizing concepts. Thus I became increasingly more adept at viewing the same phenomena (embedded in detailed case histories) from alternative perspectives. This same attitude was transferred to my continuing attempts to understand the nature and use of meaningful coincidences from alternative perspectives.

Applying Kuhn's Criterion for Scientific Anomalies to a Naturalistic Theory of Meaningful Coincidences

In Kuhn's identification of a scientific anomaly as recognizing "that nature has somehow violated the paradigm—induced expectations that govern normal science"[18] lies the potential Achilles' heel of Jung's supernatural theory of synchronicities. This is so because—according to Kuhn's guidance—if the paradigm of the moment is insufficient to adequately explain an apparent scientific anomaly, it is all together well and proper to consider changing the existing paradigm. However, and this is a big however, changes in the conceptualization of a given paradigm are not necessarily restricted to one and only one of its elements.

Thus Jung's elimination of causality as an inadequate concept for explaining the link between the inner and the outer halves of a given synchronicity does not necessarily mean that the only alternative explanation remaining is to substitute a principle of a-causality in its place.

Indeed, before adopting the extreme substitution of a principle of a-causality in place of a conventional causal explanation, the question is raised, is it not theoretically tenable to imagine that there might be some other form of causality—as yet unidentified—that might validly serve as an adequate explanatory linking principle?

This book contends that in fact there is at least one plausible revision or extension of causality— an expanded psychological causality (experiential or psychodynamic causality) that may be utilized in explaining synchronicities from a naturalistic perspective.

A Common Theme: "Rashomoning" Experience

A careful look at these two themes described above reveals an additional theme uniting each of them. This theme is the fact that any event (i.e., a synchronicity) might be viewed from alternative perspectives no matter how "obviously" one sided the matter would seem to be at first glance.

Thus if asked the question: what is the answer to one plus one most people would unhesitatingly answer two. However if asked what else might one plus one equal—the answer might validly be: eleven. If asked one more time—those who like to think "out of the box," and have knowledge of esoteric logic of correspondences (i.e., Hegelian dialectic), will answer 1 + 1 = 3. Such is the philosophical computations underlying the mystery of the trinity and interpreting the Tarot.

This concept of multiple interpretations of the same phenomena will be more thoroughly discussed in a later chapter with respect to the selected fields of knowledge associated with attempts to understand the nature of synchronicities including speculative philosophy, depth psychology, the esoteric occult, spirituality, and advances in theoretical science. Many of these concepts when combined are used to generate filters of experience in processing the raw data associated with synchronistic events.

For now, an apt example that illustrates this concept of multiple interpretations is what will be referred to as "Rashomoning" experience. I derived this concept from an unexpected attitudinal shift experienced in watching the Japanese film *Rashomon.*[19]

The story line is deceptively simple. A bridegroom is seen walking through a field of tall grass guiding a horse upon which his new bride is sitting. Suddenly a man leaps up from the field, ties the husband up, and rapes the wife. The camera then focuses on another man who, picnicking in the tall grass hidden from view, also witnesses the crime.

The rest of the film replays the same set of events from each character's unique point of view. Each new perspective yields a significantly different interpretation of what initially had appeared to be an open and shut case. The viewer (a fifth perspective) is left to decide for himself which point of view reflects the truest "truth" of the matter.

Despite Jung's insistence that an a-causal principle adequately "explains" synchronicities, increasing familiarity with the literature makes it clear that

Jung and his followers are in fact interpreting the material by processing the raw data through selected organizing concepts (filters of experience) thereby foreclosing other filters of experience that might potentially view these same anomalies from a radically different perspective.

Among the core Jungian organizing concepts used to interpret the nature of synchronicities are the transcendent realm of absolute meaning, archetypes, archetypal experience, the collective consciousness, numinosity, the principle of a-causality, compensation, spirituality, and the transcendent function.

"Rashomoning" synchronicities by deliberately changing the first assumption about the nature of reality and the acquisition of knowledge followed by revising and creating new organizing concepts to make sense out of the apparent non sense that synchronicities present,yields a naturalistic perspective in contrast to the supernatural perspective of Jung and his followers.

Among the revised and created concepts used as a composite filter to generate a naturalistic explanation of meaningful coincidences are: the collective consciousness, the personal unconscious, projected final authority, a continuum of states of consciousness of the self (kaleidoscopic consciousness, symbiotic consciousness, transcendent consciousness, transitional consciousness, ego consciousness, and unity consciousness), binary black-white/either-or thinking, ambivalence, zero point, despair, object constancy, self constancy, convergence, layering, pleasure principle, reality principle, resonance, attunement, a "grounded" spirituality, unity, perfesion (perfect ease), and incremental changes.

Thus my research strongly indicates that to do justice to the complexity of these mysterious happenings requires an objective researcher to "Rashomon" the core facts associated with the production of meaningful coincidences. In other words, the objective investigator will keep an open mind, understanding that the primary assumptions and the organizing concepts chosen to interpret the experience of synchronicities will yield either a supernatural or a naturalistic perspective depending on which assumptions and derived cluster of concepts is chosen to make the best sense out of the available data.

Ultimately it is the individual's choice as to which perspective feels most resonant with his or her direct experience. What is at issue here is that the preference be made with the understanding that there are at least two radically different perspectives from which to choose: a partially naturalistic and partially supernatural theory of synchronicities or a purely naturalistic theory of synchronicities.

Important Questions Raised

Once my doubts deepened my research took the form of exploring one challenging question after another until it became undeniably clear that Jung's seemingly obvious supernatural conclusion was, upon careful analysis, not as obvious and clear-cut as I had first believed.

Following is a list of questions I began exploring in depth and breadth, each of which is intimately associated with Jung and his follower's theoretical understanding of the nature of synchronicities. The list is in no particular order.

- Are there other forms of causality besides that of conventional scientific causality?
- If other forms of causality are existent, might any of them be utilized as an adequate linking principle?
- What is the meaning of meaning to which Jung is alluding?
- Are there alternative definitions of meaning?
- What is the relationship between meaning and causality?
- Are there other sources of meaning besides the Jungian formulation of a realm of absolute meaning?
- What is an example of so called direct unmediated knowledge?
- Are there alternative operational definitions of the term a priori?
- Does a priori necessarily imply transcendence in the "heavenly" sense of that term?
- Are there different meanings of the concept of transcendence?
- What exactly is meant by the concept of spirituality?
- Assuming that synchronicities are self generated messages what are the implications for the felt sense of spiritual feelings associated with them?
- Can a naturalistic perspective of synchronicities incorporate spirituality?
- Are there alternative perspectives associated with the experience of simultaneity?
- Assuming the Jungians are accurate, what specific knowledge is transmitted from a connection to the realm of archetypal meaning?
- Are there alternative definitions of the concept unity?
- If there is no common "mind stuff" or nous then what are the implications of synchronistic experiences?
- What specifically changes in the concept of significant change associated with synchronicities?
- What is the criterion for significant change and /or transformations?
- Are the changes (transformations) associated with synchronicities permanent?

- Do different clusters of organizing concepts or clusters of organizing concepts with alternative meanings alter our understanding of the nature and perhaps use of synchronicities?
- Do alternative perspectives of synchronicities yield different information?
- Are synchronicities revealed, discovered, or created?
- What is the self and where is it located?
- Does the self evolve?
- What is the distinction between the personal unconscious and the collective unconscious?
- What is the operational definition of the "creative process" and how it related to the evolving self, and the personal unconscious?
- Are there alternative forms of consciousness?

The deeper I probed the more it appeared that the phenomena that seemed at first reading to be a clear cut member of the supernatural club of inexplicable phenomena was beginning to shed its mysterious garb and looked to be increasingly more explainable as a potentially knowable byproduct of natural processes.

Some Questions and Unresolved Issues Raised by Other Researchers

In addition to my own questions listed above, I have selected a few suggested issues raised by adherents of the Jungian point of view to be explored. These are as follows:

- What are the factors that initiate synchronicities or give them their crystallized form?
- Are there specific characteristics by which we can recognize synchronistic events as they are preparing to occur? What are the processes by which synchronistic events take place?
- Is it correct to speak of process where the principle involved is a non-causal one?
- Do we require new terms to replace concepts like process in the light of synchronicity and the transcausal factor?
- Will it be sufficient to define these terms more closely and in new ways?[20]
- One specific hypothesis that is worth investigating is whether the lives of those individuals who can be classified as "creative persons" show a

particular tendency toward the occurrence of synchronistic events. If this turns out to be verified in any degree, the implications may be of great importance.[21]

- Repeatedly we have seen that the factor of integrative orderedness is of primary importance in synchronistic phenomena, and it is not reflected at all in the term, nor in any part of the nomenclature that Jung developed. Progoff (1973) says "this is one major point where a sharper formulation with a more specific terminology may be helpful in extending the universe?[22]
- Aziz (1990) states: "Although the literature on synchronicity that has followed Jung's principle essay is quite broad in its scope, a comprehensive study of the synchronicity concept in relationship to the individuation process has yet to be undertaken."[23] He proceeds to make this task the central aim of his book. He does so relating the process of individuation with religious and spiritual aspects. Implied in Aziz's task is himself or someone else doing the same thing, that is, undertaking "a comprehensive study of the synchronicity concept in relationship to the individuation process" from a purely naturalistic perspective.

M. D. Faber's Naturalistic View of the Nature of Synchronicities

On the other side of the ledger—namely the naturalistic point of view—M. D. Faber (1998) in his seminal work called *Synchronicity: C. G. Jung, Psychoanalysis, and Religion* offers a compelling first attempt to demystify meaningful coincidences. He does so by viewing the problematic elements associated with the production of synchronicities as essentially centering on the first two years of a child's life—pre-oedipal—early years of childhood psychological self development. In so doing Faber asserts that Jung's conceptualization can be viewed as a regressive naturalistic tendency of children and adults to return to the roots of their primary experience seeking a passive perfect union with the original good primary care giver. Faber's line of reasoning will be thoroughly explored in chapter 4, Naturalistic Interpretations of Synchronicities.

My perspective does not disagree with Faber, but believes he has only accounted for half of the naturalistic perspective—that is, viewing synchronicities as regressive phenomena. In so doing, Faber fails to identify, describe and explain the other half of a naturalistic theory of synchronicities. This other half is viewing synchronicities as progressive phenomena evidenced by expanding consciousness, increasing cohesion of the self structure, and an increasing capacity of the self to connect with one's idiosyncratic creative process and it expression.

One of the most interesting and compelling aspects of this challenging subject matter is that it continues (even after forty four years) to generate new possibilities for further study. Thus I consider my endeavor to be a work in progress. In this light, synchronistic phenomena, considered as a whole, are like luminescent sparkling diamonds composed of many overlooked facets. A slight turn in one direction or another presents additional facets (viewpoints) pointing to a potentially deeper and broader understanding of the whole complex. Each additional organizing question generated from an intimate experience with the material acts like a focused beam of light illuminating the as yet unexplored totality of facets.

In other words, doing justice to the complexity of the undeniably perplexing phenomena that meaningful coincidences present means that investigators should attempt to understand their nature and use, utilizing each and every new slant associated with the material.

In this connection, I believe that a serious investigation of these wondrous events invites the investigator to study the raw data from composite lenses derived from such diverse fields of knowledge such as speculative philosophy, depth psychology, science, the esoteric occult, spirituality, and perhaps others as well.

The one trick magic show warning conveys an attitude that gets to the heart of investigating meaningful coincidences and other such seemingly paranormal, transpersonal, and or supernatural phenomena. This attitude concerns an individual's experience of mystery characteristically associated with the experience of a synchronicity, combined with what one explicitly or implicitly makes of this mysterious aura.

Alternative Attitudes to the Concept and Experience of Mystery

There are basically two pathways in a person's attitude towards mystery: (1) accepting it as such, enjoying the accompanying feelings of awe and the uncanny; and /or (2) using it to spur one's analytic curiosity to understand how the "hidden" process works.

Representative of the first of these attitudes towards mystery, characteristic of the Jungian point of view towards synchronicities, is that of Jean Shinoda Bolen, M.D. (1979) in her book *The Tao of Psychology: Synchronicity and the Self.* Says Bolen: "[An] intuitive knowledge that there is a patterned universe, or an underlying meaning to all experience, or a primal source, to which "I" am connected, always evokes a feeling of reverence."[24]

Thus the mystery associated with synchronicities from Bolen's point of view is a just so story. It is just the way it is—no need, no reason, and no way to analyze anything more than what intuition and the feeling of the uncanny conveys.

The alternative attitude (pathway) to exploring mystery from a naturalistic point of view is acknowledging the "mysterious" as an incentive to understand what process makes the "watch" tick? This is accomplished by utilizing scientific method—to learn how the apparent mystery is a logical outcome of potentially knowable cause and effect chains of experience—but, at the moment, due to lacking crucial intellectual conceptual tools, such that a naturalistic explanation might provide, eludes the grasp of one's present capacity to make rational sense of what seems to be baffling "non-sense."

Thus the naturalistic attitude towards the mystery initially associated with synchronicities motivates the curious to redouble their efforts to understand how the apparent "magic trick" is done. The following summary of a *Nova* science program shown on public television is an apt illustration of both of these attitudes to mystery.

The subject matter of this program called Stardust involved an airplane (named Stardust) that crashed fifty-three years ago, mysteriously disappearing and then equally as mysteriously, reappearing some fifty-three years later.

Before arriving at the true answer, clearing up the mystery, there was widespread belief that the plane had first been abducted by aliens and then returned by them to send a teasing message to earthlings. Painstaking research concluded that the plane had crashed into a mountain, setting off an avalanche completely hiding the plane until it melted some fifty-three years later. The ice having melted exposed the remains of the crashed plane providing tangible clues enabling the researchers to reach an objective accounting of what actually occurred, thus demystifying a seemingly opaque mystery.[25]

In this light, perhaps Jung and his followers are accurate in their supernatural conclusion. However the findings of my investigation of these seemingly a-causal events indicates the mystery associated with them, like with Star Dust, strongly indicates there is reason to believe that what seems to only promise an occult explanation at first glance, upon further reflection and scientific investigation has, in fact, a rational naturalistic explanation.

This author agrees with the pragmatist philosopher C. I. Lewis's (1929) attitude toward mystery: "The mind—and particularly its purpose and activity—is, of course, ultimately mysterious, just as concentration upon the presentation of the starry heaven reveals it as something ultimately mysterious, when all those prosaic and familiar correlations of this and that, which constitute its explanation, are shorn away, and we stand before it in its pristine glory. But the mind is mysterious in no different sense than this one in which reality altogether is ultimately mysterious."[26]

The accumulating evidence directly leads to the following list of the objectives of this book.

The Objectives of This Book

- To present an overview of the subject introducing the intellectual challenge and emotional power of synchronicities
- To provide a summary of Jung's seminal research findings along with his provocative and challenging conclusion and implications
- To explore in detail questions raised in critiquing Jung's formulations concerning his basic philosophical, psychological, scientific, spiritual and esoteric occult first assumptions concerning the nature of reality and knowledge of reality
- To explore the processes leading to the production of synchronicities, viewing and reviewing organizing concepts including causality, space, time, meaning, meaning making, logic, alternative logics, experiential logic, and spirituality from the alternative viewpoints of a supernatural and a naturalistic perspective
- To attempt to reconcile the mysteries of these seemingly a-causal events utilizing an alternative causal linking principle, viewing the production of these occurrences as self-generated messages marking significant change as byproducts of one's idiosyncratic creative process
- To present and discuss the alternative naturalistic perspectives of Faber and Williams with respect to their implications in understanding, decoding and best utilizing the assumed embedded information
- To provide alternative concepts and methods for the reader to decode his own synchronicities
- To indicate how synchronicities are useful as generating organizing concepts as well as functioning as organizing experiences thus useful in synthesizing seemingly disparate internal and external information into meaningful wholes (this is particularly pertinent with respect to providing a model for the convergence of multiple points of view among seemingly disparate fields of information) for the purpose of a deeper, and richer integration
- To enable readers to view their own synchronicities from multiple perspectives by utilizing selected resonant organizing concepts, as an aid to tracking and perhaps facilitating significant psychological change

It is my experience that making the effort to really think about the primary assumptions and the selected core concepts associated with synchronicities—

relating them to one's personal experience—yields significant results. In so doing this endeavor is quite likely to result in one's experience of their psychological boundaries significantly stretching for the better and the richer.

Creating "trouble" for oneself by daring to "Rashomon" their primary ontological and epistemological first assumptions and their associated core concepts of either the supernatural or the naturalistic perspective forces the bold researcher to confront head on the most important questions of their lifetime. These questions are who am I really, what do I really want, what is of ultimate significance to me, how do I gain knowledge of this vital information, and how can I best utilize this information to live a meaningful life?

In this light, the primary aim of this book is to explore the nature of meaningful coincidences from the depth psychological/supernatural perspective and the depth psychological/naturalistic perspective identifying and exploring (1) alternative primary assumptions about the nature of reality, knowledge about reality, and ways in which this knowledge is accessed; leading to (2) identifying alternative organizing concepts (lens, filters) to be used in the service of enriching the specificity of detail applied to better understanding one's self. This self-knowledge is partially derived from decoding the embedded "messages" in one's synchronicities.

Having two distinct points of view in mind should enable the interested researcher to be more objective in his or her attempts to determine for themselves how to get the most out of their synchronistic experiences.

Logically there is no better bridge to a naturalistic theory of synchronicities than to critically examine Jung's personal and professional life defining experiences motivating him to construct his seminal supernatural theory of synchronicities. This task is the content of chapter 2, Jung's Psychological/Supernatural Theory of Synchronicities.

I

THEORETICAL PERSPECTIVES

2

Jung's Psychological/Supernatural Theory of Synchronicities

"If Jung was a man of science capable of expressing his discoveries in the ordinary language of men, he was also a strange being who narrated improbable experiences in a language that was at odds with that of official science. . . He gave new terms to those mysteries which emanate from the eternal tradition of man."

—Michael Serrano, *C. G. Jung and Hermann Hesse*

MEANINGFUL COINCIDENCES (SYNCHRONICITIES) appear to defy conventional laws of cause and effect (psychic determinism). Classical psychoanalysts (and other likeminded scientists), aware of the radical implications of the Jungian perspective, are likely to be disturbed and perhaps challenged by its clear threat to the traditional understanding of the nature and knowledge of reality and the use to which this knowledge is applied. Delighted (indeed, over-awed) by his personal experiences of synchronicities, hyper aware of their religious implications, Jung created a challenging supernatural theory of meaningful coincidences held together by an explanation of a-causal connectedness (the principle of synchronicity.) His radical and provocative point of view has garnered wide spread appeal dominating the synchronicity scene culminating in his provocative categorical assertion that a causal explanation of synchronicities is not even conceivable in rational terms. It will be demonstrated that Jung's a-causal synchronicity theory, while emotionally compelling, raises more challenging questions than providing definitive answers.

Further it will be demonstrated that all the factors that lend Jung's synchronicity a distinctly supernatural cast such as the transcendent function and the a-priori realm of absolute archetypal meaning will be accounted for from a purely naturalistic theoretical and psychodynamic perspective. Thus the interested reader will be left with two distinct theories of synchronicities—one supernatural (transpersonal), the other a theme and variation of a purely naturalistic point of view—which may be employed in satisfying his own understanding and practical utilization of these puzzling events.

It should be noted that psychoanalysis was in its infancy when Jung met Freud at his villa for a critically important meeting in 1909. During this meeting they experienced a shared synchronicity whose ripple effects significantly contributed to their eventual breakup in 1912.

Jung, Freud's heir apparent, having initially embraced the Master's monumental breakthrough in treating mental patients suffering from neurosis by means of the new method called psychoanalysis, was—at the same time of this meeting—realizing that major doubts about Freud and aspects of his theory had undeniably surfaced. A major concern of Jung's, which have major implications with respect to their alternative attitudes towards synchronicities, is made explicit in his (1961) commentary about this meeting: "Above all, Freud's attitude towards the spirit was highly questionable."[1]

At this time, Freud and Jung were in agreement that their primary aim was to free their patients from the grips of neurosis expressed in the form of debilitating symptoms such as panic anxiety, hysteria, and obsessive/compulsive attitudes and behavior. The particular method chosen to treat a given patient's complaints is based on the practitioner's explicit or implicit assumptions about the nature of symptom formation.

Freud's theory of symptom formation, assumes that the origin of psychological problems can be traced to unresolved traumatic childhood sexual conflicts, the details of which are initially unavailable to the patient's present awareness due to a defensive process of purposeful forgetting (repression). In this view repressed pathogenic material is thought to be unconscious, another way of saying that it is outside the patient's conscious awareness.

Following the formula that in an accurate description of a problem lies an embedded solution, successful psychoanalytic treatment consists of the analyst helping his patient to make the disturbing unconscious material conscious by verbalizing it. In so doing, the patient is able to identify the essential components of his conflicts, thereby potentially enabling him to make informed choices instead of feeling like a passive victim of internal or external forces beyond his control.

By contrast Jung observed that Freud's method of tracing symptoms back to assumed unresolved childhood conflicts simply did not apply for the majority of *his* patients. Instead, he observed that virtually every one of his patients over the age of thirty five (presumably the age of the majority of his patients) complained about such issues as feeling divided, detached, dissociated, and devitalized at their core. These are symptoms associated with patients initially suffering from moderate to severe identity disorders.

Jung viewed these symptoms as a religious problem with each of these patients ultimately seeking a reconnection with a lost sense of "wholeness." Jung (1943) conceptualized the origin of this religious problem as a lost connection with the transcendent function he defines as: "the union and harmonious fusion of opposites formerly split apart by the division of the psyche into consciousness and unconscious."[2]

Thus the thrust of treatment for those who suffer from this problem is geared to create the optimum conditions whereby the lost connection is reestablished. This is accomplished by the therapist keeping the patient focused, not on analyzing the unconscious historical origins of his problems, but in reestablishing a connection with the transcendent collective unconscious.

In this connection Jung became increasingly aware of many of his patients reporting meaningful coincidences accompanied by intense feelings of awe (numinosity) and a sense they were profoundly important. Impressed with the powerful experience of numinosity, akin to a "spiritual charge," Jung believed that a synchronicity marked a patient's successful reconnection to his previously lost transcendent "religious" function.

Clearly Jung viewed synchronicities as steeped in religiosity. Speaking to this point Aziz (1990) says, "The religious need, as Jung puts it, longs for wholeness, and here the wholeness to which one must open oneself is a wholeness that is not only transmitted intrapsychically, but transmitted to the individual through the synchronistic patterning of events in one's environment."[3]

As will be shown, significant differences in understanding the nature of synchronistic events was apparently a major reason leading to the decisive break between Jung and Freud in 1912. Subsequent to this break, Jung became increasingly immersed in the perplexities and implications that synchronicities present. Jung's (1955) scattered ideas were crystallized in a unified account with his paper on synchronicities, "Synchronicity: An Acausal Connecting Principle."

Synchronicities and Understanding Jung's Epistemology

Unable to explain how in any synchronicity A and A' connect utilizing the conventional definition of causality, Jung inferred that the connection is by means of the unconscious. Further that the unconscious provides a person with an entrance to a realm of transcendent, self-subsistent knowledge, which Jung (1955) prefers "to call "absolute."[4]

It is important to note that even though Jung indicates that his identification of this transcendent realm of absolute knowledge is inferred he nevertheless treats it as if it is a categorical irrefutable actuality.

Speaking to this point A. Jaffe (1971) an interpreter of Jung's works explains: "Synchronistic phenomena . . . led Jung to infer the existence of a transcendental meaning independent of consciousness."[5] Jung (1970) amplifying this idea says: "Synchronicity postulates a meaning which is a priori in relation to human consciousness and apparently outside man."[6] Further it is evidence of the "spiritualization" of reality.

Although Jung's conception of the realm of absolute knowledge is inferred, thus a hypothetical construct, he nevertheless is convinced that it is real, universal, and irrefutable. Jung rationalized this apparent logical inconsistency by insisting that true knowledge of spirituality can only be accurately accessed by mean of an "experientially based knowledge, a spirituality based on a genuine self- knowledge."[7]

By contrast, it is a basic assumption of this book that Jung's theory, as are all theories, is based on selected explicit or implicit first assumptions about the nature of reality (ontology), knowledge of this reality, and how it is known (epistemology); and the use(s) the obtained knowledge of reality may best be put. Thus theories are the byproducts of personal interpretations of a given theorist's imposing order on the raw data of their experience.

This means that a given synchronicity theory (as are all theories) being the byproduct of the particular theorists' conscious and unconscious interpretations of his experiences, is necessarily biased. Biases are not problematic as long as they are clearly stated so that the reader is able to make adequate compensations in arriving at his or her own judgments on the matter at hand.

In this light, chapter 2 will explore selected themes associated with Jung's basic assumptions including selected biographical details related to his keen interest in synchronicities; the psychological origins of Jung's perspective on synchronicities; a powerful confrontation between Jung and Freud centering around a startling shared synchronistic event; the seminal scarab coincidence that is representative of the type of subsequent synchronicities addressed in this book; a discussion of Jung's three anti-causal arguments whereby he attempted to add scientific legitimacy to his provocative partially anti-scientific theory; the identification of the composite "filters" of experience from which Jung derived his supernatural theory of synchronicities; and a discussion of core questions raised and their implications for further research as to the nature and use of these fascinating and challenging anomalous phenomena.

The conclusion is reached that a careful analysis of the available evidence leaves the door wide open for a naturalistic interpretation of these seemingly mystical events.

Basic Assumptions

Jung believed that the essence of his theory, including such organizing concepts as archetypes, archetypal absolute knowledge, individuation, self, were derived from his direct personal experience of an assumed extended layer of the unconscious Jung refers to as the "collective unconscious."

From a naturalistic perspective it will be shown that Jung's a-causal formulation may alternatively be viewed as a synthesis of organizing concepts selected from the realm of the *collective consciousness*, the repository of the totality of all actual and potential conceptualizations. Further that the specific organizing concepts chosen by Jung were derived from the knowledge bases of speculative philosophy, depth psychology, quantum physics, mythology, the esoteric occult, and spirituality. Jung's belief that his concepts were derived from his direct connection with the "collective unconscious" and treated as if this is an absolute truth, may alternatively be viewed as a highly imaginative and compelling hypothesis inviting scientific scrutiny. Further it will be shown that these particular concepts and the way they are interpreted and synthesized by Jung were a logical outcome of his life long struggle to grow and to maintain "a balanced, unified self that was constantly threatened with disintegration."[8]

Utilizing a method they refer to as "psychobiology" Stolorow and Atwood (1979) demonstrate how Jung's idiosyncratic metapsychological system "may be fruitfully analyzed . . . as a psychological [product] rooted in the formative life [experience of its creator]."[9] Stolorow and Atwood (1979) conclude that "[Jung's] subjective world was organized around the wrenching issues of self-dissolution, self-division, and never-ending conflict, it follows that his ideal self-image would be one of integrated harmony, reconciliation, and transcendent wholeness."[10]

Likely anticipating that Freud would no doubt adopt a theme and variation of this psycho-biographical point of view as to the origins of his theory, Jung (1955) in *Modern Man in Search of a Soul* launched a pre emptive attack: "The psychologist, to be sure, may never abandon his claim to investigate and establish causal relations in complicated psychic events. . . . That neurosis [or a work of art] have a causal origin in the psychic realm—that they take their rise from emotional states and from real or imagined childhood experiences . . . Any reaction to stimulus may be causally explained; but the creative act, which is the absolute antithesis of mere reaction, will forever elude human understanding."[11]

Extending his thinking on the difference between the byproduct of his creative process (the artist's "vision") as distinct from the psychological origins of his idiosyncratic creative process, Jung (1952) states, "If we insist on deriving the vision from a personal experience, we must treat the former as something secondary—as a mere substitute for reality. The result is that we strip the vision of its primordial quality and take it as nothing but a symptom. The pregnant chaos [taking the form of archetypes experienced when a person is connected to mythological consciousness] then shrinks to the proportions of a psychic disturbance."[12]

Perhaps Jung is right. However, the facts appear to indicate that by considering his theory to be a reconstruction of selected raw data from his personal and professional experience—hence the outgrowth of his interpretations—his supernatural point of view, although compelling, is only one of a number of conceivable theories of synchronicity.

In this connection it is potentially illuminating to note the speculations of Stolorow and Atwood (1979) tracing the origin of personality theories of Freud, Jung, and other theorists to the development and vicissitudes of their own personalities.[13]

Jung's theory rests on the following assumptions: (1) there is a collective unconscious that is not only at the core of every individual but is also transpersonal and universal; (2) the collective unconscious is the location of archetypal knowledge equivalent to a realm of absolute meaning; (3) the way an individual gets linked to this realm of archetypal knowledge (the collective unconscious) is by means of an a-causal connecting principle (the principle of synchronicity); and (4) once having connected to this realm of absolute knowledge, it may then be utilized in the service of enhancing individuation expressed as increasing wholeness, unification, and integration of the self. A more precise understanding of individuation is offered by Jaffe (1983) who states: "The goal of individuation is the synthesis of opposites, once they have become conscious, in the self."[14]

Stolorow and Atwood (1979) convincingly suggest that seemingly no psychological theory springs fully made out of the mind of a disembodied intellect no matter how brilliant the theoretician might be. Many theorists, including Freud and Jung, struggle with developmental vicissitudes resulting in the creation of their original theoretical perspectives by identifying, facing up to, and successfully mastering seemingly intractable psychological impasses.[15]As will be seen this process is definitely so in Jung's case.

Careful scrutiny of the pertinent details of Jung's life presents persuasive evidence to conclude that his adult interest in and particular understanding of meaningful coincidences is indeed no coincidence.

Jung's Interest in Synchronicities

Various accounts of the defining biographical details of Jung's life may be found in Ellenberger's *Discovery of the Unconscious* (1970)[16] and Jung's (1961) autobiography: *Memories, Dreams, and Reflections.*[17] For the purposes of this book the following selected biographical facts will be those associated with Jung's interest in and formulation of synchronicities.

Jung was born July 26, 1875, in Switzerland, the only son of a Protestant clergyman. Many of his relatives were theologians or doctors. There is some evidence that he was distantly related to the writer Goethe. This heritage probably influenced his combined interest in science and religion. Before becoming a psychiatrist Jung studied a great many subjects.

His multi faceted interests included: "zoology, paleontology, and geology; in humanities to Greco-Roman, Egyptian, and prehistoric archeology."[18] Additionally he explored mythology philosophy, Gnosticism, and alchemy.[19] Hence Jung's wide ranging interests provided him with a wealth of information which would be put to good use in formulating his original theory of synchronicity.

Student Years

As a young man Jung was not a "happy camper." He felt painfully at odds and uniquely different from his compatriots and family. Indeed there was justification for his experience of intense estrangement as he was, in fact, exceedingly "different." For example, in his autobiography Jung (1955) says, "Everywhere in the realm of religious questions I encountered locked doors, and if ever one door should chance to open I was disappointed by what lay behind it. Other people all seemed to have totally different concerns. I felt completely alone with my certainties. More than ever I wanted someone to talk with, but nowhere did I find a point of contact; on the contrary, I sense in others an estrangement, a distrust, an apprehension which robbed me of speech."[20]

He was preoccupied at an early age in trying to order his personal chaos by turning to speculative philosophy and the esoteric occult in search of absolute answers to his ultimate questions. Additionally he was hopeful that science might be the key to obtaining objective knowledge of himself. But before his twenties he came to feel that while science was useful it had its limitations in providing the kind of "absolute knowledge" he craved.

Note the unique perspective Jung (1961) brings to understanding the same two subjects that captured Freud's attention as well—"the problem of archaic vestiges" and that of "sexuality." With respect to the later interest Jung (1961) states, "My main concern has been to investigate, over and above its personal significance and biological function, its spiritual aspect and its numinous meaning, and thus to explain what Freud was so fascinated by but was unable to grasp."[21]

In this context Jung (1961) discovered and eagerly devoured the literature of spiritualism, it resonating with many of the early experiences that had fascinated him as a young boy. Much of this occult subject matter had to do with mysterious forces purportedly accounting for the presence of malevolent occurrences in his daily life. These included such events as "clocks mysteriously stopping at the moment of a person's death, or glasses which shattered at the critical moment."[22]

Jung (1961) believed he had been led into a secret and mysterious world that he alone was privy to such esoteric knowledge and information. But, while making him feel superior, this rather unusual interest also reinforced his sense of uncomfortable "differentness" increasing his vulnerability to estrangement and isolation. Thus as satisfying was the awareness of an occult realm of reality, leading to a feeling of "specialness," it also led to an increasing problem in maintaining his self-esteem. Jung (1961) said, "This insight proved dangerous, because it tricked me into fits of superiority, misplaced criticism, and aggressiveness, which got me deservedly disliked. This eventually brought back all the old doubts, inferiority feelings, and depressions— vicious circle I was resolved to break at all costs."[23]

It will be shown that the synchronistic aware people highlighted in this book describe themselves as initially suffering from similar qualities as those which Jung refers to have. This complex of personality traits characterized by an inability to adequately regulate their self-esteem will be intimately related to their interest in and use of meaningful coincidences as an adaptive process in the service of healing divisions in their internal reality (sense of being) and in synthesizing, integrating, and directing their previously scattered forces— doing and becoming— toward meaningful pursuits.

Jung's positive attitude towards wholeness, unity, and expansion of the self coupled with a growing aversion for analysis was carried over to his practice of psychiatry. Jung was concerned that psychiatrists he observed were more like disembodied intellects, over analyzing their patients instead of empathetically trying to understand their sufferings in breadth and depth as whole persons. Note the implied criticism of Freud. This same attitude is central in his understanding of synchronicities as a concept, an experience, and a pathway to even higher and deeper meaningful "spiritual" connections with the self, others, and all of reality.

In 1896 Jung gave his first talk "On the Limits of Exact Sciences." Says Ellenberger (1970): "It was a vehement attack against contemporary materialistic science and a plea in favor of the objective study of hypnotism and spiritism."[24] In this talk, Jung adamantly states his conviction that the esoteric occult offered knowledge and insights complementing that which was obtained in more acceptable areas of experience considered such by conventional scientists. Ellenberger (1970) says that Jung was becoming increasingly more unconventional "[as] an outspoken advocate promoting the idea of the reality of the soul [conceptualized as] . . . immaterial, transcendent, outside of time and space—and yet to be approached scientifically."[25]

At twenty-three, Jung's fascination with the occult was channeled into formally investigating scientifically spiritism and parapsychology. In a small group Jung conducted experiments with his fifteen year old cousin Helene Preiswerk, respected as a gifted young medium. Initially an observing participant Jung rapidly became a full-fledged participant observer.[26] These occult experiences had so much impact on him that he came to have an increasing overlapping of psychological and spiritual (transcendent) points of view. This mixture of the psychological and the spiritual would later become the essential elements in Jung's combined psychodynamic/supernatural (mystical/magical) theory of synchronicities.

Professional Life

In 1900, at age twenty-five, Jung became an assistant physician at the Burgholzli Psychiatric Clinic at the University of Zurich. In 1902 he got an M.D. degree completing his dissertation, "On the Psychology and Pathology of So-Called Occult Phenomena." In this research Jung asserts his definite ideas as to what psychology should be. Ellenberger (1970) says that Jung defined it "as the scientific study of the human soul, taking manifestations that he called psychological reality as a starting point."[27]

Also in 1902, like Freud, Jung heard Janet's lectures on the personal unconscious and its connection with the formation of hysterical symptoms which were relieved by the introduction of hypnotism. Thus he became intimately aware of the reality of the strong association between unconscious causation and psychological symptom formation.

Psychiatric Activities

Jung was preoccupied by the question of what actually occurs in the psyche of the mentally ill (their phenomenological experience). He observed that what mattered most to the pre Freudian psychiatrists was the diagnosis (the classification of the illness from the outside in) not the understanding of the actual psychodynamic processes (how the illness works and how it is experienced from the inside out). It was in this context that Jung was attracted to Freud's theories and treatment method as he strongly resonated with Freud's major concern which was to understand the question of what symptoms mean to the individual patient who complained of them.

Freud's Influence

Jung initially applied Freud's methods in his attempts to understand particularly those patients suffering from schizophrenia. Application of Freud's method led Jung (1961) to uncover relevant information from the unconscious in his patients, each of which "revealed a dark and tragic story."[28] For Jung (1961) the key to successful treatment of a schizophrenic patient was in viewing the patient as "a whole person, never the symptom alone. It is the patient's secret, the rock against which he is shattered. . . . We must ask questions which challenge the whole personality."[29]

Here then is another link to Jung's increasing interest in the subject of synchronicities, thought by him to be events that are associated with questions and experiences that "challenge the whole personality." Synchronicities appear mysterious, pointing to a realm of knowledge above or below associated with people's attempts to answer the large questions about their whole life. These questions include: What is the self? Where is it located? Does my life have an overall purpose? How do I access it, and actualize it?

In 1905 Jung (1961) became a lecturer in psychiatry at the University of Zurich assuming the position of senior physician. He "lectured on psychiatry, and also on the foundations of Freudian psychoanalysis," clearly establishing himself as a follower of Freud.[30]

Jung and Freud

Jung's fascination with the reality of the unconscious complementing the conscious mind is what drew him to Freud's work. Freud first confirmed this layering of inner space as similar to an ice berg (the topographic model of the mind) consisting of the conscious layer (the most visible tip of the iceberg), the pre-conscious layer, and the personal unconscious (the major portion of the iceberg hidden from direct sight). Freud asserted that in the unconscious there are un-verbalized contents found to motivate present attitudes and behavior.

Freud's unconscious came to be known as the personal unconscious. The content of the personal unconscious is mainly populated by memories that have somehow etched themselves to the psyche but are initially unavailable to recall for various reasons. They become accessible in dreams, fantasies, emotional eruptions and the likes and in the free associations of the patient in therapy sessions with their analyst. While Jung shared Freud's compelling interest in exploring the realm of the personal unconscious, he began to strike out in a new direction.

Jung, while noting the reality of the personal unconscious, became fascinated with what he observed was an additional factor in both his and his patients' contents of consciousness. Specifically he noticed that the unconscious contents assumed the form of myths, mythological characters, and the likes.

Impressed with Jung's observations, Ellenberger (1970) says that Freud "encouraged Jung, and other psychoanalysts, to investigate myths for their psychoanalytic interpretations." [31] In so doing Jung was well on the way to believing he had discovered an unchartered realm of the unconscious he would later name the collective unconscious to distinguish it from what he believed was Freud's too limited preoccupation with the personal unconscious. The unconscious was considered different from the personal unconscious as it was thought by Jung to be transpersonal, transcendent, and universal to all men.

Jung (1943) differentiating the collective unconscious from the personal unconscious says, "The personal layer ends at the earliest memories of infancy, but the collective layer comprises the pre-infantile period, that is, the residues of ancestral life. . . when psychic energy regresses, going even beyond the period of early infancy, and breaks into the legacy of ancestral life, then mythological images are awakened: these are the archetypes. An interior spiritual world whose existence we never suspected opens out and displays contents which seem to stand out in sharpest contrast to all our former ideas."[32]

Other differences began to emerge between Jung and Freud. One key difference was Jung's belief that the roots of neurosis lie not in a person's remote childhood but in present situations. Additionally Jung rejected what he came to believe was Freud's "obsession" with pinning all psychological symptoms on physical and, or "psychic sexuality."

However, despite these growing differences Jung still was a strong advocate of Freudian psychoanalytic theory and methodology believing it to be a major advance in exploring inner reality. Said Jung (1961): "I went on defending Freud and his ideas. But on the basis of my own findings I was still unable to feel that all neuroses were caused by sexual repression or sexual traumata. In certain cases that was so, but not in others. Nevertheless, Freud had opened up a new path of investigation, and the shocked outcries against him at the time seemed to me absurd."[33]

Jung Meets Freud

Jung, age thirty-two, first met Freud, twenty-five years older, in 1907. Highly taken with him, Jung (1961) records in his autobiography that Freud was "the first man of real importance I had encountered in my experience up to that time, no one else could compare with him. There was nothing the least trivial in his attitude. I found him extremely intelligent, shrewd, and altogether remarkable."[34] Yet, despite being deeply impressed by Freud, Jung's (1961) attitude was mixed at best; Jung (1961), summing up the visit, stated "my first impression of him remained somewhat tangled; I could not make him out."[35]

A key sticking point exciting Jung's intensifying ambivalence was what he believed was Freud's personal and professional "myopia" in dismissing the religious function as an important if not the central contributor to understanding symptom formation (teleological concerns). This point will be seen to be the central difference between each theorists' conceptualization of synchronistic phenomena. Still another very large difference between them was their opposing interpretations as to the understanding and implications of so called "occult" occurrences such as spiritism, apparitions, poltergeist phenomena and especially meaningful coincidences (synchronicities).

Critical of Freud's views on this subject, Jung (1961) said of Freud's attitude towards spirituality: "Wherever, in a person or in a work of art, an expression of spirituality (in the intellectual, not the supernatural sense) came to light, he suspected it, and insinuated that it was repressed sexuality."[36]

The Clash of the Titans: The Library Synchronicity in 1909

In 1909 Jung went to Vienna to visit Freud. He was particularly interested in hearing once again Freud's views on the occult and related matters. It is noteworthy that just at the time, when Freud was to confer onto Jung the official mantle of "heir apparent," Jung was preoccupied with challenging Freud as to their differences concerning so called supernatural subjects.

Despite Freud's doubts about Jung's "eccentricities," he believed him attractive enough to be the best person to take over the leadership of the psychoanalytic movement. But undeniable differences in personality and philosophy soon became apparent which were the precursors of a major rift. Relationship-defining differences between these two titans took the form of a dramatic clash of heated opinions centering on opposing points of view emanating from their joint experience of a shared coincidence located in Freud's library.

Jung asked Freud what he currently thought about parapsychological and occult matters. Apparently critical of the whole area of "occult" phenomenon, Jung (1961) states that Freud, bluntly rejected "this entire complex of [parapsychological] questions as nonsensical."[37] Jung (1961) inflamed by Freud's categorical dismissal of his treasured point of view, felt as if his "diaphragm were made of iron and were becoming red-hot – a glowing vault." Jung was outraged. At that precise moment there was a large report coming from the bookcase. Jung told Freud that the sound was "an example of a so-called catalytic exteriorization phenomenon." Freud exclaimed: "Oh come . . . That is sheer bosh." Defiantly Jung exclaimed: "It is not. . . You are mistaken, Herr Professor. And to prove my point I now predict in a moment there will be another such loud report." Sure enough, as if the scene was scripted by Jung, there was a repetition of another loud report. From this time on the relationship between Freud and Jung turned increasingly more distant.[38]

In his autobiography Jung (1961) reflecting on his experience of this momentous encounter, said, "To this day I do not know what gave me this certainty. But I knew beyond all doubt that the report would come again. Freud only stared aghast at me. I do not know what was in his mind, or what his look meant. In any case, this incident aroused his mistrust of me, and I had the feeling that I had done something against him. I never afterward discussed the incident with him."[39]

Jung's assertion that this was the end of the matter is not accurate as Freud responded in detail to this incident in a letter to Jung dated April 16, 1909. In this communication Freud indicates that initially he was quite impressed with the "occult" book case synchronicity. However, in an unsurprising Freudian move, Freud analyzes the event as explainable in naturalistic terms. In essence, without the presence of Jung, Freud observed that aperiodically the same loud reports were heard emanating from the bookcases. Freud reasoned they were the aperiodic sounds of dry wood stretching. Said Freud: (1909) "The furniture stands before me spiritless and dead, like nature silent and godless before the poet after the passing of the gods of Greece."[40] So at least on this occasion, for Freud sometimes a coincidence was just a coincidence with the addition of a heightened attention to detail.

Freud goes on to tell Jung about his own fascination with numerical meaningful coincidences with a decidedly malevolent turn to them. Freud had for many years believed that he would die either when he was 61 or 62. At a time when he was preoccupied with this negative thought he took a trip with his brother to Athens. He was surprised to see the frequency of the numbers 61 and 62 popping up all over the place particularly on vehicles. Depressed he went to his hotel room to give himself comfort only to discover that the number 31 was on the door.

Since 31 is half of 62 he felt haunted by these runs of numerical "ghosts." (Freud was clearly more than a little superstitious.)[41]

True to form, Freud (cited in Jung 1961) did not let the matter rest. He went about interpreting it using his own method of psycho-analysis. His associations led him to the conclusion that this predicted date of his death was associated with him having completed his first major work: *The Interpretation of Dreams* in 1900 along with being assigned a new telephone number: 14362.[42]

Freud understood and conveyed to Jung his understanding that this interpretation revealed a superstitious streak in himself. So be it. Freud (cited in Jung 1961) concluded the following about this odd coincidental run of repeated numbers and by implication all such similar events:

> I only want to say that adventures such as mine with the number 62 can be explained by two things. The first is an enormously intensified alertness on the part

> of the unconscious, so that one is led like Faust to see a Helen in every woman. (In a state of high emotionality it is not unusual to extend the concrete and particular into an abstract universal—an implied understanding of the possible psychodynamics of perceiving the individual experience in terms of archetypal experience.) The second is the undeniable "co-operation of chance," which plays the same role in the formation of delusions as somatic co-operation in hysterical symptoms or linguistic co-operation in puns.[43]

Freud, cited in Jung (1961), ends the letter with a condescending view of the whole matter: "I therefore look forward to hearing more about your investigations of the spook-complex, my interest being the interest one has in a lively delusion which one does not share oneself."[44] Indeed Freud's undisguised alarm at what clearly was Jung's unequivocal challenge to the first assumptions of psychoanalytic theory (hence an attack on Freud himself) was forcefully brought home to Jung in 1910. Freud (1961) said to Jung in the strongest of terms and tone: "My dear Jung, promise me never to abandon the sexual theory. *That is* the most essential thing of all. You see, we must make a dogma of it, an unshakable bulwark."[45]

In response to Jung's question as to what the bulwark was against, Freud (1961) answered: "Against the black tide of mud of 'occultism.'"[46] Jung (1961) responds in his autobiography:

> This was the thing that struck at the heart of our friendship. I knew I would never be able to accept such an attitude. What Freud seemed to mean by "occultism" was virtually everything that philosophy and religion, including the rising contemporary science of parapsychology, had learned about the psyche. To me the sexual theory was just as occult, that is to say, just as unproven an hypothesis, as many other speculative views. As I saw it, a scientific truth was a hypothesis which might be adequate for the moment but not to be preserved as an article of faith for all time.[47]

In the light of the above paragraph, it is interesting to view Jung's assertion of synchronicities defying intellectual explanation as an absolute fact rather than as just an intriguing hypothesis. However, Jung isn't the first researcher nor is he likely to be the last to contradict himself.

Freud's Attitudinal Shift

Reflecting on the book case synchronicity, Jung (1961) two years after it occurrence concludes that Freud was obsessed with his sexual theory. Thus he later notes with obvious pride that Freud's next two communications to him on the subject matter of the occult indicate that the "Master" was apparently more affected by the bookcase synchronicity than he realized at the time of the above communication. "Dear Friend [Jung], . . . I know that your deepest inclinations are impelling you toward a study of the occult, and do not doubt that you will return home with a rich cargo. There is no stopping that, and it is always right for a person to follow the biddings of his own impulses.[48] And "Dear Friend [Jung], . . . In matters of occultism I have become humble ever since the great lesson I received from Ferenczi's experiences. I promise to believe everything that can be made to seem the least bit reasonable. As you know, I do not do so gladly. But my hubris has been shattered. I should like to have you and F. acting in consonance when one of you is ready to take the perilous step of publication, and I imagine that this would be quite compatible with complete independence during the progress of the work."[49]

Popular opinion has it that Freud was too steeped in overly rational, nineteenth-century hydraulic/mechanical conventional science (psychic determinism/causes), preventing him from acknowledging what Jung believed to be the undeniable power of the "spiritual" aspects of reality, defining and directing man's purpose in being alive (prospective teleology/ends). In this connection, I believe it noteworthy that a careful reading of the literature associated with these two men indicates a much more complicated picture than that which is generally referred to in oversimplified black /white terms. As indicated in the above letters written to Jung, Freud was not narrow when it came to so-called occult matters. Instead of totally dismissing Jung's perspective on the occult, Freud instead was moved enough by Jung's ideas to develop a more open mind when it came to investigating the mysteries associated with the uncanny.

Indeed he went on to write a number of important papers on the subject concluding that with respect to parapsychological phenomena, telepathy is a fact. Freud (1921) was so fascinated in occult subject matters that he said in a letter to Carrington, "If I were at the beginning rather than at the end of a scientific career, as I am today, I might possibly choose just this field of research, in spite of all difficulties."[50]

Jung's Growing Estrangement from Freud

Following this relationship defining event in 1909 Jung's (1961) ambivalent attitudes about Freud intensified, expressed as a mixture of reverence and contempt. Aware that he was projecting a "father" transference onto Freud, desiring both acceptance and freedom from dependency, Jung was unable to break free from Freud's shadow despite his growing belief that his ideas were superior to Freud's.[51]

In this connection Jung was convinced that successful therapy meant more than Freud's assertion that a successful analytic experience enables a patient to convert neurotic suffering into an acceptance of everyday common misery.

Strongly opposed to Freud's starkly realistic attitude Jung (1961) states, "my whole being was seeking for something still unknown which might confer meaning upon the banality of life. . . . To me, it was a profound disappointment that all the efforts of the probing mind had apparently succeeded in finding nothing more in the depths of the psyche than the all too familiar and "all-too-human" limitations."[52]

Highly motivated to strive for something better than the "all-too- human-limitations" reinforced Jung's increasing preoccupation with the content and themes associated with the esoteric occult, spirituality, and sexuality.

With respect to the issue of sexuality that preoccupied Freud, Jung's (1961) alternative credo was to move beyond the "biological function" towards its spiritual aspect and its "numinous meaning" and "thus explain what Freud [to repeat] was so fascinated by but was unable to grasp."[53] Jung advanced the notion that there is a fundamental division in the psyche: the lower personal unconscious sexuality, and biology, and the higher collective unconscious, in the realm of the archetypal and the spiritual.

In his questing for the numinous, the transcendent, the occult, and absolute meaning Jung's interest in meaningful coincidences was born and nurtured. Says Jaffe (1970): "The synchronistic phenomena arranged by the archetype arouse wonder and awe, or an intuition of unfathomable powers which assign meaning."[54]

It now becomes clearer that the essential differences in Jung's and Freud's attitudes as to the nature and understanding of synchronistic (occult/spiritual) events are due to a combination of a number of influences. These influences are: undeniable differences in their personalities; their focusing on differing patient populations (Freud's "neurotics patients" and Jung's "identity diffused patients"); primary differences in their ontological and epistemological assumptions concerning the nature of reality and the acquisition of knowledge of reality; and differences in their selection of alternative concepts from the realm of the collective consciousness used to impose order on the raw data of their experience. All of these factors contributed to a major break in their relationship in 1912.

Some believe that the break with Freud directly led to Jung suffering, a "nervous breakdown" soon after, characterized by Ellenberger (1970) as a "creative illness."[55]

Jung's Self-Imposed Isolation

Following the break with Freud, Jung (1961) in 1912 "entered a "space" he refers to as "a period of inner uncertainty."[56] This period was characterized as such because, rejecting Freud as his "guru," he had no one to turn to for guidance except himself, but was too unclear of what he stood for to feel he could be his own reliable final authority. Unable to definitively identify his personal guiding myth, Jung experienced a seemingly intractable impasse.

In the midst of this protracted four year "psychological grid lock" experience Jung had a series of dreams and fantasies that for him, was a mother lode of potentially significant material. Jung's response, parallel to Freud's experience of his own breakdown, was to commit himself to embarking on an inner journey, confronting the contents of his unconscious mainly using his dreams and fantasies as his primary analytic material.

Extreme love and hate feelings intensified after his break with Freud preceding his nervous breakdown. Commenting on this fact Jung (1961) states: "One of the greatest difficulties for me lay in dealing with my negative feelings."[57] Thus he diagnosed himself as suffering from a serious ambivalence conflict.

Paralleling and identifying with many of his patients' complaints Jung feared that in facing these feelings (often expressed as terrifying destructive fantasies) he feared being overwhelmed resulting in a possible loss of whatever shaky sense of self he had been able to muster up to that time. It should be noted that in my research with synchronicity prone patients virtually all of them initially shared Jung's fears of confronting negative emotions (intense ambivalences) often associated with panic anxiety derived from experiencing an accompanying fear of loss of self.

Jung's Creative Illness

Generalizing from Jung's and others' similar experiences (including Freud and William James), Ellenberger (1970) describes the criteria for a creative illness as follows:

> A creative illness succeeds a period of intense preoccupation with an idea and a search for a certain truth. It is a polymorphous condition that can take the shape of a depression, neurosis, psychosomatic ailments, or even psychosis. Whatever the symptoms they are felt as painful, if not agonizing, by the subject, with alternating periods of alleviation and worsening. Throughout the illness the subject never loses the thread of his dominating preoccupation. It is often compatible with normal, professional activity and family life. But even if he keeps to his social activities, he is almost entirely absorbed within himself. He suffers from feelings of utter isolation, even when he has a mentor who guides him through the ordeal (like the shaman apprentice with his master). The termination is often rapid and marked by a phase of exhilaration.

> The subject emerges from his ordeal with a permanent transformation in his personality and the conviction that he has discovered a great truth or a new spiritual world.[58]

During his "creative illness" Jung contacted a particularly vivid and rich realm of his unconscious characterized as mytho/poetic which he named the collective unconscious. Jung relying on his direct experience as his guide, believed that the collective unconsciousness when connected to the archetypes yields "absolute unmediated knowledge." This assumed uninterpreted absolute archetypal knowledge (when channeled by intuition) may be used in the service of individuation of the self. Jung came to believe that the archetypes play a major role in the formation of symptom formation particularly that of dissociative disorders and schizophrenia. Jung operationally defines the importance of archetypes as follows: "The archetypes, which are pre-existent to consciousness and condition it, appear in the part they actually play in reality: as a priori structural forms of the stuff of consciousness. They do not . . . represent things as they are in themselves, but rather the forms in which things can be perceived and conceived" (note the parallel to Plato's forms).[59]

While aware that emotionally charged images had personal historical associations from an individual's early psychological development (one of Freud's core observations), Jung was more inclined to see them as a bridge to universal mythological knowledge. Indeed Jung was so awe struck by the quality and other worldly experience of his "archetypal" dreams and fantasies that it may account for why he tended, at such occasions, to link his associations to myths rather than to his own developmental history.

Often fearful and confused by his discoveries, Jung refers to them as if he were alone in the darkness with all the dreadful and frightening connotations that this image stirs up for most people. In the midst of his ordeal Jung was aware that it would have been nice to have had a spiritual guide to sort out the wheat from the chaff. This undisguised wish for good guidance from a wise and trusted authority—either on the earth plane or in the realm of "spirit" is central to the experience (and I believe understanding) of synchronicities referred to in this book. Said Jung (1961), "I could have wished for nothing better than a real, live guru, someone possessing superior knowledge and ability, who would have disentangled for me the involuntary creations of my imagination."[60] Extending this idea Jung (1961) states, "Philemon and other figures of my fantasies brought home to me the crucial insight that there are things in the psyche which I do not produce, but which produce themselves and have their own life."[61]

Jung vacillates as to whether or not he believes this communication with "spirit guides" (i.e. Philemon) is just a byproduct of his active imagination or that his imagination is unconsciously connected to a realm of independent subsistent transcendent spirits who literally act in the role of good guides. An example of this lack of clarity is seen in the following summary of a brief conversation between Jung and an educated man who was a friend of Gandhi.

The friend, after telling Jung (1961) that he believes himself to be personally guided by a real spirit guide, goes on to say: "[While] . . . most people have living gurus [there] are always some who have a spirit teacher."[62]

One of the most impressive experiences associated with synchronicities is the sense that the experiencer is being guided by messages sent by some mysterious "caring" force located in a transcendent "spiritual" realm. A naturalistic interpretation of synchronicities would have to account for this experience in non mystical terminology. This task will be attended to in further chapters.

Jung might have put more weight on science and scientific method as the more reliable bridge to the "objective" truth if it wasn't for the insistent presence of odd, uncanny, anomalous occurrences happening all through his life. Its powerful impact on him was undeniable. For example, as his ideas were being shaped, Jung (1961) recalls a particularly "ominous atmosphere" in 1916 when he felt the air was filled with ghostly entities actually believing his house to be haunted. Other odd occurrences happened repeatedly such as his oldest daughter believing she saw a ghost in the house at the same time the doorbell rang when no one was visibly present.[63]

Experiences like these reinforced Jung's belief that conventional science including Freud's psychoanalytic theory was woefully inadequate in explaining these undeniably perplexing phenomena. Thus he struck out on his own path to attempt to correct the perceived deficiencies of Freud's conceptualizations. However while opposing many of Freud's fundamental ideas, Jung's scientific voice needed to be heard.

The scientific part of Jung (1961) connected these events with "a state of emotion . . . favorable to parapsychological phenomena." He went on to interpret it as "an unconscious constellation whose peculiar atmosphere I recognized as the numen of an archetype."[64] Yet just as it would seem that the scientist was in command of his observations, he would encounter another set of seemingly irrational and inexplicable events rendering him once again awe struck and almost speechless.

Irrespective as to the objective truth of the issue, Jung believed that everyone has this layer of experience and it is important to personify these fantasies, integrating their power into a balanced whole. Thus he, like Freud, once identifying the essential structures of their personalities, including a map of what makes them tick, tend to over-generalize their personal findings to all mankind.

In this connection Jung (1961) states that his life work was to be "drawing conclusions from the insights the [collective] unconscious" had given him. He believed that "this is the fund of unconscious images which fatally confuse the mental patient. But it is also the matrix of a mythopoetic imagination which has vanished from our rational age."[65] Jung (1961) extending this idea says, "Only here, in life on earth, where the opposites clash together, can the general level of consciousness be raised. That seems to be man's metaphysical task—which he cannot accomplish without 'mythologizing.' Myth is the natural and indispensable intermediate stage between unconscious and conscious cognition."[66]

At this time in his career, 1916, Jung was aware of a major gap between his thinking and that of Freud. Says Jung (1961): "When I parted from Freud, I knew that I was plunging into the unknown. Beyond Freud, after all, I knew nothing; but I had taken the step into darkness."[67] Jung struggled to integrate his ideas and experiences into a coherent theory. His difficulty was largely due to the fact that his insights challenged the basic assumptions upon which conventional science was constructed. Thus he was in conflict as to which source would offer the most objective truth of his larger questions: science or religion. Jung's creative solution in surmounting this impasse was to substitute the word *or*, in the question of science or religion, to the word *and*, thus his answer was science *and* religion. This blend of science and religion resulted in the creation of Jung's unique brand of psychoanalysis he named analytical psychology.

To assert, that for Jung, the exploration of the archetypal contents of the collective unconscious of which synchronicities are thought to be their visible manifestation became his primary concern is no exaggeration. For Jung the study of their nature, anti-causal assertions, and their implications of a spiritualized realm of transcendent reality that is the source of vital absolute meaning that can and should be reconnected to by all mankind, became Jung's life-long preoccupation.

It was during his "breakdown" that Jung (l961) created/discovered the core concepts of the collective unconscious, archetypes, the archetypal experience, and the transcendent function relating them to his own personal experience. Upon emerging from his "creative illness" Jung became deeply preoccupied with the experience of and attempts to understand meaningful coincidences.

The Seminal "Scarab" Synchronicity

On the face of it, Jung's seminal "scarab" synchronicity, most likely occurring around 1925, is quite striking in and of itself. However, as will be shown its significance for Jung, was undoubtedly both personally and professionally a pivotal experience for him. The important details of this "scarab" coincidence are the following. Jung notes that he had all but resigned in helping a patient resolve her therapeutic problem. This is so because of her (defensive) overreliance on "Cartesian rational thinking." Jung (1961) said she had a compulsive need to be right and thus fought off getting in touch with what today might be thought of as allowing herself to experience ambiguity and so called irrationality more generally thought of as a "feminine" trait.[68] In Jungian terminology she had too much animus and too little anima.

Jung believed the cause of her need to be "over controlled" was due to a disconnection from her "transcendent function." To bridge this disconnect, Jung believed that she was in need of some unexpected life experience that would shake her up, so to speak, providing what might be thought of as a kind of "spiritual shock treatment."

Presumably, the experience of Jung's patient being handed the scarab by him during her therapy session following the dream of the night before, wherein she was handed a golden scarab, was such a positive shock to her system that it had the effect of dramatically breaking through her defensive rigid attitude (a positive trauma).

This breakthrough, so records Jung, had the net effect of transforming her, in the sense that she was finally able to make a felt connection with her "spiritual" self presumably providing a pathway to the significant change she had hoped to experience in her therapy.[69]

The Awe Response

The initial reaction of both his patient and Jung to the improbable confluence of the dream scarab, the parallel live scarab appearing at the window the next day, and being handed a scarab by her therapist was presumably experienced by her as intensely awesome—a quintessentially numinous experience.

An important element of Jung's synchronicity theory is that a meaningful coincidence occurs when the experiencer has made a meaningful connection with an activated archetype experienced as an awe-filled aura of numinosity. Perhaps then, having this particular patient in mind, Jung (1978) speaking of numinosity states, "With archetypal content, [and] a mystical aura about its numinosity . . . it has a corresponding effect upon the emotions. It mobilizes philosophical and religious convictions in the very people who deemed themselves miles above any such fits of weakness."[70]

Says Aziz (1990) exploring Jung's theory of synchronicity and religion states that the numinosity "imparts through the affect, a nonrational experience of transcendent [absolute] meaning . . . It infects the ego with a sense of wonder."[71] J. Jones (1993) speaking about this same feeling state says, "Because the experience of the sacred evokes feelings of awe, dread, incomprehension, and mystery in us, the object of that experience must be mysterious and beyond comprehension."[72]

As to the effects on his scarab patient, Jung (1978) says that the numinosity of this seminal coincidence was powerfully impacting: "'transforming' her personality from rigid to significantly more open to her feelings. . . . Her natural being could burst through the armour of her animus possession and the process of transformation could at last begin to move."[73] I believe that Jung's awe reaction upon experiencing this and other meaningful coincidences should not be underestimated. This reaction of awe most likely accounts for the mixed rational and irrational structure of his dualistic: partially religious/partially scientific, psychological/supernatural/ mystical theory of synchronicities.

In this connection, it is important to note that Jung was clearly of the opinion that knowledge vital for development of the soul would make its presence known mainly in bodily sensations, feeling, and intuitions (and only secondarily) to whatever ideas and insights were generated in the mind. Emphasizing this point Jung (1976) says what is most important about this process is "not how explicitly an archetype can be formulated but how much I am gripped by it."[74]

At the same time that Jung was aware of feelings of numinosity in his patient, he was aware of it in himself as well. While it is a fact that this "scarab synchronicity" was presumably an important life defining event for his patient, it is an absolutely certain that it was an equally life defining occurrence for Jung himself. This event was so important to him both personally and professionally that, although he would later contradict himself, Jung states, "never before nor since has he ever experienced an event quite like that one was."[75]

Just viewing the surface it is easy to understand how he or anyone for that matter might feel the same way about synchronicities. Imagine being a perplexed Jung, obviously deeply engaged in trying his best to understand his patient's core issue so that he could help her find the best path to resolve what seemed to her and Jung to be an intractable problem. Probably unknown to his patient, both she and her therapist were simultaneously stuck in a treatment impasse (transference resistance?) neither of them able to find a way to get her to penetrate her intellectualized defenses.

It is in this context that his patient receiving a gift of a scarab in her dream of the night before her next session, paralleling Jung's hearing, seeing, grabbing, and handing over the scarab beetle to her in the following day's session, was experienced by both of them as an intensely emotional and a wondrously awesome (numinous) shared experience.

In this light, it is interesting that this event touted by Jung as having had unmatched significance for him is not dated. He does indicate that he treated this young woman patient in the early 1920s describing the scarab occurrence. But aside from these few facts there is no indication of a specific time nor other pertinent details.

Given the powerful importance of this event for Jung, I believe that what was not recorded is in fact equally as important as what was recorded. All attempts by this author to find the specific date of the scarab synchronicity have resulted in failure. This fact is particularly intriguing, as Jung seems to have dated most everything he produced. It should be noted that the author corresponded with Diedre Bair (2003) who wrote an eight hundred page biography of Jung and his life and works. In a letter received from her, she wrote that the omission of this crucial date was very curious and was as puzzled by its absence as is the author of this book.[76] It is also noteworthy that aside from Jung's assessment that his patient experienced a major break-through, presumably benefitting her, there are no known follow up notes indicating whether or not her progress was sustained, or perhaps short lived.

In this connection I am reminded of a psychotherapy patient, J, who entered treatment in despair, lamenting the fact that she had been born wanting desperately to die but too afraid to do so. She wished she had a belief in God but this was out of the question. One day, a few years into treatment, she called, unusually upbeat, saying she would have to cancel her session. She said that she was in the back seat of a car driven by her father when on a rain slick New Jersey highway the car flipped over and landed straight up adding "no one in the car was hurt." Feeling as if she had been "miraculously" saved, her reaction was to uncharacteristically assert that there must be a God. She sounded as if her deep depression had finally lifted. Her enthusiasm conveyed the unspoken belief that she had been cured by her connection with divine intervention. I was pleased for her. However, it is to be noted that the positive effects of her spiritual transformation lasted for about two weeks when she plummeted back into the depths of despair due to some unanticipated disappointment. It is unfortunate we don't know if Jung's "scarab" patient experienced a similar fate or perhaps had a more fortuitous outcome.

Summary of the Importance of the Scarab Coincidence for Jung

It is valuable to summarize the reasons for Jung's high ranking of this seminal scarab synchronicity. These reasons are as follows:

1. Whereas Jung believed that this "scarab" synchronicity and his interpretation of it purportedly had the effect of shattering the over intellectualized defenses of his patient resulting in a positive acceleration of

her treatment, there is no doubt that this same synchronicity experience was a profoundly moving event for Jung. This particular coincidence, appearing to be the first one of its kind to be experienced by him, is conjectured to have dynamically brought together in a single event the core concepts he had explored in his period of self-imposed isolation. Thus this synchronicity may be considered to be a marker experience of a notable progression (crystallization) of Jung's creative powers notably in the area of synthesizing and integrating previously disparate abstract concepts into a dynamically lived concrete experience (cathexis).

2. Another point of interest is the fact that Jung, a protégé of Freud, familiar with the theory and practice of psychoanalysis, in working with his patient, apparently completely overlooked the three most important conceptual psychological "tools" in psychoanalytic interpretation. These tools are the concepts of transference, resistance, and a combination of the two known as a transference resistance.

When working to understand the unconscious contributions to the formation of a particular patient's symptoms, these psychological tools have been found to be of invaluable help in resolving complicated issues that on the surface appeared inscrutable.

Implications of the Jungian Perspective

At this point, the reader may wonder if I'm being a bit too picky. Concerning synchronicities, why not just accept the implications of a mysterious connection with occult forces and let it go at that? Who really knows the truth of the matter anyway, and isn't it ultimately a question of personal preference?

For those who accept the Jungian half naturalistic and half mystical/magical formulation as an article of faith there are no troublesome issues. But for those who are skeptical of this supernatural account, Jung's formulation presents a profound intellectual challenge. The key issue is answering the most basic question of being alive: who is the final authority in your life?

The answers range from a person assuming the final authority and responsibility for their life versus consciously or unconsciously projecting the final authority onto some other real or imagined person in the "real" world or in the world of "spirit." Additionally something of felt importance is happening. These occurrences are real, often profoundly impacting, and challenging. If they are not "messages" from divinity then where do they come from?

Viewed in this light, the positing of these two linking principles—one causal and the other a-causal—places synchronicities square in the middle of an historical debate beginning with the pre Socratic philosophers framed as a dialectic between alternative views of the acquisition of knowledge as well as alternative views as to the nature of the knowledge acquired. These two views are that the content of objective knowledge of reality and the means by which we acquire knowledge. Either knowledge is (l) discovered (deduced) or (2) it is created (induced). Further,that the knowledge accessed is either revealed or is realized. Thus, continues a dialogue between the adherents of Plato (Jung) versus the adherents of Aristotle (Freud) with respect to determining whose perspective provides mankind access to the truer truth.

Freud's Warning to Jung

In the following passage Freud sounds a strong note of caution in facing the anti-analytic seductive lure of the occult (including organized religion). Freud (1933) chooses the pathway of science over the pathway of religion as the primary gateway to the "truth." "It is hard for us to avoid the suspicion that occult interests are really religious ones, and that it is one of the secret motives of the occult movements to come to the aid of religious belief, threatened as it is by the progress of scientific thought."[77]

It might be asked, how Freud would have interpreted the Scarab synchronicity if he had been the analyst. Most likely he would have insisted that he strip away any of the supernatural filigree. He would most likely have viewed the scarab material as embedded in the psychological and situational contexts of his patient to determine causality.

Jung would probably argue that while Freud certainly makes sense from his own frame of reference, the crucial point is, that when it comes to these particular events, Freud's psychoanalytic method utterly fails as it is simply not up to the task. This is so because these events apparently defy comprehension when exclusively utilizing Freud's psychodynamic formulations.

Freud would likely counter that there is something yet to be understood that would make a logical explanation valid implying that what is still admittedly mysterious is potentially understandable in scientific terms, yet to be named. In this connection it is interesting that Jung either chooses to dismiss his knowledge of a likely transference resistance of his patient in not analyzing the material given to him; or is so emotionally carried away by his own experience of the scarab coincidence that he appears to have lost his professional objectivity. Instead of being the conventional analyst interpreting the material he treats it as only a "real and present" event. He also emphasizes the connection between her the patient and him the analyst as two people participating in the shared magical "numinosity" of the moment (participation mystique).

Whether it was done intentionally or was a "Jungian slip" his omission of taking note of his patient's probable transference resistance in his interpretation of the "scarab" coincidence—is a clear rejection of the core concepts utilized in classical "Freudian" psychoanalysis. One can only conjecture what the outcome would have been if he had asked this patient a number of important questions. These questions include: what the meaning of this event was for her? What else was associated with the golden scarab? What was the meaning(s) of her being given a gift? And, indeed, a special gift from perhaps a special man—in this case her analyst?

And all of that might have been a propitious occasion for him to explore with this patient the nature of her probable idealizing and or father transference to Jung at this particular time in her treatment.

The above is not meant as a condemnation of Jung. He was of course free to do what ever he thought was in the best interest of his patient. He might in fact have done all or at least some of the above—we will never know as apparently it was not recorded. These questions are mainly raised to indicate that there is considerably more to be observed about these events than just the surface of the typical reaction of awe referred to as a numinous experience. This is so particularly, when such meaningful coincidences occur in the context of a therapeutic relationship.

Observing this de facto debate between the Jungians and the Freudians (as is often the case with such matters), we witness partisans lining up, steadfastly insisting their point of view is the more correct one, thus if one side is essentially right then the other guy's must be essentially wrong. The question is raised: is there a way to break this seemingly intractable I'm totally right/you're totally wrong theoretical and methodological impasse?

Jung's Scientific Response to the Scarab Coincidence

Although Jung was emotionally enthralled with the religious implications derived from his numinous feelings associated with the scarab synchronicity, he could not permit himself to totally luxuriate in a bath of numinosity treating this synchronicity (and presumably all subsequent synchronicities) as if it was only a wondrous "just so story." As a scientist schooled in Freudian psychoanalysis he felt obliged and challenged to make rational sense out of what clearly was experienced by both him and his patient as patently irrational. Thus he embarked on a multi - year investigation to make the seemingly irrational co-incidents rationally explainable.

Jung's Initial Attempt to Explain Synchronicities Using Freudian Psychoanalytic Concepts

Two organizing questions guided Jung's scientific research in this area. Question 1 is: what process best explains the presence of the scarab given to her in a dream preceding her next therapy session with Jung? Question 2 is: what process best explains the link between the subjective event A and the parallel objective event A'?

Question 1

Jung reasoned that when viewed independent of each other, it possible to analyze the dream scarab as a byproduct of his patient's idiosyncratic psychological process (psychodynamics). Thus the image of the scarab appearing in the patient's dream had associations to her personal history that could be viewed as symbolic material connected to other material associated with her current therapeutic concerns. For Freud the associations would likely to have been viewed as a repressed sexual symbol arising out of the patient's personal unconscious unsurprisingly derived from some unresolved sexual conflict from her childhood. For Jung, the dream scarab was viewed as the activation of an archetype of rebirth and transformation arising from the patient's recent connection with the collective unconscious.

While differing as to the source of the psychic imagery, both Jung and Freud would have likely agreed that the dream scarab was adequately explainable in terms of psychodynamics and may therefore be thought of as psychically determined material obeying laws of conventional cause and effect (psychic determinism).

Question 2

It is in the consideration of the second organizing question: What process best explains the union of the patient's scarab with the parallel scarab at Jung's windowpane, that a major controversy erupts. It is this thorny problem that Jung dared to meet head on and wrestled with for the rest of his life.

On the face of it, this would be no easy task as any investigator who has attempted to rationally explain the nature of these anomalous events will surely testify. Take the present example: the key question raised in this coincidence is how to rationally explain the link between scarab 1 and scarab 2: two obviously meaningful parallel events occurring almost simultaneously but seemingly having no apparent cause and effect connection.

To say that the dreamer accurately predicted (foretold the future) seems fanciful at best. How could she possibly have dreamed up the "scarab" beetle appearing at her therapist's windowpane at exactly the same time she was either dreaming about the scarab experience and/or in the conscious activity of describing her scarab dream to Jung? By the same token it is too great a stretch of anyone's imagination to conjecture that Jung's part of the scarab experience could somehow have been foretold by him and that the content of this perplexing experience could somehow have been psychically telegraphed back to her.

If the dreamer didn't read the future and Jung didn't influence her past then on the face of it there is no apparent causal connection between scarab 1 and scarab 2. And yet, this is the compellingly sticking point—there is clearly an undeniably strong connection of meaningful significance connecting scarab one and scarab 2 made all the more uncanny by the proximity of the two scarabs occurring so close together.

Jung, the scientist, like others who attempt to explain these events exclusively utilizing the organizing concept of conventional scientific cause and effect (psychic determinism), inevitably run up against this same logical impasse. Trying to adequately explain the link between the dream scarab and the scarab appearing the next day at Jung's windowpane defies explanation utilizing an exclusive use of conventional scientific cause and effect concepts.

Jung's way out of this theoretical impasse was to concede the point that if no causal linking principle could adequately explain the link connecting A and A' then causality should be discarded as a linking principle, followed by logically substituting his radical a-causal linking principle in its place.

However, as a seeker of truth and respectful of the pressures of politics, Jung was aware that in order to stand a chance of gaining adherents for his radical anti-causal point of view he would have to use scientific method to argue his point persuasively. With this aim in mind, to make his case in rejecting the use of an exclusively rational cause and effect explanation of meaningful coincidences scientifically valid, Jung asserted three anti-causal arguments he believed were irrefutable.

Jung's Three Anti-Causal Arguments

1. Rare and Spontaneous Events: A problem concerning method
2. Necessity and Relativity: A problem of meaning
3. Simultaneity: A problem of time

These three anti-causal arguments will be carefully examined in chapter 3. However, before undertaking this task it is valuable to understand the reasons for challenging Jung's near intellectual monopoly on this puzzling subject matter.

Among the reasonable arguments that can be made for challenging Jung's presumably irrefutable arguments are: (1) an intellectual challenge to all those who affirm a different set of ontological and epistemological primary assumptions from those of Jung and his adherents; (2) In the spirit of objectivity a need to answer a whole host of questions that are derived from Jung's often "fuzzy" mystical formulations; (3) numerous warnings by Freud that to uncritically accept Jung's mystical magical anti-intellectual theory of synchronicities is escapist, and possibly delusional; (4) his provocative categorical assertion flies in the face of the continuing dialectic of history; and (5) there is compelling evidence that Jung's psychology, by his own admission, is responsible for his remarkable theory. Thus like all human beings—categorical assertions to the contrary—Jung's theory is but one of a number of conceivable theories of synchronicity.

Undoubtedly, Freud's commentaries concerning the "lure of the occult" have a great deal of validity as it has been a half a century since Jung published his paper "On Synchronicity." It is no coincidence that during this lengthy time period only two naturalistic theories of synchronicities have been published. We live in an age of crisis and uncertainty. We long to be enveloped in a cloud of fog so that our senses don't have to continually be exposed to the multiple horrors all around us. World War I, World War II, Korea, Vietnam, Iraq, and the War on Terror are but a few examples of what motivates many of us to believe with all our hearts and minds that there is—or should be—some transcendent conscious force that is good, loving, and comforting. We feel that this force can and often does violate the laws of conventional cause and effect and miraculously intervenes on our personal behalf at times which are unpredictable but do apparently happen—the "faithful" will say in the presence of meaningful coincidences (synchronicities) thought by many to be nothing less than hard evidence of "God's small miracles."

How can we begin to understand how masses of men and women are so quick to hand themselves over to the most brutal and sadistic dictators over and over again even though the script has been played and replayed hundreds of times. Must not it be as Eric Fromm has gently pointed out in his seminal book *Escape From Freedom* that people who should know better are willing—perhaps eager—to project their final authority onto one who promises they will be taken care of in order to avoid taking responsibility for one's self in order to avoid the pain of experiencing inevitable anxiety.[78] Life is hard and terribly difficult and it takes courage to face the daily struggle for survival let alone aspiring to thrive. It is comforting to believe there is an answer man who transcends us and has all the capital A answers if only we open our hearts and passively channel the coded communications he, she or it is continually sending us in the form of synchronicities.

In this context—Freud insists that our delusions to the contrary be stripped away and for us to not close our critical minds and be lured by the soporific siren call of the occult. Freud (1941) continues to warn:

> The occultists . . . will be welcomed as liberators from the irksome obligation of thinking rationally. . . . It is a vain hope that analytic work would escape this collapse of values simply because its object is the mysterious unconscious. If the spirits, with whom man is familiar, provide the final explanation, then there will be no interest in the laborious approach of analysis to understand unknown psychic forces. Even analytic technique will be forsaken when hope beckons that occult measures will enable one to enter into direct communication with the spirits who determine everything, just as one forsakes patient detail work, when there is hope of winning riches at a single stroke, through speculations.[79]

In looking over the salient facts of Jung's struggle to develop and to maintain a solid identity (self) it is evident that meanings generated from the earth plane for him were vastly inferior to the absolute meanings he believed were both a-priori and transcendent. Thus when Jung (1961) says that "he was seeking for something still unknown which might confer meaning upon the banality of life" and that this meaning is to be found in mythological consciousness; and still further, that, for him, the highest form of acquired knowledge is connecting with archetypal knowledge (a religious experience), he is leading himself and his adherents towards an inevitable supernatural interpretation of meaningful coincidences.

Add in the fact that he apparently dismissed any attempts to understand his Scarab patient's seminal synchronicity utilizing the concepts of transference and resistance, combined with his apparent need to prove Freud wrong and himself right, and it appears that Jung may well have had had a major blind spot, both intellectually and experientially, greatly biasing his attitude toward these anomalous phenomena as a mixture of natural and supernatural elements. From this perspective, Jung's radical conclusion that he doubted "whether an exclusively psychological approach can ever do justice to the phenomena in question" is not a coincidence but is an inevitable fait accompli given his particular psychological problems, his personality and character, all predisposing him to select from the collective consciousness those organizing concepts that were most congruent to his direct experience and belief system.

In short, although a genius, he was still a flawed and troubled man (as are most of us mortals) and for this reason was limited in his vision to what he was able to see determined by his attained level of consciousness at any one time. In this connection the following quotation from R. D. Laing is particularly apt: "The range of what we think and do is limited by what we fail to notice, and because we fail to notice that we fail to notice there is little we can do to change until we notice how failing to notice shapes our thoughts and deeds."[80] Agreeing with Laings that we all see what we are capable of seeing at any one time it follows that, when Jung asserts his doubt about "whether an exclusively psychological approach can ever do justice to the phenomena in question" it is fair and reasonable to doubt his doubting.

To assert doubt is to indicate that one lacks certainty about claiming possession of absolute knowledge of some issue in question. It does not mean that what is doubted is absolutely in error, only that one questions it. In Jung's case the crux of his doubting is the nature of the linking principle connecting the subjective psychological state (A) with the objective so called objective event (A'). His specific doubt directly challenges an inferred Freudian purely psychodynamic interpretation of the connecting link replacing it with Jung's partial supernatural perspective resulting in the radical principle of a-causality. What Jung does not do is to consider that there may be another form of causality other than that of conventional causality that may adequately provide a naturalistic account of these acknowledged anomalous phenomena.

Jung's three anti-causal arguments are the intellectual crux of his supernatural theory of synchronicities and signal an implied intellectual challenge to all those skeptical investigators who simply do not feel his provocative therefore intellectually challenging conclusion resonates with their own direct experience. Thus, if it can reasonably be shown that, despite Jung's categorical assertions to the contrary, his three anti-causal arguments are indeed refutable, then the way will be cleared for the potential emergence of one or more naturalistic theories of synchronicities.

It is important for the reader to know that if my own initial de facto identification and concurrence with Jung's perspective, followed by my subsequent doubting due to significant changes wrought from taking seriously the meanings generated from my own direct experience, this present intellectual challenge would not have come about. But doubt I did, and as a result this de facto challenge is accepted and forms the content of chapter 3, Refuting Jung's Three Anti-causal Arguments.

3

Refuting Jung's Three Anti-Causal Arguments

Argument 1: The Problem of Rare and Spontaneous Events (Methodology)

SYNCHRONICITIES ARE LIKE RANDOM FLICKERS OF LIGHT emanating from the bodies of fireflies therefore it seems impossible to pin them down. Because of the unpredictability of their occurrence it does not seem feasible to investigate them scientifically as systematic research requires the "subject" in question to be observable in a specified location at a specified time.

The randomness of synchronicities permitted Jung (1955) to assert his first anti-causal argument—an argument about methodology—as follows:

> Scientific method assumes that all phenomena obey laws of cause and effect. Knowledge of these relationships comes from subjecting events to controlled experiments. This presumes that the phenomenon to be investigated is repeatable on demand. Since synchronicities are always spontaneous and rare, their unpredictability would seem to resist meeting this basic requirement of scientific method. Thus it follows that events like these are inexplicable from a causal perspective.[1]

Implied in this argument about methodology is Jung's foreclosing the possibility of ever finding a way to subject these events to scientific scrutiny. My research indicates that Jung's categorical conclusion is unsupported by some significant facts of which he was either unaware or perhaps chose to overlook.

A Rebuttal of Jung's First Anti-Causal Argument

Science aims to establish order out of chaos seeking to discover regularity in apparent randomness. When applied to synchronicities, Jung concedes that there is a certain amount of order present even in the apparent randomness of synchronicities up to a point. So that while each synchronicity is spontaneous, and unique, each and every synchronicity, as previously described, has a common structure. However, order and regularity fail to materialize when the researcher attempts to explain the nature of the link connecting the internal A psychic event with B, the external event. Therefore, to formulate an adequate naturalistic theory of synchronicities obligates the theoretician to bring this perplexing and seemingly inexplicable connection between the two halves of any synchronicity into the realm of scientific investigation—a task which Jung categorically believes is doomed to inevitable failure from the very start.

In this light, the first anti-causal argument is the most crucial one. For if there is no adequate methodology which can pin down these phenomena enough to be able to examine them scientifically then the positing of an irrational connection has to be seriously entertained as the most valid conceivable conclusion to be reached however distasteful this seems to those who would like to believe otherwise.

Johnson (1996) convincingly points out in *Fire in the Mind* never underestimate the ingenuity of curious minds to fashion new organizing concepts that find serendipitous openings in seemingly impassable walls. "Instead of regarding complexity as a fixed platonic essence sitting in the middle of a neat scale, perhaps we should think of it as an ever-changing relationship between observer and observed. The implication, of course, is that there may be no preexisting, canonical order woven into the universe, waiting to be found. The orders we alight upon are, at least in part, human inventions; they depend on the lenses we use."[2]

Freud's Inferred Response

One such creative mind was that of Freud (1934) who in 1919, reflecting about supernatural phenomena, issued a challenge to all open minded people to answer the question: Is what the occultists tell us true or not?—a thinly veiled challenge to Jung, meaning, is what Jung tells us true or not?[3] Mindful of this thorny issue of problematic methodology Freud (1934) offers the following guidance: "We will further our suspicion that the application of psychoanalysis may throw a light on other so called occult facts."[4]

Freud would likely insist that even though there is an apparent mystery at hand when considering the nature of synchronicities it does not necessarily mean that no rational explanation is possible. What is called for is not a resigned attitude of passive surrender but a renewed attempt to make seemingly "just so" existential occurrences into data that can be viewed as problems to be solved. While there are other sources that could be mined, one rich addition to the realm of the collective consciousness that has important theoretical and practical applicability in enabling synchronicities to be scientifically investigated is the philosophical movement known as pragmatism.

Pragmatism: Principles and Methodology

Pragmatism is a method of inquiry that applies scientific method in identifying and resolving mundane human problems. In this connection pragmatism, says Kaplan (1961) "is an instrument for . . . change, formulating new values and providing a conceptual framework by which they can be grasped and realized."[5] Pragmatism assumes that direct experience is the core focus of human beings. While people strive to survive and to thrive they often find themselves besieged by internal and external interferences of one sort or the other resulting in a state of relative imbalance. This state is often characterized as one having "problems."

The pragmatic method is one approach to identifying, exploring, and resolving these problems. In so doing it employs two conceptual attitudes in guiding those who engage in problem solving. Synchronicities arise in the context of a person experiencing themselves hopelessly stuck in fruitlessly trying to resolve a seemingly unresolvable psychological problem.

There are two core principles in pragmatic thinking which are relevant in formulating an adequate rebuttal to Jung's naturalistic methodological challenge. These principles are (1) contextualism and (2) the genetic method.

Contextualism views all problems as embedded in a "particular biological and cultural matrix" and, further "the conceptions that grow out of and tested by experience are inevitably conditioned by that matrix."[6] Contextualism also implies "that data and solutions are ultimately concrete, rooted in the particular existents that make up the context, not in the abstract generalities of a fictitious world of ideas."[7] Another way of saying this is that in an accurate description of a problem lies an embedded solution. For example, if you accurately define a particular problem as a person suffering from a feeling of psychological emptiness, an apt solution is to fill the emptiness up with experiences of meaningful connectedness.

Applied to studying synchronicities, contextualism says look for the answers to the mystery of the linkage of A with A' in the particular context of a given person's concrete experience. Stay grounded in the particulars of that material and don't get diverted by vague, transcendent, speculative imaginings such as speculative realms of "absolute meaning."

Thus when considering the scarab patient, the pragmatic perspective would have the therapist focus on where she currently is in her treatment, the state of her relationship with her therapist, Jung, the nature of the transference, what she wants with and perhaps from him; what she thinks are the reasons preventing her from changing, and the likes. In technical psychoanalytic terminology, the contextually aware therapist would analyze the state of the transference between his "scarab" patient and Jung.

The Genetic Perspective

In addition to defining contexts, the pragmatist is interested in both the historical origins of a given problem as well as in ascertaining its significance, purposes, and function. A therapist, for example, is most interested in knowing the concrete particulars with respect to "how did the context in which [the problem] arose shape the character it now presents to us?"[8]

Applied to investigating the nature of synchronicities I think it worth repeating what Freud (1919) had to say in differentiating his methodology from that of the "superstitious": "The difference between myself and the superstitious person are two. First he projects outwards a motivation which I look for within; secondly, he interprets chance as due to an event, while I trace it back to a thought. But what is hidden from him corresponds to what is unconscious for me."[9]

It is important to note that in the seminal "Scarab" synchronicity, Jung overlooks any historical material about his patient. Jung is clearly interested not where this woman has come from (analyzing her developmental origins) but to where he thinks she needs to be going—specifically reconnecting her to her lost transcendent function, a decidedly religious or spiritual goal.

Additionally, Freud would no doubt be interested more in the idiosyncratic associations of this patient—eliciting the meanings of the various scarabs to her—rather than focusing exclusively on his own associations, that is, Jung's conviction that the scarab double is a symbol of rebirth and transformation assumed to have the same meaning for his patient as it obviously did for Jung.

Thus a naturalistic approach to understanding the psychological process leading to the production of meaningful coincidences would necessitate: (1) an interest in the developmental origins of this patient's problem and (2) eliciting the concrete meanings a given synchronicity has for this particular patient.

These two pragmatic principles, contextualism, and historical origins, taken as a compressed attitude in viewing problematic material, when applied to investigating the nature of synchronicities, views them as byproducts of a yet to be identified naturalistic psychological process omitting any notion of a supernatural or transpersonal connection with some assumed realm of absolute meaning.

Towards this aim, Devereux (1953) in his book *Psychoanalysis and the Occult* makes the critically important point that because it necessitates a human being to identify and process a given synchronicity "this indicates that [these phenomena] are psychological phenomena, which must be studied in terms of the psychological frame of reference."[10]

Speaking to this point, Helene Deutsch (1926) pondering the difficulty of explaining occult phenomena, spells out the concrete details of such a "frame of reference" providing critically important guidance in conceptualizing a methodological breakthrough for scientifically investigating synchronicities even though they are rare, spontaneous, and seemingly random events. Deutsch's intriguing idea was to demystify so called "occult" phenomena, such as synchronicities, into a person's stream of experience.[11] In so doing, Deutsch believed that these kinds of mysterious events would be transformed from incomprehensible to comprehensible, by filling in the gaps that come to light in the analytic process.[12]

When the pragmatic principles listed above are combined with the conceptualizations of Deutsch, Devereux, and Freud, the resulting mix may be utilized as an organizing methodological filter to make naturalistic sense out of the seemingly supernatural phenomena of synchronicities. This means that synchronicities may now be scientifically investigated by viewing them as embedded in potentially knowable psychological contexts.

My research suggests that when viewing these perplexing events arising out of potentially knowable contexts psychological causality will be sufficient to adequately explain the conditions under which synchronicities arise, will illuminate the psychological process which produces them, and will adequately explain how this naturalistic process links the internal event to the parallel external event despite Jung's insistence that this task is inconceivable in rational terms.

Freud's Metapsychology as a Schema for Contextual Analysis

There are a variety of possibilities when thinking about fitting synchronicities into a continuum of one or more contexts. It is my view that the most comprehensive schema for contextual analysis is the "outmoded" Freudian Metapsychology. The Metapsychology is an ingenious set of overlapping contexts in which any piece of psychic material may be viewed. Unfortunately it is out of vogue and generally dismissed as a passé construction of "metaphysical abstractions."

The following is a brief outline of Freud's six metapsychological principles representative of the types of principles that might profitably be used, singularly or as a composite set of lenses, by which opaque material—that is, the seemingly mysterious conjoining of A and A'—might be potentially illuminated. Freud's six metapsychological principles are (1) the dynamic, (2) the topographic, (3) the structural, (4) the genetic, (5) the economic, and (6) the adaptive.[12]

The essence of each of these principles follows.

- *The dynamic point of view* "assumes that mental phenomena are the result of the interaction of forces."[13] Symptom formation is an example of the dynamic point of view. It is assumed that a naturalistic theory views synchronicities as the surface manifestation of a potentially knowable psychodynamic process.
- *The topographic point of view* identifies inner reality as composed of consciousness, the preconscious, and the personal unconscious. The topographic point of view "describes the different modes of functioning that govern conscious and unconscious functioning."[14] The primary process holds sway over the unconscious. The secondary process directs conscious phenomena.
- *The structural point of view* "assumes that the psychic apparatus can be divided into several persisting functional units."[15] The major units are: the id (basic instincts of libido, and aggression), the super ego (the internalization of the law expressed as shoulds and should nots); the ego (the internal traffic cop mediates between the pressures exerted by the id and the super ego); and the self represents the total person.
- *The genetic point of view* "concerns the origin and development of psychic development. . . . It brings into focus the biological-constitutional factors as well as the experiential."[16]
- *The economic point of view* "concerns the distribution, transformations, and expenditures of psychic energy."[17] An example of the economic point of view is the concept of sublimation.
- *The adaptive point of view* states that "the implied assumption that all psychic behavior is directed serves conscious and un conscious purposes."[18]

These six principles constituting the metapsychology may be utilized as a composite lens of overlapping contexts by which complex psychological material may comprehensively be viewed. Additionally, it will be shown that selected metapsychological concepts will yield alternative theoretical perspectives regarding the nature of synchronicities. When applied to understanding the process that leads to the production of synchronicities it is hypothesized that these six principles—the meta psychology—may be utilized as an effective way of potentially understanding the whole process by which synchronicities are produced from an exclusively naturalistic perspective.

For example: Faber's emphasis on taking into account the earliest experiences of the newborn focuses the investigation of synchronicities towards the origins of self development—the pre-oedipal stage—the first two years of life. Faber's core constructs, utilized as a composite lens to illuminate what he believes to be the relevant contexts out of which synchronicities are processed, are derived from object relations theory, a relatively new development in the realm of depth psychology. The point is, whether utilizing the metapsychology schema or Faber's object relations schema, it is rationally conceivable that the entire process that leads to the production of these seemingly elusive anomalous phenomena become fit subjects for scientific scrutiny.

On a practical level, to fulfill the requirements of this task requires the researcher to keep a carefully annotated journal recording relevant contexts in which synchronicities are embedded. These contexts may include: the surface situational context, that is, identifying where the person is located in time and space; the present psychological context: that is, identifying the major psychological problem preoccupying the person; and identifying the developmental/historical psychological context, that is, identifying origins, and vicissitudes of the identified core psychological problem assumed to underlie each and every meaningful coincidence.

A Practical Application of Contextual Analysis

One implication of utilizing contextual analysis in understanding the nature of synchronicities for a given theorist is that different ontological and epistemological assumptions and associated organizing concepts yield different theoretical conceptualizations about the process assumed to explain their occurrence.

To test the validity of utilizing contextual analysis to investigate the psychological origins of Jung's half psychodynamic (naturalistic), and half supernatural theory of synchronicities a contextual analysis of Jung's personal and professional life relevant to his preoccupation with synchronicities follows.

In chapters 5 and 6 a contextual analysis of my personal and professional life leading to my own purely naturalistic theory of synchronicities will be described in detail.

Contextual Analysis of Jung's Theory of Synchronicities

In Jung's case, an application of contextual analysis is to see how knowledge of the salient facts of his developmental history have played a crucial role in both determining his interest in, and the shaping of, his particular psychodynamic/supernatural perspective. Before embarking on this task it should be noted that Jung (1955) most likely anticipating this kind of an approach directed to himself, wrote the following comments in an article called "Psychology and Literature." In this article Jung draws a distinction between himself and Freud with respect to their differences in understanding the causes of a given creative artist's production, presumably including theory construction as well. "Freud thought that he had found a key in his procedure of deriving the work of art [theory] from the personal experiences of the artist. . . . For it was conceivable . . . that it might be traced back to those knots in psychic life that we call the complexes. It was Freud's great discovery that neuroses have a causal origin in the psychic realm—that they take their rise from emotional states and from real or imagined childhood experiences."[19]

However, while granting Freud credit for determining the poet's (theoretician's) psychic predisposition permeating his work, Jung warns that the created product cannot be explained causally. Instead, says Jung, it comes about only when the artist makes a direct connection with the archetypal collective unconscious. This assertion is precisely the same one he makes concerning the apparent a-causal connection between the internal psychic event A and an assumed transpersonal supernatural external counterpart (A').

By contrast, in a particularly relevant and persuasive book, *Faces in a Cloud*, Stolorow and Atwood (1979) embrace the reverse point of view. Agreeing with Ellenberger, these authors assert that the theoretical thrust of a given theorist, such as Jung, Freud, or Rank may be most profitably understood as their dedicated attempts to resolve their core psychological problems. These authors state that their particular metapsychological systems "are in part reified expressions of their creator's most problematic subjective experiences."[20]

Following this path what follows are the salient details of Jung's personal and professional historical and psychological contexts most related to the development of his theory of synchronicities.

Jung's Early Life

Beginning with the foundation of Jung's personality development it is clear that the two major authorities is his formative years—his mother and his father—presented major obstacles in his need to grow and maintain a solid sense of himself.

Jung's mother went into a sanatorium suffering from debilitating depression when he was three years old. He experienced her loss as a traumatic abandonment. As a result he was quoted as saying that he had a lifelong distrust for women, equating the word woman with "innate unreliability."[21]

Whereas he might have been expected to use the relationship with his father as a substitute or complement to the rupture with his mother, that one failed as well. His father, filled with religious doubt, left Jung with a fundamental sense of basic estrangement blocking the way to a much needed nurturing relationship.[22] Frustrated in his attempts to maintain a basically favorable connection with his two parents, Jung had a lifelong problem in tolerating normal ambivalent feelings (love/hate). His way of dealing with them was to split his experience into all good/all bad categories.

This splitting of all good/all bad is representative of Jung's lifelong obsession with "the reconciliation of opposites, the problem of wholeness and integration."[23] It is noted that this issue is intimately associated with each one of the synchronicity identified patients in this book.

Jung had a "lasting wish for a regressive restoration of the original relationship."[24] This early rupture between Jung and the experience of a union with an idealized good mother and subsequent regressive wish for a reunion is the basis for Faber's regressive naturalistic theory of synchronicities. This point will be discussed in detail later on in this chapter.

Jung's frustrated need for good guidance from a respected father and mother left him feeling essentially isolated and alone with his inquiring, imaginative but often confused and insecure self.

The Psychological Roots of the Collective Unconscious

In this framework it is no coincidence that Jung turned to the occult with its sense of mystery, transcendence, perfection, promise of eternal meaningful connectedness, and absoluteness as a substitute for the needed but frustrated meaningful connections with his parents and with himself. It was in this context that Jung created the concept of the collective unconscious, located by him in the realm of transcendent reality that was assumed to be universal and transpersonal. Concepts such as the collective unconscious became the equivalent of a psychological life preserver for Jung.

Commenting on this idea Stolorow and Atwood (1979) state, "[Jung's] work on the theory of the collective unconscious represented an attempt to prove that the finite and fragile phenomenon of individual consciousness rests upon and derives from a timeless, imperishable foundation located deep within the psyche [Jung's psyche]."[25] Stolorow and Atwood (1979) conclude, "Contact with the collective unconscious [populated with organizing archetypes functioning like the stones of his early childhood] provided a sense of eternity, changelessness, and stability transcending the threatening forces of the interpersonal milieu."[26]

Like many theorists, Jung was not prepared to simply account for his own experience as only applicable to himself. Instead he assumed, as many theorists tend to do (notably Freud) that what he experienced in himself was also assumed to be universal. Commenting on this point Stolorow and Atwood state, “By reifying the image of the interior foundation and by trying to demonstrate its reality through empirical investigation, Jung transformed a fantasized source of stability, continuity, and transcendence into an actual, objective, entity existing independently of the trouble world of external–object relationships.”[27]

In asserting his supernatural point of view, Jung was now clearly at odds with Freud. But being a truth seeker dedicated to the rigorous reality testing that science demands, he was determined to find scientific validity for his anti-conventional scientific discoveries.

In this connection Jung (1961) said,

> It was clear to me from the start that I could only contact with the outer world and with people if I succeeded in showing—and this would demand the most intensive effort—that the contents of the psychic experience are real, and real not only as my own personal experiences, but as collective experiences which others also have. Later, I tried to demonstrate this in my scientific work, and I did all in my power to convey to my intimates a new way of seeing things. I knew that if I did not succeed, I would be condemned to absolute isolation.[28]

Stolorow and Atwood (1979) conclude, “From the fact that [Jung's] subjective world was organized around the wrenching issues of self-dissolution, self-division, and never-ending conflict, it follows that his ideal self-image would be one of integrated harmony, reconciliation, and transcendent wholeness.”[29] If these authors' conjectures be taken as reasonable, it must be concluded that it is no coincidence how the particular mystical coloration associated with Jung's theoretical point of view assumed its particular slant. Thus, it is conjectured, that synchronicities may be understood from a number of alternative perspectives depending upon the nature of the psychodynamics and the vicissitudes of a particular investigator.

Because I initially identified with Jung and his belief system but gradually found myself consumed by doubt, I felt personally challenged to answer for myself as to whether or not his three anti-causal laws were indeed, as he insisted, irrefutable. At the same time, my psychoanalysis was forcing me to realize that each and everything of which I am preoccupied in the “here and now” may be profitably viewed in the light of overlapping situational and psychological contexts. Viewing the surface—the story—in embedded contexts—the plot—illuminates the personal meaning of what one is aware of at any one time. The literary critic E. M. Forster (1956), in his book called *Aspects of the Novel*, says: “The Queen died is an example of the story. The Queen died of a broken heart is an example of the plot.”[30] Whether it be the contents of a book or the material of a patient in treatment—an analyst is always trying to illuminate the motives of a given character/patient to explain how a certain event came about.

In my case, I was trying my best to understand the nature of my serious doubts concerning the nature of myself and what was really real. With this all consuming task in view I began to understand how the salient facts of my life, mined in my psychoanalytic sessions, clearly demonstrated an intimate connection between my primary psychological conflicts and the associated overlapping contexts (situational, psychological, historical, and temporal) in which my experience and interpretations of synchronicities were embedded. A detailed analysis of my nineteen major synchronicities and the contexts in which they were embedded are discussed in chapters 5 and 6.

Anti-Causal Argument 2: The Problem of Necessity and Relativity

Conventional physics believed that there are necessary relationships connecting events with each other. That is, that event B could be demonstrated to invariably follow from event A. Modern physics has demonstrated that necessary is replaced by probability theory. Since there is no apparent necessary connection between A and A' of a given synchronicity then once again causality is eliminated.

By eliminating (conventional) causality, Jung concludes: "[this] leaves us only with equivalence of meaning and simultaneity."[31] While this formulation is apparently clear to Jung, this researcher believes that these terms—meaning and simultaneity—raise more perplexing questions than provide definitive answers.

Before rebutting Jung's second anti-causal argument it is reasonable to conjecture that a naturalistic understanding of these anomalous events is likely to be found in a careful examination as to what is meant by the meaning associated with the Jungian phrase "an equivalence of meaning" and the still unaddressed relationship between causality and meaning.

Jung's Conceptualization of "The Equivalence of Meaning"

"Equivalence of meaning" is assumed by Jung to be a direct pathway to the acquisition of vital self knowledge. It is important to recall that the acquisition of knowledge associated with synchronicities from a Jungian perspective assumes that it issues from an assumed realm of absolute meaning that is both transcendent and transpersonal with respect to human beings. Hence meaning, as in the phrase "equivalence of meaning," is assumed to exist a priori to human experience. This line of reasoning is the basis for Jung's (1955) radical and challenging assertion: "However incomprehensible it may appear, we are finally compelled to assume that there is in the unconscious something like an a priori knowledge or immediate presence of events which lacks any causal basis."[32]

Jung's phrase "the equivalence of meaning" refers to the similarity or double (twin) nature of the subjective and the objective events comprising any synchronicity. For example: being handed the scarab in his patient's dream is equivalent in meaning to the scarab beetle Jung handed his patient in her next day's therapy session. However, Jung implies that meaningful connectedness associated with synchronicities is much more than simply an exact duplicate of each scarab reference. What is of most importance to Jung, is not only that both "scarabs" together add up to an equivalency of meaning; but, that the parallel scarabs are surface manifestations of an individual connecting with an activated archetype originating in the assumed realm of absolute meaning.

For example, the two scarabs experienced simultaneously and somehow felt to be meaningful, derive their meaningfulness, according to Jung, because they are external manifestations of an activated archetypal symbol the knowledge of which is supposed to further the individuation of a given experiencer. Most importantly, connecting to this realm of absolute meaning is assumed to occur directly, that is by passing the five senses, hence it is unmediated knowledge that is passively acquired (channeled), whole and pure, without needing to be subjected to interpretation of any kind.

Extending his conceptualization of the realm of absolute meaning Jung characterizes it as equivalent to mythological consciousness regarded by him as the substrate of human knowledge. Aziz (1990) describes this mythological dimension in the following way:

> The mythic function . . . analogous to a symbol . . . draws the individual to a higher level of consciousness—a synthesis in which the personal is enriched by the transpersonal . . . This assumes that each person's life has a pre-formed "cosmological meaning." Note the widespread belief that everything that happens for good or for ill may be conceived of as having a preordained purpose according to some unknown but palpable plan. With the collective unconscious, archetypal knowledge, Jung extends this idea of a pre ordained "plan" into the realm of spirituality and concludes that each person is on a "spiritual journey."[33]

In this light, synchronistic events are religious experiences. Says Von Franz (1966), "Synchronistic events constitute moments in which a 'cosmic' or 'greater' meaning becomes gradually conscious in an individual; generally this is a shaking experience."[34]

The naturalists believe such a mystical conceptualization of the nature of meaning is not only inaccurate but potentially dangerous. Shamanism and spiritualism notwithstanding, such a view of meaning fosters the fanciful notion of angels, communication with master teachers and guides, miraculous divine intervention, with or without a collaboration with the receiver. Irrespective of one's belief system the conceptualization of Jung's meaning in the phrase "equivalence of meaning" is truly awesome, but is it true?

Freud's Psychodynamic Perspective

Freud's scientific attitude at such impasses was not to concede to a defeat of reason but to press on to construct new concepts that would act as beams of light in an otherwise dark forest. The location for these new concepts was for him not to be found in the collective unconscious but rather to locate their origin in the realm of shared mundane experience of the collective consciousness. This means that whatever experience initially appears to be unintelligible can be made potentially comprehensible when subjected to analysis via the lenses of new organizing concepts.

An apt quotation by C. I. Lewis (1929), in *Mind and the World Order*, amplifies this point of view:

> Even "the unintelligible" is a sort of category, a temporary pigeon-hole in which items are filed subject to later classification when we have some further light on them or it becomes more imperative to understand them. . . . Intelligibility is always a matter of degree. [See *Fire in the Mind* and Kuhn's *The Progression of Science.*] Nothing is completely understood. . . . The ascription of intelligibility and unintelligibility is always relative—relative to our present powers and relative to those interests which make interpretation in some particular way momentarily important or desirable.[35]

Applied to Jung's second anti-causal argument—the problem of rare and spontaneous events—what is needed, to refute it, as Freud implies, is an infusion of new organizing concepts enabling these random events to be brought under the scrutiny of scientific investigation.

Rebuttal of Jung's Second Anti-causal Argument

It is conjectured that some of the difficulties involved in the argument as to whether causality is, or is not adequately able to be used to explain the nature of the nexus linking A and A' of a given synchronicity is largely due to a lack of specificity as to what is precisely meant by the terms causality and meaning and their interrelationship.

In this light, Jung rests this second anti-causal argument on three debatable assumptions. These assumptions concern the nature of causality; the nature of meaning; and an implied relationship between causality and meaning. Specifically, (1) Jung assumes that there is only one kind of causality that can be conceptualized to explain the link between A and A' and that this one and only conceptualization of causality is found to be irretrievably inadequate; (2) Jung assumes that by replacing causality with the concept of "an equivalence of meaning" that this operational definition of meaning is unquestionably clear; and (3) Jung further assumes that there is no direct nor indirect relationship between causality and meaning. A discussion of each of these three assumptions follows.

1—The Possibility of an Alternative Form of Causality

The elimination of conventional causality as an explanation of the way in which the two halves (A + A') of a meaningful coincidence are linked, does not eliminate the possibility of an alternative form of causality from being an adequate explanation. Speaking about the nature of telepathic dreams, Devereux (1953) asserts that before adopting a psi principle of causality what is called for is not a revision of basic psychoanalytic laws but, rather, a deeper understanding of the particular logic determining the nature of their cause and effect relationships.[36] It seems reasonable to apply the same guidance in understanding the nature of synchronicities.

Devereux (1953) makes the following additional points. Since it takes a human being to register a synchronicity this means it should be treated as a "psychological phenomenon" that is viewed from the perspective of a psychological matrix implying the idea of conceptual analysis.[37] In so doing, the investigator looks for the particular psychodynamics which motivate a person to assume that the two events in question are linked.[38]

It is to be noted that Jung would argue that most assuredly the two events are connected by means of the collective unconscious resulting in his radical half psychodynamic and half transpersonal a-causal synchronicity principle. By contrast, a naturalistic understanding of the nexus would hypothetically result if the collective unconscious is replaced with the personal unconscious.

The point is that even if conventional causality initially seems to be an inadequate explanation when it comes to understanding the nature of synchronistic anomalies, we should not quickly jump on the band wagon of Jung's adoption of his radical a-causal principle.

Addressing this issue is Johnson (1996) strongly supporting the argument advanced by St. Thomas Aquinas and others that we should not stop looking for causal explanations until we have exhausted all reasonable attempts to do so. In this connection he says: "The point of science is to expel miracles, to explain the world through natural law."[39]

Causality as a Psychological Construct

According to Mach's dictum, "There are no laws in nature. We put laws in nature." In this connection causality may aptly be viewed as " projections on the part of the mind of the [investigator] who imposes the patterns of his own thinking upon the world which he believes himself to explore."[40] This strongly suggests that different "minds" (consciousness) may well have differing conceptualizations of causality.

If this assumption is accurate then the conceptualization of causality explicitly or implicitly utilized by a given theorist to explain the linking principle connecting A and A' is intimately related to the theoreticians' attained level of consciousness. Thus it is hypothesized that alternative forms of consciousness will conceptualize alternative forms of causality utilized as linking principles. For example, a theorist (or any experiencer) who perceives synchronicities through kaleidoscopic, or transcendent consciousness contrasted with a theorist (or patient) who perceives synchronicities through unity consciousness will be expected to have alternative conceptualizations of causality. The main point is there appears to be no getting around the fact that one's psychology is always playing an intimate role in whatever conceptualization of causality or a-causality one conceives.

Devereux's Critically Important Conceptualization of Causality and Occult Occurrences

A close inspection of the term causality reveals that the causation referred to in Jung's anti-causal arguments is conventional scientific causality thought of as "mechanical-hydraulic causality" commonly associated with nineteenth-century Newtonian science. Jung apparently assumes that Freud's operational definition of causality is essentially the same one as that described above. This strikes the investigator as exceedingly curious given the fact that Jung was fully aware of Freud's psychodynamic formulations in which the concept of causality (psychic determinism) appears to be infinitely more complex than "mechanical hydraulic causality." Assuming this to be the case, then the evidence suggests that Jung did not do justice to Freud's conceptualization of causality—a form of causality which might aptly be referred to as psychodynamic causality or, simply, psychological causality.

Expanding on the nature of psychological causality Devereux (1953) asserts that there are essentially two different conceptualizations to account for causality as a linking principle in the observation of so-called occult (including synchronistic) phenomena: The usual one is when A and B parallel each other because they are both identical to C or are both derived from C. But an alternative view of causality is when A parallels B because A causes B to be that way.[41]

Such a concept of the process is patterned upon communication between two individuals (or between a me and a projected me). Devereux (1953) expanding upon this intriguing idea indicates that whereas it is true that event A occurs before event B it functions as the structural model for the parallel event it induces in B.[42]

This means that the conventional notions of causality and classical Freudian psychic determinism are now conceptualized as a process of structuring that which is perceived.[43]

In this connection, a number of alternative forms of causality have been conceptualized which lie in between conventional causality and Jung's principle of a-causality. Presumably one or a possible combination of these alternative conceptual forms of causality might be utilized as adequate linking principles in naturalistically explaining the link between A and A' in synchronicities.

An Alternative Form of Causality and Synchronicities

Devereux (1953), speculating about the nature of the relationship between causality and synchronicities observes that while not obeying conventional laws of conventional causality (i.e. mechanical causality), events such as synchronicities appear to have their own unique forms of logical relatedness. Implied is a different order of logic yet to be identified.[44]

Following Devereux's lead, a theorist who is attempting to propose an adequate naturalistic theory of synchronicities has to propose a conceptualization of causality that has a logical relatedness but is not one that is associated with conventional mechanical causality. In this connection, another form of causality that appears to adequately account for the link between the two halves of a given synchronicity is a composite of three alternative forms of causality; namely, teleological, immanent, and transient causality—each form of causality having its own unique form of logic—which if joined together might aptly be referred to as psychological or psychodynamic causality.[45]

Psychological causality (expressed in the form of psychodynamics) may be viewed as a composite of overlapping causes being deterministic in the conventional mechanical sense; producing changes in itself as in the immanent sense; and being purposefully directed as in the teleological sense. This composite or hybrid causality might be aptly referred to as synthetic, psychodynamic, or as psychological causality.[46]

Psychological Causality

If psychological causality is hypothesized to be an adequate replacement for both conventional "mechanical" causality, as well as Jung's radical a-causal principle the question arises: what is the operational definition of psychological causality when it is applied to adequately explaining the nexus linking A and A' in a given synchronistic occurrence? While there are probably other possibilities, the following operational definition of psychological causality is proposed. Psychological causality obligates a researcher to delineate some "sequence [repetitive patterns of sequential relationships], under definitely known conditions."[47] (See the findings in chapter 9.)

In this framework: known conditions applied to synchronicities means searching for repeated psychodynamic patterns. Knowledge of these patterns is obtained by an examination of selected overlapping contexts (including current situational preoccupations; current psychological problems; and developmental historical contexts) from which meaningful coincidences emerge. The important point in the discussion above is that Jung appears to be premature in his categorical assertion that there is no way to rationally explain the link between A and A' thus eliminating causality. The major thesis of my research, is that there is at least one alternative form of causality—psychological causality—that may be utilized in the service of adequately explaining the seemingly unexplainable from a naturalistic perspective. If this proves to be accurate then Jung's half supernatural, magical, mystical theory of synchronicities will be demystified.

The Relationship Between Causality and Meaning

Additionally Jung sparks another unresolved issue by glossing over the meaning of meaning. He does so in the following way. Convinced that the nature of the perplexing nexus is to be "explainable" only by utilizing the principle of a-causality leaves all interested parties with a connection of only an equivalence of meaning and simultaneity. However, contrary to Jung's assumption that the meaning in the phrase equivalence of meaning is or should be unquestionably evident, a closer inspection indicates that this is simply not the case.

2—The Nature of Meaning in the Phrase "An Equivalence of Meaning" Is Open to Alternative Definitions

This investigator takes the position that synchronicities might be profitably viewed from the broader perspective of the way in which the self and the object world are connected. In this view synchronicities are connections distinguished from other events only by virtue of the special meanings attributed to them but share with all other events the same process eventuating in their construction. The way in which the self connects to either itself or to that which exists outside the self is the major focus of the process of acquiring any knowledge. The process whereby human beings gain knowledge—knowing—will be viewed from two perspectives: (1) the general issues and (2) the specific issue.

The General Issue

The general issue seeks to understand how any subjective state A' gets linked to an objective event A' irrespective as to whether the nature of the link be thought of as due to a principle of causality or a-causality. An example of a general issue is identifying one's reflection in a mirror as oneself. Three elements should be noted and distinguished: There is the observation made that one's face (A) is reflected in a mirror (A')—(a) indicating that a connection has been made, (b) conscious and/or unconscious meanings may or may not be attributed to the connection of the reflected image, and (c) conclusions reached about what has been perceived will determine subsequent attitudes and behavior. Additional concepts derived from the collective consciousness, particularly in the last fifty years, have shed much light on this complicated issue.

Linking the subjective with the objective (A + A') philosophically can be thought of as imposing order (meaningful connections) out of the seeming random raw data of experience. Philosophically, this task falls under the province of epistemology—theories of knowledge. Representative of new directions in understanding the nature of meaning and its relationship to causality is that of the Pragmatists John Dewey, Pierce, William James, C. I. Lewis, Polyani, and Frosch. For example, in *Mind and the World Order*, C.I. Lewis (1929) operationally defines philosophy as "the study of the a priori, and is thus the mind's formulation of its own active attitudes."[48] This naturalistic conceptualization of the a priori is one hundred and eighty degrees at variance with Jung's transcendent view of the a priori. Says Jung (1955): "Synchronicity postulates a meaning which is a priori in relation to human consciousness and apparently exists outside man."[49]

C. I. Lewis, an advocate of the naturalistic perspective of the a priori, states: " although the a priori represents the contribution of mind itself, to knowledge, it does not require that this mind be universal, absolute, or a reality of higher order than the object of knowledge."[50] With respect to obtaining knowledge he continues : "there is no knowledge merely by acquaintance; that knowledge always transcends the immediately given."[51]

If it is true that there is no knowledge merely by acquaintance then it follows that knowing anything is an active process that always involves some form of interpretation. To interpret means to impose some order via some form of conceptualization onto the raw data of experience. Speaking to this point, C. I. Lewis (1929) states: "For the validity of knowledge, it is requisite that experience in general shall be in some sense orderly—that the order implicit in conception may be imposed upon it. And for the validity of particular predictions, it is necessary that a particular order maybe ascribed to experience in advance."[52]

It is further assumed by C. I. Lewis (1929) (and other pragmatists) that the "interpretation is an attitude . . . which serves practical action and relates to what is not given."[53] Concepts are used to aid individuals solve problems that are initially experienced as gaps or discontinuities in experience. These gaps are felt to be "stuck" points or forks on the road of one's life journey.

Applying this pragmatic view applied to the acquisition of knowledge associated with synchronicities, the above assertions by C. I. Lewis (1929) means that "it is the function of mind to bridge gaps or discontinuities in experience by assigning to the present given an interpretation though which it becomes related to, or a sign of, a correlation between certain behavior of my own and the realization of my purpose."[54]

Support for this philosophical point of view applied to understanding the nature of synchronicities are concepts added to the collective consciousness, specifying what knowledge is, where it comes from, the ways it is constructed, and describing uses to which it is put—all of it from a naturalistic or scientific perspective. In this connection, perceptual, developmental, cognitive, and depth psychologists generally agree with the philosophical position of pragmatism that the process of knowing always involves an interpretive (personal) element in establishing all such meaningful connections.

Findings indicate that facts (the raw data) to be known are not passively received but are, instead, selectively chosen out of the flow of streams of experience. Sometimes the selection is made consciously but more often the selection is apparently made unconsciously, or preconsciously both below and /or outside the level of total awareness. Whether a selection of data from the flow of personal experience is made consciously or unconsciously, it is a response to (purposefully) satisfying some potentially knowable human need.

In this formulation, acquiring knowledge of something is an active process involving a particular individual always adding something of itself in the selection of "facts" and in the interpretation of those "facts." In so doing the process of knowing always involves some causal agent (the self) generating links between some subjective state A with some objective state A' resulting in a link of meaningful "significance."

Links of significance will be referred to as meaningful connections. This active process of meaning making is also known as psychological causality (psychodynamics). An apt description of psychological causality is that of Kaplan (1961) in his book *The New World of Philosophy*: "The facts of experience are not "data"—what is given—but rather what is taken: a "fact" is etymologically something made. The perceptual experience from which knowledge issues is more like reading the expression in a face than it is like solving a cryptogram or a crossword puzzle. What is at work is not a process of sheer ratiocination, but processes of identification, introjection, and other such mechanisms, largely unconscious and preconscious."[55]

Thus, a naturalistic interpretation of meaning takes the position that each person is ultimately stuck with accepting final responsibility for the idiosyncratic meanings that govern his life giving it value.

This means "that in the final analysis, ultimately there is your experience, your experience of your experience, the conscious and unconscious meanings attributed to your experience, and the role these meanings play in a persons' psychic economy expressed in the form of attitudes and behavior" (personal communication, Rudolf Wittenberg).[56]

By contrast, Jung believes that really absolute "meaning" is assumed to be located "out there"—transcendent, a priori, in its own absolute realm of existence. Further, for Jung, this realm of absolute meaning is equivalent with mythological consciousness regarded by Jung as the substrate of human knowledge.[57]

Meaning Is or Is Not A Priori to Human Experience

Braude makes some important points with respect to analyzing both the meaning of meaning as well as analyzing the relationship between synchronicities and meaning making. Braude's second argument is a refutation concerning Jung's (1955) assertion that "Synchronicities postulate a meaning which is a priori in relation to human consciousness and apparently exists outside man."[58]

Disavowing Jung's conceptualization of ultimate reality being a homogenous unity equivalent to philosophical concepts like mind stuff, Plato's *nous*, or Leibnitz's pre-established harmony, Braude (2002) says, "This [concept of a realm of absolute meaning] assumes that nature has a structure intrinsic to it (whether macroscopic, microscopic, subatomic, or logical) just waiting to be discovered."[59]

Braude believes this assumption to obviate the facts as we know them as he tacitly supports the pragmatic philosophical position that meaning is not something to be passively swallowed whole but must be actively interpreted. Braude

(2002) states: "[Nature] does not have a structure waiting to be discovered and transcending any perspective or point of view one might have."[60]

Finally, Braude supporting a contextual (pragmatic) perspective indicates that the particular ways that history (past, present, or future) is divided depends on the purposes of a particular individual in question. Braude (2002) says: "the meaningful similarities or connections between events are not built into nature independently of any such perspective or guiding set of purposes."[61] Thus Braude implies that an adequate naturalistic (causal) explanation of synchronicities is most likely to come about when there is a clear understanding of the process of meaning making—an amplification of a linking principle known as psychological causality.

Psychological causality means that there is no un-interpreted knowledge. Meaning presupposes a self that actively selects facts and then adds something of himself by way of interpreting the selected facts determining what Wm. James refers to as the "cash value" or purpose to which the idea(s) is put. In this connection Braude (2002) says: "As we have seen (a) history has no intrinsic structure or meaning; (b) attributions of either structure or meaning presuppose a perspective or point of view or history; and (c) these perspectives are not autonomously existing things, but presuppose instead an interpreter or consciousness who owns (so to speak) the point of view."[62]

It Necessitates a Person to Have a Synchronicity

The difference between these mundane connections and a synchronicity is the special meaning we attribute to the connection enhanced by the typical experience of "numinosity" accompanying these events. Without a live person reacting to the external stimulus/event as a synchronicity, there would be no synchronicity. In this frame of reference, if an individual must necessarily note the stimulus that will be the basis for a given synchronicity this clearly fits the operational definition of psychological causality.

Even Aziz (a strong advocate for the Jungian point of view) in his important work called *C. G. Jung's Psychology of Religion and Synchronicity* highlights Jung's "fuzzy thinking" on this matter. Aziz (1990), first responding to a criticism of Rao, who says: " some examples of synchronicity given by Jung himself, devoid of their symbolism, appear to be no more than mere coincidence,"[63] then comments: "Here I think Rao puts his finger on a critical shortcoming in Jung's presentation—that Jung does not consistently demonstrate how the symbolical meaning of the synchronistic event specifically relates to the psychology of the individual."[64]

Aziz (1990) continues raising some serious questions about Jung's logic: "If these events are understood to have a special meaning for the subject, something that a chance coincidence by definition does not have, it is of the greatest importance . . . to know in what exactly this meaningfulness consists, specific to the subject. This is something, however, which Jung does not consistently demonstrate."[65] Chapters 5, 6, and 7 will examine in great detail the nature of the meanings of each synchronicity described as it is related to the overlapping contexts out of which each synchronicity springs.

Fully agreeing with Aziz, it is a major task of this book to begin to fill in the specific psychodynamic gaps alluded to above, and in so doing provide interested parties with an alternative naturalistic theory of the nature of synchronicities and their use. Further, by accomplishing this task the vital information assumed to be associated with synchronicities will be shown to be indeed vital but person specific.

3—The Relationship between Causality and Meaning

The above discussion may well stir a degree of confusion in the reader. This is due to Jung's assumption that meaning and causality are two separate entities. This is valid in his half psychodynamic and half supernatural theory of synchronicities. However, from the perspective of a naturalistic interpretation of the nature of synchronicities, there is an assumed intimate connection between meaning and causality.

William James (1895) says that if a newborn could describe his experience of being alive it would most probably describe it as a "buzzing, blooming confusion of sensation." The task of each individual is to find or create order out of his initial personal chaos.[66] In this light, indicative of the close association between causality and meaning, C.I. Lewis (1929) implies that there is an inevitable causality-meaning continuum stating, "[The] experience of reality exists only because the mind of man takes attitudes and makes interpretations. The buzzing, blooming confusion could not become a reality for an oyster. A purely passive consciousness, if such can be conceived, would find no use for the concept of reality, because it would find none for the idea of the unreal; because it would take no attitude that could be balked, and make no interpretation which conceivably could be mistaken."[67]

Extending this idea, it is a fact that no two people are likely to register a synchronicity in exactly the same way. Nor is the same individual likely to experience the same synchronicity if repeated in the same way. In other words, the meaning of a given synchronicity is relative to the observer in question and arises out of potentially knowable overlapping situational and psychological contexts which are continually changing. Consider the reactions to the September 11 terrorist attack on the World Trade towers. A typical and understandable response was shock, dismay, fear, and sadness for countless millions of people across the whole world. And yet, there were many other millions of people at the same moment celebrating with joy that the United States had finally suffered a deserved blow. The same stimuli (planes crashing into the Twin Towers) elicited opposite reactions. This suggests that meaning as Jung indicates is a linking principle connecting inner and outer events. However meanings may be expected to vary relative to the contexts with which an individual consciously and unconsciously experiences the stimulus in question.

However, instead of the assumption that the meaningfulness associated with synchronicities is a connection with a realm of "absolute meaning" that is transcendent, subsistent, and universal; rather it is more likely to be meaning that is highly person specific therefore pluralistic and relative to the meaning maker under consideration engaged in a creative act experienced as an especially meaningful coincidence. Viewed in this light meaning and causality are both linking principles joining intrapsychic reality to the external object world. Thus there is not just one absolute logic—defined as a linking principle—but several logics ("markedly different, each self consistent in its own terms.")[68]

In support of this claim, Phil Phenix (1964), in his seminal work called *The Realms of Meaning,* offers a perspective on meaning helping to clarify the confusion between causality and/or meaning as the primary linking principles in explaining synchronicities. Says Phenix: (1964), "There is no single quality that may be designated as the one essence of meaning."[69]

In the place of fruitlessly attempting to settle on one operational definition of meaning Phenix (1964) asserts that it is far more objective to consider the concepts of "realms of meaning." Phenix (1964) outlines six individual but overlapping realms of meaning. These six realms (patterns) of meaning are (1) symbolics, (2) empirics, (3) esthetics, (4) synnoetics, (5) ethics, and (6) synoptics.[70] For my purpose I will only focus on three of the six realms of meaning most applicable towards understanding the nature of synchronicities from a naturalistic perspective. These are empirics, synoetics, and synoptics. Operational definitions of each of these realms of meaning follows:

- Empirics "includes the sciences of the physical world, of living things, and of Man . . . [meanings are generated] in accordance with certain rules of evidence and verification and making use of specified systems of analytic abstraction."[71]
- Synnoetics "embraces . . . 'personal knowledge.'" Synnoetics signifies "relational insight" or "direct awareness."[72] It is analogous in the sphere of knowing to sympathy in the sphere of feeling.
- Synoptics refers to meanings that are "comprehensively integrative. It includes history, religion and philosophy. These disciplines combine empirical, esthetic, and synnoetic meanings into coherent wholes. Historical

> interpretation comprises an artful re-creation of the past, in obedience to factual evidence, for the purpose of revealing what man by his deliberate choices has made of himself with the context of his given circumstances. Religion is concerned with ultimate meanings, that is, with meanings from any realm whatsoever, considered from the standpoint of such boundary concepts as Whole, the Comprehensive, and the Transcendent. Philosophy provides analytic clarification, evaluation, and synthetic co-ordination of all the other realms through a reflective conceptual interpretation and in their interrelationships."[73]

Viewed from the context of realms of meaning, both the principle of causality and the principle of a-causality may be viewed as alternative combinations of these six realms of meanings. Thus "causality" may be validly viewed as a linking principle connecting the self with the object world comprising various combinations of realms of meaning derived from the personal biases of the theoretician and or experiencer of a synchronicity in question. This observation has significant implications in generating a naturalistic theory of synchronicities. It means that by changing the mix of alternative realms of meaning into a composite filter from which to impose order on chaos differing conceptualizations of linking principles will result. These alternative principles might best be thought of as hybrids or composite forms of causal linking principles composed of overlapping classes of meanings.

Thus, the causality Jung is referring to is mechanical, conventional scientific causality expressed in the form of linear logic. The equivalent meanings associated with synchronicities obviously point to the presence of some additional factor—other than linear logic, connecting the two halves of a given synchronicity. This additional something extra might best be thought of as one or more different classes of meanings combined into a hybrid linking principle.

In this connection, adding synnoetic meanings into the mix seems like an apt candidate towards the construction of an alternative form of a naturalistic principle of causality. Says Phenix (1964): "Synnoetic meanings relate subject to subject—objectivity is replaced by inter subjectivity. Meanings are concrete rather than abstract and stress a logic of feeling or experiencing."[74] It is worth repeating what Devereux (1953) says concerning the relationship between causality, meanings and synchronicities: "While defying conventional causal explanations, the synchronistic event, appears to have some 'logical relatedness' though perhaps a logic of a different order than that associated with mechanical causality. Implied is a functional or causal nexus of a particular kind."[75]

Specifically Devereux proposes the concept of synthetic causality as his solution to the "logic of a different order" idea. Synthetic causality, then, may be viewed as a composite or hybrid linking principle composed of synnoetic, empirical, and synoptic meanings. It is further proposed that the logic associated with this alternative naturalistic principle of causality be thought of as experiential or synthetic logic, and, or psychodynamic causality. This proposed synthetic causality will be applied to a naturalistic theory of synchronicities inferred in Faber's psychodynamic/naturalistic/regressive theory and is explicitly asserted in Williams's psychodynamic/naturalistic/progressive theory.

Anti-Causal Argument 3: The Problem of Simultaneity (an issue about time)

Jung (1955) states his third anti-causal argument as follows: "Conventional causality presumes some kind of transmission of energy occurring over time and in space between interacting bodies. But synchronistic phenomena occur simultaneously apparently eliminating and relativizing conventional notions of time, space, and energy exchange. This suggests the need for some principle of explanation other than conventional causality."[76]

By eliminating conventional linear time and conventional causality Jung is left once again with a seemingly unobstructed pathway in adopting his radical a-causal principle of synchronicity as the only theory adequately taking into account the supposed "supernatural facts" associated with these uncanny events. Therefore it follows that to adequately rebut Jung's third anti-causal argument—an argument about temporality and synchronicities—it is necessary for the investigator to demonstrate that there are alternative conceptualization of the "time" factor which can be utilized in generating a causal theory of synchronicities. It will be shown that was discussed about the meaning of meaning can be fruitfully applied in understanding the nature of temporality and its relationship to a naturalistic theory of synchronicities.

Synchronicities and the Experience of Simultaneity

For Jung the key notion about time is the experience of simultaneity which occurs when A and A' appear to happen at exactly the same moment. The experience of simultaneity added to the experience of an "equivalence of meaning" always accompanying the occurrence of a meaningful coincidence lends these odd occurrences an uncanny and mysterious aura Jung refers to as numinosity.

This is important as Jung believes that the experience of numinosity indicates that the experiencer has connected with an "activated archetype." Connection with an activated archetype is thought by Jung to be the source of potentially vital information to be used in the service of furthering a person's individuation.

It is to be remembered that for Jung the power of synchronicities is associated less with an intellectual understanding of the "message" being received than the numinous feelings that are "gripping" the person's total being. When a synchronicity is experienced, for a moment there is a felt sense of time having stopped, accompanied by an all pervasive feeling of at-one-ment (merging) both with oneself and the external world.

The familiar experience of linear time (past-present-future) and bounded space (a differentiation between internal reality from external reality) is suddenly and decisively overridden by an altered state of consciousness in which conventional space seems unbounded, and conventional time nonexistent (durational). Ordinary mundane experience in the midst of a synchronicity is typically experienced as extraordinary. The temporary absence of time and space boundaries is referred to as the "now."In the midst of a synchronicity ordinary experience supplanted by extraordinary experience is the reason why many experiencers view these anomalous events as magical, mystical, and spiritual.

To repeat, Progoff (1973) describes numinosity as "an awareness of special light, carrying a sense of transcendent validity, authenticity and essential divinity."[77] Jung (1955) describes the effects of numinosity as often transforming: "[Numinosity] mobilizes philosophical and religious convictions in the very people who deemed themselves miles above any such fits of weakness . . . [Via an amplification of feelings it imparts a sense of] depth and fullness of meaning that was unthinkable before."[78]

Thus for Jung and his adherents the experience of the numinosity associated with experiencing a synchronicity is evidence enough that external reality is spiritualized and the experiencer has made a direct connection with an assumed "spiritual ground" of reality. Eliminating conventional causality in explaining the time factor associated with synchronicities appears to reinforce Jung's mystical magical esoteric occult conceptualization of the nature of reality. On the face of it, Jung's argument appears persuasive. However, a careful look at the facts present a much different picture.

Jung's Conceptualization of Time Associated with Synchronicities

The uncanny feeling of numinosity for Jung only appears when internal and external co-incide (registered as) an equivalence of meaning. What is implied is that conventional time ceases to "exist" and that in its place is experienced no time or timelessness (simultaneity.)

In this connection it is interesting to note that Aziz (1990), an avowed Jungian adherent, says that Jung has major problems in his discussion of time. This is so because the two halves of a given synchronicity do not always occur at exactly the same time.[79] For example, a notable passage of time elapsed between the patient's dream of being handed a scarab (A) and actually handed a scarab in her session the next day (A'). Therefore although the two scarabs were equivalent in meaning they did not happen simultaneously.

To account for this discrepancy Aziz infers that Jung is referring not to microcosmic linear clock time but to macrocosmic durational timelessness associated with his assumed archetypal spiritual realm of absolute knowledge. The distinction between linear microscopic earthly clock time and macroscopic durational transcendent eternal time is clearly in line with Jung's particular coloration of his partially naturalistic and partially supernatural theory of synchronicities. The experience of simultaneity added to the experience of an "equivalence of meaning" always accompanying the occurrence of any synchronicity lends the synchronicity event its uncanny and mysterious aura experienced as numinosity.

A Naturalistic Conceptualization of Time Associated with Synchronicities

What is not mentioned by Jung, Aziz, and to my knowledge any of the other Jungian adherents, is that there is an alternative conceptualization of time which will be utilized in adequately explaining the temporality factor associated with synchronicities from a naturalistic point of view.

In this connection, what Jung refers to as macroscopic transcendent time is viewed by self theorists as the inferred normal timelessness experienced by pre-oedipal babies. An awareness of linear (clock) time gradually happens as the sense of self develops.

It is proposed that the concept of "psychic time" might profitably be utilized to identify the experience of simultaneity being an overlapping of both linear (past, present, future time) and the experience of durational timelessness. This concept might be helpful in explaining the process involved in the experience of (1) mirroring, and (2) reversible images wherein connecting the dots in alternative ways results in the creation of alternative patterns of perception.

Quantum Physics, Time (Simultaneity), Consciousness, Causality, and Synchronicities

For Jung (1955) the crucial criterion for identifying the presence of causality is that "the cause must contain those conditions that are necessary for the occurrence of the effect, those conditions in the absence of which the effect would not have come into being."[80]

Toward accomplishing this aim, an article by Bach (1972) called "Jung's Relationship to Synchronicity" is thought provoking. Bach (1972) substantially agrees with Jung that (mechanical) causality cannot explain simultaneity.

However he adds an intriguing addendum that points to the possibility of some alternative causal explanation. He states: "space and time appear in synchronistic events as if they were related to conditions of the psyche, as if they were only demanded by consciousness and did not exist in their own mind."[81]

What needs to be elaborated is what is implied by Bach's intriguing speculation concerning the role of consciousness, conditions of the psyche, and the experience and role of simultaneity as they relate to alternative theories of synchronicities. Jung and his followers believe that psychological inner reality (subjective state A) and external reality (objective state A') are best conceptualized as a connected psycho-physical co-existent reality both manifestations of a greater unified singular source, which Jung refers to as the unus mundus.[82]

In this connection, Pauli (1955), a noted physicist who together with Jung wrote their seminal monograph called *The Interpretation of Nature and the Psyche* (Jung/Pauli, 1955), is representative of those Jungian adherents who believe that advances in theoretical quantum physics offer a "scientific" validation for this "psycho-physical" parallelism. The concept of simultaneity related to consciousness is a core consideration of quantum physics.[83]

An informative discussion of quantum physics, time, consciousness, and its implications for the understanding of synchronicities is found in a comprehensive paper called "Quantum Physics, Depth Psychology, and Beyond" by Thomas J. McFarlane (2000). What follows are highlights of the core concepts of quantum physics and their relationship which are pertinent to understanding the supernatural part of Jung's synchronicity theory.

The essence of quantum physics is that any quantum (a bedrock building block of matter) may be described either as a wave or as a particle depending upon certain conditions. In this connection McFarlane (2000) says "quantum theory . . . forced a revision of the concepts of causality, determinism, and locality . . . and suggested to some thinkers that the psyche may be involved, in some mysterious way, with the determination of the observed properties of matter."[84] What is most significant in applying quantum physics to understanding the nature of synchronicities is that in the act of measuring, the consciousness of the observer is seen to effect what is perceived. When a quantum is perceived (the observer adding his consciousness in the act of perceiving) the quanta " is a particle having a definite localized position . . . [However] when it is unobserved, in it is a non local wave of probable dimensions."[85] Since both particles and waves are necessary organizing concepts to adequately describe the quantum's behavior this fact is the basis for the principle of complementarity. This principle has been carried over to Jungian depth psychology primarily by Pauli.

Pauli (1955) reasons that the affect of the observer measuring any observed system, has the net effect of "invalidating the deterministic conception of the phenomena assumed in classical physics"[86] This observation is the basis for his and Jung's formulation of an a-causal principle later used to explain the seemingly inexplicable acausal linkage in each meaningful coincidence.

Jung applies the principle of complementarity to understanding the nature of synchronicities in the following manner. Says McFarlane (2000): "Because the phenomenon of synchronicity involves an a causal coordination of the inner and outer worlds in a meaningful way, it is not exclusively a psychological or physical phenomenon, but is 'psychoid' meaning that it somehow essentially involves both psyche and matter."[87]

Both the internal psychological subjective state (A) and the external "physical" objective state (A') are both considered to be derived from the same "transcendental unitary reality" Jung (1955) refers to as the "unus mundus." It is inferred that the unus mundus is a domain that has "orderedness and [absolute] meaning."[88]

What is significant about this conceptualization as it relates to the temporal factor and synchronicities is that simultaneity by means of the complementarity principle is now thoroughly located in an assumed transcendent state of spiritualized reality. Assuming this to be true then the principle of complementarity is useful in explaining many of the seemingly "mystical" other worldly aspects associated with both the theory and the experience of the supernatural part of Jung's theory of synchronicity. Says McFarlane (2000): "Viewed in its subjective aspect, this unified reality [unus mundus] takes the form of a psychic domain containing psychological archetypes that manifest in our inner experience. Viewed in its objective aspect, the unus mundus takes the form of a physical domain containing the archetypal laws of nature that govern manifestations in our outer experiences."[89]

Additionally, McFarlane (2000) delineates a parallel between the particle/wave complementarity with the conscious/collective unconscious complementarity in depth psychology. In this framework: "Just as the wave is the unobserved aspect of the quantum and the particle is the observed aspect, so the (collective) unconscious is the unobserved aspect of the psyche and the conscious is the observed aspect. [Similarly], the area of unconscious is enormous and always continuous [analogous to the wave function], while the area of consciousness is a restricted field of momentary vision."[90] He further adds: "the archetypal structures of the unconscious represent fundamental potentialities of psychic manifestation [analogous to the un-actualized probabilities of the wave function]; while conscious contents are actualizations of these potentialities [analogous to the actualized particle]."[91]

Vic Mansfield (2002) a professor of physics and a Jungian investigator of synchronicities extends the principle of complementarity applied to synchronicities still further. He spells out the role of reflective consciousness in bringing the potential archetypal knowledge into actuality experienced as a synchronicity. Mansfield infers that a given synchronicity is evidence of reflective conscious bringing "the transcendental into the empirical world of multiplicity."[92]

Quantum Physics and Its Implications for a Naturalistic Theory of Synchronicities

The complementarity principle indicates that our view of objective reality is "an imperfect imaginative construct, and not an actual mirror of some real, objective reality."[93] However, and this is a big however, the parallels between (1) the principle of complementarity applied to the interplay of consciousness, the personal unconscious, and the collective unconscious constituting inner reality and its connection with the physical world related to the principle of synchronicities; plus (2) the principle of complementarity applied to the interplay between the focus of seen particles versus unseen waves in quantum physics, are compelling analogies but not absolute parallels with the human experience of generating personal meanings.

Whereas the quantum argument is used by the Jungians to reinforce the supernatural part of Jung's theory of synchronicity, this same quantum argument could just as well be used to validate a naturalistic theory of synchronicities. The essence of the quantum argument is that an observer's consciousness is thought to greatly influence the outcome of what is observed. Granted. But with synchronicities the issue is not simple measurement of random data but a process by which significant meanings are acquired either by passive "channeling" or by actively generating them.

What is most important to consider is the assumption of the experiencer and/or investigator of synchronicities as to their understanding of the meaning of meaning as well as their understanding as to how meanings are processed and acquired. It has been shown that alternative conceptualizations of the meaning of meaning and whether or not meanings are thought of as revealed or realized will result in the formulation of either a supernatural or naturalistic theory of synchronicities. Whereas the parallels between the quantum physicist observing quanta and a person experiencing a synchronicity are seductively appealing, the fact remains that synchronicities add the extra element of either channeling or generating personal meanings whereas the observation and measurement of waves and particles do not. Thus the leap from the strange effects of observing quanta to observing synchronicities does not strike this investigator as even remotely parallel.

What Jung's third anti-causal argument suggests is that by eliminating clock time thereby relativizing time, conceiving linear time to be a useful construction of the mind—what remains, for Jung, is a connection (in synchronicities) of only an equivalence of meaning. The meaning, for him, is absolute being a manifestation of an activated archetype. However, if, as has been advocated, meanings always involve some contribution of an individual self—then meanings are generated. What follows is that time (linear or durational) may be reduced to the following formula: "time = libido" (Wittenberg, personal communication). Libido equals basic energy that is either conscious or unconscious that continually faces the givens of reality with the unending task of making choices in the service of surviving (being) and, or thriving (becoming).

There is apparently no necessity for doing anything at all other than fulfilling the tasks necessary for one's survival and acting in such a way to sustain a chosen lifestyle. But in either case, whether a person is primarily engaged in being and/or becoming, they are forced to make choices to resolve inevitable "problems." In this connection, this researcher contends that what we refer to as time is, in actuality, filling up emptiness with meaningful connections usually in the service of consciously or unconsciously resolving problems of daily living.

In this view, consciousness, if, as the proponents of quantum physics want us all to be aware, is crucial to whatever we observe and measure: it logically follows that different consciousnesses will observe the same reality in different ways (Roshomoning experience). Additionally, it is conjectured, that even the experience of simultaneity, and related experiences such as unity, togetherness, attunement, on the same wave-length and the likes are subject to different interpretations.

The Self, Time, and Synchronicities

To illustrate the above points, consider various perspectives in attempts to understand the complex interaction between the self, time, and synchronicities. Aziz says that in analyzing the seminal scarab synchronicity there are three significant events: (1) his patient's dream of being handed a golden scarab; (2) the patient's discussion of her dream with Jung in therapy session of the next day; and (3) the simultaneous connection of the golden scarab content of the dream and Jung's hearing, catching, and giving the scarab beetle to his patient.

For Aziz and presumably Jung as well the "simultaneity" that occurred that was most important was the scarab dream apparently coming true the next day. (The reader will note the liberty Jung took in operationally defining the "simultaneous occurrence of" the scarab in the dream A and the scarab beetle in the next day's session A' as not exactly what is usually thought of as simultaneous—two events occurring at exactly the same time.) It can be conceded that in special instances like this a stretch of time can occur between event A and A' to be considered close enough to fulfill the criteria of simultaneity but in so doing, what emerges in the foreground is the contribution of alternative points of view.

What Aziz omits is the following that, I believe, deepens the issue and makes understanding the nature of synchronicities much more complex than Jung would have us believe. This is particularly the case when the synchronicities are those of patients in treatment.

In this connection it is instructive to consider Aziz's comments on the joint participation of synchronicities in which it is easy to overlap boundaries in what is a union of projections known as a "participation mystique." In this view it is necessary for the analyst to underscore the independence of the various factors of a synchronicity. For example it is pure projection to conclude that the patient made the scarab in the office appear to suit her psychological needs. Thus both the patient and the scarab beetle at the windowpane are seen to have independent existences. From Jung's point of view both he and his patient are sharing a common archetypal patterning that is manifested in the scarab synchronicity. Thus there is or should be "the recognition that subject and object are interrelated as complementary players in the larger archetypal pattern."[94]

When this differentiation does not occur for Aziz this is evidence of an abnormal reaction to a synchronicity. Abnormal, in this sense, means "the subject thus would not distinguish what "belongs" to him, in the compensatory sense, from what belongs to the object."[95] This attribution of self to other is the operational definition of projection and a lack of clearly established psychological boundaries.

Jung's omission of specific details about the contexts from which the scarab coincident was derived plus his great amount of personal detail suggests that Jung may have been talking more about himself than his patient. Therefore, while both he and his patient experienced the union of the two scarabs it is reasonable to conjecture that the meaning(s) associated with this important event was not absolutely identical but was colored by what each one of the participants brought to the table.

In the next chapter, Naturalistic Interpretations of Synchronicities, it will be shown how additional concepts in the realm of the collective consciousness related to consciousness and the experience of timelessness, results in a plausible naturalistic theory of meaningful coincidences.

It should be noted that the search for an adequate naturalistic theory of synchronicities is an ongoing adventure. Just when you think you have the mysteries all neatly accounted for, there comes along another organizing concept that adds another nuanced dimension into the incomplete picture.

Representative of the types of concepts to which I am referring are Faber's identification of timelessness as a primary experience in the consciousness of the pre-oedipal child (the first two years of life essentially pre-verbal); Bach's hypothesis of the development of primary process implying an expansion of consciousness along a continuum of attained level of self-consciousness; Spitz's research detailing the importance of concept of psychic organizers and the development of the self structure; the powerful effect of positive and negative transferences; the experience of quality connectedness expressed in such concepts as attunement, resonance, positive reverberation oscillation; the concept of a GPS (global positioning signal), and the entire movement of self theory.

Having successfully refuted Jung's three anti-causal arguments, the next task is to present alternative naturalistic theories of synchronicities. Two such naturalistic theories of synchronicities are Faber's *Naturalistic Regressive Theory of Synchronicities* and Williams's *Naturalistic Progressive Theory of Synchronicities.* Faber's theory will be discussed in chapter 4. Williams's theory will be discussed in chapters 5–8.

4

Naturalistic Interpretations of Synchronicities

> The names of our categories may be very old and stable [time, space, and causality,] but the concepts, the modes of classifying and interpreting which they represent, undergo progressive alteration with the advance of thought.
>
> —C. I. Lewis (1929)[1]

Overview

SUCCESSFULLY REFUTING JUNG'S THREE ANTI CAUSAL ARGUMENTS provides the scientific rationale for formulating one or more naturalistic theories of synchronicity. Two such naturalistic theories, M. D. Faber's regressive naturalistic theory and G.A. Williams's progressive naturalistic theory, will be described and discussed in the present chapter 4 and in chapters 5–8.

But before discussing Faber's and Williams's synchronicity theories I think it is valuable to fill in the space between Jung's partial supernatural (occult) theory and Faber's and Williams's purely naturalistic theories of synchronicities.

The Progression of Science

Kuhn makes it clear that science progresses to the degree to which an investigator(s) attempts to account for why nature appears to have violated the generally accepted paradigm currently in vogue. This task is accomplished either by (1) challenging primary ontological and epistemological first assumptions; and/or (2) redefining (translating) existing organizing concepts, currently utilized as filters of experience connecting the seemingly random data associated with the phenomenon being investigated, and/or creating new organizing concepts.

Jung's understanding of the nature of synchronicities led him to tacitly conclude that synchronistic anomalous occurrences appear to violate the generally acceptable paradigm of psychic determinism—lending strong support for the esoteric occultist's supernatural perspective.

The combination of the special meaningfulness when experiencing synchronicities, plus the exquisite timing in which they occur, lend these events their characteristic sense of the uncanny aura accompanying them. Add to the mix the intense feelings that one is being guided by transcendent invisible forces contributes to the sense that these occurrences have a "spiritual" or "religious" origin. Jung was utterly convinced this is surely the case. Indeed the formulation of Jung's partly supernatural theory of synchronicities was greatly fueled by his increasing preoccupation with the subject matter of the esoteric occult, particularly that of alchemy. It might be asked what it was about esoteric occultism that Jung thought it to be so compelling, whereas Freud thought it to be so potentially harmful?

Jung's Total Embrace of the Esoteric Occult

To accept Jung's partly supernatural theory of synchronicities is to tacitly accept his philosophical first assumptions about the nature of and acquisition of the knowledge of absolute reality. This is no insignificant issue. This is so because Kant (1957) reasoned that because of realistic limitations due to the structure of our minds, humans are forever restricted from having certain knowledge of the nature of absolute reality he refers to as the noumena. This means that the best we can know of reality is that which we directly perceive, referred to as phenomena. We may theorize all we wish, fervently believing our strong faith about our conceptions of absolute reality are coincident with objective reality, but we can never really know for certain as to the capital T truth of this categorical claim.[2] Jung thinks otherwise, writing as if he is utterly convinced that synchronicities support the cosmology of the esoteric occultists.

This means that for Jung the ontological and epistemological primary assumptions he makes about the nature of reality and knowledge of its contents, as well as the ways in which knowledge is acquired, plus the derived organizing concepts he uses to order the raw data associated with synchronicities is for him, not simply theoretical speculation, but instead, are equated with absolute fact.

Thus his core conceptualizations including the collective unconscious, archetypes, archetypal reality, a realm of absolute meaning, the nature of the apriori, the primary archetype of the self, and a level of subsistent meaning are asserted to be transcendent facts existing independent of human interpretation. In Jung's (1952) words:

> We mean by the collective unconscious, a certain psychic disposition by the forces of heredity; from it consciousness has developed. In the physical structure of the body we find traces of earlier forms of evolution, and we may expect the human psyche to conform in its make-up to the law of phylogeny. It is a fact that in eclipses of consciousness—in dreams, narcotic states, (synchronicities) and cases of insanity—there come to the surface psychic products or contents that show all the traits of primitive levels of psychic development. The images themselves are sometimes of such a primitive character that we might suppose them derived from ancient, esoteric teaching. Mythological themes clothed in modern dress also frequently appear.[3]

C. Wilson (1988) describes such an "occult" suffused reality as consisting of "a sense of 'hidden meanings'" lurking behind the apparently impassive face of everyday reality.[4]

Freud's Concern about the Lure of the Occult

In and of itself Freud was encouraging when it came to Jung's interests in mythology and archetypal influences. However Freud drew a line when it came to Jung's wholesale rejection of the primary assumption of psychic determination as the way in which human beings acquire objective knowledge of reality. Thus Freud's and Jung's major difference with respect to understanding the nature of synchronicities—occult like phenomena—is primarily a difference between alternative epistemological alternatives: namely that knowledge is either revealed or is constructed.

Freud essentially believed that immersion in the occult was "escapist" providing a too easy way for human beings to delude themselves by denying that reality on the earth plane isn't as harsh, complex, and realistically limiting as indeed it is.

Representative of his tacit warning to Jung concerning the lure of the occult Freud (1953) wrote, "The occult allows us to bypass feelings of 'aversion, doubt and uncertainty' . . . a general human inclination toward credulity and belief in the marvelous. . . . when life imposes its stern discipline upon us [realistic limitations] there grows up in us a resistance against the restlessness and monotony of the laws of thought, and against the need for putting things to the test of reality."[5]

In addition to promoting escapism, Freud was concerned that an immersion in the esoteric occult runs the risk of obviating critical thinking. For example: Jung stresses that the important parts about the experience of synchronicities are (1) the connection the self makes with a transcendent realm of "absolute meaning" ("archetypal knowledge") assumed to subsist over and above one's psyche which provides vital knowledge for the purpose of enhancing a person's individuation, and (2) the transcendent vital knowledge of absolute meaning is passively received (channeled) intuitively by passing any interpretation.

Addressing himself to this point Freud (1953) says:

> The occultists . . . will be welcomed as liberators from the irksome obligation of thinking rationally.... It is a vain hope that analytic work would escape this collapse values simply because its object is the mysterious unconscious. If the spirits, with whom man is familiar, provide the final explanation, then there will be no interest in the laborious approach of analysis to understand unknown psychic forces. Even analytic technique will be forsaken when hope beckons that occult measures will one to enter into direct communication with the spirits who determine everything, just as one forsakes patient detail work, when there is hope of winning riches at a single stroke, through speculations.[6]

In this light, the implied war of theories between the Jungians and the Freudians over the nature of synchronicities is a battle between two different approaches in dealing with anomalous events: the supernatural versus the scientific.

Synchronicities for Jung, tacitly viewed by him as anomalous events, were thought to be understandable not in terms of the generally accepted psychoanalytic explanation of causation associated with the *personal unconscious*; but, instead, was thought to be only adequately understood as a byproduct of the "uncaused' pre-existing *realm of the collective unconscious.* These two views are most clearly differentiated by the concentrated use of their primary organizing concepts: that is, Jung's collective unconscious and Freud's personal unconscious and their alternative conceptualizations of meaning, and time. Differences in their frames of reference as a starting point for their research is crucially responsible for the radical differences in their respective attempts to understand the nature and use of synchronicities.

Jung's supernatural theory of synchronicities as the prevailing point of view to this day represents nothing less than the cutting edge of a new paradigmatic shift referred to by him as "The New Age." This new paradigm is thought by Jung and his adherents to be a definitive of the religion versus science debate—presumably combining the best of both.

What makes Jung's point of view particularly provocative and challenging is his categorical assertion that there is no need to attempt to continue the dialogue as these particular anomalies are rationally inexplicable. This assertion is a powerful one. For if Jung is right, in the light of the sweep of history, as reviewed in the comprehensive works of *Fire in the Mind, and Fits, Visions, and Trances* this will be the first time in recorded history wherein this assertion of absolute finality is equated with incontrovertible unchanging law. A case in point is Freud's revolutionary view of the psychodynamic understanding of hysteria as an example of a scientific "breakthrough."

Freud's Revolutionary Breakthrough

Freud's identification and treatment of hysteria as a de-facto scientific anomaly initiated a revolution in thinking resulting in a paradigmatic shift from a decidedly religious to a scientific explanation—the psychoanalytic revolution. Similarly, Jung's identification of meaningful coincidences—as another scientific anomaly (defying adequate psychoanalytic explanation)—swung the understanding of these perplexing events back to what many believe to be another paradigmatic shift characterized by a decidedly occult and religious perspective.

In what follows, it will be shown that added concepts in the realm of the collective consciousness provides a viable new pathway to successfully countering Jung's challenging and provocative assertion implying that his psychodynamic/supernatural formulation puts an end to the meaningful coincidence debate for all time.

Alternative Naturalistic Approaches in Understanding Scientific Anomalies

Tacitly agreeing with Kant, that because of realistic limits due to the structure of our minds, it is assumed that the most we can know about the nature of reality has to be derived from synthesized knowledge obtained from the organized data accumulated by the various sciences.

Scientific knowledge is the byproduct of processing the raw data of experience. This process involves selecting organizing concepts from the collective consciousness and utilizing them, individually and collectively, to filter and organize raw data to generate meaningful connections. Logically, then, selecting alternative organizing concepts to be used individually or collectively in generating meaningful connections will result in a partial or wholesale paradigmatic shift.

In this connection, Johnson's (1996) book: *Fire in the Mind,* subtitled *Science, Faith and the Search for Order is* an impressive work surveying the historical dialectic between opposing perspectives in their questing for knowledge of the nature of reality.[7] Johnson contends that in virtually all fields of knowledge including speculative philosophy, psychology, science, and religion there is seen to be assertions crystallized in the prevailing "cannon" for a period of time, inevitably followed by counter assertions that eventually supplant the existing paradigm, that in turn are countered by yet another swing back in the opposite direction and so on. (See also *Trances, and Visions,* and Kuhn's monograph *The Structure of Scientific Revolutions.*)

Speaking to this issue C. I. Lewis (1929) states: "Categories and concepts do not literally change; they are simply given up and replaced by new ones. [C. I. Lewis pre-dates Kuhn] . . . Such new and recalcitrant datum which bring about the change, complicate the problem of comparing the 'new truth' with the old. The factors which need to be considered are: (1) the two sets of concepts, old and new; (2) the expanding bounds of experience in which the novel has come to light; (3) the conditions of the application of the concepts to this new body of total relevant experience."[8]

Applying the Dialectic Schema in Formulating a Naturalistic Theory of Synchronicities

A naturalistic theory of synchronicities is obligated to strip away, (demystify) the supernatural coloration of Jung's psychodynamic/supernatural perspective. To accomplish this task requires an open minded person to consider that what Jung asserts as proven fact may just be a brilliantly imaginative but unproven hypothesis.

A naturalistic theory of synchronicities begins with the ontological assumption that absolute reality can never be directly known but only induced (constructed). What is induced are the findings derived from various fields of knowledge that in turn may be utilized as singular and/or composite filters of experience.

C. I. Lewis (1929) summarizes this point of view as follows:

> In experience, mind is confronted with the chaos of the given. In the interest of adaptation and control, [which is what patients are seeking to change, transformation from psychological pain—compulsion/impulsion] it seeks to discover within or impose upon this chaos some kind of stable order, through which distinguishable items may become the signs of future possibilities. Those

> patterns of distinction and relationship which we thus seek to establish are our concepts. These must be determined in advance of the particular experience to which they apply in order that what is given may have meaning. Until the criteria of our interpretation have been fixed, no experience could be the sign of anything or even answer any question. Concepts thus represent what mind brings to experience.[9]

The inescapable limitation placed on the extent to which we limited mortals may hope to have absolute knowledge of the "real" nature of reality does not mean all attempts to accomplish this worthy task are meaningless and futile. It does mean that in attempting to do so it is important to state alternative assumptions (inevitable biases) so that all interested parties have access to the full range of possibilities from which to make their own independent judgments.

With this caveat, chapter 4 invites truth seeking readers to suspend final judgment about the issue at hand. Adopting an attitude of purposively limiting ourselves to what we know for certain (factual knowledge by way of direct experience versus belief by way of channeling), calls into question many of the core Jungian concepts and primary assertions underlying his non-natural theory of synchronicities. In so doing the way is prepared for a naturalistic interpretation of meaningful coincidences. In this light the following questions are raised:

- What if reality is not "spiritualized" in the Jungian sense of this term?
- What if there is no personal intercession by a conscious god, spirit guides, angels, master teachers, and the likes leaving us mortals essentially on our own to be our own final authorities?
- What if there is no realm of transcendent absolute knowledge or meaning?
- What if, instead, meanings are constructed as byproducts of the self always adding something of itself rather than already preformed, out there, and passively channeled?
- What if unity does not exist in the form of a "preformed patterning" but instead is the result of a convergence of a spectrum of various perspectives?
- What if the self is not already preformed and whole but must be grown as a byproduct of systematic struggle with struggle?
- What if significant change is possible but is the result of an evolutionary not revolutionary process dogged by resistance, the major one being the need to repeat the familiar?
- What if synchronicities do in fact indicate the actuality of significant psychological change but are conceived of as less a single event than as a

progression of an expanding self connecting with, harnessing, and directing its available powers?
- What if transformation of the self comes about not in the "twinkling of an eye" but as the result of persistent hard work in which the "patient" struggling with struggle to make meaningful connections with himself and the object world such that a synchronicity marks the integration of the various connections resulting in an expansion of consciousness?
- What if the ultimate benefit of these remarkable occurrences further the subject's connection with their own creative process?

These questions will be addressed in this and subsequent chapters.

Chapters 4, 5, and 6 present some naturalistic theoretical interpretations of these seemingly inexplicable phenomena. For our purposes naturalistic means that attempted explanations are derived from the application of scientific method that presumes knowable (either already known or potentially knowable) cause and effect relationships establishing order and clarity in place of randomness and vagueness. The preceding chapters indicate that the operational definition of causality used to explain synchronicities calls for a revision of its basic structure.

Essentially there are four naturalistic theories of synchronicities. These are

1. The statistical (sometimes a coincidence is just a coincidence)
2. The parapsychological: the chief form of which is telepathy (telegraphy)
3. Faber's psychological psychodynamic regressive theory
4. Williams's psychological psychodynamic progressive theory

Only the last two theories will be discussed in breadth and depth.

Identifying Two Naturalistic Theories of Synchronicities

There are at least two identifiable naturalistic theories of synchronicities. These are (1) M. D. Faber's regressive psychodynamic/naturalistic theory of synchronicities, and (2) G.A.Williams's progressive psychodynamic/ naturalistic theory of synchronicities.

M. D. Faber's Regressive Naturalistic Theory of Synchronicities

M. D. Faber's (1998) book *C. G. Jung, Psychoanalysis and Religion* is one of the few attempts to view synchronicities from a naturalistic perspective, done so in comprehensive detail. Faber indicates that "hard synchronicities" is the subject of his book describing a hard synchronicity as one which "raises the discussion to lofty religious and philosophic heights."[10] He reiterates the important point that Jung's theory is a combination of psychodynamic and occult concepts resulting in its decidedly supernatural perspective.

Faber focuses on "the golden scarab" coincidence as representative of Jung's supernatural attitude towards synchronicities. However, unlike Jung's view of it as a "spiritual" breakthrough, enabling his patient to commence a spiritual rebirth; Faber, instead, views this seminal coincidence as evidence "of [Jung's] therapeutic manipulation and authoritarianism."[11] This strong assertion is Faber's opening salvo advocating a naturalistic rather than a supernatural point of view.

Faber says that his book is not a refutation of Jung but a viable alternative, however his hard hitting analytic approach to this subject pulls no punches. His stated aim is to "strip away" by "unpacking" and "deconstructing" the magic and mysticism that Jung militantly believes is absolutely essential in accurately appreciating the nature of and wondrous implications of these extraordinary events.

Faber's method is to take each one of Jung's core supernatural, mystical, and transpersonal concepts and convert them into organizing concepts derived from the Object Relations school—an offshoot of classical psychoanalytic theory. Thus Faber's aim is turning Jung's half- naturalistic and half supernatural theory of synchronicities into one which is purely naturalistic.

Faber's Naturalistic Perspective

Without using this explicit formulation, Faber (as does Williams) derives his organizing concepts from the collective consciousness, unlike Jung who derives the majority of his concepts from the realm of the collective unconscious. In so doing Faber selects a number of psychological concepts recently added to the collective consciousness to explain the mysteries of synchronicities from a naturalistic perspective. Further, in selecting and synthesizing these psychologists' ideas, each an adherent of the object relations school of thought, Faber (1998) believes that his "psychodynamics of interpersonal development strips synchronicities of their [transcendent] spiritual implications."[12]

Faber's Focus on the Pre-Oedipal Origins of the Self

In all theories of synchronicities be they supernatural or natural, the self is a primary organizing concept. However, there are important differences. The

Self for Jung is preformed and originally whole and balanced whereas for the naturalist theorists the self is initially unformed and therefore must be grown and developed.

Since Jung's day, Faber notes that there has been a shift from "instinct theory to attachment theory [in which] the self and its development is of central concern . . . . And of central concern to the formation of the self is the process of internalization."[13] Schaffer (1968) defines the internalization process as: [a process by which we] "transform real or imagined interactions with the environment, and 'real or imagined characteristics of the environment' into inner relationships."[14] Faber says "It is the thesis of [his] book . . . that the conflict (separation merger) never ceases."[15] Faber believes this to be the case because: "It is the infant's sense of helplessness, his long period of dependency to master and to control a world at odds with his wishes and threatening in itself that goads the internalization process to life."[16] Logically then, from a strictly psychodynamic perspective, Faber believes that the key to a naturalistic theory of synchronicities is associated with the psychodynamics of the developing self and its vicissitudes originating in the pre-oedipal (first two years) of self development.

In this connection Faber (1998) conjectures that: "Jung's theory emerges just as it is needed to shake the bitter thirst for connection and meaning"; and (2) "as part of the growing trend to replace God the Father with God the Mother."[17] Faber is alluding to the notable shift of patient's complaining less about oedipal issues than with pre-oedipal problems associated with identity formation and the vicissitudes of self development such as not being able to adequately regulate one's self esteem.

Faber's aim is to demonstrate how "synchronicity is rooted in the individuals' actual developments past and how it manifests as a naturalistic psychological reflection of that past. There are no mysterious 'something,' 'no subtle body,' no hidden process, or principle waiting for our discovery. There is only the human being expressing his/her fantasies, wishes and fears."[18]

For Faber and the object relations theorists, the self grows and develops in direct proportion to the presence or absence of meaningful connectedness with the primary care giver (usually the mother). In Freudian psychodynamic theory the emphasis on origins and development constitutes the genetic (developmental) point of view. Faber's list of object relations theorists he deems as the major contributors towards formulating a naturalistic theory of synchronicity includes Bolby, Mahler, Stern, Bollas, Melanie Klein, Fairbairn, Winnicott, and Stephen Mitchell.

Object Relations Psychodynamics

Whereas Freud's formulation of psychoanalysis emphasizes the assumed crucial role of the "oedipus complex" as the key concept in understanding the meaning of neurosis, object relations theory focuses attention on the child's real relationship with the primary caretaker—typically the mother. Thus for Faber a major characteristic associated with the process and experience of synchronicities are themes and variations of attachment theory.

For example, Faber (1998) identifies Bolby's formulation of the "decisive role of attachment and loss in maturational growth."[19] and Mahler's description of the developing child's "struggle in separation and attachment [wherein] differentiation and merger is the elemental struggle of our being."[20]

Extending this line of reasoning, Faber converts merger with divinity (Jung's formulation of unity) into the mundane realm of merger with the mother. That is, Faber transposes merger of his subject from the spirit plane to the human plan (the province of modern self psychology.) Faber refers to concepts such as attunement, resonance, and empathy to describe in naturalistic terminology, the exquisitely meaningful connectedness that the baby who is well loved probably experiences, thought to be absolutely necessary for the healthy development of his or herself.

These inferred meaningful connections experienced by the baby with adequate parenting are, for Faber the same kinds of feelings experienced by those who have synchronicities. Thus when Jung speaks about numinosity and awe as typical reactions to synchronicities often experienced as extraordinary moments in time, Faber understands them to be the normal "ordinary" experiences of a baby who is highly attuned to his primary care giver.

To account for the belief that synchronicities are "messages from divinity," Faber (1998) utilizes Bollas's conceptualization of the "transformational object" whereby "maternal care turns to self care."[21] This same concept is thought, by Faber, to account for the felt sense that a person is receiving good guidance in the form of coded messages. In so doing, Faber reasons that what was once a direct experience with the early mother stimulating, acknowledging, accepting, and instructing her baby is displaced into the experience of a synchronicity.

Faber also suggests that Jung spiritualizes the transformational object by transposing the meaningful connections with the mother (and subsequent connections with known and unknown authorities that come to populate the child's collective consciousness) into the occult, unseen, universal and transpersonal realm of absolute meaning and knowledge Jung refers to as the collective unconscious.

Additional Psychoanalytic Concepts Selected from the Collective Consciousness

Faber (1998) utilizes additional concepts from the British School of object relations including those of Melanie Klein's "internalized object relations";

Fairbairn's tension reducing concepts; Winnicott's "good enough mothering"; transitional objects, negotiating transitional space and transitional experience in furthering psychodynamics, in understanding the natural process that leads to the production of synchronistic phenomena.[22]

For example, in speaking about Winnicott's concepts Faber switches from his focus on the genetic or developmental point of view to that of the adaptive point of view. Faber (1998) quotes Winnicott who says that the healthy self develops as one "fashions a reality from the creative capacities of his own mind as they interact with the environment."[23]

Thus Faber is explicitly taking the position that the meaning in Jung's phrase "meaning equivalence" is a dynamic process of active meaning creation. This activity associated with creating meaningful connections with the object world is contrasted with Jung's belief that the meaningful connections associated with synchronicities are accessed through an implied passive "channeling" of the assumed information derived from the realm of "absolute meaning." Williams picks up this point utilizing it as a key part of his progressive naturalistic theory.

By emphasizing the experienced level of quality connectedness, Faber challenges the Jungian assertion, that conventional notions of causality omit issues of purpose, meaning, values, ends, and goals. The pre-oedipal baby is preoccupied with attaining and sustaining meaningful connections with representatives of the object world not simply to reduce tension but to participate in a process that leads to an ever increasing realization of the reality and value of the self in terms of its being and in its strivings. By emphasizing the experience of quality connectedness linked to purpose driven behavior, Faber sets the stage for an explication of his regressive theory of synchronicities.

Faber's Critique of Jung's Supernatural Theory of Synchronicities

The importance of synchronicities for Jung is accessing vital information used in the service of the development of the self. In this connection Faber quotes a letter written by Jung on July 19th, 1939, sent to a psychotherapist which summarizes the essence of Jung's supernatural (esoteric/occult) theory. Jung (1980) wrote, "originally we were all born out of a world wholeness—in the first years of life are still completely contained in it. . . . There we have all [archetypal] knowledge without knowing it. Later we lose it and call it progress when we remember it again."[24]

Faber believes Jung's concepts of activated archetypes, a realm of absolute knowledge and absolute experience, the spiritualization of reality, numinosity, a prepatterned reality, the transcendent function, unus mundus and the likes are too far from ordinary mundane experience. Thus he believes that Jung's adoration of mythological consciousness is second best to person specific knowledge gained from understanding concrete psychodynamics derived from a person's unique experience.

Having stated his naturalistic perspective, Faber moves on to applying his theory in working with patients. In this connection, he implicitly asks a crucial question. If the role of the Jungian therapist is to view synchronicities as aiding a patient to make a reconnection to their lost transcendent function, once stripping away the "mystical" trappings, what then should be the most appropriate attitude of the non-Jungian therapist in responding to the reports of his patients' meaningful coincidences? The implied answer is for the therapist to be aware of the regressive implications of the experience.

For Faber synchronicities occur when a patient makes a conscious connection with a good object. In the case of a patient this connection is likely to be an idealized transference to his or her therapist. The origin of this idealizing transference is either a displacement of a real person from the patient's past or a fantasy construction of what they would liked to have experienced.

Thus Faber's (1998) core thesis is that synchronicities reported by patients receiving psychotherapy are re-experiencing a regressive connection to the original or wished for good care giver(s). Further, that the quality of this psychological regression is "to a time when higher powers [parents] could miraculously discover and respond to one's needs, to a time when the universe did have the capacity to copy one's requirements in a mysterious, inexplicable way."[25]

In the case of the scarab coincidence Faber believes the most accurate interpretation is that the synchronicity marks the conscious experience of a "positive transference" to Jung—the now idealized, good father. Implied is the idea that his patient has transferred a memory of at one-ment feelings with her actual good father/mother onto Jung—her symbolic father in the present.

From this perspective, Faber agreeing with Freud, understands the transcendent or religious function to be an extension of awe and good guidance originally experienced with the good Father now displaced and projected onto the archetypal God the Father.

Faber selects additional organizing concepts he believes strengthens his position that a naturalistic theory of synchronicities is valid. For example Faber (1998) utilizes Mahler's stages of the developing self. These stages of self development include the autistic, symbiotic, separation, rapprochement, and individuation. The developing child experiences increasing mixed feelings of love and hate (ambivalence) towards the primary care givers. The child prefers harmony and disdains conflict.[26]

One positive effect of experiencing synchronicities is that for a few brief moments there is a felt sense of unity transcending dichotomous ambivalent feelings. Thus it is no wonder that individuals experiencing synchronicities are impressed by their apparent power to evoke "pure" feelings of meaningful connectedness even if short lived.

Spitz: Psychic Organizers—The Mother as a Reflecting Mirror

Another uncanny characteristic associated with synchronicities is the "doubling phenomena" that occurs when there is an equivalence of meaning between the internal and the external event made even more mysterious by the fact that inner and outer often appear to occur simultaneously.

In order to explain the apparent uncanny and other worldly experience of this doubling phenomena, Faber (1998) utilizes Spitz's organizing concept of the Mother as mirror. Applying this concept to the nature and experience of synchronicities the doubling phenomena is explained as the baby and the mother (1) sharing an equivalency in meaning with the objective event (A'); and (2) the child (B) and the mother sharing a meaningful connection simultaneously (at the same time).[27] Faber (1998) employs Stern's concept of "affect attunement" to explain the sense of excitement that is generated in people experiencing synchronicities. The excitement reinforces the sense of having experienced something extraordinary (fostering self-esteem).[28]

In explaining Jung's assumed archetypal/ mythological transcendent realm of absolute knowledge, Faber uses Winnicott's concept of "evoked companions." Says Faber (1998), "God, Mary, guardian angels, aliens, shamans, guides, channeled entities, Jesus, may be regarded projective psychological expression or complex multi layered symbolifications of those longed for inward companions associated with the dynamic affects included in the dual unity situation, the baby's delicious, regulating, invariant and internalized encounters with the care-giving figure of the early period."[29]

Another example of substituting Jung's transpersonal synchronistic explanations for naturalistic explanations is the anatural explanation of simultaneity and the often uncanny aura surrounding it. Thus Faber's (1998) understanding of the experience of simultaneity accompanying synchronicities has its origins in the baby's experience of its needs being met without undue delay as if its wishes were instantaneously obtained (like magic). He states: "The parent knows intuitively, telepathically, clairvoyantly the affective meaning of the infant's signals, and the parent provides a response in a timely fashion, magically echoing or mirroring the infant's inner world as the infant makes the world manifest. . . . Once we discover or re-discover an attunement, an evoked companion, an energetic affective mix, we often feel transformed."[30]

Attunement, Meaningful Connectedness, and Religion (Spirituality)

Faber alludes to the fact that the religious or transcendent function central to Jung's supernatural theory of synchronicities has its naturalistic origins in the pre-oedipal period of the foundational development of the self.

It is this exquisite sense of just right timing between the painful experience of the (frustrated) need (distress) and the need satisfied in a timely way (from the vantage point of the baby) that evokes the experience of extra special meaning associated with synchronicities.

In this connection: Faber—commenting on Jung and his patient's scarab experience—is not highly favorable: "In psychoanalytic terms, Jung fosters an electrifying projection 'making' during the course of which his shocked, startled patient has internalized objects out into the environment where it may serve as a supernatural substitute for the relinquished parent." This faith healing "fosters a religious outlook," a transformation of attitude, "a kind of intellectual rape precipitated by the rigidity of Jung's religious outlook." The infantile unconscious sends feelings of being "secretly guided by other worldly influences, feelings that originally personal and subsequently projected into a 'deity.'[31]

Faber is confident that his use of the composite list of organizing concepts selected from the stream of the collective consciousness has adequately and naturalistically accounted for the magical, religious, and the uncanny feelings associated with the experience of synchronicities.

Says Faber (1998), "the sacred and the spiritual are loaded with pre-verbal feelings of fusion and transformation, connection and change, union and the wondrous sense of the self's alternation. One is tied uncannily to the other who is numinous, magical because specific pre-verbal memories rooted in the dynamic unconscious awaken affects that 'say so.'"[32]

Thus what Jung calls apriori in unus mundus for Faber (1998) is "the internalization of the early period in which the parental object functions as the dynamic, emotive, [for] 'all those centers of the neonates existence.'"[33]

When needs are experienced as perfectly met, the feeling of at-one-ment characteristic of those who describe their reactions to synchronicities is equivalent to the mystical feelings associated with those who feel as if they have been the recipients of divine intervention. In this light, it is easy to understand how many who experience synchronicities typically believe they are "heavenly signs"—verifying the wondrous powers of God intervening in a given person's behalf.

"Boundaries are dissolved, an experience of at-one-ment...projected power. . . . Needs are perfectly met."[34] Thus for Faber the experience of synchronicity is like reliving or living presently in the experience of the hope for and needed at-one-ment experiences of pre-oedipal consciousness. Speaking to this point Faber says, “In synchronicities we see (experience) the return of the repressed. If religious, the care-giving is assigned to a deity. Miraculous, divine intervention is judged to be the case.”[35]

In this light, the synchronicity is taken to be a sign—a verification of the wondrous powers of god violating the “normal” laws of time and space in the service of intervening on the person’s behalf.

In so far as treatment is concerned, Faber suggests that after stripping away illusions, the end of a good analytic experience would be . . . “For some of us at least, it is exciting to take a deep psychological breath . . . and confront life just as it is and not what we would wish it to be.”[36]

A Bridge to Williams’s Naturalistic Progressive Theory of Synchronicities

Faber makes a valuable contribution in demystifying seemingly inexplicable synchronistic anomalies. He provides reasonable naturalistic concepts as replacements for the more mystical concepts used by Jung pointing to a potential naturalistic understanding of the intricate psychological process assumed to produce these seemingly acausal events.

However, whereas synchronicities for Faber appear to function as nothing more than regressions to pre-oedipal consciousness re-creating a real or fantasized merger with the “good primary care giver”; for Williams, synchronicities function as progressive events arising out of the need for human beings to continually resolve inevitable life problems of being, doing, and becoming by connecting to their idiosyncratic creative process.

While there is every reason to believe, as Faber asserts, that synchronicities do involve a regression to pre-oedipal consciousness, unlike Faber the regression for Williams is not an end in itself but a radical beginning of a much more complicated psychological process. Therefore where Faber ends, Williams continues.

In this connection, a detailed discussion of the origins and development of Williams’s progressive naturalistic theory of synchronicities is the subject matter of chapters 5–8.

II
THEORY CONSTRUCTION

5

Synchronicity Challenged

The major problem of man is to have a clear idea of what he wants to do. Then to activate his will power. He needs imagination to know what to turn his will power to therefore his awareness of relative values. In the classical occult sense consciousness raising means the slow evolution of individual man to reconcile the splits in himself—to control his will so to be able to take his place with others to move towards fulfillment of the grand plan which is working back to an experience of the union with God and ultimate self control.

—Colin Wilson[1]

Do not follow where paths may lead,
Go instead, where there is no path and leave a trail.

—Ralph Waldo Emerson[2]

A Shift from a Supernatural Perspective to a Naturalistic Point of View

The Colin Wilson quotation above both captures the essence and the essential difference in my experience and understanding of synchronicities. The essence of synchronicities is that they are markers of a vital connection with one's idiosyncratic creative process evolving over time. The creative process in this connection is a byproduct of systematic work on the self in identifying and reconciling fundamental splits perceived as problematic in internal reality. These fundamental splits are most noticeable in the areas of being, doing, and becoming.

In this view, synchronicities are intimately associated with an individual's need to provide essential answers to ultimate questions such as who am I, what do I really want, how do I acquire such knowledge, and how best do I put it to use? In short, synchronicities are associated with a strong desire to make significant changes in one's life even to the point of fashioning wholesale transformations. But, while characteristically appearing to have mysterious, mystical, and magical origins, I believe them instead, to be naturalistic byproducts of human beings making important adaptations in their all too human struggles to both survive and thrive.

What follows in the remainder of this chapter and in the one that follows is an account of how my theoretical perspective gradually shifted from an initial de facto concurrence with Jung's position to a wholly psychodynamic non supernatural point of view.

It should be noted that at the time I recorded these particular synchronicities, and the sixteen others that will follow which were to become initial raw data of my research, I found them to be truly remarkable in terms of the impact they initially had on me.

Looking back over them, from the perspective of decades later, I find most of them to be hardly worth noting. The significance of this observation is that for a person experiencing what for them is a coincidence perceived as evoking little or no particular meaning; the same occurrence for another person (or the same person at a different time) may be perceived as a pivotal life defining experience.

My Initial Interest in Meaningful Coincidences

As seen above, my earliest experiences of meaningful coincidences were accompanied by the awe response that Jung describes is a typical reaction to such odd occurrences. Jung further states that this state of awe—numinosity—signals the presence of what might be thought of as a spiritual force pervading all of Reality.

I initially believed that it was entirely plausible that my meaningful coincidences were actual transmissions from a realm of spirituality that was transcendent (a priori) to my personal experience. Unknowingly, at the time, with respect to my attitudes about synchronicities, I was a de facto Jungian.

De facto means that initially I unknowingly paralleled Jung's intellectual and experiential attitudes of his own and others' synchronicities accepting his combined psychodynamic and supernatural explanation as the definitive voice of authority.

It is important to recall that Kant persuasively established the fact that because of realistic human limitations it is seemingly impossible for human beings to be certain that they are actually in contact with the Noumena—the name that identifies the absolute ground of experience. This is important because Jung initially agreed with this position.

But in Jung's formulation of his half psychodynamic and half supernatural synchronicity theory he overrode Kant's argument asserting that those who experience synchronicities are in fact directly connecting to and receiving absolute knowledge from the Noumena—Jung refers to as the realm of "preformed harmony" that is also "spiritualized" (also known as the Unus Mundus).

Spiritualized, in this connection, means an unseen substrate of "absolute meaning" once contacted presumably provides vital information to the self. Thus for Jung it is a given that there actually exist some unseen force actually "out-there," transcendent to the self—a priori, providing vital information obviating interpretation—that can, under certain special circumstances, intervene in the lives of human beings. (This force has many names including God, manifestations of spirit, angels, spirit guides, activated archetypes, and spirit.)

Jung and his followers consider the mysterious phenomena of meaningful coincidences (synchronicities) topping the list of "special circumstances," presumably signaling that a vital connection has occurred between an individual and the assumed realm of absolute meaning via an activated archetype.

Hypothesized transcendent realms of absolute whole meanings, activated archetypes, connecting with "divine" intelligence (spiritualized consciousness) implies the actuality of a "grand plan" respectfully alluded to and actively subscribed to by many sophisticated members enrolled in esoteric occult circles. (One such active organization is the *Lucis Trust.)*

Where I differ with the C. Wilson quotation at the top of this chapter, is the idea that such growth and development enables a person to connect with this hypothesized "Grand Plan." Why so? Perhaps there is in fact a Grand Plan. If there is, so be it. But what I know for a fact is only my ongoing struggle to fashion and to sustain the form and content of my personal life path. What I know for certain is that there are inevitable "forks in the road" that are experienced as critical choice points demanding the most informed judgment I am able to muster. It is at these forks in the road where and when synchronicities are observed to occur with both myself and in virtually all of my synchronicity prone patients I have come to know in breadth and depth. These choice points are characterized by a great deal of ambiguity.

Those of us who have never connected with the certain knowledge of a "Grand Plan" are forced, whether we like it or not, to fall back onto our own experience to guide us through this mystery called life. Given this state of affairs, Emerson's guidance to "go . . . where there is no path, and leave a trail" is a pithy alternative naturalistic attitude.

Although, as was said, that Jung initially vacillated as to whether or not human beings are able to have absolute certainty about the true nature of the noumena, the essence of his supernatural theory rises or falls on tipping his hand towards the assumption that we are both capable of and do in fact know the truth of the matter. Further, that the knowledge of Absolute Reality is by way of connecting with what Jung refers to as the collective unconscious.

For Jung, the collective unconscious is an established reality, not as some believe, just an ingenious imaginative unproven hypothesis. In so doing, Jung apparently considers it acceptable to treat hypothetical imaginative speculation co equal with proven fact. In this connection it is important to note what a confidant of Jung says in speaking to this point: "He [Jung] established through a way no scientist can deny that this collective unconscious within man was objective, that the visions and dreams and imagery in which it communicated with man's conscious self were utterly objective facts, however subjectively they are experienced."[3]

This quotation indicates that Jung took the position that not only is knowledge of the noumena possible but that, in fact, he was able to describe its nature in fine detail. Jung's questionable position is secure as long as he and like-minded adherents assume that their primary implicit ontological and explicit epistemological assumptions are equivalent to objective reality. If, on the other hand, it is assumed that the nature and certain knowledge of ultimate reality necessarily eludes us because of realistic limitations (such as the way we are psychologically wired as Kant persuasively shows us) then, whatever viewpoints we consciously or unconsciously assert with respect to our understanding of reality (including synchronicities) must necessarily be relative to our own experience.

This realistic limitation restricting our capacities powers to have certain knowledge of absolute Reality means that we can only have a relative understanding of the phenomena we actually experience (including the experience of synchronicities).

If this second, alternative primary assumption is embraced, it means that in attempting to understand the nature of reality we must acknowledge that something of the self is always added to our so–called objective observations in understanding the nature of any phenomena—including synchronicities. Further, this something added by a participating self are one's individual interpretations; wherein, interpretations refer to all of the conscious and/or unconscious meanings attributed to a person's idiosyncratic experience including experiencing a synchronicity.

It should be noted that even if Jung is absolutely correct—that is, that indeed if there are supernatural elements intimately connected with the process, the source, and the meaning of the content of meaningful coincidences—this fact does not exempt human beings from their responsibility to understand what meanings they themselves consciously or unconsciously attribute to these awesome events.

If the messages are in fact being transmitted by a divine intelligence then the receivers of this assumed vital knowledge should be actively engaged in translating the concrete data of this communication as accurately as possible. This active approach is contrasted with the passive attitude of simply channeling the transmissions while the receiver is passively standing in awe.

An additional issue comes to light. What if the receiver of a divinely inspired "message" either doesn't like what is being sent or disagrees in part or in whole as to its significance?

Forced to take a position about this and other complex questions associated with attempts to understanding the nature of meaningful coincidences, forces the serious student to face up to the central most important question any human being can ask: Who is the final authority in my life?

Having reached a point in my mid thirties when I was more confused than I had ever been with respect to answering this most important question, I began my third therapy experience—this time a psychoanalysis with a classical Freudian analyst.

Previous to starting anew, despite my best efforts to get to the root of my issues, nothing substantial got to the heart of the matter as whatever knowledge I had about myself failed to accrue. This was because there was a fundamental detachment between me and my sense of reality that I could not bridge. Although I longed to make a meaningful connection with myself and the object world, most of what I actually experienced, disappointedly, was a profound sense of meaningless disconnectedness.

Unlike my previous failed attempts to order my personal chaos, my analyst both accepted and validated my sorry self-assessment. In so doing he adopted an attitude of encouraging me to take whatever my experience was felt to be: good, bad, or indifferent, as my experience.

This was in contrast to whitewashing, denying, embellishing, omitting, lying, over simplifying and the like. Thus the one rule in my analytic sessions was to speak my truth (free associate—that is just say what comes to mind and try not to censor) no matter how difficult the task seemed to be, and then we would see where it would lead.

Implicit in this attitude is that one's self is the final authority in this life; therefore, for the self in question, even though that self may not like to acknowledge this truth, one is stuck with one's final authority.

A statement whose authorship is unknown, repeated by my analyst, Dr. Rudolf Wittenberg, on numerous occasions is pertinent to this discussion. He said: "In the final analysis we are left with our experience, and our experience of our experience. We then attribute conscious and unconscious meanings to our experience. Then we draw conclusions from these meaningful connections that play a role in our psychic economy greatly influencing our attitudes and behavior."

Learning to take my experience seriously greatly influenced my attitude about synchronicities. For as I actively struggled with the big questions of my life in my analysis including: what is myself, where is my self located, what do I really want, and what interferes with my obtaining and sustaining it: I applied my accruing self knowledge to reapproaching the complex questions that had previously been raised concerning the nature of synchronicities.

In so doing, the previous abstract "intellectualized" interest I had had in speculative philosophy began to come alive for me in a personal way. Thus I was newly able to begin to apply meaningful concepts to my direct experience resulting in viewing the nature of synchronicities in a fresh way. For example, I was now able to verify the truth of William James's pragmatic method applying it to my own direct experience.

In technical terminology, I had begun to cathect my experience wherein cathexis means making a previously abstract or "dead" concept, idea, and/or experience, come alive. For example: It is one thing to feel that one has an important book to write, it is quite another to initiate a process that eventually results in a finished manuscript. Ideas are a dime a dozen, struggling with struggle to produce a respectable project is quite another undertaking.

The ultimate test of any theory, as Williams James so cogently refers to the "cash value" of a theory—is inextricably associated with the direct experiences of the theorizer in question. Any theory about anything is acceptable until and unless a person's direct experience conflicts with the primary assumptions and operational definitions of the inevitable array of associated organizing concepts supporting the theory in question.

That is, when what is, clashes with what is supposed to be, something has to give one way or the other. Either the experience has to be denied, or there has to be a revision of the initial theory and the core organizing concepts associated with it.

An important qualification should be considered. It is one thing to note experiences that clash with long held beliefs. It is quite another to fully acknowledge that this clash is real, and that the implications for the possibility of significant intellectual and affective (experiential) changes in both primary assumptions and in the associated organizing concepts utilized to make sense out of the raw data, is actually occurring.

This last sentence is a long way of spelling out what is meant by both taking one's experience seriously and gradually acknowledging that one's personal reality is really real for them.

Jung would wholeheartedly agree with the statement above. He takes great pains to point out that his radical theory was derived not from neatly constructed thoughts from his disembodied intellect but because he dared to descend and to explore the largely unfamiliar "dark" complexity of his conflicted whole self.

In this light, if the following account is to be taken as testimony of Jung's most ardent beliefs on this subject, he would have no other choice than to fully endorse and support my current endeavor even though the ideas I affirm, radically conflict with his own point of view.

Laurens van der Post (a confidant of Jung's) reflecting on this issue in his book, *Jung and the Story of Our Time* states: "Experience is before and beyond argument. One of the gravest indictments of the intellectualism of his and our age is a strange determination to deny human beings the validity and dignity of their own experience and to subject it to some external, preconceptualised devaluation."[5]

Gradually learning in my psychoanalysis to take my direct experience seriously led me to shift my understanding of synchronicities from (1) an initial uncritical de facto acceptance of Jung's psychodynamic/supernatural theory to (2) a de facto Faberian regressive psychodynamic/naturalistic theory to (3) my own progressive psychodynamic/naturalistic theory of synchronicities and the uses they serve.

Viewing synchronicities from a naturalistic perspective means searching for what the self brings to the table not only in determining their content but their structure, and the process that leads to their creation. The self's contribution in these three areas is clearly noted when a given synchronicity is viewed as embedded in a matrix of overlapping personal-situational-psychological and temporal contexts. (I refer to this process as contextual analysis.) The interested reader is encouraged to refer back to the section in which I rebutted Jung's three anti-causal arguments. In the first argument concerning method, I believe I have successfully made a persuasive case for the efficacy of scientifically investigating these anomalous events by fitting them into sets of overlapping contexts.

My research indicates that when synchronicities are viewed as embedded in overlapping contexts what initially appears to be supernatural in its origin as well as its nature, soon reveals itself to be a byproduct of an undeniably marvelous but totally human naturalistic process.

Applying the method of contextual analysis to the pertinent data, I have reached the following conclusion. That for myself, initially, a subject of one, in attempting to do justice in comprehending the exceedingly complex material associated with meaningful coincidences, it has been infinitely more illuminating and concretely efficacious in utilizing organizing concepts whose source is the collective consciousness rather than in utilizing organizing concepts whose source is the so-called collective unconscious.

This contextual analytic approach to investigating the nature of synchronicities identifies the essential difference between Jung's psychodynamic/supernatural perspective and a psychodynamic/naturalistic approach such as Faber's and my own. This difference is found in our respective alternative understandings as to the source of the "special meaning" that differentiates a mere coincidence from an especially meaningful coincidence. Whereas Jung attributes the source of the "specialness" to a direct connection with an activated archetype that is transmitting vital information to the self from a realm of absolute transcendent "a priori" (un-interpreted) meaning; I understand the source of the "specialness" to be found in a purely immanent location—the byproduct of the human being attributing personal meanings attribution of meaning and projecting them onto a selected external event that is mirrored back, and is experienced as a coded message received from some external "transcendent" source.

In effect, my position is that the "coded messages" associated with synchronicities are generated from a given person's idiosyncratic creative process for the purpose of effective accommodation with no need to posit any supernatural elements at all.

Freud's conclusion as to his interpretation of the nature of occult phenomena is applicable in understanding the hypothesized psychodynamic/naturalistic process resulting in a synchronicity as well as in providing implied guidance as to effectively decoding them. (These words have been quoted before in this book but are deemed worth repeating). Says Freud: "The differences between myself and the superstitious person are two: first, he projects outwards a motivation which I look for within; secondly, he interprets chance due to an event, while I trace it back to a thought. But what is hidden from him corresponds to what is unconscious for me."[6]

Following Freud's guidance, my research indicates that what makes two events perceived as coinciding into a synchronicity is the special meaning which is consciously or unconsciously attributed to them by the subject in question. Thus, while Jung looks to an assumed realm of absolute meaning for divine guidance, I cast my lot with Freud, who finds that it is more profitable to assume the final authority for what I believe is always the truth of any meaningful connection. This means we human beings are the ultimate source of whatever significance we happen to experience in any and every aspect of living our lives. Even if what we believe is attributed to God all mighty it is still up to a given person to determine what if any meaning is associated with the communication in question as well as in determining what if any action is to follow.

In my investigation of these remarkable events I have observed that it is no coincidence that they occur when they do, nor is it coincidental that they are associated with highly personal content. Therefore I agree with Barbara Honneger that they are best interpreted as if they are waking dreams wherein the analysis can often reveal a rich mine of potentially vital person specific information about one's self (see B. Honneger).[7]

Viewing synchronicities from a naturalistic prism, the remainder of this chapter charts the journey I took that led me to gradually shift from a decidedly Jungian psychodynamic/supernatural perspective to what I refer to as a progressive/psychodynamic naturalistic perspective in my attempts to understand the nature and use of meaningful coincidences. In the service of attempting to make my naturalistic approach to this complex subject as clear as possible, utilizing the method of contextual analysis, I am detailing relevant events from my personal and professional life associated with the production and experiencing of what I took to be a number of especially meaningful coincidences.

Following then are the pertinent details as to the historical, situational, and psychological contexts from which my selected synchronicities arose.

My Initial Interest in Synchronicities

This investigation of synchronicities is not simply the byproduct of my disembodied intellect whose curiosity had been sufficiently stimulated to begin to actively explore the nature of a scientific anomaly (synchronicities) with my primary goal being that of advancing the progress of science. Rather, my interest has its roots in the soil of personal struggle to sort out the truth of the matter as a lived experience. Thus a summary of my personal connection with synchronistic events is pertinent to this discussion.

As my research indicates a naturalistic theory of meaningful coincidences necessitates viewing these wondrous events as embedded in the personal situational and psychological histories of the subject in question. For this reason I am summarizing what I believe to be the most relevant facts of my life associated with my interest in synchronicities.

At the age of nineteen I began keeping a journal that was to span the next thirty-five years. Reviewing the entries from the perspective of an adult I can see the emergence of clearly visible themes. Starting with the first entry I see that I was driven to making sense out of what primarily was experience as my disordered life. In this connection the main theme of the journal is a quest for identity and negotiating obstacles put in the way.

Note: For those seriously interested in conducting their own research into this most fascinating of topics I urge you to keep your own critical incidents autobiography in the form of an ongoing journal. An example of this particular approach follows.

My Early Years

Before commencing on detailing the pertinent facts of my life associated with my involvement with synchronicities, it is of value to take note of Redfield's (1997) *Celestine Prophecy* (perhaps the most popular book on the subject of synchronicities to date). What is of interest at this point is his sixth of ten insights (used as a guide to interpretation) which he titles *Clearing the Past.* This insight states:

> The more we stay connected, the more we are acutely aware of those times when we lose connection, usually when we are under stress. In these times, we can see our own particular way of stealing energy from others. Once our manipulations are brought to personal awareness, our connection becomes more constant and we can discover our own growth path in life, and our spiritual mission—the personal way we can contribute to the world.[8]

Redfield makes the point that to be free to understand the "mystical" messages that he (and many others) believe are the coded essence of meaningful coincidences, it is first necessary to free oneself of psychological interferences from the past. A key interference is a child having to work out his own identity often feeling caught between the competing demands of his parents.

I agree with Redfield that freeing the self from the psychological entanglements of the past is intimately connected with obtaining the greatest amount of benefit from one's own meaningful coincidences. However, unlike Redfield, my research indicates that unresolved childhood conflicts predispose an individual to synchronistic awareness and thereby greatly contribute to the idiosyncratic meanings imputed to them.

My Mother

My mother was beautiful and remote. My memories of her till this day are sketchy at best. She was an active clubwoman who enjoyed great respect even awe to the many who knew, and adored her always uplifting way. I saw her tired and depressed side. She and my father rarely seemed in tune. The later years of their marriage were stormy. When she was 35 years old she contracted breast cancer and died five years later. I found it nearly impossible to go into her bedroom as she was getting sicker and sicker. I suffered from constricting shame and guilt believing I was an imperfect son.

My Father

My father was handsome, smart, and unbalanced. We were like oil and water. He was a lawyer who was upset that neither my brother nor I wanted to take over his practice. He was obsessed with his need to know what I wanted to be. He said he would support whatever I wished to be but when I told him I wanted to be a teacher he bitterly exclaimed: "Those who do, do; those who don't, teach." I found him to be excessively narrow minded, impatient, argumentative, fatuous, and generally abusive. I wanted him to love and approve of me but not at the expense of my losing what hard won self I had managed to muster.

My Brother—Ambivalent at Best

My brother, who is four-and-a-half years younger than myself, and I were relatively close until our mother died. After our father remarried six months later my brother became the favorite son. Approaching adolescence we became increasingly more estranged.

My Adolescence—Confused and Lost

The central fact of my adolescence was the death of my mother when I was fifteen years old. Losing her led to an increasingly stormy relationship with my father and stepmother. I found myself in the midst of two battles, a revolution and a civil war. Although I was a good student and agreeable on the outside, I felt increasingly more alienated and estranged on the inside.

Perhaps because of the high degree of estrangement from my family, I was preoccupied with trying to find essential answers to ultimate questions such as What is the meaning of life? What is the meaning of my life? Is there a God? and What is the Nature of Reality? My salvation was a deepening love of great ideas. I read Will Durant's *Story of Philosophy* in which the words of the great speculative philosophers such as Socrates, Plato, and Aristotle seemed to speak to my direct experience. While their ideas and experience were comforting and validating, they could not prevent the onrush of my growing intensity, alienation, and smoldering that I was increasingly aware was nearly engulfing me.

At nineteen years old, my preoccupation with trying to organize my chaos motivated me to begin what was the beginning of a thirty-five-year journal. My first entry read: "I must begin to write. But I find it painfully difficult to begin anything anymore due to the realization that nothing exists in a vacuum. What a grand surprise to realize that behind all external manifestations lies a real (or at least) motivating internal cause. This awareness opens up worlds never dreamed of; yet, at the same time, causes new complications. Before it was simple to act. There seemed to be no choice. Now there seems to be nothing but choices. Before the question was to act or not to act. Now the question is what actions are best? This question paralyzes me. My English teacher is fond of quoting Plato: "The unexamined life is not worth living." But I have discovered that the overly examined life is incapable of being lived.

Not understanding what I wanted at the time, I see now that it was a desire to live naturally—to be true to my nature—to have peace of mind. Instead I was experiencing myself as increasingly divided, confused, tormented, alienated, isolated, and insecure. There was a notable gap between the surface me and the increasingly chaotic me beneath my skin. Initially I thought my main problem was due to a dissonant atmosphere. Thus I thought that the solution was to get away as far as I could. I looked forward to going to New York City and Columbia College.

College Years: The First Two Years—A Crisis of Trust Is Brewing

Initially feeling liberated and excited I plunged into my assignments. But within the first six months I became increasingly depressed, isolated, and alienated. I intuitively understood that the "geographical solution" of getting away to a new change would not in and of itself be the answer to effectively healing my "divided self". I was weighted down with excess baggage from my past.

In a memorable conversation with the mother of my best friend she put her finger on what was most troubling me at that time when I was nineteen years old. The occasion was a trip home from college, Ms. B said: "Don't analyze so much. You are a boy of extremes. You have to learn to play with time. Play it by ear. Be able to praise in spite of. We need each other to tell us who we are. You are very sad."

I didn't like hearing what she told me but down deep I knew that I lacked courage to be myself, and, instead I was feeling terrified, afraid, and alone. I began to realize that my problem was not outside, it was in me.

A Wish to be Rescued by a Good Guide

As the journal entries were to reveal, I had a clear sense of what I needed but I didn't know how or where to find resources that would be helpful. Representative of this awareness, I wrote: "When one has to confront his own contradictions and try to overcome his own impasses he may try to change the outside or he may go into himself and attempt to change his inside. To do so alone, however, soon leads one into circles. A bridge is necessary to go from the fog into the clear light. There must be 'an essential other' to guide the way."

Without knowing it at the time I was seeking an absolute answer to each essential question preoccupying me. The current essential question then, was, what is the nature of the good life for me? Searching for good guidance I avidly drank the words of some acknowledged "greats" of Western literature.

At first I would get "high" on each thinker's ideas but inevitable contradictions had the net effect of canceling each other out. The discovery of the realm of the collective consciousness—the great repository of seminal ideas—that initially had been hope inducing was now causing me unexpected despair. Instead of my experiencing a path of clear thoughts that would hopefully lead me out of my personal dark prison; I was, instead, experiencing a crisis of information overload reinforcing my dreaded states of confusion making me feel more stuck than ever.

Information Overload

A crisis of information overload was recorded in my journal (September 24, 1956, Columbia College): "All is confusion! Plato is right (the good life is "A sound mind in a sound body"). Aristotle is right: the good life is finding your own golden mean. Spinoza is right: the good life is the intellectual union with all things. Each of them is right but how is this possible? How can each of them be right (and different) at the same time?

Later that day: "I went into Salter's bookstore today looking for something interesting to read. I went to the philosophy and psychology sections as I always do. I first picked up one book, then another, and another. None of them seemed to have all that I was looking for. Finally I stood in the middle of the bookstore paralyzed. I couldn't choose."

Quintessential "Stuckness": A Major Fork in the Road—1956, 19 years old

The bookshop event made me realize that although I had traveled some 1700 miles to get away from my parents and that part of my society that I had despised, yet I still felt bound to my psychological umbilical cord.

The crux of this depressing realization was recorded in a journal entry: "The start of my freshman year was a depressing haze. I am isolated and lonely. I can't act. I felt I could do anything and everything. But I have discovered that emotionally everything equals nothing. I have reached an emotional and spiritual crisis."

Summary of My Predominantly Kaleidoscopic Consciousness

I desperately sought unity and wholeness in the place of a protracted sense of division and chaos. Instead of lightness and freedom there was a predominance of heaviness and constriction. While I longed for transcendence and transformation I mainly experienced negative inertia expressed as tedious repetition. I felt as if I had come to a grinding halt. I actively wished for a sign that significant change was possible.

It was in this context of feeling quintessentially stuck that I recorded the first of what I considered to be nineteen especially meaningful coincidences.

> *# l "The Sun at Midnight" (a double synchronicity) December, 1956*
> *The Synchronicity*:
> I am in my dorm room at Columbia College. (A) I paint a picture of the sun bursting at night. I finish it and call it "The Sun at Midnight." Checking the time I see it is exactly midnight. (B) Shortly after, in reading an occult book on the Upanishads, wherein I had randomly come upon a section describing the four basic elements: fire, air, earth and water, I was "shocked" noting that I had only a few moments earlier just read about the same concept in a book called the *Mystical Kabalah.*
> *Reaction*: I experience a sense of wholeness and meaningful connectedness. Implications: This experience reinforced feelings of being in contact with a 'spiritual' force.

This synchronicity being associated with an intellectual pathway to wholeness resulted in a short lived but notable lifting up of my spirits.

A Fateful Fitful "Vacation," December 1956

I had mixed feelings going back "home" to visit on vacations. It was always with the hope that this time things would be vastly different, that I would finally be accepted unconditionally and I also would accept all of them unconditionally as well. This always proved to be a "grand" illusion.

During Christmas break during the middle of my sophomore year it took only an hour for me and my father to become embroiled in a bitter argument.

He had insisted I do something I didn't feel I should have to do. Uncharacteristically I held my ground. This served to infuriate him to a fever pitch. Standing toe to toe he faced me down yelling: "We are happy all year long until you come home. You are nothing. Never were. You are a snot nose, an idiot, a selfish prig. Take that you jerk. . . . First time I've hit you in twenty years. I should have done it long ago." I broke down and cried and put my head on his lap. "Good," he said. "Now you're my boy. Now I know you need me. For the last year I haven't been able to get to you."

I recorded in my journal: "I should try to accept Dad as he is. But I can't. There is too much friction between us. Although he says he acts in my best interest he makes too many impossible demands." Later on: "My father talks to me about my mother, his wife: 'You were her whole life.... You were never neglected. She neglected both of us. She was the tyrant.'" I wrote into my journal: "I stood in his bedroom writing down notes of things he said to me. He grabbed the paper out of my hands. He ripped them up bit by bit. He marched into the bathroom and threw them into the toilet (saying), 'This is where this bull shit belongs.'" And then I entered into my journal: "What drunken madness is growing up! Ideas! Ideas! Ideas swarm around tormenting my brain leaving me defenseless against myself."

My interior reality felt more and more like a hot bed of "negative" emotions. Yet simultaneously there was a burning desire to find the truth. I wrote: "I see myself in the mirror. I see a piercing, probing, intense, lean look. I want to see right down into the guts of life and flesh. I demand to find the truth. Nothing will conquer me in my search. If I am mad, then the whole world is mad! [Before] No choices. Now there seems to be nothing but choices. Before the question was to act or not to act. Now the question is what actions are best? This question paralyzes me. My English teacher is fond of quoting Plato: 'The unexamined life is not worth living.' But I have discovered that the overly examined life is incapable of being lived."

If my goal was to be like an efficient engine that purred, I was finding myself increasingly inefficient. I was more and more feeling less in control. I either couldn't turn myself on; or once on, I couldn't easily turn myself off. I would often sputter and short circuit. In short, I had no solid center that would enable me to find and maintain a personal balance point. Without a solid self, I over or under reacted.

Therefore, informed choices that necessitate delay, judgment, and planning were nearly impossible. I was like a top that either couldn't spin or once spinning couldn't seek and maintain a focused direction.

Not knowing it at the time I was becoming aware that my troubled self was complaining about the same core issues as did Jung. I, like him, was preoccupied in trying to attain and sustain a personal balance point. But in so doing I was daily preoccupied with threats to my cohesion both with myself and with others. Mini and many small but sharp breakdowns in self-esteem were increasing in quantity and in the debilitating toll they took on my spirit.

I experienced this whole negative vortex as a "spiritual crisis." I described it as my self: "caught in a titanic struggle for my soul (as I am unable) to resolve the question of whether to be or not to be. And if to be— to be what? Nothing seems important except to know [but] to know leads [only] to increasingly confusion."

Thus I experienced what I have come to call a quintessential fork in the road along my particular life path. As I could not look to myself for adequate answers, I looked outside for any significant signs of even the faintest hint of good guidance and salvation.

The Appeal of the Collective Consciousness

In this context of overwhelming confusion, it is no coincidence that I was attracted to speculative philosophy, depth psychology, spirituality, the esoteric occult, and science. Reading the words of truth seekers made me feel they were speaking to my direct experience. Two such seminal works were Colin Wilson's *The Outsider* and J. Campbell's *Hero With a Thousand Faces.* At nineteen I quoted Colin Wilson: "Man stripped of his externals…. is an outsider because he stands for Truth… He sees too deep and too much, and what he sees is absolutely chaos… Truth must be told, chaos must be faced… The outsider's business is to find a course of action in which he is most himself, i.e. in which he achieves the maximum of self expression."[9] Quoting Campbell: "The hero's act is to delve into the unconscious mind, bring it up, and make it one with the conscious mind."[10]

Their words and others like them identified a path that resonated with my direct experience. However, while the goal seemed clear enough, exactly what path to take in getting there was not.

Meaningful Coincidences Are Noted: The Summer of My Freshman Year

A friend of mine who knew I was depressed asked me if I have ever heard of psychoanalysis. Curious, I thought that he asked me this particular question exactly at the same time I had just begun reading Freud's Interpretation of Dreams. I wrote my reaction in my journal: "This is but one of a number of coincidences I have noted in my life I have reacted to with fascination and curiosity. Coincidences like this evoke a feeling that suggests the presence of something higher—transcendent or in back of these apparent co–incidences.

I desire to know the truth about coincidences in a context of feeling 'driven' to search for the nature of truth, integrity, purpose, wholeness, and meaningfulness."

On September 27 I woke with a depression I couldn't shake. I wrote: "I feel as if there is a thin sheet of glass between me, and the world. All I want to do is sleep. . . . The world lies outside my 7th floor [dorm] window. I desire to be at one with it. I need to take hold of myself and put me in order. I have to find myself." The next day I called my friend's therapist for an appointment to enter my first psychotherapy experience. I recorded my hopes in my journal: "[I] want to rise above the contradictory, ambivalent, ironic, paradoxes of myself and the world [to be able to] grasp the essential absolutes. There is something missing in me."

My First Psychotherapy Experience: Enlightenment Eludes Me, 1956–1960

My first attempt to find myself in psychotherapy traversed 4 years, twice a week. While there were some gains for the better, I wound up essentially at the same point where I had entered. This first psychotherapy attempt failed as I unwittingly repeated with my therapist the basic relationship I had had with my father. They both erroneously thought they had absolute answers to my troubling questions.

My therapist enjoyed interpreting my dreams. I would go back to the dorm after my therapy session, go to sleep and quite often record two page dreams. I dutifully brought them to each session reading them to him as if they were gifts. He routinely analyzed them with what often seemed to be "brilliant" interpretations frequently leaving me in a state of awe but often without consulting me at all except for me to confirm the wisdom of his interpretations.

While his words sounded impressive they left little emotional impact on me. Secretly, (even to myself) what did make an emotional impact on me, were my own private explorations of spiritual ideas. One such exploration was my strong reaction to having read Zimmer's *King and the Corpse.* I wrote into my journal: "[Zimmer] talks about the veil of illusion that covers reality like a thin transparent tissue.[11] I know this veil. It seems to be ever present. I feel I can see the contradictory, ambivalent, ironic, paradoxical nature of reality and to somehow rise above these antimonies in an intuitive grasping of the really real—to capture the Truth with a capital T. I am feeling alone with my penetrating insights."

I wondered in earnest whether the Indian philosophers are right. Was there, is there, a way to transcend our own human contradictions or are we fooling ourselves? I know they existed. The question is what could be done about them? I felt addicted to words and ideas. I doubted if I was really making any significant progress in my therapy.

I wrote: "I know that if feeling exists in me at all it is in the forms of . . . the fighting parts of me, fighting for wholeness and integrity."

My therapist grows a mustache and reminds me of the way my father looks with a mustache. Doubts about him grow but I characteristically blame me for my failure to progress. Myself is experienced as a collection of intense negative feelings that go mainly unexpressed except to myself and my private journal.

My Secret Self

This "material" concerning my feelings towards my therapist needed to be expressed openly to him, but instead, was expressed only to my secret journal. After one of my therapy sessions in which he said that I had successfully separated him from my father, I wrote my secret response: hardly a confirmation of his handiwork: "I am reborn out of the shit and slime of my past: war, threats, unloved, abandoned, used, seduced, manipulated, phony, lonely. Now to be able to rise above it all and be transformed into a new person . . . to be able to recapture the kidnapped child of my youth—to recapture 'him' and liberate my feelings."

There was a clear wish for transcendence, to be able to feel vitally, to have a sense of purpose and clear sense of meaningful connectedness, to feel whole and solid at my core, to feel liberated and free from the invisible chains that kept me pinned to the ground like Gulliver tied to Lillaputia, and to experience a true sense of unity without losing myself. How ironic, whereas my therapist was thinking I had cut the psychological umbilical cord, I was feeling as tightly bound as I had ever felt.

I was struck by how resonant I felt reading Hesse's *Steppenwolf*: "There are times when a whole generation is caught… between two ages, two modes of life, with consequence that it loses all power to understand itself and has no standard, no security, no simple acquiescence. Haller belongs to those whose fate it is to live the whole riddle of human destiny heightened to the pitch of a personal torture, a personal hell [Hesse]."[12]

I wrote my response to this powerful book stating: "I identify with Haller, the Steppenwolf. I wish I could reconcile the overlap of romanticism and intellectualism, nostalgia and cold cynicism, division and compulsion at work in my soul. I long to be objective; but how to be objective if the acquisition of knowledge is based on my subjective self selecting 'facts' out of the flow of the raw data of experience to order reality? How can I ever hope to penetrate to the nature of reality when I feel so confused half the time? I find this problem becoming more and more central to me as I come closer to the essential facts of my life. I feel bound to a wheel that inevitably repeats itself, and, although I wish to get off, I am unclear as to how to do it."

I tried clarifying this matter with my therapist. He said that my problem is that I am afraid to act as I fear I will be like my father. Thus I have developed a defense of non-action or illusory impotence to protect myself. He says further that I am afraid to express my anger—mainly at him. I try to connect with the unexpressed anger he insists I am holding back, but my truth is I don't feel what he insists I do or should.

A few days later I record what my actual experience was four years into my therapy: I listened to Wagner, and felt a mood of mystery. I wrote: "I wish I could capture that bigger than life quality that good art transmits. I want to capture that sense of a clearer reality. Instead I find myself bound to a wheel. I operate in the same pattern: hope, frustration, detachment, isolation, depression, sadness. Why I get caught up in the same circle? What can I do about it? I am almost totally blocked in action. ... Even after four years of therapy I seem to have the same problems as when I begun. I am still afraid or unable to get involved. Le Misanthrope."

In my senior year I had a summary dream that clearly reflects the state of my soul at the time: "It's my father's birthday today. He is 54 years old. I had a terrible dream last night. I dreamed that Dad's birthday is being celebrated by him and others. He says that as soon as it is 12 AM. I am to slap him and he'll make all of my decisions for me. He says the trouble with me is that I thought I was able to make decisions for myself. I resist violently. I feel a terrible struggle going on inside. Part of me wants to go along, the other side says no. I yell no – no – no. I realize the fight is not as much with him as it is with me."

My own interpretation recorded in my journal is: "I see that most of the negativity is a reenactment of a struggle that is going on in me. I am frustrated—caught between the desire for and against being a free man. I can't seem to break the psychological umbilical cord. I punish myself for daring to be a man. To be a man I somehow have to give him my soul, the very thing that defines me. I realize that my life is an endless stream of problems to be resolved. And to do so I have to be able to rely on my inner resources. But I am rightfully concerned that my inner resources at this time are insufficient to do justice to the inner and outer complexity I am experiencing."

My Attempt to Reconcile the Opposites in Myself Winds up in a Failure

Despite my highest hopes and best intentions I leave my therapy feeling as though I have failed. While there were some surface gains, I feel that the core of me was left essentially untouched.

A journal entry reads: "It is the same pattern over and over: high hopes, frustration, detachment, isolation, depression, sadness. What do I do with this? I am tied to a psychological umbilical cord and unable to cut it despite four years of psychotherapy.... My soul is slowly gripped and squeezed until all feeling is strangled out of it."

Despite four years, twice a week, trying my best to order my chaos I left my therapy with the same core problem I complained about the day I called for my first appointment: a divided self desiring to experience and to sustain a feeling of unity. I was facing a clear fork in the road of my life's path with unanswered questions: To where does it all lead? Anywhere? What is the answer to where we come from and to where are we going? I have passed the point where I want to be labeled in one philosophical group or join up with only one psychological theory. I was aware that I needed a pathway that would enable me to connect with my soul, defined as "a unifying principle" that would help me to integrate my feelings and make them conscious. I was dedicated to taking what I referred to as my personal "spiritual odyssey." I wrote: "Perhaps my problem is 'spiritual'—a hole in my soul—I need to connect with a higher authority—divinity, an essential , whole, united meaningful connectedness, [with] myself, others, the all."

6

Immersion in the Occult

Experience ... is not mere awareness of a succession of presented objects, it is a awareness of a succession determined by a controlling interest or purpose. The order of my experience is not something simply given from without, it is controlled and determined by subjective interest from within.[1]

A Memorable Trip to Europe—Summer of 1959, 22 Years Old

DESPITE INTENSE FEARS I SOMEHOW MANAGED TO TRAVEL around Europe on my own (on my beloved Lambretta motor scooter). The trip covered 7,000 miles. I started in Italy, then to Yugoslavia, Austria, Switzerland, France, Germany, Denmark, Sweden, Finland winding up in England. What began in terror wound up in an overall feeling of surprising mastery. Amazingly I put it all together—the stars were in alignment—but I couldn't sustain it.

New York State Employment Service—End of 1959–1961

I became an employment interviewer in civil service. At first I was enthusiastic about my work. But by the end of the second year I was feeling under-challenged. But despite my clear dissatisfaction I felt stuck—uncertain as to what else to do.

The Lure of the Occult—1960–1961, 22–24 Years Old

After graduating from college and my therapy, I was still preoccupied with trying to make meaningful connections with myself, others, and the world. However, having "failed" psychotherapy and having suffered a crisis of information overload, I was ripe for the lure of the occult.

I had to make important life choices. But feeling more divided than ever—confused, and riddled with doubts—I needed something solid to hold onto transcending myself. It was in this context that I first came upon a bookshop specializing in the esoteric occult; it was love at first sight.

The first day I discovered Mason's psychology and occult bookshop in New York, I instantaneously fell under his spell when he referred to the fact that my Mercury was in Capricorn. He said that was a good place for it to be, predicting that I should look forward to becoming a teacher, adding that teaching was indeed a "noble and important profession." I noted his 360-degree difference from my father.

Mason said that occult phenomena was interesting but of more importance is the esoteric philosophy. He said all you have to do is to believe that its first assumption of the oneness of everything being spiritualized is absolutely real and all else follows. In this context, phenomena such as astrology, tarot, kabala, numerology, are each systems by which the fundamental spiritualized unity is revealed to mankind.

I thought of other men I had known who, like my ex-therapist, had initially excited me me and stirred the depths of my soul. As I turned to leave the magical atmosphere of Mason's occult bookstore I knew I was instantly hooked.

My girlfriend at that time was not as thrilled as I was to have met Mason and his strange world. In fact my girlfriend found him to be decidedly off-putting. I was decidedly disappointed that she did not share my same degree of intense enthusiasm. This difference stirred already strong ambivalent feelings I had been having about her. When people asked me if I was serious about her, I jokingly answered that we were nine-tenths engaged. The one-tenth nagging me was filled with what I thought of as sickly emotions, all too distressingly familiar whenever I became too intimate with someone, particularly a girlfriend.

For me the esoteric occult, by focusing on the whole of me instead of parts of me, provided a fruitful method for potentially integrating disparate pieces of my experience including intuitions, feelings, and thoughts internally and the effects of destiny, luck, chance, serendipity, and possibly even karma externally. In utilizing occult concepts hope was kindled that I might realize my long sought illusive goal of attaining and sustaining "infinite variety in perfect unity." The language, the concepts, and the attitudes associated with the esoteric occult were what I intuitively felt I had needed but failed to get in my psychotherapy experience. Believing my job in civil service was a dead end I was relieved to be drafted into the army.

My Army Experience 1961–1963—The Lure of the Occult Intensifies

In the army, an unexpected amount of free time allowed me to go to the public library where I discovered the mysterious case V. It was mysterious because it was locked up. And when I asked what was behind the lock I was told that it contained all of the occult books in the library that were certain to be stolen if not put under lock and key. I greedily devoured the contents for days on end as if I had been starving for years and had suddenly discovered an oasis in the middle of the Sahara. Absorbing the language and concepts of wholeness; divinity behind all manifestations; the law of correspondence: as above; so below; we all "bathe" in a common sea of mind stuff; that there is in actuality an invisible world filled with vital contactable information that might be used in the service of providing helpful and effective good guidance; there are unseen forces that are caring, compassionate and understanding: all of this—and more was balm and manna for my all but nearly dried up parched soul.

I plunged into learning all I could about the esoteric occult. As the result of my studies, I concluded: "I feel sufficiently convinced that there is something more than just [simply] remarkable correspondences between birthdates and the positions of the planets only due to coincidence and random chance." Further:

> If one assumes that the world, that is reality, is a unity—that all is truly one; that all that is, is directed towards some teleological end—that end being the unfolding spiritual development of the individual: then it follows that various so called "occult" systems like astrology might in fact be able to tap into an assumed "divine" plan. This idea offers exciting possibilities for further study. I am a skeptic but not an ardent one. I feel more like a receptive analyzer.

I concluded, "Am I not truly on the path taken by the mystics, the kabbalists, the esoteric astrologers, the men of mystery and religion, all of them peepers into blackness, no better, the grey fog?" Later that month, my enthusiasm with the esoteric occult intensifying, I wrote: "I have plunged into the study of the occult. I feel caught up in it as if I were possessed. I can't read enough. I am drunk in the wine of the content. I see a new way of viewing reality, [so that] internal and external is vastly expanded. … The astrology chart is a symbol of the way I wish to view myself. Each of the 12 houses of the horoscope is an aspect of the total unity of myself. If only there was something like this in psychology. Why isn't there? Is there? Where is it?"

In addition to the significant theme of everything is interconnected, another theme emerged in the journal that partially explains the initial burst of excitement that was associated with my initiation into the mysterious world of the esoteric occult. I had finally found an area all my own that allowed me to make a stand with my father. In this connection I wrote:

> Isn't it about time I start to do what I want to do instead of always doing what I feel I should do? Isn't it time to make a choice? Suddenly in my mind I have a memory of being in English class in the 11th grade. That day I discovered [for myself] the law of threes. I was struck then and now by a powerful intensity. ... as if a thunderbolt or a rainbow of lightning had stuck me. I realized in a blinding flash that everything is united—that there is a unity [connecting] all things.

I decided to experiment for myself. I bought a book on how to construct your own astrological charts and interpret them. Armed with powerful new organizing concepts, I plunged into the arcane realm of the esoteric occult. I picked a famous person, Wagner, whose music I had liked but was unfamiliar with any personal details of his life history. After erecting his astrological chart, I interpreted it using five respected classical and modern astrological authorities. Upon completing a forty-page workup I read three biographies about him. I then compared and contrasted the two sets of distilled reports. I concluded: "The congruities between the facts of the two reports was astonishingly similar."

This initial immersion into astrology quickly led to an exploration of the tarot, kabbala, numerology, Ouspenski, Alice Bailey, and the like. Best of all, by coincidence there was a spiritualist church directly in back of the building I worked in when I was in the army, stationed in Springfield, Massachusetts. The head of the church, Paul Spencer, was very real and accepting—soft-spoken, alert, and joyously alive. The force of his personality impressed me more than anything else. I felt as if there might be something of real value for me so I began attending church on a regular basis. My impressions were as follows:

> I feel as if I have made an active break with skepticism. I am far from a true believer but I am not an adamant agnostic either. I long for proof that occult teachings reveal an intelligence that is in fact knowable and that I am on the path. It is one thing to say that I am psychologically motivated to being attracted to this church at this particular time in my development out some need to resolve a conflict ... but another possibility exists (perhaps not contradicting the other) to say that I am being guided in this direction by forces that are unseen yet are real and are looking out for my best interests. These two realities are not necessarily

> mutually exclusive. Free will theoretically could coincide with fate. Who knows for sure where the Truth lies hidden? It is found in all places and in all things. Blake said: "Everything is Holy."[2]

I was enthralled with immersing myself with the mysterious, the fantastic, the miraculous. All of these states of consciousness were associated with the atmosphere of the spiritualist church. Attending each Sunday I had "a feeling of something transcendent pulling me out of myself."

Twenty-Six Years Old: My Immersion in the Esoteric Occult Deepens Even More

I was swept up in exploring all I could get my hands on related to the esoteric occult. Among my varied projects was reading Edgar Casey, Swedenborg, Blavatsky, viewing materializations, attending spiritualist churches in New York City, sending for information on the two Rosicrucian groups: the AMORC, and the Heindel group who gave out free astrology lessons. During this time of my life I was the most excited I had been in years. I wrote: "I feel I am on the path whatever it is and to wherever it seems to be leading. It is not enough to reduce this statement to one of psychological meaning—for example, that I am feeling satisfied and in harmony with my questing. That [while perhaps accurate] it doesn't strike me as an adequate enough explanation for my motivation. I believe there is a calling—a purpose to all of this—a pulling towards something greater than myself." Jung wrote: "How can I be substantial if I fail to cast a shadow? I must have a dark side also if I am to be whole. . . . The horror which we feel for Freudian interpretations is entirely due to our own barbaric or childish naiveté, which believes that there can be heights without corresponding depths, and which binds us to the 'final' truth that, when carried to the extremes, opposites meet."[3]

Jung had pinpointed the issue of ambivalence that I had been plagued with all my conscious life. Now he was saying that it is front and center. He also indicated that it was not only acceptable but that it was indeed a necessary fact to be reckoned with if one were to be whole. This idea of the "Shadow" struck me with great force. He also inferred that there was another way to view psychic complexity. For me this new way was later to be viewed as a different conceptualization of logic complementing conventional linear logic.

The notion of a different form of logic was evident in my explorations in the sophisticated literature of the esoteric occult introduced to me by Mason. For example a book by Sadhu called *The Tarot* was written in a style that made perfectly clear and good sense to me. It pointed to an alternative logic that differed from the conventional one of linear cause and effect: that is conventional scientific logic. This book was representative of advocating what I have come to calling experiential logic. Sadhu wrote: "*The Tarot* is a guide to creative thinking for development of the ability of concentrated, deliberate thinking . . . an approach to the ultimate mystery of the . . . magic unity, the un-manifested spirit . . . the unknowable."[4] My research indicates that the esoteric occultists such as Sadhu are the precursors of what is currently referred to as self psychology.

The First Spiritualist Church of New York (Consonance and Dissonance), 1963

After my discharge from the army, I returned to New York to work at the employment agency and to obtain a master's degree. Even though I was elevated to the role of employment counselor, I still believed that my job was a dead end. However, despite my having obtained a master's degree in general psychology, I felt there would be no jobs open in the field. Thus I was at another fork in the road. I needed guidance.

During this time, I became an active member of the First Spiritualist Church of New York. Among the parishioners were a number of highly intelligent truth seekers all of whom unconditionally accepted and encouraged me to explore any and all aspects of the esoteric occult. My favorite member was Larry, a psychiatrist. I experienced an instantaneous rapport with Larry's infectious charisma. We sat together at the back of the service every Sunday alternatively cracking jokes and talking serious talk about the intriguing phenomena we were witnessing together. As I felt more in tune with Larry and spiritualism, I was feeling increasingly more distant from my soon to be ex-girlfriend.

I asked Larry if he would be my psychiatrist. He said no but invited me up to his apartment on a few Saturdays to discuss whatever I wished to talk about. During these times he would go into a trance state and purportedly channel messages from Freud and Jung. In one message he said that in a past life I had been a Chaldean scientist, a priest in Atlantis, and also a priest in ancient Egypt. He often spoke in a philosophical style. A representative example of his style follows: "Communication means to commune. It is a means to obtain cosmic consciousness: the attainment of the realization of the unity within and without."

In these talks with this unconventional psychiatrist who was also a medium, the core concept of unity within and without struck me with a gripping force. I was impressed with the awareness of the possibility of wholeness and unity by way of self-healing leading to a potential synthesis of myself. The question remained: how best to obtain this prized objective?

A few months later in church I received the following message from a guest medium: You are a man of the Aquarian age: restless, intelligent, seeking balance. You have to seek your own meaning. You probably will not settle down in the conventional sense of the world—not a sedentary life. . . . You have enthusiasm but don't cast your pearls before swine... You will create opposition by your stands.

Spiritual Consciousness Raising—26 Years Old

I joined a spiritual consciousness-raising group. I sat in a circle with ten other people.

The experience was described in my journal as follows:

> We were given instruction to report whatever we heard or saw in the pitch black room. Soon I sensed lights, and a flickering candle. They felt to me to be obvious projections stemming from a wish to make a spiritual contact. I saw an image that looked like a battleship in the water and a pilot–less wheel of a ship with a face behind it reflected in a window. The medium, Agatha, is a little old woman in her late 70s who is pleasant and cheerful. She interrupted my productions saying that my images are evidence that my personal guide will get the wheel turning and I shall learn to steer myself. Then a voice seemed to come through Agatha sounding like a child. Agatha said "This was Crystal" who would give everyone in the room a personal "message".

When she came to me the voice spoke softly and sweetly in such a way that I would expect my mother to sound if she were to speak to me. The message was that Sylvia (my mother's name) was near me and she would help me and that she was glad I was in this work and that I should continue in it. Still I remained skeptical.

On November 7, 1963, at the second meeting of the spiritual consciousness raising group I experienced the first part of what I have come to judge my most significant meaningful coincidence.

Synchronicity #2 The "Lazarus Rising" Synchronicity: "Lazarus Rising," November 1963, gap of five years since Synchronicity #1

The synchronicity: Participation in a spiritual consciousness- raising group. The leader says to say what comes to mind. Despite my initial skepticism I see an oval circle of yellow light. In the oval is a grandmotherly face. She has thin-wired granny glasses. I say that she is the grandmother of a woman (D) sitting next to me. D says the fact of the granny glasses makes it a fact. Later on in my apartment I ask myself the question: are miracles real? I open the Bible and read the first words I see. I read a passage about the raising of Lazarus. Excited I call D and tell her about my exciting find. D says: "Isn't that an interesting coincidence." She tells me that just this past afternoon her unconventional psychiatrist and herself were walking together in the park and he revealed the details of a past life in which he had attended the raising of Lazarus.

Reaction: Intense awe and excitement—

Implications: I feel as if I am in contact with a mystery that holds out the possibility of divine guidance. Coincidences appear to be connected with an unseen "occult" realm reality that is spiritualized. Whatever else these events may mean they add breadth and depth and point to something higher and more meaningful than most events experienced in my more ordinary life.

A significant reverberation of this remarkable event was my heightened attention in taking note of both my own as well as others' meaningful coincidences. There was no question in my mind that they were indeed remarkable events particularized by the felt experience of special meaning that characterized them.

The Meaning of Meaning

I experienced the content of the Lazarus Synchronicity as one of the most meaningful events of my life. But, of even more importance to me were the startling and perplexing implications. Clearly defying conventional cause and effect explanations this event was a true scientific anomaly. As I soon discovered, Jung asserted that these kinds of events were incapable of being rationally explained at all. Jung concluded that what we are left with, once removing causality as an inadequate linking principle, is only an equivalence of meaning and simultaneity.

The two nearly simultaneous references to Lazarus: 1- the random reference in the Bible presumably answering my question as to whether or not miracles were real; and 2- the reference to Larry having revealed to Diane that in a past life he had been present at the raising of Lazarus although clearly defying conventional scientific explanation was clearly meaningful—at least to me.

While the part of me that needed to feel I was in the presence of divinity was in awe; the scientific-rational part of me was perplexed. I became near obsessed with attempting to understand the meaning of meaning. A related question was, what was the relationship between meaning and causality.

Increasing Runs of Meaningful Coincidences (Synchronicities)

My experiences in the séances strongly suggested that meaning is something more than just the result of a psychological process. I wrote: "I feel that meaning is more than just made, it is also [something] to be revealed. It has to be continually rediscovered."

Additionally, the "piling up of coincidences" were experienced as especially meaningful events. Commenting on their increasing impact, I wrote: "Whatever the reasons for the 'runs of coincidences' that have been occurring almost daily: whatever be the reason(s) for the uncanny accuracy of the spiritual messages; whatever be the true source of my 'visions' and psychic experiences—surely no one can deny that they add a dimension to life that in turn gives breadth and depth, zest and enthusiasm, knowledge and joy to the living and experiencing of life."

Discussions in church frequently discussed the nature of meaning from an occult perspective. For example, Reverend Clifford Bias, sermonizing about the problem of meaning stated: "Meaning is creative development. One must extract significance from experience. [This process] leads to development and expansion which [in turn] leads to consciousness."[5]

Synchronicities appear to be a confluence of perceptions, ideas, feelings, intuitions, and sensations. I discussed these and similar ideas with Larry, the receptive psychiatrist. I wrote: "Larry and I discussed my experience of an 'invasion of intuition and feelings.' He said: 'There are many modes of apperception that are deeper and equally as meaningful as the thrusts of the intellect.'" It was relatively novel for me to discuss these ideas that I had been mulling for years but had rarely revealed them to others let alone having them validated as well.

The Esoteric Occult Promises a Pathway to My Salvation

The realistic possibility that reality is "spiritualized" evoked a surge of hopefulness and positive momentum. I enthusiastically looked forward to attending the Sunday church service and the Tuesday night séance. Although part of me remained skeptical about Agatha's attribution of past lives to me and others; there was a larger part insisting that I draw no absolute conclusions at the moment. This was particularly so in the light of my experience of the Lazarus synchronicity—a truly remarkable event. Challenging the skeptical part of me, I asked myself the question: how could I be so sure that Agatha and the other spiritualists like Larry and Clifford were not in touch with essential truths about aspects of reality that while occult might still be real?

I recorded some ideas I had about the relationship between reason, irrationality, and what I had understood at the time to be mystical experience: "The mystical perspective is essentially a religious approach. It is a feeling of at-one-ness that transcends all opposites. . . . That which is irrational need not be below reason or unreasonable: it can be a conscious awareness of the totality and unity of whatever context we [find] ourselves to be a part of."

Although I held myself back from totally accepting a supernatural/magical explanation to account for these remarkable occurrences, I was still drawn to the possibility that mysterious forces greater than myself were operating in salutary ways that as yet eluded scientific understanding. Furthermore, the apparent reality of these unseen forces held out the realistic possibility that I might have finally discovered the pathway to obtaining my long sought but elusive goal of wholeness, unity, and transformation. During this time I was supercharged with hope for my present, vitality, and even higher hopes for my future. This expansive state of consciousness, characterized by a sense of exquisite hopefulness and high energy, lasted about one year.

But even as I felt a strong resonance with this spiritual atmosphere, I had one nagging concern—the issue of final authority. An entry in my journal reads: "One must take responsibility for one's own actions and not ascribe them to some external authority ('spirit' included)."

Politics in Spirit Land—Disillusionment, 27 Years Old

I was in a state of relative harmony with spiritualism until I attended a weekend summer camp for spiritualists. In various tents there were held numerous and varied spiritualist manifestations. Among them were individual readings of tarot cards, astrology, cabala, and numerology; message services delivering "messages" from dead relatives, master teachers, spirit guides and the likes; and demonstrations of spirit photography, voices coming from "trumpets," and demonstrations of ectoplasm appearing as thin white material glowing in darkness. But what started out as exciting and intensely pleasurable rapidly became depressingly disappointing.

Internecine warfare came to a head the day of the camp outing. There was enormous pressure by two warring factions for me to either join the splinter group St. Germaine or stay the course. Most depressing was being told by a spirit guide, Morning Glory, that if I rejected the mantle of St. Germaine one more time the door will be shut to me for the next 2,000 years. I winced wondering what kind of spiritualism was this absurd nonsense? The coup de grace was a message from spirit categorically stating that "spirit is not political". But even sweet, old Agatha was applying not too subtle pressure for me to fall in line.

Feeling caught in the middle of an unexpected war resulted in the return of the suspicious part of me full force. As my antennae automatically came out and up, I also noted that what had been my passionate interest in the occult simultaneously waned. (Years later I would realize that this event was experienced by me as truly traumatic. I associated to a time just before my mother died when my father came into my brother's and my room asking us a question—a question that was an impossible one to even hear let alone come up with a good enough answer. He said: if your mother and I get a divorce who would you boys want to live with?) Now openly irate and suspicious I wrote: "They said spirit is not political. How absurd! The whole tenor of tonight's group was one of cajoling, imploring, threatening, with the clear undisguised implication that if one were fortunate enough to have been given an invitation to join the St. Germaine group one better honor it or else." I oscillated between a wish to continue to believe in the philosophy and manifestations of the esoteric occult, warning myself not to confuse the message with the messenger, coupled with deep doubts about the whole point of view.

Depressingly familiar waves of highs and lows followed in short order. I wrote: "I am experiencing a growing disillusionment with the occult [and spiritualism in particular]—a repetition of meaninglessness once again drowning my soul."

Who Is The Final Authority in My Life?

Although I longed for the special knowledge that the occult promised I began to wonder if its attainment was to be found in some other unknown location. I wrote: "I am a stranger in a crowd, passive, unaware, negatively inert, lacking concern, anxious, pained, feeling tortured, [experiencing] human relationships as too complex for me to handle." My aim was clearly in view but the path to getting there was shrouded in fog: "I wish to have synthetic thinking… that is to be able to entertain a multiplicity of facts [so that I can] act on reality on many different planes and levels of reality simultaneously…. I know I am split and feel trapped … I even know what I need but I lack a map and the right tools [to be able to release myself from myself]."

Clifford, the reverend leader of the First Spiritualist Church of NY, told a fish story in a sermon in church that captured the essence of what my immersion in the occult and spirituality had revealed as to what I wanted to know but could not seem to find:

> Two fish heard that a great man who could perform miracles was in a certain place. They swam to the brook where he was instructing a crowd of people and

> swam near him. They saw him come to the water's edge, scoop some into his hands and say how water was a great creation of God. It was cleansing, purifying, vivifying, essential for life. It was in fact God's greatest gift. The fish touched by the teaching looked at each other and both said: I wish we could find some water.[6]

Clifford added: "If one knows the laws of nature—he is able to change the environment [psychological atmosphere] and rearrange the context." This idea seemed to describe the essence of the aim of white magic—making things change significantly by knowing how to use the laws of nature. Clifford appeared to actually have the "know how" whereas I could only imagine (having and using it).

For example, during a Christmas sermon Clifford placed blank cards into a hat surrounding them with colored pencils and chalk. He covered the hat with a cloth. Within five minutes the cover was removed and at least twenty of the cards had pictures and messages on them for many of those in the congregation. I thought that if this phenomenon was on the up and up I had indeed witnessed an amazing event.

In the Thick of Ambivalence

Although skeptical I was open enough to my new found pathway hopeful that the phenomena I was experiencing and the concepts I was exposed to would reveal some deep esoteric truth. This hope in the possibility of contacting some potentially transforming vital information kept me actively participating in the séances and attending church on a regular basis. But, as had been the case in my past, doubts depressing my enthusiasm, once again having crept into my consciousness were rapidly intensifying. I wrote:

> I have been reaching a point where my contact and confrontation with the "realm of spirit" has now forced a new realization of consciousness. As with most events and major studies in my life I have approached spiritualism, séances, soul growth as an idea—an intellectual exercise, a game, a sport- a competition that was initially novel, stimulating and pleasurable. I believe that in those first few séances I actually did see something besides images of my own projections. That in fact I did have and do continuously experience the kinds of [meaningful] coincidences that Jung refers to as synchronicities. However, the bloom is off the rose, i.e. the bloom associated with the first meetings. I feel a strong sense of resistance—that is somewhere deep inside me comes that part of me that says: what are you mad? Spiritualism!—the idea—the hubris—the egotism that Jung could or would speak to you directly. And yet, there is this other part that "sees" evidence clearly in the form of accurate "messages" that

> ring out not only factually true but psychologically, emotionally, realistically and personally true. [I was negative about my increasing negativity.]

Soon after I found a reassuring letter written by Freud (1989):

> I have found little that is "good" about human beings on the whole. In my experience most of them are trash, no matter whether they publicly subscribe to this or that ethical doctrine or to none at all. That is something you cannot say aloud, or perhaps even think, though your experience of life can hardly have been different than mine. If we are to talk of ethics, I subscribe to a high ideal from which most of the human beings I have come across depart most lamentably.[7]

I Broaden My Horizons in the Esoteric Occult

A few months later I went to the Church of Light astrology classes. The teacher, Don Conte, introduced me to the details of the Alice Bailey books that had been frequently mentioned in church. Alice Bailey was an uneducated farm girl who purportedly was contacted by the Master Teacher DK for her to both channel and to disseminate his teachings to the world.

The teachings are an elaborate exposition of a so-called Grand Plan that outlines the gradual but inevitable evolution of man's consciousness on this planet. In spelling out the details of this spiritual unfolding, Bailey relates astrology to expanding levels of consciousness. In so doing, she offers new dimensions of astrological interpretation culminating in a new field referred to as esoteric astrology.

Conte, describing the attitude of mind that is necessary to make one curious about the Occult, said: "That which was previously 'obvious' now becomes full of mystery and the surface phenomena no longer appears as they are."[8]

He presented this material in a lucid, logical, and crystal clear style. Additionally, his obvious enthusiasm conveying his attitude towards the esoteric occult as absolutely factual had the effect of renewing my respect for this arcane subject matter. Representative of the type of material he presented was outlining the seven principles underlying the esoteric occult. These principles are as follows: There are not two worlds but emanation and vibration. Occult philosophy has seven major principles: (1) karma and reincarnation (cycles of rebirth), (2) pairs of opposites, (3) light, (4) sound (created by motion-vibration-speech-word), (5) heat (the principle of blending and cohesion), (6) the law of attraction, and (7) the law of repulsion (orderliness in the universe). All lead to balance. The basic assumption underlying esoteric occult is that this is an orderly universe: meaningful and governed by knowable laws. As Emerson said, "Every man feels the furthest star and that star feels him."

Although I was highly re-stimulated in church by the teachings and the curious phenomena; at the same time, I experienced a lack of intellectual precision. Thus it was significant that I had initiated going outside the familiar to broaden and deepen my learning about the esoteric occult. Going outside the fold underscored the importance that reason has always had for me in my attempts to objectify any of my experiences particularly those experiences that are highly complex like meaningful coincidences. I found it irritating to just passively oooh and aaah at the admittedly impressive phenomena like the Lazarus Rising synchronicity. For me the experience of what Jung refers to as numinosity was not the end of the line but a starting point for further rational investigation. In short, I had the sense that all of these teachings and the phenomena were trying to give me a message of vital importance. But try as I might I couldn't break the code.

Some months later: I had an insight that all of my questing up to the present moment, including my reading great works of literature, entering psychotherapy, exploring various pathways in the esoteric occult, being an active participant in spiritualism, taking synchronicities seriously, all constituted an all out attempt to find my own identity. Believing my insight to be an accurate one, I was aware that the central questions concerning myself were still left essentially unanswered. These continuing questions were: Who was I really and what did I really want?

My Need for Good Guidance—1965–1966

In 1965, I fell in love. But as I got more intimate, "sickly emotions" once again got stirred up converting purity of feelings into a dizzy internal whirl of rapidly shifting feelings of intense love and hate. Despite my working as a vocational guidance counselor and obtaining a masters degree in general psychology, I continued to feel confused, lost and isolated both personally and professionally.

There was a clear need to transcend the stultifying confines of my constricting experience. But I felt bound to a wheel of boring repetition both by a lack of external opportunities and by an all-pervasive sense of being stuck in an atmosphere of internal negative inertia. In this context there was a dawning realization I needed to seek out good guidance once again. I had done so in the past with mixed results. What was different this time was more clarity as to the specific characteristics I wished from my guide(s): I was clearer that I needed a role model that would provide some concrete example of how and what I could and should be who would also resonate with my true nature. This role model would be the embodiment of a spiritual good father with whom I could make a positive identification. (My psychoanalyst some years later was to fulfill this need for me.)

I wasn't looking to make a connection with an activated archetype; I was looking to make a significant connection with a real live person. In my search for transcendence I wasn't looking to ascend into the heavens but simply to find a pathway and a method for extending my spatial boundaries on the earth plane. I wanted to make and to sustain meaningful connections in my loves and in my work.

On May 16, 1966, I rediscovered the kind of person I wanted to be like. It was William James, whose responses to his life experiences were once more making a strong impact on me. I wrote: "I am reading Williams James' biography. His dialogue of a life and personal synthesis—intellectual, emotional, spiritual, philosophical, psychological lights me up. It seems to me to be of supreme import to articulate so terribly clear that which he so passionately feels and has taken such obvious pains to think out: to advance in good faith the quest for truth and greater awareness of the meaning of existence for himself and all mankind."

Themes embedded in the paragraph above, including the search for an integrated self, identifying with a resonant role model that aids the self to transcend its restrictions, and constrictions in its desire to make meaningful connections, are intimately associated in both intellectually understanding and in my experiencing synchronicities. James' whole life was dedicated to showing how it is possible for one person to find his own pathway to synthesize multiple interests and points of view into an integrated whole. He also was a living embodiment of a person who was able to effect a naturalistic transcendence, escaping his own personal wheel of repetition compulsion by harnessing and directing his energies to pursuits and goals he deemed were significant. In so doing, he was able to move from a realm of meaningless disconnectedness to a realm of meaningful connectedness.[9]

I Aspire So High—Fall So Low—And Aspire So High Again

It dawned on me that I should go back to graduate school and get a Ph.D. but I had no extra money. Therefore, needing financial aid I reluctantly requested a loan from my parents. By coincidence, my brother in law, who was in New York on business, invited himself over to my apartment to deliver my parents' response. He said that they turned down my request as they believe I was a n'er do well and would likely waste the money thereby "throwing good money after bad." He also insulted my apartment and rhetorically asked if I ever planned to leave the 'sh.t' hole I was living in. Stung and defenseless I wanted to scream: they don't know who I really am, but all I could do was to remain mute and head bowed.

At 4 A.M. I woke up in a rage feeling like a caged lion. I was experiencing the familiar feeling of quintessential entrapment with no foreseeable way out. Suddenly another idea popped into my consciousness. If I couldn't afford to go back to graduate school then I could at least try to get a part-time job at night in psychology using it as a bridge to both freeing myself from the employment service and enabling me to transcend into my desired realm of psychological services. The next day at work I asked a friend of mine who worked next to me on the part time desk, to let me know if she ever heard about a part time job as a psychological tester. I figured the odds of this happening were next to zero but reasoned nothing ventured, nothing gained.

In this context of negative inertia, and perceived failure, but with a new determination to change my fate, I experienced my third major meaningful coincidence: "Saved by the Rabbi."

Synchronicity: #3 "Saved By the Rabbi" June, 1966—a gap of three years
The Synchronicity: An eleventh hour coincidence.

I had just that afternoon asked a co-worker in the employment service where I was working as a counselor that if she ever got a part time job as a psychological tester to tell me about it instantly. A few hours later she tapped me on the shoulder and said "you'll never believe what job I just got."

Reaction: I felt elated and in a state of awe. I was in the right spot at the right time. It felt like an answer to my prayer. Implications: I noted that there was an apparent connection between my troubled state of mind, great need, and the appearance of meaningful coincidence. This coincidence resulted in my obtaining a part time job as a psychotherapist in a therapeutic community treating heroin addicts in Queens, New York. The two principles were a Priest who wore cowboy boots under his hassock and a jovial rotund Rabbi.

I wrote into my journal:

> I found this to be a startling event.... Amazing this coincidence coming as it did. [Exquisitely good timing]-This has infinite possibilities and may turn out to be a major turning point in my life. This observation confirms others I have had: synchronicities occur at major stuck points. They indicate that a clear pathway has been opened. In adaptation theory: assimilating a problem is converted into accommodating a problem—The not me is conjoined to the me...A creative solution has been discovered/created freeing the blocked energies... This results in a significant change of attitude and action... both in consolidation of the self (beingness) and in the self's capacity to strike out on a path with a clear direction and sense of purpose and meaning. It is also an enlivening experience. Out of nothing comes something.... Despair is converted into hopefulness—the dead

> rises and regains the lost vitality... One cries out in the wilderness and feels so terribly alone and then when the time is ripe their prayers are answered. Thank you, God.

This is a clear statement that my initial reactions to synchronicities like this was a felt sense that I had made a direct connection with "spirit" who was in fact intervening on my personal behalf. It didn't occur to me until decades later that Roslyn, my friend, who told me about the job had no doubt called the Rabbi and asked if he might have a job for me. If I had figured it out at the time I am certain that I still would have regarded the timing [simultaneity] between my need and an actual job opportunity as an especially meaningful coincidence.

Aftermath of the "Rabbi Saves Me" Synchronicity—July 30, 1966

I didn't realize it at the time, but there was a shift in consciousness associated with this synchronicity. I wrote:

> A flood of feeling has broken through—streams of feeling: There is a certain quality which is the simultaneity of my experience. Each [separate] experience has its own unique value. It is as if I was in the center of a huge wheel [the astrological glyph wheel] when suddenly from the perimeter were to come at me a simultaneous profusion of different colors—each color representing a different experience—each experience having its own value. Each value having its own intensity, hue, chroma, but taken together [mixing all of the individual colors and their mixed values] there is an overall feeling of harmonious unity. Thus simultaneity is an attempt to experience difference in unity—shifting from focusing on a detail to experiencing the whole—as if in directing a movie where there is a choice of a close up, mid range, or wide angle. The effect is like the last two scenes in the movie: Wild Strawberries wherein the final scene is shown in two different ways: (1) a tableau that is impressive as it is; and (2) the same impressive tableau enhanced. It is like a movie that begins in black and white were to unexpectedly switch into technicolor.

The Beginning of a Shift in My Ideas about the Nature of Synchronicities, 1966

Without realizing it at the time, the foregoing ideas were the beginnings of a shift from a Jungian supernatural perspective to one that was decidedly naturalistic. An example of this shift was a journal entry I made responding to a book, *The New World of Philosophy* (1961) by Abraham Kaplan, which is about modern philosophy. I was in agreement with him that it was foolish to try and separate the philosophical from the religious and the aesthetic.[10] Applying this idea to my thoughts about the nature of synchronicities I wrote:

> What I am doing with my naturalistic perspective re synchronicities is extending Jung's insistence of thinking in wholes: that is considering both determinism and teleology. He leaves off by excising [arbitrarily abstracting] both the understanding and the experience of philosophy from the mix. I agree with Kaplan that it is foolish to do this . . . Therefore I include it: challenging Jung's first assumptions and thereby rearrange his dots into a naturalistic configuration . . . I reasoned: Alter the first assumptions and what is perceived looks entirely different to the viewer. In this connection note the phenomena of reversible images. The same dots when viewed from a different angle [perspective] are perceived with entirely different patterns. The patterns evoke different sets of feelings, thoughts, imagery, meanings, interpretations, and conclusions.

I discovered additional concepts of related interest reading Szuki's *On Zen*: Transformation: metanoia equals new perception equals reframing: relatedness on multiple levels of perception simultaneously... Include new dots viewed at different angles of perception processed through different organizing concepts (singular and/or collective) yield different configurations.[11]

Again, without quite realizing it at the time, whereas Jung emphasizes the interconnectedness of all things in an "absolute spiritualized unity" I was becoming increasingly more aware of individual differences converging to make a unity. From *Zen*: "Spiritual training starts with the purification of vision . . . Allow things to solve themselves-beyond categories. [images and analogies will spring up and out of silence.] The third eye: the things he sees are no different than before, he just sees them differently. His vision—as well as perhaps himself—have changed [Satori—metanoia—reframing—transformation]."[12]

These ideas were applied to my re-thinking about the theory and the experience of synchronistic phenomena. In summary these ideas were moving in the following direction: synchronicities are thinking and experiencing outside the box. The same dots are connected in a different way leading to a new configuration taking the form of a new pattern. It is apt to refer to the phenomenon of reversible images; wherein, a first view of images on a page are experienced as a candle stick whereas a second view perceives the same dots as two women looking at each other. (This is the concept of "Rashomoning" in the process of being cathected.)

Thirty-Two Years Old—High Hopes Dashed

After years of doubt and indecision I was finally certain that I wanted to be a psychologist. With this goal in mind I diligently studied for the Graduate Record Examination, applied to ten graduate schools, received ten rejections, and fell into deep despair. I got a very high score in the verbal part of the test and a very low score on the math. To escape my feelings of being an utter failure I went away once again to a summer resort to work as a bus boy and lick my wounds. Coincidentally a guest who was also a psychiatric nurse thought her boss might be interested in possibly hiring me as a psychologist in her new program. Thus, once again out of the jaws of defeat fate seemed to propel me to an opportunity for potential glory.

Contextual Summary of the Eight Years Preceding My Job at Odyssey House

1959: "Identity-less, overwhelmed with 'sickly' emotions. I identified with the Steppenwolf (wild man of the steppes), searching for meaningful connectedness, within and without—occasionally finding it—but unable to sustain it. Too much uncertainty, rootless, directionless, without clearly defined goals. Passion without precision."

1960: "I am a compulsive reactor who longs to act from within—a self imposed isolate. My world view is perpetual warfare in which I play the role of a Marine whose motto is: kill or be killed, and who seeks a kindred spirit for love."

1961: "I desperately seek a sense of purpose. I am addicted to intensity, my essence is like diffuse energy. I long to be dedicated to a meaningful goal. I respond positively to structure—e.g. a girlfriend and the army."

1962: "I want to be free from my bondage, but part of me likes it. I am unable to free myself from the grips of an unresolved ambivalence conflict (love-hate). I plunge into the structure, language, and mystery of the esoteric occult."

1963: "The esoteric occult speaks to my need for unity. I experience a logic of unity. I am drawn to Spiritualism. I feel a calling. I plunge even further into the occult. I am awe-struck by a run of meaningful coincidences—a growing appreciation for the power of the intangibles of fate, chance, luck, destiny, synchronicity. The Kennedy assassination jolts me back to nitty-gritty reality. It he can die, I can die. I feel at a crossroads."

1964: "I have to choose a concrete direction. I try to correlate levels of consciousness. I am drawn to the idea of a spiritual science. I found Clifford

Bias: (a spiritualist leader) 'The purpose of systems of the occult are that they all point to the fundamental unity of all things.' I have an increased drive toward unity and synthesis."

1965: "I meet my wife to be and by the end of the year get engaged in one year. The marriage will turn out to be a great mistake [my escape into marriage]. My analysis will eventually reveal I have unwittingly married my transferred father. The 'failure' is mine, I did the choosing."

1966: "I stand alone — confused. I can't rid myself of obligations toward my father. I identify with Munch's painting of a man shrieking in front of a bridge. All around me is the lonely crowd, passive, bored, inert unconcerned, anxious, marked with pain. I must have a goal! I must make a leap of faith—a sense of a growing dedication to "pure" ideas. I wish to be like William James. But I am shaken by a confrontation with my brother-in-law, who says my parents think I'm a ner-do-well, just wasting my time-going nowhere fast, spinning in endless circles. I aspire so high, but always seem to fall so low. An eleventh hour coincidence: I get a job offer from The Samaritan Half-Way Society, a narcotics addiction treatment program. I associate to Joyce's comment: "The longest way round is the shortest way home." I identify myself as a scientist-healer. I feel saved by God. W leaves me. I mourn the loss and my incapacity to sustain intimacy."

Three months before Odyssey: "I experience a generalized anxiety (insecurity) deep in my core, I am unable to. Despite my best efforts, I am still spinning like a top."

March 31, 1967 on the cusp of entering Odyssey House:

- I feel on the path. I need to be concrete.
- A confluence of the energies of five major planets all in conjunction.
- I conceptualized a philosophical position which I call pragmatic idealism, comprising the essence of Pierce, James and Dewey, plus Freud (the personal unconscious.)
- I agree with McCluhan who said: "Never let going to school interfere with getting a good education."
- At this same time, another part of me was shifting once again towards embracing a belief in the possibility of a personal divinity.

Two hours before Carolyn called: "I feel as if I am the instrument of a higher power that I freely choose to obey. I experience my reality as magical and full of revelations. [In time I will come to realize that Odyssey House, for me, was an absolutely 'perfect' fit on multiple levels.]"

In summary, by 1966 my reoccupation with philosophy, depth psychology, the esoteric occult, science, and spirituality, developed as a result of my discovering that there were splits in my inner reality. I began unknowingly searching for a pathway to clarity, vision, certainty, dedication, aliveness . . . I was searching for a method to free myself from bondage . . . a way to resolve my seemingly intractable problems of stultifying ambivalence, information overload, and overwhelming complexity. In this light, my growing interest in synchronicities both intellectually and experientially was fueled by my experience of them—at three critical occasions—showing me pathways out of darkness into the light of day.

Without at the time having identified it as such all of the events of the preceding eight years culminating in the first interview with the director of Odyssey House, Dr. Judi, were experienced by me as predestined events. While I did not name it as such, the meeting with Carolyn had all the earmarks of an especially meaningful coincidence. Perhaps it could only feel that way after but not before the fact. It was no coincidence that I instantly resonated with Dr. Judi and Odyssey, as for many years I had been preparing inwardly and outwardly for just such an opportunity. As some say about the existence of God, if Odyssey had not existed, I would have had to invent it. I was in a state of near perpetual ["born again"] ecstasy for about two months.

Odyssey House—A Pivotal Life Defining Experience, 1967–1970

The reader must be convinced by now that in utilizing the method of contextual analysis to understand the nature of synchronicities is one that I take quite seriously. What comes next chronologically along my road of life is an opportunity to be a psychologist at a therapeutic community for the treatment of heroin addicts called Odyssey House.

During a span of seventeen months from October 1967 through March of 1969 I experienced a titanic struggle—internally and externally—that was nothing short of a fight for the ownership of my soul. I wrote an unpublished book about my experience called *Odyssey: Personal and Professional Perspectives in Addiction* (later titled *A Head of Changes: My Odyssey of the Turbulent Beginnings Treating Heroin Addicts in the Sixties*).

My stay at Odyssey was a life-defining experience, mixed bag, allowing me to develop my skills and talent as a budding psychotherapist while at the same time repeating the worst traumas of my life. Odyssey House was both a tangible place and a confluence of innovative ideas about healing addicts, which were formalized and expressed through the Odyssey Concept. The Odyssey concept was based on the principle that one's final authority is the self but if that self is either hidden or missing, it must be rediscovered (reborn) or constructed (born). To accomplish this objective, the new inductee must choose to systematically work on his self, in a program organized and focused to provide the optimum conditions for maximizing the probability of success. In this light, Odyssey is both an example of a concrete institution that provided a structure for accomplishing this goal and also represents a microcosm of the best and the worst of the sixties.

I entered Odyssey consciously aware that I was lacking a professional identity and was increasingly amazed to discover that I was lacking a personal identity as well. My consciousness gradually shifted from an initial experience of at-one-ment to a state of chronic fear, distrust, and paranoid-like feelings. My reality of Odyssey became a confused, dizzy whirl of positive/negative—good/bad experiences. I became obsessed with attempts to make sense of this radical shift. With my sense of reality in doubt, I couldn't trust my judgment leaving me feeling profoundly insecure. A journal entry made when I was twenty-one summarizes the state of mind I had both then and nine years later when I began working at Odyssey House. I again wrote:

> I identify with Haller, the Steppenwolf. I wish I could reconcile the overlap of romanticism and intellectualism, nostalgia and cold cynicism, division and compulsion at work in my soul. I long to be objective; But how to be objective if the acquisition of knowledge is based on my subjective self selecting "facts" out of the flow of the raw data of my experience to order my reality? How can I ever hope to penetrate the nature of reality when I feel so confused half the time? I find this problem more and more central to me as I come closer to [confronting] the essential facts of my life. I feel bound to a wheel that inevitably [circles round and round] and, although, I wish to get off, I am unclear how to do so.

At Odyssey House, this problem resurfaced with a vengeance becoming the central preoccupation (obsession) of my life. In place of a reality I had [previously] thought was black and white [dichotomous], I now saw as complex, multi-leveled, multi-dimensional, perhaps best described as a messy profusion of colors on an artist's palette.

Thus during a span of seventeen months from October 1967 through March of 1969 I experienced a titanic struggle—internally and externally—that was nothing short of an all out fight for the ownership of my soul. It was at Odyssey that I had unwittingly repeated the worst experiences of my past with hostile authorities. I experienced the core of me as dis-eased. I described my self-diagnosis in my journal: "My sickness is one of no center. It is not a sickness of my head rather my soul. Who am I and what do I want are my central questions. I need to be able to trust but I don't know if I am capable of trusting."

Reflecting further on my journal summaries, I was astonished to realize how radically my feelings and thoughts had shifted from an unquestioning idealization of Judi and Odyssey to a near all-consuming cynicism and bitterness. I identified with Yeats (1996), whose earliest poems reflect romantic themes such as nature's perfection, as in "The Lake Isle of Innisfree."[13] But, with the passage of time he made a one hundred and eighty degree shift in his view of the world, expressed in one particularly biting and painful line, "I spit into the face of time."

Except for a few waves of resurgent feelings to return to the glory days of my intense interest in the esoteric occult, I emerged from Odyssey with my unwarranted need to idealize shattered with an accompanying long overdue period of disillusionment upper most in my consciousness. My falling back to earth, so to speak, forcing me to face up to the nitty-gritty concrete facts of mundane daily existence, greatly influenced by attitude towards both my experience and understanding of meaningful coincidences.

I had come to Odyssey seeking salvation and for a while believed I had found it. I left both as clear and as confused as I had ever been in my whole life. It was during this span of time I date my making my theoretical shift from viewing synchronicities as part psychodynamic and part supernatural to viewing them as purely naturalistic phenomena. When viewed out of context each synchronicity above is highly congruent with a Jungian supernatural interpretation. Each synchronicity was experienced with the same feeling state that Jung refers to as numinosity felt to be a connection with a transcendent, spiritualized higher power. Further, this power was felt to be transmitting vital information in coded form that if and when interpreted could be used in the service of providing desired help to guide if not rescue me on the road of my life's journey.

However, when these same synchronicities are viewed as embedded in overlapping contexts (situational, psychological, historical, temporal) what initially appears to be supernatural now appears to be a logical derivative of a person struggling to overcome complex but relatively transparent psychological and practical, mundane problems. The first three synchronicities each arise out of a climate of crisis experienced as quintessential stuckness at a point described as a fork in the road on my life's journey. The synchronicities viewed from this naturalistic perspective signal that a new pathway through the stuckness had been found. Whether the discovery of a new pathway was revealed or created was—upon leaving Odyssey House—still open to question. How this issue was resolved will be thoroughly explored in the next chapter.

In chapters 7 and 8 the remaining sixteen of the total nineteen synchronicities used as the raw data of my research will be described as well as the contexts in which they are embedded. In so doing the switch from concepts derived from the collective unconscious previously used to organize my experience (both affectively and intellectually) with respect to the nature and use of synchronicities shifts to an exclusive reliance on the collective consciousness for the source of my organizing concepts.

7

My 19 Synchronicities and Freud

> Concepts share the potential of language and words for unfolding new meanings, for changes of meaning, returning to earlier meanings.
>
> —Loewald[1]

> The true beginning of scientific activity consists. . . in describing phenomena and then in proceeding to group, classify, and correlate them. . . . Everything depends on their not being arbitrarily chosen but determined by their having significant relations to the empirical material, relations that we seem to sense before we can clearly recognize and demonstrate them. . . . The advance of knowledge, however, does not tolerate any rigidity even in definitions. Physics furnishes an excellent illustration of the way in which even basic concepts that have been established in the form of definitions are constantly being altered in their content.
>
> —Sigmund Freud (1915)[2]

> The range of what we think and do is limited by what we fail to notice and because we fail to notice that we fail to notice there is little we can do to change until we notice how failing to notice shapes our thoughts and deeds.
>
> —R. D. Laing[3]

THE PRECEDING CHAPTERS 5 AND 6 SUMMARIZED the key events in my life (pre–Odyssey House) predisposing me to a fascination for, a curiosity about, and an initial adoption of Jung's mystical/magical position about synchronicities. The present Chapter 7 and Chapter 8 which follows summarize the key events and their significance in my life (post Odyssey House) that contributed to a gradual shift away from Jung's psychodynamic/ supernatural perspective to a wholly psychodynamic/ naturalistic/progressive perspective. It is important to note that this shift in perspective did not occur in a straight line from point A to Z, rather, like World War I, it advanced and retreated circuitously over time.

My View of Synchronicities Pre–Odyssey House

Eleven years before my life-transforming experience at Odyssey House I was impressed by what seemed to be the mysterious power associated with certain coincidences that appeared seemingly at random in the ongoing flow of my life. In this connection, I recorded three specially meaningful coincidences in my journal I referred to as "The Sun at Midnight" (1959), "Lazarus Rising" (1963), and "Saved By the Rabbi" (1966). My initial experience of all three was that they were episodic random events—apparently uncaused—surprising my consciousness like noting a firefly's random flashes of light in a dark sky.

What impressed me most was the feeling of the uncanny that accompanied each one of these "numinous" events. By some logic of feelings, these uncanny occurrences confirmed the presence of actual occult forces. Further, these occult forces appeared to be spiritualized leaving me with no doubt that I had made a direct and highly personal connection with an unseen but palpably important "spiritualized" realm of reality.

Further, connecting to this realm of reality gave me a desired direction just at the time I needed it the most—at forks in the road of my life's journey, critical points, I experienced as quintessential stuckness. This external guidance took the form of validating that I was unconditionally accepted, cared for, protected, confirming that I was on the right road, and encouraging me to just keep going in the same direction—a cosmic green light.

Thus, pre-Odyssey I was virtually on the same track as Jung with respect to my attitude towards synchronicities. However, this attitude radically changed as a direct result of my life defining experience working at Odyssey House (1967–1969). Odyssey was an innovative therapeutic community for the treatment of heroin addicts beginning in the late sixties. I was a budding psychologist and thankful that I was hired "chosen" to become part of the staff. Initially, I played the role of a relatively detached observing participant, but quickly became enmeshed in its half healing and half noxious atmosphere, resulting in a shift of my perspective to that of a hyper-emotionally involved and a progressively more confused participant observer.

Before, during and post Odyssey House I felt as if I was a "house divided"—an extremely unpleasant feeling that adversely affected all areas of my life. I was like a six cylinder car that was perpetually running up hill on only four cylinders. Although I managed to function seemingly well enough, the constant strain was wearing me down. I, like Jung, was preoccupied with persistent frustrated attempts to answer seemingly unanswerable questions: who am I, and what did I really want, and can I find a way to make myself whole and purposeful?

My central issue, as was Jung's, was how to obtain and sustain a cohesive self that could and would remain solid in the midst of internal and external pressure. In this context, synchronicities played a major role. For, like Jung, I too discovered that in paying close attention to and repeatedly attempting to understand their nature, I found invaluable guidance pointing to new pathways helping me to get a handle on these very largest and previously unanswered questions of my life.

Pre Odyssey, the numinous awesome uncanny feelings associated with the experience of synchronicities combined with the implication that I was being guided by some unseen transcendent benevolent spiritual force—was enough to counteract my tendency to sink into despair and negative inertia when facing a fork in the road.

However at Odyssey House good feelings alone were not enough to sustain me at critical stuck points as I was realistically contending with an atmosphere of rampant hostility. Because I could not afford to drop my guard, passively luxuriating in a state of wondrous at-one-ment, I instead, had no other choice than to actively develop my critical faculties to be able to make informed judgments in the service of adequately protecting myself.

Additionally, as I desired to be the most effective psychotherapist I could possibly be, I had to be clear as to what I was doing and why I was doing it. This desire to be competent reinforced my determination to develop my largely overlooked capacity to utilize linear logic (cause and effect) that would complement my highly developed intuitive abilities.

Summarizing, three main reasons contributed to shifting my theoretical perspective: (1) My Odyssey House experience deepened my fundamental distrust of practically all authorities, particularly those who acted as if their way was the one and only, pushing me back onto my own direct experience as the final authority in such matters; (2) a growing disenchantment with what I experienced as an over generalized lack of clarity and specificity characteristic of concepts associated with Jung's supernatural "explanation" of synchronicities. Examples of these types of concepts are a priori meaning and a-causality as well as archetypal knowledge and the collective unconscious; and, (3) a growing respect for the clarity and "cash value" of organizing concepts derived from the collective consciousness such as individual psychodynamics, the metapsychology, ego weakness, self esteem regulation, and the transformational object.

Exposure to concepts derived from the collective consciousness differentiated from the collective unconscious were the result of my extensive and intensive immersion in learning to be an effective psychoanalytic psychotherapist. Specifically I was introduced to them in graduate school and clinic classes, in supervision discussing my cases, in my clinical practice in working with patients, in my second psychotherapy experience with a Gestalt therapist, and eventually, in my psychoanalysis with a Freudian psychoanalyst.

Post–Odyssey House, synchronicities continued to play a central role in my thinking about my core issues but—as will be seen—were gradually stripped of any supernatural explanatory concepts. In this chapter, I will draw attention to those experiences and organizing concepts that most contributed to this shift in my theoretical perspective.

An Additional Sixteen Synchronicities

From 1971 through 1976 I recorded an additional sixteen meaningful coincidences. What follows is a description of these sixteen synchronicities along with pertinent autobiographical details constituting the overlapping contexts (situational, psychological, temporal) in which they are embedded.

Meaningful coincidences (synchronicities), viewed both singularly and as collective "runs," are profitably viewed as clues in a complex psychological treasure hunt. In this game, an identified synchronicity is a marker that a leg of the journey (i.e., the desire to transcend into a realm of meaningful connectedness) has occurred. A given synchronicity marks both the ending of one leg of an individual's life theme and the beginning of the next. Thus synchronicities might profitably be viewed as markers of the self's evolving consciousness as it progresses into chosen realms of meaningful connectedness.

In describing the following sixteen synchronicities and their significance in formulating my naturalistic theory, the reader should note that the format is the same as the one used as in chapters 5 and 6. That is, pertinent contextual material is provided leading up to the synchronicity in question. Each synchronicity is then described, along with reactions, interpretations, and pertinent associated material.

The following material constitutes the pertinent overlapping contexts before synchronicity #4.

Situational and Psychological Contexts Pre Synchronicity #4, March 1969–March 1971—a 4-Year Gap

After Odyssey, I experienced a mixture of clarity and confusion that intensified my need for guidance and structure. I recorded:

> I experience the best and the worst about reality. Odyssey repeated the worst of my traumatic past. I once again idealized the authority to discover that it is corrupt. I leave feeling bereft . . . tossed inside and out, confused, abused, betrayed, filled with fantasies of revenge. It has the net effect of leaving me once again drowning in a vat of distrust with nothing solid to hold onto. . . Yet at the same time, I am able to use the occult to maintain a certain degree of hopefulness that my life can become considerably better. . .I experience my reality as magical and full of revelations.

My next job as an addiction counselor repeated many of my experiences from Odyssey. What begins with high aspirations once again degenerated into abject despair. I was satisfied with my challenging work but I soon grew to distrust the authorities—wolves in sheep's clothing. This unsettling familiar experience recapitulated the best and the worst of my Odyssey House experience in six months time. I suffered a severe crisis of trust and self-doubt. The tenuous balance between hopefulness and hopelessness shifted way over to the negative side.

In February 1970, I enter psychotherapy with a gestalt psychotherapist as well as starting a private practice. I also enter private supervision with a Freudian psychoanalyst who specializes in psychopathology of the self. My experience at Odyssey, and continuing professional training equipped me with a deeper understanding as to what constitutes effective psychotherapy from two perspectives: (1) that of the therapist and (2) that of the patient. In so doing I experienced the crucially important concepts of the *therapeutic alliance* in which the therapist and the patient work together as a team; and the therapist as *a transformational object* who mirrors (tracks) that which the patient most needs at any given time in the therapy. I wrote: "The psychotherapist performs the function for the patient of participating on the same plane but [simultaneously—at the same time-] stands outside . . . extending his perspective. [The therapist is a reflecting mirror—but a mirror whose reflection adds something new to the patient's experience—this is the operational definition of the therapist acting in the role of transformational object.]" I also recorded: "I begin to see how the one experience can mean many different things depending on the context in which it is embedded. Meaning is dependent on one's scale of observation. Meaning not causation is the glue that holds the world together. Once meanings can be changed expect revolutions to occur."

During this time I also struggled to complete my dissertation. Commitment to completing my dissertation has many positive residuals. By providing a self-imposed structure and discipline I force myself to both face and cope with inevitable frustrations. This discipline gives me increasing confidence that I am capable of persevering even in the midst of previously debilitating fears, negative feelings, and nearly overwhelming situational pressures. But despite an increase of positive momentum I encounter another seemingly impassable obstacle.

While seemingly on the right professional track I was aware of persisting undeniable psychological issues that were hampering me personally and professionally. While I longed for sustained unity and good feelings I too often felt fragmented, scattered, and pained. While my occult experiences and concepts offered a certain measure of relief—it was temporary at best. I intuitively knew that I needed greater specificity and concreteness but I was uncertain what it was or where I might find it.

At this time, my professional training and psychotherapy exposed me to the concept of psychodynamics: enabling me to have a personal psychological "fingerprint" of my patients' functioning as a map of their psyches. The first step in knowing the particulars of my psychodynamics was to become aware of and to name the contents of my consciousness—my inner reality. These contents include, feelings, thoughts, sensations, intuitions, desires, intentions, fears, and the likes. The discovery of psychodynamics provided me with the potential of mapping my own inner reality. It also held out the hope that I might be finally able to identify my core psychological problem.

I intuitively knew that my core problem straddled psychological, spiritual, occult, and philosophical boundaries. In this connection I was deeply moved by a new patient's words which spoke to my direct experience: The sickness today is the experience of no center. It is not a sickness of the head but of the soul. Who am I is the central question. What is the point of it all?

Reinforcing my need for external guidance I wrote:

> When one has to confront one's contradictions and try to overcome his own impasses he may act out and try to change the outside or he may go inside and attempt to change himself. To do so alone however soon leads one in circles. A bridge is necessary to go from the fog into the clear light. There must be an "essential other" to guide the way. My dilemma is who to trust when the outside seems to be populated by psychopaths and con men. Much of my history seems to have been in fog—I have operated on sheer guts and intuition. I have often felt slammed on the head not understanding how people work. I have been cut off from my feelings.

My strong feelings of inadequacy expressed as self-doubt and distrust of others, generated and reinforced an obsessive need for external rescue and guidance. As rescue on the earth plane seemed impossible, I looked to the invisible world of occult forces. Rescue seemed near at hand each time I experienced one of my nineteen meaningful coincidences.

Whatever else might be said of meaningful coincidences their character speaks of a real or imagined need (wish?) for external guidance. To seek external guidance implies a person who is in a state of lack. This state of profound lacking most assuredly characterized my state of being in my thirty-third year.

Each of my nineteen synchronicities were feelings of negative inertia that were instantaneously converted into an unexpected burst of exhilarating kinetic energy at the moment that each synchronicity was experienced. The entire experience seems to occur in no more time than a flash of a firefly's light. This short but highly significant experience is akin to what Colin Wilson (1988) refers to as a peak experience.[4]

I Recommitted Me to Healing Myself

I was aware that in order to be an effective psychotherapist I had to heal myself. To accomplish this task I had to have an accurate diagnosis, not just in the clinical sense of an official classification such as Borderline Personality Disorder, but in the sense of what at core was most troubling me. In this connection, I became increasingly aware that certain organizing concepts that I was exposed to in my therapy, supervision, and research spoke to my direct experience—instantly providing me with meaningful connections where previously there were only disconnected thoughts, feelings, sensations, and intuitions.

These organizing concepts functioned like searchlights illuminating a given problem at hand. Among the current concepts that resonated with my direct experience were the concept of ego weakness (a core organizing concept in the British School of Object Relations—Winnicott, Guntrip, Fairbairn, et al.),[5] "the frozen introject" (Giovanchinni),[6] and the self (Guntrip).[7] For example, the self concept, conceptualized as a totality (not simply a collection of parts), evoked the same initial excitement I experienced when I first made an acquaintance with the astrological wheel composed of houses, signs, and planets. The astrological wheel symbolized for me unity in the midst of diversity (complexity) that was a visual image of an integrated (synthesized) self. This view of the self, along with associated concepts including that of self-esteem regulation, shame and guilt cycles, pathological narcissism, resonated with my direct experience enabling me to make meaningful connections with the real truth of the matter at hand.

Similarly, the concept of ego weakness, expressed as devitalization of the spirit associated with a profound sense of isolation and inadequacy, concretely described exactly what I had been experiencing. Similarly, the concept of the frozen introject (a feeling of the self—"dead"—frozen in psychic time) provided an experiential rationale for what I was coming to realize was my self-imposed isolation. It explained why my self imposed isolation was a likely and understandable reaction to the death of my mother when I was fifteen.

The importance of these (and other) concepts was that I was beginning to experience myself as if I was a complicated jigsaw puzzle whose pieces had been tossed and turned many of them disconnected from each other either singularly or in sections. Intuitively I sensed that if I was indeed like a mixed up jigsaw puzzle then my task was to fit the pieces together. Concepts such as psychodynamics, the self, ego weakness, and the frozen introject strongly suggested that my "dis-ease" had a potentially knowable structure therefore would be expected to have a potentially knowable experiential logic. Further, that if and when this logic (my idiosyncratic psychodynamics) would come to be known it would provide a map for recognizing the particular contents of my internal reality providing me with "directions" for guiding my efforts in potentially reassembling myself.

Not quite understanding the significance of this crucial idea at the time, I intuitively pressed on to understand specifically what constituted my own and my patients' idiosyncratic experiential logics. Organizing concepts like these gave me a growing sense that perhaps my problem was concretely definable which sparked hope that my confused self was potentially comprehensible.

This shifting from associating with fuzzy generalities to specific particularities resulted in my stopping—almost completely—my immersion in the pursuit of occult knowledge, to focusing almost exclusively on concrete facts of my own and my patients' mundane experience.

I wrote:

> Perhaps because of the concepts I am exposed to in my therapy my attitude [preoccupation] with the occult is changing. Enough of the mystics—enough of the "other" (unseen) world.— It is this world I am in. It is through identification and struggle and patience that all real permanent changes are possible. Enough of these untested short cuts. . .. One of the major concepts (that is powerfully fruitful) is that of psychodynamics which equals the structure of my unique psychological fingerprint—(the idiosyncratic way a person processes the contents of their consciousness through psychological structures—including the id, the ego, the super ego and the self.) I am more than a tabula rasa—I have inner contents of consciousness that are responsive to internal and external stimuli.

> This is a different emphasis from Jung's emphasis on passive reception of absolute knowledge [with his tacit endorsement of no great need to understand the structure, or developmental origins and vicissitudes of a patient in question.]

February 1971—An Unexpected Experience of Meaningful Connectedness

I experienced a significant change in my psychotherapy. I wrote: "I am aware of feelings that are soft and tender towards my therapist. [This unusually positive experience carries over to an unexpectedly good time on a vacation wherein] I experience a [highly pleasurable] sense of timelessness [pure being without any intrusions or expectations]. I long to have the confidence to be my own authority [a desire for self confidence.]"

Armed with evidence that I am able to change in significant ways excites my interest in understanding the nature of change. Central in this pursuit is understanding the concept and the experience of meaning. In this connection I was aware of oscillating from meaningful connectedness to more frequent states of meaningless disconnectedness. Thus, like Jung my core problem has been associated with threats to both attaining and sustaining the cohesion of my total being (self).

I noted that the experience of meaningful connectedness is the core experience associated with meaningful coincidences (synchronicities). I was puzzled by Jung's assertion of a realm of absolute a-priori meaning transcendent to personal experience. This puzzlement led me to explore the meaning of meaning.

March 21, 1971—The Meaning of Meaning Becomes a Highly Meaningful Pursuit

A patient said a memorable thing to me today: "Meaningful things I forgot are now meaningful again." Meaning is connected to personal history (time). Further that memory, as Freud persuasively points out, once forgotten (either by suppression or repression) can become conscious once again. My therapy is filled with recalling memorable memories of times past.

Positive Feelings are Short Lived

The good feelings don't last as I experience myself oscillating between relative clarity and confusion. I hate the confusion and condemn myself for having it, judging myself to be woefully inadequate and stupid. Although I know it is possible for me to be clear headed the issue is how to sustain it? I feel at wit's end in my frustrated attempts to find a clear pathway to obtain the answer to this critical question. All of these entries between the last synchronicity and the one that will shortly follow culminate in what I have previously referred to as a "fork in the road." These forks in the road are characterized by their being experienced as seemingly intractable psychological problems. All attempted solutions initially fail to dislodge a person—in this case, me—from experiencing themselves as "quintessentially stuck" in a state of permanent entrapment.

In the present case, I wanted to be able to sustain the experience of being centered—to will myself to be in the now, i.e., in a state of relative pure "being"—grounded in the present, but I was unable to find a way to do this. Although I was certain that I was lacking specific knowledge about the way myself works, I was uncertain as to whether it was obtainable at all, as well as where would I look to find it?

03/28/71 Synchronicity—a gap of 4 years—34 years old
#4 "Sun and the Moon"
Immediate Situational Context:

I am aware of a major split in myself. I am aware of a wish to be rescued. In supervision I have become conscious of the experience of focused awareness. I want to free myself [at will] from the restrictions of what I refer to as linear time (past— present—future). I try to imagine what my life would be like if I could experience myself in "cosmic" time—(the now.) If I could experience myself in the now I believe I could control myself as I would be centered. Then I could start or stop at will instead of feeling as if I am caught up in forces beyond my control.

On impulse I buy a book of Patanjali's (2003) *Aphorisms,*[8] and Nicoll's (1984) *Living Time.*[9] I am preoccupied with an active search to make my life meaningful by trying to understand the nature of absolute reality. Psychologically I need to understand the concept of central psychodynamics.

The Synchronicity:

I have an urge to meditate on the positions of my astrological sun and moon in the 8th house (the house of birth, death, sex, creativity, change, and regeneration). Randomly I turn to page 67 of Patanjali. It states: "concentrate on the sun, know the world—whatever is in man is in the sun; whatever is in the sun is in man; concentrate on the moon; know the planets."[10]

My Reaction:

I take this synchronicity as a need to gain knowledge of my inner reality. Specifically I need to gain knowledge of my idiosyncratic psychodynamics. This means I have to be able to identify the contents of my consciousness and understand how they are processed through various psychological structures (i.e. id, ego, super ego, self). This synchronicity was validating my idea of the path I should take providing myself with good guidance, and encouragement.

In the past I had attempted to explore my inner space but had no clear idea of what I was seeing. The impressions were vivid but unrelated. It was like being on a trip to a foreign country without a map resulting in my experiencing each new place I visited as episodic and disconnected from all other locations. This synchronicity validated my need to have a map of my psyche. It also pointed to the fact that I should take the occult planets and concretize them in terms of facts of my idiosyncratic self.

Follow up:

After this synchronicity there was a decided shift in my consciousness due to my recognition that a search for the knowledge of my patients' (and my own) central psychodynamics was a major priority. I now had a clear overview as to where I was and where I wanted to go expressed as an increasingly more focused and purposeful way of thinking about and working with my patients.

I understood the need to integrate linear (cause and effect) reasoning along with an awareness of my feelings, intuitions, and sensations. This was good in theory but I became increasingly aware of unforeseen complexities. This directly led to the subject matter of the next synchronicity # 5, four months later.

Situational and Psychological Contexts Pre Synchronicity # 5 (March, 1971–July, 1971) 4 month gap; I Am Thrown Off Balance by Overwhelming Feelings 04/06/71

My therapist announced he is getting a divorce and is leaving for California. This stirs up enormous sense of loss that further stirs memories of other traumatic losses and my reactions to them. These feelings include abandonment, betrayal, fury that I can't directly afford to express as I am dependent on these authorities.

The announcement of my therapist's pending move triggers off long buried and previously unexpressed feelings associated with my mother's "sudden" death. It is increasingly clearer to me how myself has lacked clear definition because of my unwillingness (incapacity?) to experience the intensity of these negative feelings. I also begin to realize that to become a whole person I will need to face up to, and integrate that part of my experience that I have previously found too painful to bear.

04/08/71 Increasing Awareness How I Generate Personal Meanings

I record:

> I am experiencing my own logic of experience. . .. Experience is defined as a combination of feelings and ideas—perhaps it also includes intuitions and sensing. I am experiencing what is referred to as my psychodynamics. . .. My symptoms are correlated with specific fantasies. These in turn are connected with specific defense mechanisms. All of [this data] is correlated with a specific developmental level. . . The terms such as ego, id, developmental levels, resistance, defenses, developmental levels speak to my direct experience. I experience my inner world as truly onion skinned with levels of overlapping experience. [My inner reality has both breadth and depth and is alive and pulsating. Much of what is in there is snarled and in conflict . . .]

I became aware that there is a distinct difference between my intellectual awareness of a concept and the more full bodied experience of it. This is particularly so with respect to distinguishing theorizing about, versus experiencing the psychodynamics of myself and of my patients. It is one thing to observe psychodynamics as if I were observing an operation through a one way glass as an observing participant; it is quite another thing to be emotionally engaged in the process whether the engagement be with myself and myself and/or with one or more other people in the role of a participant observer.

I recalled that this distinction between detached theorizing and active experiencing had been one of the major lessons I learned at Odyssey House. I also learned that if the engagement was benign it would bring out the best in me and indeed enhance it; however, if the engagement was in an atmosphere of hostility, it would bring out the worst in me setting me adrift. When adrift I would lose my sense of cohesion. Thus I needed to find a way to understand the specific psychodynamics that would enable me to sustain my sense of cohesion no matter what atmosphere I would happen to be in- benign or hostile.

I Enter Private Supervision with a Freudian Analyst—May 1971; Out of Confusion Comes Wisdom: Processing Content Through Structure

My supervisor accepts me unconditionally. I feel safe and therefore free to reveal to him my mixed experience including my excitement and my doubts.

I am exposed to a great many powerful organizing concepts including the therapeutic alliance, repetition compulsion, and the principle of multiple function. Above all, he shows me a method of approaching my patients that combines both linear cause and effect thinking with compassion, and empathy.

My early days in supervision were marked by my many confessions that I was feeling more confused than clear, more doubtful than certain. My supervisor reassured me, saying, "There is a long tradition from Heraclites to Freud (advocating) that the world coheres because of psychological cause and effect relationships (Reality) is a process and is knowable by way of understanding linear causality (conventional scientific logic.) We have to move from the why to the how. . . Focus on the structure (processing content through organizing concepts) gives orientation and perspective. The how equals the identification of structure and function. If one or the other is changed, then the other changes. The why equals explanation not understanding."[11]

June 1971 A Significant Shift of Attitude

My supervision with Dr. L greatly aided me to become increasingly more appreciative of precise details and structure in my efforts to understand my patient's material. This focus on specificity led to a significant shift in my attitude to the occult.

I wrote:

> I have taken back some of the energy I put into the world of mysticism and now placed it in the world of concrete facts. . .. I can begin to understand my obsession with occultism. It is a wish for self-sufficiency –an attempt to obliterate a disappointing past; an attempt to deny an [anticipated] meaningless future; a wish to be able to [foretell the future] and thereby control [it]; and perhaps a reaction to my feeling isolated. The language and the concepts [associated with it] are different from ordinary usage and may function like a secret code does for kids.

I felt as if I had taken a major step by committing myself to learning my craft from a master teacher. But with each exposure to concrete knowledge I found myself increasingly flooded with information overload. Feelings of increasing adequacy were counter balanced with equally strong feelings of inadequacy. Frustrated that I was unable to immediately see what my supervisor saw made me feel stupid and inadequate.

Although he reassured me that my worry about inadequacy was really a realistic fact of inexperience, I knew that was not the whole story. I intuited that I suffered from an inability to synthesize the analytic material in a way that did justice to its complexity.

The frustrated need for an ability to synthesize complex material became my central preoccupation. Although I kept looking for new pathways, I had become convinced I had reached the limits of my ability to extend my boundaries in this particular area. By the end of July, 1971, my frustrated attempts to attain the unifying experience I craved, culminated in another fork in the road event, directly preceding synchronicity #5.

07/29/71 Synchronicity—a Gap of 4 months—34 years old
#5 "Crossword Puzzle"
Immediate Situational Context:

I became aware of the complexity of living. I now realized that behavior and events are multilayered and overdetermined [have multiple causes]. I connected with feelings of helplessness, hopelessness, generalized fear, hostility, and impatience, both with myself and with my patients. These realizations enabled me to experience reality as imperfect; particularly so, when experienced as a complex of negative feelings. Associated with this new awareness was a reduction in the intensity of grandiose and omnipotent fantasies expressed as a loss of magical thinking. While more level headed I experienced the material as too impressionistic. I needed to have a way of organizing these realizations so that I could work on them sequentially.

The synchronicity:

I had just completed a session with a patient that highlighted a problem with commitment expressed as an inability to take a clear position. She oscillated between being half in and half out of treatment. At the moment that I identified her problem as indefiniteness, I simultaneously realized that I too had the same problem as she. After she left my office I noticed a half completed crossword puzzle in my wastepaper basket. With no apparent purpose in mind, I glanced at the directions for filling in one of the empty sets of spaces. The directions read: choose a concept that means "to become definite."

My Reaction:

I believed that I had received a message that there are no short cuts to understanding. I feel as if I have reached the outer limits of my capacity to synthesize so I need some kind of external guidance. It is positive that I find myself less guarded about exposing what I feel are my lacks, inexperience, inadequacies, and ignorance. In short, I am more comfortable in asking questions to aid me in defining that which is unclear. I need clarity to adequately define myself.

Follow Up:

I am determined to be clear and concrete about the concepts I use. I reserve the right to challenge all fuzzy thinking whether it be my own or others. In feeling free to asking for help especially from my supervisor, risking his negative judgment, I became a more open rather than a more closed system. Instead of feeling I have to know all of the answers I switched my attitude to asking challenging organizing questions. I wrote: "I am beginning to integrate the subject matter of psychotherapy. I am doing more than simply feeling my way around now. I am combining science and art—a body of knowledge with learned techniques which I am able to verify for myself."

September 1971—I Need to Define Myself

Whereas defining concepts was a major leap for me in understanding others it gradually dawned on me that I had a larger issue to deal with. This issue was to define the totality of myself. This was made clear to me each time I was faced with events that I reacted to either with an upsurge of intense excitement or a total deadening of my feelings. At these times it was as if I completely lost my sense of cohesion. At these times, I felt scattered, all over the place—the very opposite of contained and clearly defined.

I was preoccupied with a need to completely transform my basic being. The key to success was finding a way to synthesize the disparate parts of me into a totality that would remain cohesive under internal and/or external pressure.

Although I was clear in what I needed, fulfilling it eluded me. I bogged down in what might be thought of as a state of "psychological gridlock." It was in this context of quintessential stuckness that directly preceded synchronicity #6, five months after the last synchronicity.

Situational and Psychological Contexts Pre-Synchronicity #6, July, 1971– December 25, 1971—a Five-Month Gap

In August we find that my wife is expecting a baby. Although I was initially excited that I was to be a father, I was more frightened that I would not be a good one.

As I am experiencing a great deal of constant pressure, I am no longer the veritable optimist I used to be. Life is a struggle and there are inevitable ups and downs. I am nearly overwhelmed with strong emotions: multiple confusing, contradictory feelings. I have a high degree of excitement mixed with fear. Instead of accepting the mix—I find that the contradictions cancel each other out. This is parallel to a patient who is also synchronicity prone complaining that her contradictory feelings are experienced as world's colliding canceling each one out of existence.

During this time I resonate to organizing concepts of the British Object Relations School of psychology and the Self -Psychologists. Their ideas push the probable origin of my problem back to the first two (pre-oedipal years) of my life. I wrote:

> I discovered the writing and research of the British object-relations school identifying ego weakness as the core problem of today. Winnicott (1999) defines this problem as "An infantile ego that has been rejected and repressed. It remains therefore underdeveloped and weak and deep maturity of the personality comes to a standstill."[12] [This is a diagnosis of developmental arrest] I am also discovering that in a well-described problem there lies an embedded solution. . . Therefore most of what I have been about these many years of examining my interior has been to describe in as accurate detail as possible my symptoms, giving voice to the contents of my consciousness, searching for external solutions to hold on to such as spiritualism, the occult, role models such as Larry, systems such as astrology and psychotherapy. I have hoped that at least one of these systems would function as a pathway to wisdom, hopefully providing me with enough detail that would allow me to have an accurate diagnosis of my core problem.

In this connection, Jung's concept of archetypal knowledge located in a realm of absolute meaning a priori to personal experience is too vague and generalized to be of help to me. I need specificity of detail not vague generalizations.

Whereas Jung advises those with divided selves to search for their identity in transcendent experiences, my journey is leading me ever deeper into my developmental origins.

During this time, the pressure to be a good father increases. My experience in supervision is benign and freeing. I feel safe and structured. I find that this atmosphere allows me to have maximum freedom to roam around, explore, ask anything I want, expect reasonable detailed answers that are concrete and practical. This is the model of the kind of relationship I would have liked to have had with my father.

Desperately wanting to be a good father in not repeating the bad experience I had with own father, I wrote: "I want to be able to teach my child what the real is as I see it and understand it, as well how most people see reality and what they do about it. If he chooses to be different that is his choice."

What was most important in defining the essence of good fathering was an attitude of unconditional acceptance of my fantasy child's whole being. This attitude was succinctly conveyed in Guntrip's (1999) comments about this attitude: "Science never knows 'the person'; it only has information about the person. . . . There cannot be a whole complete human being without an integration of feeling with thinking and acting, provided by 'doing', arising spontaneously out of the fundamental experience of 'being.'"[13]

Intuitively I knew exactly what Guntrip was talking about. Now, the question for me was how to transform what he so well defined into my lived experience. My frustrated wish to have access to a method enabling me to transform myself into the person I wished to become resulted in another "fork in the road" directly preceding synchronicity #6.

07/29/71 Synchronicity—a gap of 5 months—Age 34
#6 "Paul Newman"
Immediate Situational Context:

Guilt—whatever I do at root is wrong and inadequate. The last year I have been preoccupied with issues of self definition. Externally, I have increased responsibilities; internally, aware of a sense of relative indefiniteness experienced as feelings of confusion, extremism, and self imposed isolation (detachment and compartmentalization). I am aware of interrupting my flow of experience. I also fear I won't be able to change. I am fearful of being a father as I dread being like my own father and doing to my child what was done to me. I fear I am doomed to repeating my past. I also fear I will never be able to stop scattering my forces by focusing at will. I experience these collective fears as extremely painful and possibly unalterable. I am frustrated in my desire to transform myself into a brand new man.

The synchronicity:

I have a dream with a synchronicity in it. Part two of the dream has someone mentioning Paul Newman. Later on I dial the wrong number that happens to be answered by Paul Newman. I get excited more about the coincidence than in speaking to Paul Newman. I am relieved to experience my mind uncharacteristically free from chatter, clutter, and even logical thoughts. Part I of the dream is my leading a prayer group in Miami Beach. Someone is upset with my long hair. I say F the length of my hair, it's what you are that counts. Someone else calls me a hippy. I'm flattered. At least I feel I am getting some respect.

My Reaction:

I see the synchronicity as an obvious wish fulfillment. I tell myself that in order to be a New Man I must have self-respect. To have self-respect I have to accept myself unconditionally. In Part I of the dream I hold my ground instead of knuckling under to criticism.

Follow up:

To accept myself I have to learn how to regulate my self-esteem. It is an intricate process that has to be understood in fine detail. The synchronicity indicates that a new path lies in front of me. It is my task to understand the details of this process.

Situational and Psychological Contexts Pre Synchronicity #7, December 25, 1971– June 27, 1972— A Six-Month Gap

Upon the birth of my first child I was forced to confront a mixture of intensely ambivalent and complex feelings. While I was excited about being a father, I equally dreaded it. In my analysis I would realize that I was in conflict as to whether I wanted more to be a good father to my child, or to be the son of a substitute good father.

I wanted to be a good guide but at the same time I wanted to be guided. I feared I would not be able to rise to the occasion. This fear was expressed in my theoretical speculations about the nature of reality and meaning. I wrote: "I wonder if it possible to hold two different views of reality simultaneously [wherein simultaneous implies holding two seemingly divergent perspectives of reality together obeying some principle of unity?] Meaning could be absolute as in the idea of truth, goodness, beauty thus discoverable; yet, at the same time, meaning could be thought of as an active and personal process of organizing chaos. This seems like believing equally in Plato and Aristotle, Freud and Jung at the same time."

During this time, the idea of overlapping alternative points of view under one unifying principle was evident to me in my increasing awareness of the complexity of what I refer to as psychic time. An aphorism of Pantanjali (2003) I had been reading at the time defines what I mean: "Time is divided into three divisions, which, when reduced mean only one undivided time. It is all one road, the part of the road that we have traveled, is called past; the part of the road that we are traveling, is called the present; the part of the road that we have to travel is called future."[14]

Another useful psychodynamic that reinforced my formulation of experiential logic, was reading Arieti's (1974) description of four solutions when faced with a hostile environment (culture, society, or family). These are: to comply, to defy, to retreat, and/or create one's own reality.[15] These four solutions is everyman's struggle: to be able to find order in himself and to be able to order the outside in conformity with his nature.

1972—A Marital Impasse and Feelings of Ambivalence

Intense ambivalence and complexity characterized the marriage feeling as if I was on a perpetual roller coaster. It was almost impossible to maintain a tenuous balance. Whatever cohesion I had been able to muster was constantly under internal and external threat. I aspired high but fell low as I felt I was a prisoner to seemingly random cycles of guilt and shame that had a life of their own.

I was aware of discontinuities and gaps in my experience. It was difficult at best to keep myself focused on practically anything except my work. I hated feeling the way I did and I hated more the fact that I felt powerless to do anything to help myself. I wrote: "My goal is to dig into the intrapsychic . . . realign it. . . create an Aristotelian balance point for myself and move my own way through the world. Spinoza (1954) says: "The impotence of man to govern or restrain the emotions I call 'Bondage' for a man who is under their control is not his own master, but is mastered by fortune, in whose power he is, so that he is often forced to follow the worst, although he sees the better before him."[16]

This was an accurate diagnosis of my inability to escape the wheel of negative emotions by facing up to and mastering ambivalence and complexity. It was also an acknowledgement of how much I was bound to the wheel of repetition compulsion.

The twin issues of ambivalence and complexity were at the forefront of my consciousness. I was experiencing them in their starkness both internally and externally. At the same time, each new awareness of the presence of either one, or both together, threatened my cohesion. Guilt and shame followed each negative thought I had about my wife and child to be. Pressure built up as tension intensified. A patient with similar preoccupations as my own asked a highly significant question that I had no good answer for that paralleled my own troubled self: "How is it possible to be a good Christian in a world that is so self consciously hostile and corrupt? Or, more specifically, [when frustrated] how not to act out destructive fantasies?"

Uncharacteristically I find myself at a loss of words. The feeling I had was utter helplessness. I connected with feelings of quintessential not knowing. Additionally, I connected my feelings of ineffectualness with memories of my mother dying of cancer and my feeling at a total loss as to what to say or do about it. This negative experience was soon followed by swings of contradictory ideas, fantasies, and feelings. I couldn't seem to keep my inner self steady and balanced.

Understanding these complex and ambivalent events as only existential occurrences, that is—simply just so stories—I believed there was nothing more to do about them except passively suffer them.

May 15, 1972— Meanings Revealed or Realized?

The mixed feelings I had been experiencing concerning my wife and baby to be plus the discoveries about myself, evoked a curious blend of both generating my own meanings while at the same time feeling as if I was being guided by some invisible transcendent force. I wrote: "I had a feeling today that I am very much the originator of my [meanings] yet, at the same time, I still hold onto that mysterious feeling of destiny. Perhaps it is a primitive wish to hope that life has some ultimate God given purpose that I can tap into. Perhaps it is holding onto some last connection with my mother. Yet, [whatever the cause], it still persists. And, in my experience it is still a logical possibility."

Spring 1972—It's a Girl: I Am a Father in Reality

The birth of our baby has "kicked" me into the present. This kick makes me realize that I had been oscillating between alternative experiences of time. I wrote:

> I am aware of [experiencing] various streams of association along with the existence of at least two independent and sometimes interpenetrating [temporal] regions—secondary process: experienced as normal clock time, past, present, future held together by conventional cause and effect relationships; and primary process experienced as timelessness—an eternal sense of now. I have to try to understand psychological time and psychological space [and its implications].

But later this spring, I discovered that when anxious I tended to fragment into various splits and parts. With this awareness I had a resurgence of interest in attempting to understand the masters of esoteric astrology such as Marc Edmund Jones,[17] and Alan Leo.[18] I believed that such knowledge might provide me with a pathway to accessing and sustaining ego synthesis.

Reinforcing my belief that the esoteric occult had something of value in such matters, I found notes I had made concerning my experiments in Astrology when I was twenty-three years old. These notes were significantly relevant to my developing theory about synchronicities. I wrote: "When one gives into the feelings that lie somewhere beyond our conscious control [awareness], one realizes that there seems to be an inner knowledge—an ineffable, non verbal, wisdom, which when translated shows us the right path to travel, the most adequate turns in the road to take."

As a summary statement covering the content and meaning of my first seven synchronicities and associated contextual material I wrote: "I experience [all of it] as an ongoing deliberate challenge, preoccupation, puzzle, that is evolving, unfolding, but a seemingly insurmountable obstacle driving me forward in a kind of compulsive quest to find my personal identity."

By June, I experienced myself as oscillating between swings of being wise and being stupid, being superior and being inferior, being worthy and being worthless. For most of my life I stayed clear from directly experiencing ambivalence and complexity. Pressures associated with the marriage and the pregnancy left me with no place to escape. I had to face up to the psychic pain I had so long avoided.

Also in June, a fateful car trip telescoped my overlapping senses of time. I wrote: "Today in the mountains my wife and I had a harrowing experience. We took a road that was leading to nowhere. We were nearly out of gas. The rains had caused a mudslide, and the ignition wasn't catching properly. The trip itself was a risk in the first place and now we had made a wrong turn [to boot]. The gas gauge read empty. I felt shocked into reality."

A rereading of this experience can be read from the vantage point of a worm's eye perspective and/or a bird's eye perspective. I thought of the distinction Spinoza makes between macroscopic universal eternal time and microscopic personal durational time.

From a worm's eye—microscopic—perspective the trip was difficult at best indicating poor judgment on both of our parts. From a bird's eye view—macroscopic—perspective this trip was an archetypal event symbolizing the near end of the marriage that had made the wrong turn and was nearly out of gas. Most importantly, for me, I was undeniably aware that I was nearly out of gas and had little to no motivation for continuing on in the relationship.

I played with the conceptualization of coincidences being explained as an intersection of horizontal and vertical modes of time: that is, horizontal being normal clock time and vertical being timelessness. I speculated that perhaps one function of a synchronicity is a cosmic confirmation of going in the right direction on one's life path—that is a kind of macrocosmic feedback—a kind of global (synthetic) right on.

Without being conscious of it at the time, my preoccupation with wishing to access and to sustain timelessness and unity was in the service of a desperate need to transcend the pain associated with ambivalence and complexity. Previous to the following synchronicity #7 I had begun to feel the full undeniable force of intense ambivalence and complexity in both my inner and outer realities but, at the same time, my attitude towards them was highly critical and negative. My desire was to rid myself of these unpleasant, intrusive, negative experiences. But all attempts to accomplish this task utterly failed.

07/13/72 Synchronicity—a gap of 6 months—Age 35
#7 "Horizontal and Vertical"
Immediate Situational Context:

I feel more at ease accepting realistic pressures. I experience myself as made up of various streams of information: i.e. thoughts, feelings, intuitions, sensations, and the like. I am aware of oscillating between states of grandiosity and worthlessness and am aware that this polarity has defined me up to this point. I am upset that I have murderous wishes towards some people I should be loving. I appreciate the power of magical thinking and relate it to a patient who has frequent synchronicities. I identify with him. I theorize that synchronicities are the self's attempts to find [creative] solutions to seemingly unsolvable psychological problems. I utilize the structure and symbolism of the cross [two vectors (horizontal and vertical) joined at their centers] as a way of trying to understand combining space and time meeting in the "now." The now is experienced as timelessness = a state of pure being. I am preoccupied with the question how to make subjective reality connect with objective reality. This is in the service of understanding the occult formula: as above, so below—the idea that everything is connected to everything else.

The synchronicity:

I walk outside my office with the image of a cross on my mind realizing that it can represent multiple meanings simultaneously. As I am mulling this idea I spot an odd looking black man pushing a cart. On the right rear end of the cart I notice a wooden case that is decorated with multi colored strips of cloth with words painted on them. My eyes were drawn to the words that read: horizontal and vertical. I felt a surge of excitement.

My Reaction:

I instantaneously understood this synchronicity to be a dramatization of my growing capacity to synthesize and to integrate my experience. I felt it was now possible for me to reconcile my subjective (internal reality) and my objective self (external reality). I felt that this synchronicity was a message that I was on the right track, that is to be able to reconcile the opposites in myself I have to be able to synthesize my experience. I intuitively felt that the secret to synthesis for me was in filling in the gaps between clock time and timelessness. Responding to an intuitive flash I associated to this interpretation. The problem of ego synthesis is aligning the creative self. My problem is how to develop my synthetic function which apparently has been greatly impaired.

Follow up:

Whereas I was conscious of the fact that my priority psychological task was to continue pursuing the pathway towards synthesis of my divided self—this pursuit was mainly experienced on a cognitive and theoretical level not on the level of my feelings. Although I was intensely aware of feelings (mainly negative) that would periodically bubble over, I was at the same time, detached from them in general. Feelings were like impurities floating around in a clear glass of water. I knew they were there, could even taste them, but finding them obnoxious I was more concerned with ridding myself of them than in accepting and integrating them into my total experience.

In order to avoid experiencing the pain associated with them I had turned to the supernatural for comfort and guidance. I had longed for a state of being I referred to as perfesion—perfect ease (a state of consciousness characterized by the total absence of feelings of frustration and other so called negative feelings and emotions). Among these feelings I experienced as aversive were: not knowing, ambiguity, complexity, vulnerability, inadequacy, anxiety, tension, depression, and the likes.

In this connection, mystical states that evoked feelings of at one ment were particularly appealing to me. At least, for a brief moment in time, they provided an experience of pleasurable totality and unity.

My primary concern at this time was the source of these "mystical" at-one-ment experiences. It mattered to me as to whether or not, once in them, I was connecting with a transcendent realm of spirituality that would provide comfort and guidance to me personally; or whether these states were self generated and were perhaps precursors to the psychological synthesis I had so long desired to obtain and to sustain.

The answer to this question seemed unsolvable thus I experienced it as another fork in the road.

Situational and Psychological Contexts
Pre Synchronicity #8, Summer 1972

In reading Lilly's (1985) book I resonated to his concept of mystical fusion states.[19] In my ongoing attempt to find a pathway to inner synthesis, I related Lilly's ideas to both Jung's concept of numinosity and parallel states in my own direct experience. I speculated:

> I wonder if the mystical fusion states described by Lilly are explainable as merger fantasies (symbiosis) and some kind of synthetic integration. In this case there would be the same goal [of unity] but two different subjective experiences [as

> to how unity would be experienced.] One would be the experience of some external power—a merger fantasy; the other would be experiencing a sense of unity—synthesis—generated from and within the individual.

Driven to find a pathway to understanding how to obtain and to sustain psychic synthesis led directly to synchronicity #8.

07/28/72 Synchronicity—a gap of 1 month—Age 35
#8 "A Patient's Coincidence"
Immediate Situational Context:
I attempt to relate basic concepts associated with synchronicities to me personally. These concepts include: space, time, matter, and causality. I am consciously looking for an understanding of how to [grow] a synthetic self. I am preoccupied with what it is that makes the self cohere. Here to fore I have experienced myself as a collection of fragments, associations, verbal contents, bursts of intuitions, and theories with no central experience of cohesion and unity. Doubting, and ambivalence have too often been able to destroy whatever meager experiences of unity and continuity I have had. I reasoned that faith in myself and in my own powers coupled with the ability to sustain this faith is the key to synthesis. These ideas seem both clear and valuable to me.

The synchronicity:
As I had just been aware of a feeling of vastness, and richness, (associated with an experience of the logical clear light of inner perception, experienced as mystical-like) my next patient banged on my office door. He was evidently in the throes of a major emotional storm demanding I see him immediately. He also said that he had to see his girlfriend at exactly 3 PM as he had a mystical feeling that he was on a cosmic mission. I took note of the fact that both of us simultaneously had a mystical-like experience, but that our reactions to it were 180 degrees different.

My Reaction:
I associated this coincidence to my understanding of synchronicities. I saw for the first time the efficacy of explaining meaningful coincidences from a naturalistic perspective utilizing psychodynamics (experiential logic) with no need to employ supernatural concepts to provide an adequate explanation. The core concept would be the self of an individual seeking wholeness, integration, and balance naturalistically.

Follow up:
The aftermath of this synchronicity marked a significant shift in my consciousness with respect to my understanding of the pathway towards

psychological synthesis. For me, the unity that I had been seeking would not be found through a passive merger with a realm of transcendent meaning or independent spirituality, but would be—if at all—by means of a convergence of the various parts of me into a totality. This convergence towards synthesis would be like a number of tributaries converging and intermixing in an ocean. The goal of psychological synthesis would not be the obliteration of my individual ego but a strengthening of it wherein all separate and seemingly disconnected "voices" would get an opportunity to be heard. *The goal would be unity without sacrificing diversity.*

Summer and Fall 1972

Increasingly dedicated to viewing the process leading to synchronicities as one that was naturalistic and having no need to depend on supernatural concepts for an adequate explanation, my appointed task was to take the organizing concepts I currently resonated to and connecting, exploring, and testing them against my own direct experience.

09/19/72 Testing Organizing Concepts Against My Own Experience

Representative of this self-testing process, in reading Colin Wilson's (1972) *New Pathways in Psychology,* I wrote: "I have discovered my will. I am reading C. Wilson's Pathways in Psychology. I am struck by the way science progresses. Each significant contribution comes from an astute observer attending to his own inner process and attempts to make sense out of it.[20]

I was beginning to take my experience more seriously. I was reminded of Yeats (1986) in his autobiography stating that it took him many years to get in touch with his primary feelings and many more years to treat them seriously, considering them as valid for him.[21]

Synchronicity #9, "Gertrude Calls"—a gap of 3 months—Age 35
Immediate Situational Context:

I speculate that synchronistic phenomena may be related to the "superconscious; and that this state of consciousness may be an altered state. I know I have to think about Giovanchinni's (1975) paper called '*The Frozen Introject.*' As I reread my notes I have memories of my remoteness immediately following the death of my mother when I was fifteen years old. Before her death I was feeling either ignored or overly praised. Production was more important than quality. My reaction to these memories was that perhaps I now have a need to be logical. That is I have a need to understand what the meaning of my experience is not just recall the feelings. I continue to speculate: perhaps I have kept myself split on purpose—one possible reason is that secondary process thinking—linear logic—may be forbidden or in some other way conflictualized.[22]

The synchronicity:

Just at the moment when I consider that I may be defensively keeping myself split my phone rang. Gertude, a professor and Jungian psychologist, with whom I have been sharing my non Jungian interpretation of synchronicities, was calling. As I was relating my current thoughts about the nature of synchronicities to her, I was keenly aware of her obvious unconditional acceptance and unexpected encouragement of my ("radical") non Jungian thinking.

My Reaction:

This coincidence reinforces my awareness of being aware. I am aware that I am being totally accepted by a person I respect who does not share my point of view. This experience makes me feel that more of my splits are coming together. If a respected person with a different perspective towards synchronicities can take both my being and my differing ideas seriously then I should do the same for myself.

Follow up:

Without quite realizing it at the time, I was beginning to experientially understand that the elusive goal of psychological synthesis has to be carried out in an atmosphere of unconditional acceptance, cooperation, alliance, and trust. It is a new experience for me to be able to be perceived as different and yet accepted at the same time. This growing awareness is a precursor for cathecting the concepts of object and self-constancy. Although the path I am walking intuitively feels right to me, there is a continuing sense of emotional detachment. I simultaneously feel these ideas are "right on the money," and yet, it is still difficult, if not impossible, for me to take myself seriously. It is as if I am going through the motions not really connected with the important implications of what I am discovering.

The issue for me is no longer to be or not to be, or to do or not to do. The issue is to believe in myself or give up the urge (compulsion) to define myself as clearly distinct and clearly demarcated from everyone else alive.

My doubtful attitude to being able to transcend these lifelong oscillating feelings is another fork on my life's road immediately preceding synchronicity # 10.

Situational and Psychological Contexts Pre Synchronicity #10, September 19, 1972–September 25, 1972—a 6 day gap

I cathect the concept of Waelder's (1945) principle of multiple function. This illuminating organizing concept states that any psychological event (i.e., symptom, psychodynamic, theory etc.) is best considered to be a convergence of various psychological determinants (causes) serving alternative functions.[23]

Freud's structural theory as a confluence of Id, Ego, and super ego is an example of the principle of multiple function. This principle when applied to synchronicities invites a researcher to consider the process that results in a given synchronicity to be one that is complex. Thus, synchronicities might be viewed as the surface manifestation of an intersection of overlapping multiple logics, i.e., primary process plus secondary process mixed together. In this view, I theorize that an adequate naturalistic explanation of the nature of synchronicities would be a synthesis of both Freudian classical psychoanalytic determinism and Jungian teleology.

Past	**Present**	**Future**
Determinism		Teleology
	NOW	
Origins		Goals

Chapter 8 completes the description of the remaining nine synchronicities and the relevant situational and psychological contexts from which they emerged.

8

My Synchronicity Theory Works

> The key to understanding the nature of the process that leads to the production of synchronicities from a naturalistic perspective entails treating them as byproducts of human beings accommodating creative solutions to resolve seemingly intractable problems.
>
> —G. Williams[1]

09/25/72 My Father Dies . . .
09/25/72 Synchronicity—a Gap of 6 Days—Age 35
#10 "Spinoza, Myself and the Will"
Immediate Situational Context:

I experience a need for both fusion and realistic boundaries simultaneously. I speculate that synchronicities may be naturalistically explained utilizing a combination of Waelder's (1936) principle of multiple function;[2] concepts from ego psychology; and self psychology—incorporating Jung's emphasis on teleology (purposeful goals) resulting in a totally psychodynamic interpretation. My father dies. My marriage worsens. (It is very difficult for me to keep focused.) I am aware that I need to put my will (desires, intentions, aims) under the control of my ego, that is, I have to be able to harness and focus them at will.

The Synchronicity:

At the very moment that I have the thought that I need to put my will under the control of my ego, I randomly turn to a page in Spinoza's *Ethics* (1954) alighting on a section that describes the concept of controlling one's will.[3]

My Reaction:

I again experience myself as being on the right path. That is, I should continue to thoroughly understand this concept as it resonates to my own direct experience.

Follow Up:

Although certain that my priority task is to continue to do all I can to further attain synthesis by harnessing and directing my powers, I am equally as certain I am unable do so alone. I also am intuitively aware that although I am learning a great deal in my supervisory experience it is mainly cognitive. I sense that I have to somehow bring my negative feelings into the picture to obtain the total integration I have been longing to have. However, this means risking once again an intimate experience with another real person in an intimate relationship wherein I am required to be absolutely open and honest.

Whereas I feel as if I have no other choice but to try this path once again, I am painfully aware that my track record has been poor. In this connection, I experience myself locked in an internal civil war: one side daring, adventurous, open to discovery; the other fear ridden, insecure, and closed. The net result was that once again I felt stuck in a cleft stick quintessentially doubting my chances of significantly effecting significant change.

I was stuck between the need to find a good father substitute and a belief that such a relationship was probably not in the cards for me. Thus, although only one day passed since my last meaningful coincidence, once again—only a day later—I found myself at another fork in the road.

Situational and Psychological Contexts Pre Synchronicity #11
(September 25th, 1972–September 26th, 1972)—a 1 Day Gap 09/23/72
I Realize My Father Is Really Dead—All Men Are Mortal, Including Myself

Upon the death of my father I felt simultaneously more free and more enslaved. I was freed forever from his negative judgment but not freed from my own. I wondered if I would ever truly be free enough to take my ideas seriously. Part of my difficulty in doing so was a difficulty I was having understanding the psychodynamic understanding of the meaning of meaning. I consulted my supervisor as to his understanding about the meaning of meaning. My supervisor gives me a cogent answer to my question: what is the psychodynamic understanding of the meaning of meaning? He explains that the problem of meaningfulness in terms of psychoanalytic metapsychology is its preconditions. To have an experience of meaningfulness a person has first to experience the internalization of positive inner objects. A precondition to have good internalized objects is the necessity to have had a relationship with one or more objects that have been substantially warm, and responsive to hold onto.[4]

Later that day I record into my journal my thoughts about two types of people, each one with a distinctly different attitude toward the unknown. Type one views the unknown as bounded, expressed as a just so story—this is the way it is—an existential point of view; the other, type two, views the unknown as a never ending mystery—a jumping off point for generating additional questions. Type one stops action; type two explores.

The Synchronicity:

I turn at random in a book called *The Unobstructed Universe* (1988) to page 45 that draws a distinction between the obstructed universe that is limited and the un-obstructed universe that is unlimited.[5]

My Reaction:

This synchronicity reinforces my ideas about the nature of synchronicity prone individuals of which I am familiar. In my experience such people have suffered from a deprivation of meaningful connectedness that predisposes them to tirelessly search for pathways to meaningful connections as a life theme. [I added]: This is story of my life.

Follow Up:

My priority was clear that I had to find an atmosphere in which I would experience an openness allowing me to bring out my best. Realizing I could no longer do it alone, I knew I would have to ally myself with someone but I wasn't ready to do so until now.

Although I knew exactly what I had to do I was gun shy, fearing that I would repeat the same negative experience that I had with practically every important male authority I had worked with in the past. I felt caught between the need to reach out once again versus keeping myself guarded.

Situational and Psychological Contexts Pre Synchronicity #12
(September 26th, 1972–January 16th, 1973)—a Gap of 4 Months

Continuing to theorize about the nature of synchronicities in terms of psychodynamics I read a series of articles pointing to childhood origins for those psychological states described by Jung as numinous. For example: I was excited reading a resonant article by Phyllis Greenacre called "The Family Romance of the Artist."

10/03/72 "The Family Romance of the Artist"

I quoted Helen Greenacre (1958):

> It is very striking how many creative people describe memories of experience of revelation, awe, or some kind of transcendental states in childhood and how regularly this is placed at the age of 4 or 5.[6]

Greenacre's observations functioned like a magnet for many of the ideas that have been on my mind. I connected Maslow's concept of peak experiences with the oedipal period. I referred to my experience as consciousness of consciousness i.e., a fusion of subjective and objective—an overlapping of primary process and secondary process.

01/04/73 I Experience Fragments of My Consciousness Connecting (Synthesis)
I wrote:

> I begin making meaningful connections in what heretofore have been gaps in my internal reality. For example: in the latest crisis with my wife I have become aware that she is like the worst of my father and that I have permitted it to be this way. In a dream I am aware that in some respects I am just like the worst parts of my father. I am painfully aware that I am playing out the Oedipus myth in my actual life: The more I seem to get away, the more I seem to head right into the grips of my problems. [I am doubtful that I can ever free myself of what seems to be an inevitable " moth to the flame complex."]

01/16/73 Synchronicity—a Gap of 4 Months—Age 36
#12 "Teaching in my Dissertation Chairman's Department"
Immediate Situational Context:

I relate the process leading to the production of synchronicities to unmet needs of the self. The most notable need is the need for warm responsive unconditional acceptance. (In self psychological theory the patient needs to experience effective therapy to be a "mirror transference"—in which the patient hopefully experiences, for the first time in his life, a meaningful connection with one other live person—the therapist—that acts as a bridge back to a meaningful connection with oneself.) I posed the following question to myself: is there a clear state of consciousness that shuts out all psychic conflict—conscious or unconscious—whether from the past, present, or the anticipated future? (Such a state would be the consciousness of pure being.)

The Synchronicity:

Two days later I was telling someone about my possible goal of teaching after I obtain a Ph.D. The person says maybe you will get a teaching job in your chairman's department. At that precise moment the phone rang. The caller was an ex-patient from two years ago who had a problem she thought I might be able to solve. She told me that she works in my chairman's department as a teacher and that she is going to resign. She knows he is likely to be sensitive to her leaving and wanted my advice as how best to break the bad news to him.

My Reaction:

Even though there was no hint of a teaching job for me I still felt a surge of excitement noting the meaningful parallel of thinking about my chairman and the simultaneous call from an ex-patient who works with him. This coincidence intensified my curiosity about the source of these odd occurrences. I asked myself are these events transmissions from some unknown transcendent force or are they messages from myself experienced as if they are transcendent to me? Despite my skepticism I couldn't shake the possibility that I was in fact vibrating in reaction to some "divine" spiritual wave length.

Follow Up:

Having never had a sustained intimate relationship with a father figure I held back on searching for another analyst. However, still in need of external guidance I rekindled my investigations of the esoteric occult with the hope that I could find a pathway to the good guidance I needed. Without knowing it at the time I was continuing to search for my "spiritual" father. The latest in a long line of hoped for "good fathers" was my dissertation chairman.

Even as I refocused my energies in researching the esoteric occult I felt split. Part of me insisted that I keep an open mind for who really knows what forces are at play in the universe; whereas, the skeptical me believed that this return to the occult was little more than a regressive childish wish for rescue. Once again, I was at a distinct fork in the road: evenly divided between the supernatural and the naturalistic points of views re synchronicities.

Situational and Psychological Contexts Pre Synchronicity #13
(January 16th, 1973–October 25th, 1973)—a Gap of 9 Months
I Straddle a Position Midway Between Freud and Jung: Determinism and Teleology

During this next nine months culminating in synchronicity #13, I traveled two parallel and divergent paths simultaneously: the supernatural and the naturalistic.

01/19/73 Contextual Analysis Tips the Scale

Supervision made it abundantly clear that symptoms and dreams were best understood as embedded in personal contexts. Why, I reasoned, wouldn't the same hold true for synchronicities as well?

I wrote:

> I hypothesize that meaningful coincidences may be best viewed in terms of specific problems of a given person. I can review past synchronicities and see out of what context they emerge. Are they attempts to resolve a specific problem? Do they serve any pragmatic purposes relative to specific goals?

01/20/73 Integrating Various Streams of Experience

The discovery of Guntrip's "rashomoning" of "being" and "doing" along with his integration of science and religion resonated with my two path walk. Says Guntrip (1969) in discussing the treatment of schizoid (fragmented) personalities:

> There cannot be a whole complete human being without an integration of feeling with thinking and acting, provided by "doing", arising spontaneously out of the fundamental experience of "being".[7]

This strikes me as a good example of "rashomoning"—an argument for synthetic thinking. I was experiencing these and associated concepts from all camps resonating to my direct experience functioning like sharply defined pieces of a jigsaw puzzle that when connected with each other began making coherent patterns filling in the gaps of my discontinuities.

02/08/73 The Pattern of My Experience Is Dynamically Alive and Patterned

I experienced the reality of repetition compulsion both in myself and with my patients—that is, how the past habitually repeats itself in the present like various themes and variations having a life of their own outside conscious awareness.

02/14/73 Intense Emotions Threaten to Spill

Additionally I became aware that in every intimate relationship, I inevitably experience intense feelings of attraction and repulsion [quintessential ambivalence].

I wrote:

> I feel as if I am emerging from a long period of isolation. I have felt caught between the there and then and the here and now. My experience has been as if I were caught in a tidal wave of feelings—a kaleidoscope of experiences—on an emotional roller coaster. . . .

In this context of emotional intensity and confusion I renewed an interest in searching for evidence of a master plan in back of reality.

I wrote:

> I am searching for evidence that a divine plan is a reality in addition to a psychological wish. . . . Thus I hope to discover for myself that Jung's supernatural theory of coincidences is in fact accurate.

With this aim in mind, I read Alice Bailey's (1934) treatise *On White Magic* that purports to give accurate "channeled" information about the nature and use of an assumed Grand Cosmic Plan.[8]

I speculated:

> If there is a plan then others who know of it, either know others like themselves, or they do not. It suggests there are secret societies with special passwords like spiritual fraternities and sororities. If so I desire entrance! This is what I experienced with the Lazarus Rising synchronicity. The meaning for me was that I was in touch with some awesome power or intelligence that had revealed its existence to me. It was as if I had been taped into a secret society.

Freud's Linear Logic and Jung's Intuition Compete for Ascendancy

The scientific part of me observed the benefit of utilizing linear scientific cause and effect logic in my continuing attempts to understand both the nature of myself and of my patients in breadth and in depth. At the same time I was aware that something was still missing that felt vital. It felt as if I needed to be reassured that there was a force that was transcendent to me—providing vital information in the service of guiding, validating, warning, and encouraging me to move in certain directions while avoiding others.

09/26/73 Combining Conventional Cause and Effect (Linear Logic) and Intuition

I wrote: "I have been plugging in missing gaps—presently I am learning how to use linear logic in conjunction with my reliance on intuition."

Although I was building psychological structure I still couldn't rid myself of a profound sense of inner emptiness. As much as I wanted to experience myself as my own man, the truth was that I was inordinately responsive even to a hint of acceptance by substitute father figures. Thus I was unable to make an objective evaluation as to who was truly trustworthy from those who only pretended to be so. Lacking clarity on this crucial issue I remained doubtful as to whether my emotional roller coaster could or would ever change. Such was the state of my affairs immediately preceding the next synchronicity.

10/25/73 Synchronicity—a Gap of 10 Months—Age 36
#13 "Vaughn's Book"
Immediate Situational Context:

I desire to be able to provide links between emptiness and fullness—meaninglessness and meaningfulness. In a class with an admired analyst I realize that my need for omniscience is a symptom of pathological grandiosity and that my search for a union with God is a wish for merger with an ideal authority. (If I can't merge with my father then I will look to God the Father as a necessary and wished for substitute.)

The Synchronicity:

I read a book on synchronistic phenomena called *Patterns of Prophecy* by Alan Vaughn. I get increasingly more excited with each new page. The excitement reached its peak intensity on page 56 wherein Vaughn recounts a prediction made by a medium. The prediction is that he—Vaughn (1973)—will be involved with a psychologist who is between 35 to 40 years old who will collaborate with him on his second book on this same subject. I am utterly convinced (deluded) that I am the psychologist he is talking about.[9]

My Reaction:

I feel shaken by my near complete loss of objectivity. While my feelings inform me that I am indeed the psychologist in the prediction, my more rational side dismisses my feelings as delusional. I am concerned that if I am capable of such "flights of fancy" then how can I be certain of the validity of any of my passionately held beliefs? Acknowledging my "crisis of judgment" revives my interest in investigating the Jungian supernatural perspective with the implied possibility of connecting with some transcendental benevolent and guiding forces.

Follow Up:

Despite my confusion I was certain that I was dedicated to pursuing the truth no matter in what direction it might be found. In this connection nothing was more important to me than being as clear as possible concerning what I referred to as vital knowledge about myself or my patients.

Although I was oscillating between hyper subjectivity and relative objectivity it seemed important to take a position as to the source of the coded "messages" presumably hidden in synchronicities. That is, I felt I had to take a definitive position as to whether or not the presumably vital self-information associated with synchronicities was revealed from a transcendent realm of absolute (divine) meaning, or was, is, in fact, self generated messages only experienced as if they came from some transcendent source. I oscillated back and forth seemingly unable to get off the fence. It appeared as if I would never be able to take a clear cut position on this issue. Deadlocked I felt hopelessly resigned to my fate.

Situational and Psychological Contexts Pre Synchronicity #14
(October 25th, 1973–March 31, 1974)—a Gap of 5 Months
10/29/73 I Begin to Side with the Position That All Meanings Are Self Generated

In my continuing preoccupation in attempting to make myself whole and stable I was zeroing in on identifying my core issue. Without naming it as such, I was describing my core problem as a lack of psychological structure. I described my current preoccupation as:

> My inclination is to rise above the feelings of sludge, doom and gloom, and alienation. I want to try and provide links between emptiness and fullness—to move from hopelessness to hopefulness. I am convinced by my own experience with myself and some of my patients that this is not an impossible task. [The essence of the therapeutic task in this issue is nothing less than creating something out of nothing.]

In this light, my interest in understanding the "true" nature of synchronicities intensified. I read extensively on the subject. I was particularly interested in understanding the way in which connections become meaningful. After reading additional sources I would test out the author's ideas against my direct experience and draw my own conclusions. For example:

> I have been checking out Vaughn's ideas on synchronicities against my own experience. My findings are: (l) My synchronicities make statements that seem to crystallize a particular psychological or philosophical problem of the moment. The coincidence seems to confirm some aspect of the problem in question as if to underscore the fact that I am on the right road. (2) My particular synchronicities flow directly out of my particular ongoing streams of consciousness of the moment. (3) There may be a common theme linking the synchronicities together. (4) The synchronicities seem to function more as problem solvers than predictors of the future.
>
> Theoretically, synchronicities are perhaps like waking dreams in that they gather together highly charged emotional material that seems logically unrelated (primary process) and at the same time [simultaneously] appears to be quite ordered and meaningful as is the case with secondary processing.
>
> Whether or not synchronicities can be explained as a byproduct of a knowable psychological process or that there needs to be an assumption of an external realm of transcendent meanings which is tapped into I am not sure of at present. Perhaps as Greenacre points out in "The Family Romance of the Artist" the child is able to have a simultaneous peak experience of both primary and secondary process experiencing.[10] [My son at 8 is convinced he will be a famous and rich professional baseball player. He is utterly convinced of the truth of his imagination, will power, and directed energy.] He would become aware of being aware—conscious of being conscious—worlds within worlds. . . . He would know that time is both linear and durational.

11/16/73 Occult Powers Are Viewed as Underdeveloped Psychological Faculties

In addition to utilizing psychological concepts in my ongoing investigation of the nature of synchronicities, I continued my reading of occult literature. In this connection I found C. Wilson's book, *The Occult*, helpful.

Reading Wilson's (2006) observations, combined with my own research concerning synchronicities, reinforced my growing awareness that synchronicities are probable markers of what is referred to as an expansion of personal consciousness.[11]

In this connection I was excited reading William James's account of what the experience of conscious expansion feels like as his words resonated with my own direct experience.

Says James (1910):

> What happened each time was that I seemed all at once to be reminded of a past experience; and this reminiscence ere I could conceive or name it distinctly, developed into something further that belonged with it, this in turn into something further still, and so on, until the process faded out leaving me amazed at the sudden vision of increasing ranges of distant fact of which I could give no articulate account. . . . There was a strongly exciting sense that my knowledge of past (or present) reality was enlarging pulse by pulse, but so rapidly that my intellectual process could not keep up the pace. The content was thus entirely lost to introspection—it sank into the limbo into which dreams vanish as we gradually awake. The feeling—I won't call it belief—that I had a sudden opening—had seen though a window, as it were distant realities that incomprehensively belonged with my own life, was so acute that I cannot shake it today.[12]

Additional Concepts Providing a Naturalistic Explanation of Seemingly Supernatural Phenomena

11/21/73 Paul's Concept of Analytic Experiences

In a book called *Letters to Simon*, the author, Paul, describes certain moments in therapy with patients that are akin to peak experiences and synchronicities. Such experiences feel like reconciliations of subjective and objective (surface and depths, story and plot, etc.) inside and outside, present and past (reconciling opposites). Paul calls such experiences Analytic Experiences. Paul (1973) describes them as:

> a feeling which is rare and profound—even shaking . . . it's the sense of revelation that really counts—the sense of something deeply valid and authentic for you. It doesn't have to be so new or startling; but it does feel rare and revelatory. . . . The patient feels wholly open to his Inner Reality, and for this reason it is likely to be accompanied by apprehension if not anxiety. . . . Analytic experiences, then . . . are events of critical importance and impact. Some therapists refer to them as peak experiences; I prefer Analytic because that emphasizes the fact that they are heightened experiences in knowing. In my opinion they are acts of acute understanding, and therefore likely to have a profound effect. Such experiences are memorable and moving, but also traumatic. They are probably the stuff out of which basic change is wrought and against which major defenses are applied.[13]

Applying Paul's concept of Analytic Experiences to synchronicities, I wrote:

> Meaningful coincidences are like analytic experiences in that: (1) They are experienced as if they are peak experiences. (2) They are felt to be intensely alive

with special meaning. (3) The particular meaning seems to join large areas of thoughts, feelings, past memories and associations plus a present "triggering" event. And (4) they serve the purpose of indicating that a resolution of a major problem has taken place.

Later I wrote: "Synchronicities are experiences of self-development occurring when the central ego makes a connection with some previous repressed split-off feelings [conflicts]."

12/04/73 I Find It Impossible to Relax
I wrote:

> I am aware that I am obsessed with constantly trying to figure things out, theorizing, endlessly problem solving. I need to relax [but I feel as if I am on overdrive and I don't know how to stop it].

Tension Mounts: I See How My Self Esteem Drops Precipitously
A trip to Miami was disastrous. Negative forces—marital, professional, and personal—were converging. I became aware of an automatic pattern of self-esteem deregulation that was undeniable and alarming. In identifying this automatic pattern I was able to see how I am capable of overreacting to frustration with anger that gets turned in to myself resulting in depression, despair, and hopelessness. The net result is that at any given moment this psychological process once triggered assumes a life of its own resulting in a wholesale temporary loss of my identity.

01/03/74
I described this pattern in my journal:

> Last night I clearly saw the process that my wife and I get locked into that leads to a silent or open war. I need only experience her suddenly turn from warm to cold, or high to low, and I automatically plunge into a mood which is edgy, irritable, and wavy. I then blame myself for her change of mood and look for the slightest confirmation of it. A frown will do it. I begin to feel a rising tension that often leads to rage. Sometimes it gets so out of hand that I explode. Other times I hawk her, or analyze, or worry, or obsess about it. Eventually my feelings build to impotent rage. The horrible part about all this is that I can [clearly] witness what is going on but I am helpless to do anything about it. Once the [negative] feelings [are triggered off and the process is activated] they have a life of their own.

01/04/74 Nightmares and Fear of Cancer
I wrote:

> I am terrified to go to sleep perchance to dream. . . .

A Clear Fork in the Road: Naturalistic Versus Occult Explanations

A seminal article in the *N.Y. Times* puts my problem in clear naturalistic perspective. The part that most resonated with my direct experience was the concept of apocalypticism operationally defined as:

> a distinctive way of managing reality is . . . a method which the imagination tends to employ precisely in those moments when the realities of history [personal] seem to be quite unmanageable. We fall back on the dramatic ellipses of prophecy and revelation, on cosmic incantation, when we no longer have what Paul Tillich called the "courage to be"—the kind of courage that permits us to reckon with the conditioned and imperfect reality of ourselves and the world to which we are committed by the logic of our history.[14]

01/14/74 I Decide to Have a Consult with a Psychoanalyst to Discuss My Fears and Consider Entering Psychoanalysis

I wrote:

> I can see many of my problems as if they were shining like blazing stars in a pitch black sky—but is awareness enough? Must I have therapy to work them out? . . . I suspect my recent cancer fear is the fact that something is gnawing at me like psychic cancer. I hope Dr. K.[consultant] understands this fear and that she is not a fraud and can be trusted.

I realize that I need professional help but I am highly distrustful; thus I am faced with another fork in the road: denying or dismissing my complaints as occult or directly facing my fears with an unknown authority. I experience both hope and doubt that this psychological dilemma can result in a salutary outcome.

01/18/74 Synchronicity—a Gap of 3 Months—Age 36
#14 "Nagera Understands Me"
Immediate Situational Context:

A confirming appointment with Dr. K notably reduced my fears of cancer generating new ideas about the nature of my synchronicities. Previously I would have treated such fears as purely existential—that is they occur at random and are experienced as overwhelming. From a spiritual perspective it was as if the devil was sticking me with a pitchfork for unnamed sins. As a result of my consultation I am seeing that it is possible to convert what appears to be existential (my cancer fear) into a symptom that signals that I have an unresolved psychological problem that calls for analysis (understanding). In this later view, I suspect that these fears are related to my new awareness of undeniable psychological issues. I name these particular fears "psychic cancer."

My heightened cancer fear, the consultation, the analyst's confirmation of my experience, and sensible guidance were associated with a marked reduction in my distress.

This experience also generated some new ideas about the nature of my synchronicities. I wrote:

> Synchronicities are markers of self-development. [They occur] when the central ego [consciousness] makes a [connection] with some previously repressed [and/or dissociated] split off feelings.

As I was mulling these ideas a synchronicity occurred.

The Synchronicity:

At the same moment I was speculating that my cancer fears are actually hypochondriacal symptoms related to the death of my mother to cancer, I reached for the 1970 book *The Psychoanalytic Study of the Child*, having noticed an article by Nagera (1970) called "Children's Reactions to Death." The essence of the article is that each of the psychologically disturbed children studied in the article had been given no emotional support before, during, or after the death of a parent, which led to massive developmental interference.[15]

Among the problems that followed were an overidentification with the mother's issues and an array of pathological symptoms that include an incapacity to mourn, a massive use of denial, an inability to grasp the reality of death, and fantasies of reunion.

My Reaction:

This synchronicity confirmed that my naturalistic perspective about the nature of synchronicities was valid. Thus a significant result of this synchronicity was to tilt my understanding (shift of attitude) of meaningful coincidences toward a decidedly naturalistic perspective.

Follow Up:

There was a marked shift in my consciousness. I could see my problems not as existential random occurrences but as psychodynamically explained symptoms. The key difference in my new perception was to view these negative events embedded in my daily situational and psychological contexts. This is my first experience of what I will eventually refer to as experiential logic.

This approach to my difficulties allowed me to bring to the table a confluence of all of my streams of information: sensations, feelings, intuitions, and thoughts. This approach was clear, concrete, factual, information specific, and real. It was distinctly different from the gauzier, overgeneralized, loosely associative ramblings associated with my experience of the esoteric occult.

I was able to clearly name the psychological problems I wanted to resolve. I interviewed a psychoanalyst who would become my analyst. Importantly, I had an instantaneous sense of attunement with him. For the first time in my life I felt I was in good analytic hands to do the psychological work I knew I had to do on myself. My undeniably positive experience enabled me to feel potentially comprehensible. Thus the way out of my last fork in the road was to make a leap of faith, daring to trust this man—who was soon to become my psychoanalyst—a stranger who I had only just met a few short weeks ago.

Situational and Psychological Contexts Pre Synchronicity #15 (January 18, 1974–April 18, 1974)—a Gap of 3 Months

01/19/74 A Clear Statement of My Goals in Psychoanalysis

I read somewhere that the goal of psychoanalysis is for the patient to cut through the neurosis of fate by taking charge and being responsible for his own fate. That is, to be able to shift from reactivity (impulsive/compulsive) reacting to (purposeful) acting from within (reflection).

Believing that my problems were intimately bound up with a spiritual as well with psychological concerns, I read an article that resonated:

> As to our spiritual state in difficult and confusing times . . . this is our task: in the darkest night to be certain of the dawn; certain of the power to turn a curse into a blessing, agony into a song.[16]

At last, my priority task was clear. I had to learn to face my direct experience—good, bad, or indifferent—and discuss the truth of it with a stranger who I had to learn to trust. Now that I knew my destination was crystal clear, the issue was, could I stay the course? As my tendency was to cut and run at crucial impasses I was in doubt as to whether my actions would outlast my intentions. I experienced this doubt as another fork in the road. I wondered if it was perhaps no coincidence that I would cut and run at predictable times.

2/21/74 I Receive Scientific Legitimacy

I passed the Ph.D. orals. I am no longer waiting for a message from the gods, but waiting for one from myself. Pain is multidimensional—existential (death, illness, prejudice); psychological (conflicts due to repression, suppression, fears real and imagined). I can no longer obliterate or deny pain so I must learn how to live with it (gracefully). (As I achieve—transcend—due to my persistent effort in struggling with struggle, the need to depend on occult intervention fades.)

In line with my increasing desire to understand synchronicities scientifically I codify my interest.

I wrote:

> I would like to do an article on the *Phenomenology of Synchronistic Experiences and Their Relationship to the Development of the Self.* Such experiences join together occult phenomena, and personal experiences, relating them to interferences in self-development (the transition between magical and experiential views of reality).

Overlapping Fields of Knowledge Appear to be Essential in Understanding Synchronicities

I quoted John Dewey (1929) from his book *The Quest for Certainty* indicating science's need for philosophy: "The need for integration of specialized results of science remains, and philosophy should contribute to the satisfaction of the need."[17]

Magical Causality: Another Important Organizing Concept

In *The Child's Conception of Physical Causality,* Piaget (1960) describes alternative ways in which a child makes sense of the world. One of them is magical causality.[18] This generates a number of questions about synchronicities: Do they signal breakthroughs of primal material? Do similar themes repeat for all people? Are synchronicities associated with people fixated at a developmental phase between intuitive/emotional/magical perceptions and linear logical sensory motor intelligence?

These concepts sweep up an enormous amount of heretofore separate pieces of experience—facts, feelings, events (present and past). This is the type of integrative statement that seems clear and comprehensive and feels central to me.

I See a Way to Incorporate the Esoteric Occult into the Mix of Knowledge Bases

The esoteric occultists appear to be the first self-psychologists. Representative of this perspective is a description of viewing the Tarot cards as a road map outlining the potential evolution of consciousness of individuals seeking individuation.

I quoted the following from *The Tarot Speaks to Modern Man*:

> When the trickster [Fool] wills [Magician] to learn of his own dichotomy [High Priestess], his actions [Empress] change. He begins to see himself in a new light, realizing that the unconscious [his personal unconscious] contains germs of the future. [Behavior tends to repeat via habit—the future begins with the next

> choice.] . . . The individual who does not take the unconscious into effect endangers himself, for where the unconscious contents are repressed or neglected, their specific energy disappears into the unconscious. The energy, in turn, serves to intensify whatever is uppermost in the unconscious. Thus can a person become a slave to passion, guilt, perversion, greed, and a thousand other demons.[19]

02/24/73 Synchronicities Appear to be Connected to Pathological Self-Development—Particularly Ego Weakness

Hypothesizing about the need of such people to have at-one-ment experiences, I wrote:

> The unbalanced [un-integrated/in-cohesive] self would have little tolerance for ambivalence, complexity, disappointment, the reality principle, limitations, separation, [loss, conflict] and differences. All of these [ego states] are experienced as [intrusive] burdens. [With such aversive attitudes] there is a need in such people to transcend these [inevitable ego states] to experience states of unity, wholeness, and perfect ease [perfesion].

03/01/74 I Feel Betrayed by My Dissertation Chairman

My anger mounts since my orals. I feel as if my chairman set me up. He told me the night before the orals that I should relax as he will start them off the next morning. Taking him at his word I relaxed as much as I was able to do under the circumstances. His first question was very complex and multileveled—anything but easy. Although I experienced a surge of tension and fury I somehow managed to contain myself coming up with an adequate answer. But I no longer felt as if I could ever speak to him again.

04/16/74 I Receive Word That My Best Friend from High School Is Dead

[Unaware that I am depressed from multiple losses] I wrote:

> I can no longer believe in magic. What passes for magic is a trick, or an illusion. It is not real.

04/17/74 I Resonate to Freud's Structural Theory

Freud's structural theory provides a way to take independent psychological data and synthesize it into meaningful wholes. Intuitively I know that this is my self-appointed task in understanding the nature of synchronicities. Specifically I aim to take the components associated with synchronicities (i.e., the self, the personal unconscious, psychic time, a meaning-making process, projection, mirroring and the like) fit them together utilizing structural theory and additional psychoanalytic principles. In this connection the following quote of Freud's (1953) resonated with full force:

> Occult powers are to be sought in the depths of psychic life and that psychoanalysis is destined to clarify this problem in the same manner in which it has previously clarified other "mysterious" happenings in the human psyche.[20]

04/18/74 I Begin My Formal Research into Synchronicities

I read Le Shan's *Physics, Mysticism, and ESP.* He makes the point that the explanation of paranormal experiences (could apply to synchronicities) is related to perceiving the world in a different way from ordinary sensory experience. Le Shan's (2003) findings bear out what my experience reveals re coincidences:

> With respect to the psychological phenomenology of synchronicities, they are accompanied by a heightened sense of perception and great excitement, making one feel as if the observer and the observed are both united in one interdependent fluid unit.[21]

I foresee the possibility of transposing Le Shan's findings utilizing the current concepts of self psychology and object relations. I am particularly focused on the primary experiences of ambivalence and complexity as core psychological issues associated with all of my previous synchronicities.

I am fired up with my commitment to research synchronicities but I am equally torn apart by my feelings concerning my falling out with my chairman. I cannot tolerate the fury but I feel I should get over it. I feel caught in what seems to be an intractable problem—one that I have experienced many times in the past beginning with my father.

04/18/74 Synchronicity—a Gap of 3 Months—Age 37
#15 "Good Judgment"
Immediate Situational Context:

I had previously felt betrayed by my chairman, who I felt had given me a double message before my orals. Sooner or later all of my encounters with major authority figures degenerated into the same disappointing state. I doubted that once these feelings took over I would ever be able to change them. In other words, once I felt betrayed, that's the end of the relationship. Is there no other possible solution?

The Synchronicity:

I listened to Bob and Ray do a parody on the radio. One of the lines goes: "the sun's rays shone on the locked door." At that very moment I was aware of reading about the symbolism of the sun associated with the Tarot deck of cards. The next card mentioned was the judgment card. The next radio piece to catch my attention was a news flash from Miami. Two men running for mayor got a tie vote. Since there was no provision for a runoff, a compromise was called for.

The men, one of them white, the other black, decided to split the term. In that way both won. Reason won the day and showed a path to transcend potentially destructive opposites. My conclusion: when all that appears to be are extreme answers to seemingly mutually exclusive problems, try cutting to the middle.

My Reaction:

I associated this synchronicity to the recent confrontation between me and my chairman. With my new insight the way was open to me to clear the air by speaking my piece and him listening and giving me an explanation for his confusing behavior.

Follow Up:

Allowing myself to speak my piece to my chairman was one of the first times in my life that I allowed myself to just be and trust my instincts. This radical change of attitude resulted in a significant expansion of my consciousness enabling me to approach my whole life from an entirely new and better perspective.

Situational and Psychological Contexts Pre Synchronicity #16
(April 18th, 1974–April 19th, 1974)—a Gap of 1 Day

The connection with my instincts had its first application in my attitude to the esoteric occult specifically consulting the I Ching and the Tarot cards. I read the following from a reading of the I Ching: "A Time of struggle—no misgivings—make the self strong. . . . Work on what has been spoiled . . . Don't recoil from work or change. . . . "[22]

I read the Tarot cards for myself but have a profound hesitation in doing so. In two successive readings the judgment card appeared. The interpretation for the judgment card is:

> [Judgment] symbolizes the higher sphere of will, intelligence and action open to man. He who is no longer governed by the instincts of the flesh, who no longer lets others do his thinking, who no longer acts for purely selfish reasons, has success at his fingertips.[23]

Resonating to this "message" I wrote:

> I am beginning to see the complexity of the [layering of] character, fate, intelligence, will, and inevitable life struggles.

04/19/74 Synchronicity—a Gap of 1 Day—Age 37
#16 "Freud and Free Association"
Immediate Situational Context:

I am aware of how other people's anxiety is contagious. I am also aware of how I project my sadistic wishes onto other people of my [unconscious] choice. I find using the Tarot to be a useful guide in stimulating my thinking about psychological matters, particularly the nature of the self and its vicissitudes. I ask myself (consulting my personal unconscious) what steps I should take to enable me to best master using the Tarot for my purposes?

The Synchronicity:

As I was consciously attempting to empty my mind of all contents a book fell from my bookshelf. I noted that it was a collection of papers by Freud on technique. Among the essays was a paper on free association. I instantly freely associated that this essay on free association was the answer to my question about how best to utilize the Tarot.

My Reaction:

I take this coincidence to be my direct experience of my personal unconscious at work. I take this synchronicity to be a confirmation of my hypothesis that synchronistic phenomena are best explained as byproducts of knowable psychodynamics obviating any need for additional supernatural concepts.

Follow Up:

Connecting with my instincts and trusting them allows me to work on learning how to relax and just be. I know that this is the pathway to my creative self and am dedicated to gaining mastery over this long sought and equally elusive goal.

Situational and Psychological Contexts Pre Synchronicity #17
(April 19th, 1974–March 11th, 1976)—a Gap of 23 Months
04/23/74 A Preoccupation with Durational, Preoedipal Timeless Time

I see that my preoccupation with timelessness may be in the service of a denial of change. The quest for a sense of timelessness may be a regression in the service of an attempt to regain symbiosis to attain ego integration and identity (this is the sense that Faber uses); or it may represent a regression to a conflictless world to avoid present conflict (oedipal); or perhaps it is a progressive attempt to capture a transcendent experience in which the self experiences itself as interconnected with the totality of all of reality.

Or, I theorize, it could be a progressive experience in which there is a transcendent experience—the result of a confluence or convergence of various streams of information with an external parallel event equivalent in meaning that reflects one's changed consciousness.

11/08/74 "Rashomoning" Experience

(A major concept in understanding the nature of synchronicities: rashomoning experience[24]—the same dots can be perceived as connected in different ways evoking different patterns that convey different associations.

The associations are connected to alternative conscious and unconscious conclusions that profoundly affect attitudes and behavior.)

Implications of meaning making are that there is our experience, our experience of our experience, the conscious and unconscious meanings attributed to our experiences, conclusions reached derived from these attributed meanings, and the role they play in our psychic economy with respect to them shaping and directing our attitudes and behavior.[25]

11/30/74

My analyst—W—contains me. I realized that with S (my first therapist) I repeated the basic lack I experienced with my father. (What was crucial to me with my father was the absence of an atmosphere that was conducive to building a cohesive structure.) He gave me too much of what he thought I should be dealing with, and too little of what I thought I should be exploring on my own. Sometimes he was there for me, but on too many occasions he was absent and remote. He was inconsistent. And when critical moments happened he gave up on me. (Listening to the good sense of my psychoanalyst objectify my painful experiences with my father eventually enabled me to gradually view the whole relationship from an entirely new and significantly less troubled perspective. Whereas notable changes occurred, it is also true to state that these major shifts in attitude were incremental.)

12/01/74

It is clearer to me that in my continuing good association with my analyst there is a growing excitement I am experiencing associated with my dedication to significantly changing myself. In the first entry of my journal when I was nineteen years old I said that I wished to live "an artistic life." In my analysis I am learning how to do precisely that. My medium is the raw data of my experience from which I learn to shape and extract personal meanings session by analytic session. To be a skilled artist I have to be increasingly conscious of the contents and structures of myself and the way they interact to form a unique psychic fingerprint—the creative essence of myself.

Brewster Ghiselin (1952) in his inspiring anthology, *The Creative Process*, describes the creative process as "the process of change, of development, of evolution, in the organization of subjective life."

Further:

> Every genuinely creative worker must attain in one way or another such full understanding of his medium and such skill, ingenuity, and flexibility in handling it that he can make fresh use of it to construct a device [himself] which, when used skillfully by others, will organize their experience in the way that his own experience was organized in the moment of expanded insight.[26]

With respect to synchronicities, there is an integration between unconscious contents passing through the preconscious on the way toward consciousness resulting in new combinations of meanings and perspectives. That which was previously viewed from one fixed position is now capable of being viewed from multiple perspectives as in the curious phenomena of reversible images.

I instruct myself to spell out research in the development of the self, meaning making, how the self generates meaning in the service of expanding consciousness, etc.

Toward Becoming My Own Good Father

The above indicates that real change is occurring with respect to the development of myself, but it is like trench warfare. Individuation is a two stage process. Once seeing I am un-free I understand that I have to separate. To accomplish this task I have to find a way to structure myself. In so doing I can identify a continuum of attained levels of consciousness. I have identified the following states of consciousness I have experienced in my identity quest. These are kaleidoscopic consciousness, symbiotic consciousness, transcendent consciousness, transitional consciousness, transformational consciousness, and ego consciousness. I imagine there are additional states of consciousness that I may experience as I keep on aspiring to more integrated levels of being.[27]

02/20/75

Today a patient reintroduced coincidences. I wrote:

> I saw at a glance that there seems to be a naturalistic way to explain these striking occurrences without resort to supernatural and mystical causes. I saw the role of wish, fantasy, idealization, the need to fuse, [project final authority] magical thinking, attempts to simplify experiences, to feel special, to personalize, to externalize, to combine unconscious and conscious material. I would like to write a paper on *The Psychodynamics of Meaningful Coincidences.* Coincidences as an adaptive integrative experience . . . sweep together seemingly disparate pieces of information, past, present, overlapping logics (past/present, durational time/linear time), not me/me associations, to mention a few dichotomous primary experiences. My naturalistic theoretical shift is clearly happening in the context of an authentic salutary experience with my psychoanalyst Wittenberg. He always asks for my meanings and extends whatever I have to say. I get knowledge from him [organizing concepts, psychological tools], but I do the work of integrating it into my own direct experience.

Additional Observations Concerning Synchronicities

Synchronicities occur in a psychological state of deprivation, devitalization of the spirit, alienation, psychological gridlock, generating a wish to be meaningfully connected with or to something or someone that is solid, trustworthy, consistent, reliable, and responsive.

With W, I experience a positive resonating atmosphere that allows me to compare the one I grew up in with the one I am presently living in—day by day. As a child I felt that my family and my culture (more often than not) were talking oranges while I talked apricots. I desperately searched for meaningful communication (shared, attuned, supportive, nurturing, objective), but the (apparent) lights in the tunnels of my experience previously led only to other tunnels. I felt increasingly trapped in mazes leading only to other mazes.

How to establish meaningful connections became the raison d'être of my life and the pathway of my particular life's search. It is this opening up of all channels)streams of information) that seems to be the precondition for triggering the creative process allowing for a suspension of belief in known categories permitting a confrontation of the split off, not me, unfamiliar parts of the self. At the very same time this is happening (simultaneously) there is both an active penetration of the unknown and a passive yielding to the same unknown.

My experience of my true self is increasingly more cohesive. Thus I have no need to idealize and project my final authority onto men or women who function as substitute parents, as I am finally learning how to be my own good set of parents.

02/11/76 I Am Moving Beyond Black-White Thinking to Complexity

(I am experiencing) new uncharted territory in myself. I feel (a mixture) of excitement, hope, and optimism on one side ; and resentment, fear, and pessimism on the other. . . . I am beginning to see that the best simplification is to describe and to experience the true complexity. Joyce (1990) says in *Ulysses*: "The Longest Way Around is the Shortest Way Home."[28]

02/20/76 The Recognition of Complexity Applied to My View of Synchronicities

I understood that my self-appointed task is to bring science to bear in understanding the nature of these apparently anomalous, supposedly unmeasurable phenomena. I read and quoted the following operational definition of science. "Science is the systematic observation of natural events and conditions in order to discover facts about them and to formulate laws and principles based on these facts."[29]

In this light it was increasingly clearer to me that synchronicities occur in a particular psychological climate. It is as if an individual in this particular psychological climate opens his entire self to whatever forces there are in the world (subtle and gross) allowing himself to enter this atmosphere and resonate.

03/09/76 I Experience the Process of Deidealizing Male Authorities

Despite my intellectual knowledge that I have to separate from the negative and depressing influences of my past, I find there is no easy climb up my internal mountain. I am increasingly more aware that it is easier for me in times of stress, confusion, and complexity to project my final authority into an idealized male authority rather than for me to determine what it is I really want and what it is I really stand for, and what it is that I am prepared to do to obtain and sustain my desires.

I tell W a fantasy that he might be a master teacher—even a member of the Great White Brotherhood[30]—and that I have longed to be part of his mission. W, in characteristic fashion, denies membership in any such lofty supernatural status.

I wrote:

> If I accept W's disclaimer that he is really not a great King and that I am not his subject then we are—in fact and not in fantasy—true equals. Then if and when I experience him as a King I must of necessity be projecting my final authority onto him. That is, I give him the power to judge me. Why? Back to historical origins. . . . The difference between Freud and Jung is that Jung eventually insists that we make a connection with absolute answers that are transcendent to the self, whereas Freud takes the position in exploring the patient's unknown guided by good organizing questions, to locate the answers to his important questions in himself.

I know that I am standing on core material. I further know that I have to assume final responsibility for myself to be the integrated man I wish to be, but I am uncertain that I can ever feel equal to—not less than—my projected heroes—like my psychoanalyst.

03/11/76 Synchronicity—a Gap of 23 Months—Age 39
#17 "Fire All Around"
Immediate Situational Context:

I theorize that synchronistic phenomena are a dramatization of the need to reconcile splits in myself by reaching outside myself for (a transcendent) organizing principle that unifies. I apply these ideas to a psychodynamic understanding of a synchronicity-prone patient, BW. I conjecture that it is out of his isolation that he projects his fantasies of omnipotence onto occult forces in the hope that someone up there will notice, accept, like, intervene, encourage, support, guide, and protect him. When he does experience one or a combination of these needs being met it reinforces his belief in the actual existence of such entities as The Great White Brotherhood, invisible Master Teachers, the power of astrology, "power objects," and the like. I also have an important insight into my own character: I am hypersensitive to certain details; that is a wish for meaningful connectedness. For example: I realize that whenever I feel I am taken seriously (a rare experience) it automatically follows that I have an intense surge of expectancy. This intense feeling of expectancy strikes me as equivalent to Jung's description of "numinosity."

The Synchronicity:

I acknowledge to myself that my psychoanalyst takes me seriously along with the awareness that I am able to be increasingly more objective. I mulled these two realizations walking away from a bagel shop on 8th Street in New York City toward 5th Avenue. I speculated that, in the expectant state I was experiencing at the moment, I might well be able to predict when I would next have a synchronicity. To accomplish this task I put myself into a clear state—freeing my mind of all extraneous chatter—instructing myself to let myself be aware of the first perception that for any reason impinged on my mind catching my conscious attention. At that very moment, I looked up to see that the 8th Street bookshop (a store I had often frequented) had been gutted by a recent fire. I began feeling dizzy. I instantly associated to a fantasy I had had in the morning traveling on a bus on 14th Street going from my home to my office on 11th Street and 5th Avenue. I remembered having the fantasy that a building on the south side of the street was missing. I recalled wondering what the experience would be like of people to notice the absence of something—like the building—the presence of which they had taken for granted. Now—back at the burned-down bookstore—my perception/fantasy had become an unexpected reality. I felt dazed, bewildered, and disoriented. Walking in the direction of my office I saw and heard fire engines going in the direction of my office. I ran along following them, ending up right next door to my office.

My Reaction:

I related this experience to my having felt accepted by my analyst. This unexpected experience of truly being accepted unconditionally coincided with the wish that it should actually happen. This implies that a heightened sense of self "realness" will be experienced when the wish to be unconditionally accepted is actualized in fact. The resulting feeling is akin to ecstasy. A parallel experience in childhood would be the likely feeling that a child would have when coming back from school—eagerly greeted by his mother—that he is the most important person in the world at that particular moment in time and space.

Follow Up: A Shift in Consciousness Leads to a New Pathway

In synchronicity #18, I experience how vulnerable I am when I feel accepted by an admired authority. I lose all capacity to make critical judgments. Realizing this makes it clear that I have to continually focus on what I need, what I want, and how I really feel and think about matters that are important to me independent of whatever are the real or imagined positions of authorities in my atmosphere.

03/15/76

W believes that I tend to look to external sources to find myself rather than to sublimate and find sources located in my creative unconscious. My psychoanalysis reveals that I have had a lifelong mix up between basic issues: i.e., pleasure equals pain; and reality equals fantasy. Talk about complexity! I wrote:

> No wonder a major thematic interest in my life has been a preoccupation [obsession] with understanding the nature of reality focusing on the anomaly of meaningful coincidences (synchronicities). I have partially used my interest to force myself to learn how to distinguish reality from fantasy.

05/28/76 Progress in Keeping Myself Whole and Balanced Is Hard Won at Best

Despite a clear conceptual grasp of my core psychological problem, I can't always control my emotions. Once again I fell into what was felt to be a psychological black hole—one from which I felt I would never be able to extract myself. It appears that every step forward is met with ten steps back. Whatever progress there is in my continuing quest to "get myself together" is more like trench warfare than dropping an atomic bomb.

W suggested I read Freud's essay "Those Wrecked by Success." Freud (1916) details the psychodynamics of those patients—like me—that have an aversion to the very goal they want the most.[31] Thus it is difficult enough to strive to change bad habits, but it is even more complex to be successful only to encounter another level of complexity: that the goal that is most desired is also one that is forbidden; thus its attainment is laden with conflict.

The key to success—assuming the right to be my own final authority without shame, guilt, fear, or apology—is to continue freeing myself from the bonds that have held me back and down much like Gulliver[32] being held captive to the ground of Lilliput by a hundred thousand threads. To accomplish this task I have to experience how I am my own worst enemy—holding myself back and down from being my own good father.

08/10/76 I Am Both Excited and Afraid of the Major Changes I Have Been Making

I have the feeling that I have been here many times in the past. At times when I was facing something new—such as going to Europe on my own—I felt both eager anticipation and sheer dread. My analyst reassured me I had a right to my fears.

I wrote:

> So too, at the present time, I feel at the crossroads ready to undertake a new voyage, although this trip is an inner one. Its destination is ever deeper into my psyche. I feel there is a key here to the eventual outer expression of a form I seek to dedicate the rest of my life too. I am in search for structure.

I am grateful for the fact that I was able to search out a reliable guide and a just-right method for helping me carry out the necessary inner work on myself that I have known that I have needed to do to become the person I have longed to be.

08/18/76 I Read a Confirming Article, "Self Objects and Oedipal Objects"

In this seminal article Tolpin distinguishes between a superstructure of neurotic conflict and the central underlying pathology of structural deficits. The deficits are in self-esteem regulation, self-reliance, autonomy, and object (self) constancy. Tolpin makes the crucial point that symptom formation (the classic psychoanalytic explanation for neurosis) does not (adequately) explain deficiency illness.

Says Tolpin (1970):

> Classical explanations of hysteria and hysterical symptoms are based on the rejection of reactivated infantile oedipal strivings. . . . Threats to self-cohesion (danger of fragmentation in loss of vitality) occur as a direct consequence of traumatically frustrating empathic failures (of parents) who fail to meet minimal needs of mirroring and idealization.[33]

08/19/76 Yet Again Still One More Confirming Article, "The Psychoanalytic Revolution"

In this article I find a key to my particular complexity—how is it that my mind, alone, has not led to greater control of my emotions that too often has made me feel as if I am being swept away.

Freud's psychodynamic formula of a patient, Schreber—diagnosed as suffering from paranoia—describes its essence as contradicting the proposition I—myself a man—love my father—also a man. Freud's psychodynamic understanding of paranoia characterized by delusions of persecution obeys the formula "I do not love him"; instead I hate him. Then by projection the active ambivalent feelings become reversed: "He hates and persecutes me, which justifies the hatred I feel for him."[34]

Upon reading this I instantly understood that the intense ambivalent feelings I have had for my father were transferred to my wife and other parallel authorities. This realization explained much of what had seemed totally inexplicable, including my aversion to complexity, feeling trapped in a seemingly intractable ambivalence conflict, a fear of success, in the chronic grips of a persistent wish to be rescued, all combined with a lifelong feeling of unreality, self-doubt, and core worthlessness.

I knew that I needed to have a solid structure, but it was hard to imagine that one would ever be forthcoming. The good part was that at least I was able to experience my lack of structure with a certain degree of objective acceptance and empathy.

09/30/76 Synchronicity—a Gap of 6 Months—39 Years Old
#18 "Captains and Kings: Spinoza and Odyssey"
Immediate Situational Context:

A greatly improved summer as my overall tension eased, mainly due to an increased ability to tolerate frustration and ambivalence. There was also a notable increase in confidence, but I was still subject to what seemed to be intractable rage reactions. I had newly found energy to begin a book about Odyssey, but I needed an organizing principle to provide my book with a unifying structure. One possibility, I considered, was to combine the essence of Homer's *Odyssey* with Spinoza's *Ethics.*

In response to my telling my psychoanalyst about how difficult it is for me to find a way to organize the various Odyssey themes together, he responded simply and directly: "The answer to the creative process will come out of your unconscious. You need to be able to suspend secondary process purposeful thought and more approximate the dreamlike state while awake."

The Synchronicity:

As I was watching an adaptation of *Captains and Kings* on TV, simultaneously thinking about formulating a structure for a book about my Odyssey experience, I heard a remarkable back-to-back reference to Odyssey and Spinoza.

My Reaction:

I leaped at the conjunction of these two particularly meaningful references. Here was my organizing principle realizing that Odyssey House was my experience of Spinoza's *Ethics* dramatized. My Odyssey was essentially (a complex journey) about liberating myself from emotional bondage. I intuitively comprehended that my own personal Odyssey would not be complete until I could once and for all reconcile the opposites in myself.

Follow Up:

For the first time in my life I understood that my central problem was viewing my self and the world from the vantage point of an incohesive self. This realization explained my lifelong experience of constant oscillation and imbalance. Now at a point that I was beginning to get truly organized, I knew my path was crystal clear. This path was to continue with my psychoanalysis to grow a cohesive self and a strong ego. This to me is the pathway to transcendence and transformation on the earth plane.

05/16/77 On The Nature of Change

I realized:

> Mere words alone nor good will banish mental illness in and of themselves, nor do they create it, but what does heal over time is understanding. In my experience understanding is slow in coming. It takes considerable patience, and struggling with struggle in a combined effort to get at the details of the issue in order to thoroughly master the material at hand.

06/06/77

It is clear from my analysis that my fascination with coincidences is based on projected narcissism. I act surprised by the messages I give to myself. They are my inventions that for some reason I can't quite accept, much like a screenwriter who watches his own play and forgets he is the writer. (This experience of nonacceptance of the creative self can be seen in a dreamer's experience of his own dream. Often is the feeling of wonder expressed in the question, where did that come from?)

06/13/77 A Key Analytic Session

The central point is that my loss of identity was related to the feared mother and the feared father. I had to regress to being passive and weak in order to get the love I desired. I also had to hold my masculine aggression in check. I had to join forces with the feared aggressor (identification with the aggressor) in order to save myself. But the price I paid for appeasement was the loss of a cohesive self.

10/17/77 A Major Realization

I have been using the world—external reality—as a reflecting mirror.

01/17/78 Forty One Years Old

I identified with the lead character in the TV series called *The Prisoner (1967):*

Here is a modern hero who has been captured by an authoritarian regime that surrounds him with an atmosphere of terror. Unbending, he devises ways to adapt to his miserable circumstances with an attitude of pragmatic flexibility, always adhering to his high principles. This to me is a believable description of a person with quintessential ego strength and a lofty character.[35] I noted some progress made in my continuing attempts to strengthen my ego. I noted a better ability to act in my best self interest.

W says the goal of my therapy is to gradually take the frustrated wish to be taken care of and convert it into accepting the responsibility for taking care of myself. [This portrait characterizes my ego ideal.]

05/19/78 A Notable Acceptance of Ambivalence and Psychic Complexity

In one fell swoop I noted the two identified core problems associated with synchronicities—ambivalence and psychic complexity—are in synchronicities experienced through preoedipal consciousness as transcended and simplified. The experience of "all is one" instantly switches the focus to unity, peace, love, cooperation, perfesion and away from unsettling dualities, separation, differences, jagged edges, frustration, missed expectations, and human limitations.

Relative to synchronicities the issue for me is to understand how to make the "messages" functional. This is the issue of spelling out the steps in decoding meaningful coincidences.

My research leads me to ever-deepening descents into the origins of the self. In this connection what is explored is not the collective unconscious but is the complex layering of the psyche consisting of various levels of consciousness, preconsciousness, and personal unconscious dimensions.

I see more and more that human beings, as W has frequently stated "will use any external stimulus for their own conscious and unconscious purposes." Extending this idea: a basic principle of psychoanalysis is that any piece of psychic material will be used for defensive and adaptive purposes.

Applying these ideas to understanding the nature of synchronicities results in the following conclusion: what initially appears to be phenomena that are conceived as transcendental, archetypal, and originating from the collective unconscious may alternatively be conceived as being transitional, personal, and arising from one's personal unconscious.

I experience myself shifting from an almost exclusive preoccupation with my own processes and contents of conscious to a recognition and interest in others outside me.

01/05/81 Taking Pressure in Stride—I Experience My Core Problem

I recorded:

> I noticed that the subway system is increasingly breaking down. But I also realized that the subways are not me and that I am not breaking down. Reality pressures have always been an enormous stress and strain for me as I have often felt I would break down or break apart. My worst fantasy is that there would be a single event, like a war, or combination of critical events that would be my ruin. My analyst interpreted my fears as a discrepancy between my viewing realistic pressure as too big in comparison with my self-image of being too small. He added: this discrepancy represents a basic experience (world view) of childhood tinged with a touch of self pity.

Later On: I Reflect on How Much I Have Clearly Changed

I wrote:

> [My attitude to struggling in a new relationship is to] . . . just continue to be open and honest and see how things evolve. When I first began my journal some twenty-four years ago, the major issue was how to differentiate myself from my father. I felt no one really understood me so I tried in my writing to figure it out for myself. [I now understand what my analyst means when he says] it is time for me to throw off the coat of the helpless, lost, needy boy wanting rescue. I know what is best for me and how to go about getting it—so I'm getting on with it because to do otherwise makes no sense at all being a total waste of time. There is still a fork in the road that is expressed as I know the way to go but I still feel I am holding myself back from doing so. Will I ever release myself?

01/16/81
Synchronicity—a Gap of 5 Years and 3 Months—44 Years Old
#19 "Closing a Circuit"
Immediate Situational Context:

I am increasingly aware that the goal I want the most I tend to reject. Thus when I am under stress I have an impulse to reduce myself to helplessness. Helplessness reinforces a need and a wish for rescue from some benevolent real or imagined external force. I can see how intricately complex my psychology is at the moment. On the one hand I am aware of what I want—to feel secure, solid, and manly—however, on the other hand, I have serious doubts as to whether I can really feel this way and sustain it. My analyst says the key to significant change is being able to be objective about reality (reality test). I finally understand what it is he has been saying to me for many years.

I understand that the key to my success is to take myself seriously, but this presumes that there is a solid enough self to take. And even if there is, there is a further presumption that one feels worthy enough to believe in. I wondered as to what my first conscious experience of being alive was really like. I mulled over what it would really be like to experience this developmental reunion.

The Synchronicity:

As I was consciously mulling over the developmental origins of psychological causality wherein the child's cry is taken seriously—experienced as "I make the world react to me,"—I ran into Diane, the woman associated with the Lazarus synchronicity eighteen years ago. Upon seeing her, I realized how far I have changed since that point. It was good to see her and especially so as I had none of the feelings I had eighteen years ago when I was hungry for something meaningful to hold onto, to excite me, to feel me up. Then I was preoccupied with an all-consuming wish to be enveloped by an experience of mystical unity.

My Reaction:

I feel as if I have completely replaced mysticism with a belief in objective reality as I am finally in touch with my core self. I accept the responsibility to be my own final authority in answering such questions as what is best for me. Evidence that my changes are substantially solid is the fact that I am able to regulate my own self-esteem—fulfilling a long-sought goal of creating and utilizing my own personal golden mean—my own personal balance point.

Follow Up:

This synchronicity marks the discovery of a path midway between the frustrated wish for instantaneous transformation and a complete "throw in the towel" passive surrender. It is the awareness and personal validation that whereas significant psychological change is possible it is not revolutionary and extreme but evolutionary and incremental. "Mountain climbing" in my inner space has proceeded through inevitable barriers of resistance I have experienced as formidable obstacles to overcome. The pathway to the attainment of my priority important objective—a solid self—has been my internalization and following Spinoza's formula in leading the good life: "Anything worth accomplishing is as difficult as it is rare." This formula can be translated as the pathway to a solid self (i.e., a clear sense of identity and a sense of purpose) comes to fruition when one dedicates himself or herself to systematically struggling with struggle.

10/01/81 The Isolated Self, Causality, and the Occult

W said he now understands why the occult had such a strong attraction for me. I had a need for reassurance with hidden forces, complexity, and vagueness. In short I needed pleasure. . . . I had a desperate need to connect with some externally meaningful experience.

10/28/81 My Self, My Journal, and Synchronicities

My journal was begun as a desperate attempt to create order out of the chaos of my confused thoughts and feelings. In this light, I view my synchronicities as manifestations of my persistent attempts in struggling with struggle to create order and meaningful connections out of the fragmented pieces of my divided self.

11/21/81 In the Midst of My Psychoanalysis I Took a Long Hot Bath

In response to my analyst's suggestion from years past, I created a "perfect" environment for myself. I filled my bathtub to the top of the sides with the temperature of the water just "right." I turned off the light, lit candles, played classical music, and rested my head on a special bathtub pillow placed behind my head on the tiled walls. I felt myself totally relax and was able to empty my head of any chatter. I became aware of part of me looking inward witnessing another part of me looking out. I then became aware of the difference of my perceiving so-called "objective" experience contrasted with my interpreting my experience with a palette of feelings, sensations, thoughts, and various temporal associations of my past, present, and anticipated future.

Sitting in the hot water I was aware of my being aware—conscious of my consciousness—and how my present conscious state has traversed (evolved) through a series of alternative states of consciousness. These states of consciousness include kaleidoscopic consciousness, symbiotic consciousness, transcendent consciousness, transitional consciousness, transformational consciousness, to the present state of the beginnings of ego consciousness.

Each state of consciousness has acted like a filter through which I have organized the raw data of my experience. Or perhaps it is more accurate to say reorganize my experience. And at each point of transition, I am certain that synchronicities, at least in my case, have been markers of shifts of consciousness. Each shift of consciousness has been accompanied by a notable increase in my perceived sense of cohesion, well-being, integration of my various "selves," an increased and increasing capacity to synthesize the various "streams of information" that constitute my daily experience of being alive, and topped off with a new-found ability to take myself more seriously, harnessing my powers, and choosing, if I so desire, to direct my libido toward making meaningful connections with myself and the object world.

Summary

I have detailed the pertinent situational and psychological contexts from which the nineteen synchronicities I have deemed most important to me have been derived. These nineteen synchronicities have been the raw material for the basic formulation of my naturalistic, nonsupernatural theory of the nature of synchronicities along with some suggestions as to the uses to which they may be put, particularly in the analyst's office.

My life, of course, has not ended with the experience of the nineteenth synchronicity. There have in fact been more of them through the years. At least for me, they continue to occur at major stuck points where I have to find an accommodation—a creative solution—to what initially appears to be an intractable problem.

I have no doubt that a synchronicity is a marker that a creative solution to an otherwise intractable problem has been found. In my experience of these always impacting events, I literally experience my boundaries stretching accompanied by feelings that I am actively processing the raw data of my existence generating purposeful behavior.

In my experience there is nothing mystical or supernatural about these wondrous events. When a synchronicity is first noted, it is like sighting the appearance of the opening of a colorful spring flower. What is first noticed is the color, and the remarkable patterning and freedom of the newly appearing object. What is less noted is the fact that this colorful, free object first began its existence as a small seed that had to be nurtured with an adequate proportion of water, sunlight, and soil. The nurtured seed then had to work its way through the earth taking the form of an evolving root system. After struggling against resistance the eventual flower appears like a miracle, but in reality it is the end product of a mundane, though wondrous, natural process of slow and steady growth and development. The seed turning into a flower is indeed a major process of transformation punctuated by significant phases of incremental change.

11/19/76 My First Attempt to Describe the Process Leading to the Production of Synchronicities from a Naturalistic Perspective

I wrote:

> Coincidences [happen] all the time. The special significance [attributed] to each one of them is likely to be caused by an overestimation of a particular detail determined by the psychological need of the person at the moment.
>
> The origin for this coincidence proneness seems to be the failure to have been unconditionally accepted channeled into an intensified need and wish to make meaningful connections. The quality of this connectedness approximates the regressive experience of adults in the face of an unwanted reality wishing to reconnect to an inferred state of bliss believed to be the experience of satisfied

newborns. This inferred state of blissful consciousness has been characterized as "perfesion" [perfect ease], states of at-one-ment, nirvana, symbiosis, unity with divinity.

Whereas synchronicities do have a regressive aspect to them, my investigation indicates they are much more than regressive phenomena. They begin with the divided self passively wishing for wholeness. Then under specified conditions, they function as indicators that the self is actively questing to grow, develop, creatively problem solve, stretch its boundaries, continually integrating and persisting in evolving and expanding its consciousness.

A number of years after I wrote the above, I synthesized my ideas about a naturalistic theory of synchronicities expressed in a paper called "A Theory and Use of Meaningful Coincidences (Synchronicities)." This paper is the content of chapter 9.

III

A NEW THEORY

9

A Theory and Use of Meaningful Coincidences (Synchronicities)

THE PURPOSE OF THIS CHAPTER IS TO SCIENTIFICALLY INVESTIGATE the phenomena of meaningful coincidences (synchronicities); specifically, to determine their nature and to delineate some purposes they serve—particularly as they occur in working with some patients receiving psychoanalytic psychotherapy. It is proposed that these apparently a-causal occurrences obey laws of psychodynamic causality and are therefore determined. Further, it is proposed that the principal issues associated with synchronicities are those having to do with the development of the self as it naturally aspires to increasing expansion of individual consciousness. It is concluded that meaningful coincidences are the surface manifestations of an individual's creative process accommodating the "best" available resolution of a problem initially experienced as being trapped in a seemingly intractable psychological dilemma. From this perspective, there is nothing mystical or divine about the origin of these anomalous events. While this analysis does rob the "magic" associated with only reacting to the surface, it nevertheless affirms a wondrous appreciation for the creative capacities of each person to order his own internal and external chaos.

Implications for an Understanding of the Psychodynamics of Meaningful Coincidences

After rebutting Jung's three anticausal arguments with my own points of view, I spelled out an alternative account of the psychodynamics of synchronistic events. In this connection, I made use of Spitz's concepts of psychic organizers, particularly the smile response of the baby at about five months old; mirroring; overlapping of two modes of consciousness (durational timelessness and no spatial boundaries/linear time and bounded space); compromise formations utilizing Waelder's[1] concept of the principle of multiple functions; Noy's[2] concept of developing primary process—a hint as to how consciousness expands?—and Winnicott's[3] concepts of transitional phenomena, negotiating transitional space, and transitional objects. All of this flows together in the psychodynamics of the creative process.

I concluded:

> What is seen in synchronistic events and the awe response is the deification of one's own psychological processes. This process is perceived as magical by those who are unable to feel validated as having a cohesive self (i.e., unable to make a meaningful connection with their own personal unconscious).
>
> For those individuals who have a cohesive self it is suggested that the psychological process leading to (the production of) synchronicities is experienced as synonymous with what is commonly called the creative process. Thus people with a cohesive self have synchronicities, but their experience of synchronicities is likely to be registered by them as a by-product of their own creative unconscious and conscious.

I ended my paper with the following remarks:

> In this connection: the awe experience associated with experiencing meaningful coincidences is like the author of an epic play who somehow forgot he is the author and who in watching an enactment of his production exclaims in wonder: "Marvelous! I wonder who wrote that?" (R. Wittenberg, 1978, a personal communication).[4]

Finally, viewing meaningful coincidences as derivatives of the personal unconscious, taking the form of projected transitional objects, supports Freud's conclusion regarding occult phenomena:

> The differences between myself and the superstitious person are two: first, he projects outwards a motivation which I look for within; secondly, he interprets chance due to an event, while I trace it back to a thought. But what is hidden from him corresponds to what is unconscious for me (Freud, 1919, *The Uncanny*).[5]

That was nine years ago. The following material is new.

In part, I used Jahn's papers *On the Quantum Mechanics of Consciousness, With Applications to Anomalous Phenomena*, and *The Science of the Subjective*[6] as a guide to what is new with my continuing work. Jahn stated:

TABLE 9.1
The Common Structure of Synchronistic Phenomena

The Subjective Event	*Nexus*	*The Objective Event*
The Intrapsychic	The Connecting Matrix Linking Principle (Causal?) (Acausal?)	The Interpersonal

> Some attempt to represent the experiences of human consciousness as it turns inward towards its center, rather than outward toward its center, rather than outward towards its environment [might] be a worthwhile step.

Responding to Jahn's challenge, table 9.1 is a diagram of the psyche (internal reality) associated with the production of meaningful coincidences, otherwise known as synchronicities (a class of anomalous phenomena).

While all synchronicities are likely to have idiosyncratic meanings, nevertheless they share a common structure. A is associated with internal reality or subjective experience (intrapsychic). A′ is associated with external reality or objective reality (interpersonal). If one views intrapsychic reality together with interpersonal reality, the resulting combination may be thought of as a "systems perspective" of reality.

The Subjective Matrix

This next section will focus on the nature of the subjective, intrapsychic matrix. Following is an outline of the salient contents, structures, and their interrelationships that appear to be most relevant to the production of these anomalous events. These include the contents of psychological inner space, the structures of inner space, some interrelationships between contents and structures, and some implications toward understanding the production of meaningful coincidences.

The Contents of Psychological Inner Space

The contents of psychological inner space are physical sensations, feelings, thoughts (fantasies), intuitions, and judgments.

The Structures of Psychological Inner Space

While there are a number of models of the psyche, the one that seems to me to be the most inclusive of the relevant facts and the most exclusive of extraneous material is that of Freud's structural theory.

The following is an overview of the central organizing concepts comprising the essence of the structural theory.

The Id

The id is a reservoir of basic instincts which may be broken down into two: libido (love—binding—moving toward fusion) and aggression (extension in space moving against—in the service of separation and differentiation). The id may be inherently strong or weak, seeks immediate discharge, is expressed in fantasy and/or in actions, and may be allowed free sway on the one hand to actively squelched (suppression, repression) on the other. The id is under the sway of the pleasure principle that asserts "I want what I want when I want it" and "I will tolerate no frustration."

The Superego

The superego is representative of "the law" (shoulds/should nots) which is internalized in the developing child and becomes the voice of moral authority. The superego ranges from primitive to mature, moderate to rigidly punitive, and in some cases is missing altogether. The superego is the representative of inevitable limitations. It often says "No" to the id. It is out of the clash of I want vs. you can't have it or can't have it now that the ego is born.

Note:

Between the forces of id and superego, internal reality is characterized by a state of seemingly never-ending psychological conflict. Out of the inevitable clash between the desires of the id and the restrictions of the superego another psychological structure, referred to as the ego, is born.

The Ego

The ego (the voice of reason) is the internal traffic cop which mediates the desires of the id with the real or imagined restrictions of the superego. The ego is under the sway of the reality principle which assesses the realistic possibility/probability of obtaining desired gratification in the context of real or imagined prohibitions. The ego may be profitably viewed as being globally ego strong to ego weak.

Further, the ego may be broken down into a defensive ego, which is the repository of defense mechanisms whose function it is to protect the system from psychological overload (i.e., panic anxiety). Defenses range from primitive (denial, projection) to sophisticated (sublimation).

Along with the defensive ego are the autonomous ego functions, whose responsibility is to connect the whole person with external reality. Among the autonomous ego functions are thinking, organizing, and synthesizing. Under certain conditions the autonomous ego, initially thought to be conflict free, becomes conflicted itself.

Current psychological mapping suggests that it is profitable to include the self as a separate psychological structure alongside the id, ego, and superego. Previously, what is now referred to as the self was considered to be part of the ego.

The Self

The self is operationally defined as something solid at the core of an individual that endures in the midst of internal or external confusion. It is also the prime moving force in the individual that would commonly be thought of as the person's vital essence. Using Kohut[7] and Spitz[8] as guides, the self is thought to grow and develop out of an undifferentiated matrix.

According to Spitz, the self spontaneously grows to the degree that the newborn develops the capacity to tolerate increasing dosages of frustration. Thus the self learns to sustain continuity despite internal and external threats to the integrity of its being-ness.

Note: It is important to note that this is but one view of the self.

In this view, the self ranges from cohesive to incohesive to practically nonexistent. The self can be strong (able to remain constant, steady, and continuous even under great internal and external pressure) to highly vulnerable (easily fragmented, decimated, destroyed, with little capacity to bounce back).

How Content and Structures Interact

According to classical depth psychology, there are six concepts utilized to comprehensively understand how content is processed through form. These six concepts are the structural (id, superego, ego), the topographic or the iceberg model, the dynamic, the economic, the genetic, and the adaptive.

The topographic depth psychology model (also referred to as the iceberg model) of the psyche asserts that like an iceberg, psychic productions may be best viewed as originating out of unconscious experience passing through preconscious to consciousness. Consciousness may be thought of as the tip of the iceberg signifying "that experience" of which we are most aware and focused upon at any given time.

The dynamic point of view asserts that the contents of consciousness (feelings, thoughts, sensations, intuitions, fantasies, judgments, actions, observed as verbal and nonverbal behavior) are actively processed through the structures of the id, superego, ego, and self. This processing is dynamic (kinetic) as differentiated from static and fixed.

The economic point of view asserts that there is a certain quantity of psychic energy associated with this processing which is either used synergistically (like an efficient motor that hums) or constricted (ranging from bottled up to short circuited, as in neurotic or psychotic personalities).

The adaptive point of view asserts that all psychic behavior serves knowable conscious and unconscious purposes including behavior which seems most random or apparently nonsensical. Thus, all behavior is considered to be an attempt (though perhaps an inefficient one) to resolve a psychological conflict.

The genetic point of view points backwards to the historical origin of all behavior. It also takes into account the fact that growing and developing individuals pass through identifiable psychological stages of development (Erikson,[9] Freud,[10] Spitz,[11] Mahler,[12] Piaget,[13] Kohlberg,[14] et al.).

Implications of This Particular Model of the Psyche for the Production of Synchronicities

This model of the mind is one which is highly complex and multilayered. It is also one that appreciates psychic origins, thus emphasizing determinism, but also takes into account intentionality (purpose), hence teleology. (Proponents of this theoretical perspective believe that behavior is both caused and purposeful. Thus there is a joint acceptance of both classical causality and "modern" teleological causality (the genetic plus the adaptive points of view).

Acceptance of this multiple point of view model of the psyche suggests that contents processed through a given individual's structure (or lack of structure) is idiosyncratic (relative) to the individual in question, and is therefore constantly in motion (capable of development).

The idiosyncratic ways in which a given person will attempt to organize his chaos, utilizing his particular complex of contents of consciousness processing through his particular structures, is the operational definition of psychodynamics.

In this view, the more a person is aware of (cathects, makes an abstract concept come alive) his own unique complex of contents and structures, and the ways in which they work together, is an operational definition of degrees of consciousness.

Extending this idea, a person who is increasingly aware of his psychodynamics (both in the sense of understanding how he got to be the person he is, as well as utilizing this information for making increasingly better informed judgments) might be thought of as being conscious of being conscious (consciousness of consciousness).

In this view, consciousness is neither static nor equal in all human beings; instead it is more or less developed and developing and is, therefore, capable of expanding.

Summary

Developmental psychology indicates that there is a layering of the psyche ranging from the most primitive preverbal sensory realm of consciousness to the most highly evolved integrated synthetic consciousness. Analyses of thousands of people suggest that if the preverbal child could share his view of reality, he might well describe it in William James's terms that the world appears to be "a busy blooming buzzing confusion of sensation,"[15] of which it is each person's lifelong task to order his own chaos. This task might operationally be defined as proactive meaning-making.

Undeveloped (preoedipal/pre-verbal/unmediated) experience is characterized as stimulus-reactive (S-R) reflexive responses, differentiated from developing (oedipal/verbal/mediated) experiences characterized as stimulus-organism-response (S-O-R) reflective responses.

Each level is associated with its own organization of consciousness and may singularly and collectively be regarded as a filtering system allowing in or screening out what it deems as significant stimuli (raw data or information) utilized in generating meaningful connections.

The realm of Being (A) is associated with the first two years of life (preoedipal: preverbal), hence preconscious at best and probably mainly unconscious experience. According to Spitz,[16] Kohut,[17] et al., the first two years, particularly the first, are crucial to the development of a cohesive self.

In order to grow a cohesive self structure, the child has to learn how to bear increasing dosages of frustration and other so-called negative affects. Among these negative affects are anxiety, depression, ambiguity, confusion, ambivalence, not knowing, uncertainty, increasing complexity, and the like.

TABLE 9.2
Realms of Experience

Being	*Point of Transition*	*Doing*
A Passive Self Task: Attain Object and Self Constancy	B	C Active Self Task: Attain Self-Directed Actions

Tolerating increasing dosages of frustration leads to the automatic development of a cohesive self. Failure to begin to process the capacity to tolerate frustration means that the chronologically advancing child is devoid of the psychological prerequisites for spontaneously growing a cohesive self. This results in a chronological grownup, but who at the time, is psychologically unable to regulate his self-esteem. This problem has crucial implications for the quality of life for people suffering from this difficulty.

Those who are unable to regulate their self-esteem (irrespective of intelligence and drive) are utterly dependent upon the object world to regulate their self-esteem for them. To the preoedipal child (under 3 years old) the object world functions as a reflecting mirror.

Thus, their self-esteem rises or falls in direct proportion to the degree to which they experience a harmonious connection to the projected authority(s) of the moment. If perceived worthy by the projected authority(s) of the moment, they will correspondingly feel all is right with themselves and the world, whereas, if perceived as disapproved of, they will feel depressed sometimes to the point of feeling crushed by an internalized negative judgment of unworthiness. In the grips of perceived negative feedback they often experience themselves as if they were to suddenly plummet into a deep hole and lose whatever hard-won identity they have been able to muster.

Successfully negotiating the developmental task leading to the spontaneous growth and development of a cohesive self is a two-step process technically referred to as (1) object constancy leading to (2) self constancy. It is in the realm of being that the central issues of object and self constancy must be initiated and worked through as necessary conditions for a cohesive self to form and to develop. An explanation of object and self constancy follows.

Overview of Object and Self Constancy

Children are under the sway of the pleasure principle. That is, they want what they want when they want it and brook no frustration. When the mother's response matches the child's desire, the child experiences a state of blissful at-one-ment with the "good" mother. This state of being is, of course, ideally desirable but doomed to inevitable aperiodic disruptions, as no "mother" can be quite so perfectly understanding all the time.

When the imperfect authority figure (usually the mother) inevitably fails to provide the expected "perfect" response, her child experiences the missed expectation (disappointment) with frustration and anger. The child now experiences the same angelic good mother of the recent past as presently frustratingly withholding, pain inducing, and therefore bad. It is normal for the disappointed child to turn his derived fury against the frustrating "object" usually in the form of actively hating and or rejecting the perceived "bad" parent.

Object constancy is the capacity of a person to experience the frustratingly "withholding" object as bad, hated, and "killed off," yet, somehow, at the same time, managing to tolerate the destructive negative affect enough to be able to repair the broken circuit, thus emotionally reconnecting with the frustrating but loved parental object. Self constancy refers to the same situation, except that the person who falls short of his expectations of himself is able to be disappointed without "completely" destroying himself (psychic or literal suicide), keeping solid, and maintaining focus and fortitude.

Thus the realm of being is primarily concerned with growing and preserving the integrity of the self structure. The "job" of the baby is just to be—required only to be given to in the form of recognition, validation, and unconditional acceptance. In the countless small but cumulative daily disappointments (frustrations) of normal living, the developing child hopefully learns how to experience a missed expectation (disappointment) as only a disappointment and not as a sign that the end of his world (complete destruction of loving feelings toward his main connections or to himself) has actually come about.

Successfully negotiating the tasks of object and self constancy leads directly to the growth and development of a cohesive self. An operational definition of a cohesive self is the capacity of a disappointed person to experience internal and external cohesion while still remaining solid at the core. Attaining self constancy is a necessary condition to enable the developing child to move from overreacting to glitches (like a paramecium might react to a live wire) to being able to reflect upon them in a balanced, even manner. A person, in this state, is able to shift from automatically reacting to acting from within.

Summary

The psychological process of self-esteem regulation has been highlighted. This process starts with newborns reacting automatically and emotionally to internal and external stimuli which frustrate them. As they gradually learn how to bear increasing dosages of "negative" affect (including frustration, anxiety, depression, ambiguity, confusion etc.) they learn to delay, and think through problems so as to be able to make increasingly more effective problem solving choices. Toward this end, attaining self-constancy is a necessary condition to enable the developing child to move from simply reacting to glitches (like a paramecium might react to a live wire) to being able to reflect upon them.

Meaningful Coincidences

Now, finally, we come to the relevance of this discussion to the topic of meaningful coincidences. The development of a cohesive self, by learning to bear increasing dosages of frustration leading to object constancy and then self constancy is, I believe, the core psychological process involved in what speculative philosophers are describing when they refer to a human being's need to order their personal chaos. The psychological progression from automatically reacting to being able to act from within is, I believe, a statement about the existence and development of consciousness.

In this light there is, then, a necessary connection between the attained level of psychological development and the degree of attained development of an individual's consciousness.

This means that if a person has failed to negotiate the tasks of either object constancy and/or self constancy, attempts by them to order their personal chaos will be necessarily filtered through the predominance of that state of being associated with the attained level of incomplete self development. Thus it is not coincidental, in the analyses of adults who are seen to be fixated (developmentally stuck) in the stage of preoedipal development, to observe them predictably preoccupied with fusion wishes and fantasies echoing the theme and variation of continuously needing and searching for uninterrupted at-one-ment (fusion) experiences.

Thus reported psychological conflicts centering on derailed dialogues, and attempts to mend broken relationships (either with the object world or with the self), are the norm. Additionally, such people are very concerned with issues of essences and ultimates expressed as a preoccupation with binary opposites including those of keeping the faith/faithlessness; trust/mistrust; hope/hopelessness; persistence/collapsing; and cathecting meaningful relationships vs. cynically throwing cold water on even the idea of having, let alone sustaining, meaningful connections.

Filters of Experience

It is suggested that each of the above modes of experiencing (individually and collectively) be viewed as filters through which the raw data of experience is selected and organized. In this perspective, each mode, singularly and in combination, has its own conscious and unconscious organizing concepts which may be expected to filter the raw data of experience in predictable ways. If this idea is extended to attempts to understand the nature and function of consciousness, it is hypothesized that consciousness is actively dynamic (not static) and ranges from an undifferentiated sensory base, gradually to quickly, expanding into ever increasing states of awake and aware. The penultimate state of awake and aware might be thought of as consciousness of consciousness.

With respect to the way in which connections are made, evidence indicates that it is done so by means of primary process linkages. Primary process logic is akin to the Salvador Dali painting *Time Bending*. In this painting there is a large pocket watch that seems to have melted and thus would be incapable of functioning; yet, at the same time, there is the sense that somehow it is still able to do so despite apparent linear logical impossibility.

Considering time and space (the mediums in which cause and effect are conceptualized), there is a radical departure from conventional scientific causality. For the baby there is no such reality as a sense of time. There is, instead, a sense of timelessness, no clock time, no awareness of a past, present, and/or future, but in its place only play or vacation time. There is also no sense of clear boundaries as, for example, being able to distinguish internal from external reality (differentiating all that is in the body, "me," from all that is outside the body, "not me"), but rather, it is a sense of fusion particularly with the primary mother. (In an important experiment at New York University it was concluded that the core concept dominating the inferred unconscious of the year one baby is "My Mother and I Are One."[18]) In the light of these findings it seems fruitful to refer to this realm of preoedipal experience as durational consciousness.

Oedipal/Linear Consciousness (three–seven years)

The oedipal mode of consciousness organizes chaos utilizing the organizing concepts (psychic filters) of linear time and bounded space (conventional causality). The language used to express cause and effect linkages is often characterized as scientific, rational, objective (exclusively of the intellect). The logic of this form of consciousness is governed by laws of secondary process. Time is thought of as clock time with a clear sense of past, present, and future. Space is clearly demarcated as defining and limiting one object from another as in the differentiation of inside from outside. Preoedipal consciousness is characterized by unmediated linkages (S-R) reactive responses to stimuli, whereas oedipal consciousness is characterized by the beginnings of mediated (S-O-R) reflective linkages.

Oedipal consciousness is also associated with the realm of doing as differentiated from the preoedipal realm of being. In this realm of consciousness desires converted into ideas are now galvanized into proactivity toward the attainment of a desired goal.

Thus passive wishes of the preoedipal state (give me) is converted into active intentionality in the doing oedipal stage of consciousness. (Bear in mind that the categories of being and doing are not absolutely black and white distinctions but are better thought of as a continuum.)

Summary: Implications of Alternative State of Consciousness (Pre-Oedipal: Oedipal Being-Oedipal Doing)

In a given individual at any one time (past the age of two years) there exists not one consciousness (linear) but rather two (linear and durational) expressed in the form of two distinct logical processes. One process is usually more predominant than the other. Additionally, these two logics may be either independent of each other or more or less overlapping. An overlapping (blending) of consciousness *a* (durational) and consciousness *b* (linear) results in a synthetic or tertiary consciousness having its own unique stamp and coloration when placed upon the raw data of experience. It is conjectured that meaningful coincidences are an external manifestation of an overlapping of durational and linear consciousness.

Fertile Conditions for the Appearance of Synchronistic Phenomena

Research has established that synchronistic phenomena are intimately associated with attempts to resolve psychological problems. What has not been done is an analysis of the specific nature of the problems associated with the production of synchronistic phenomena. Following is an attempt to do so.

The first issue is to be clear about the nature of a psychological problem. Psychological problems are experienced when a person either (a) tries to initiate or sustain some activity (mental or physical) but is thwarted, or (b) tries to stop some ongoing activity but is thwarted. In other terms, psychological problems are operationally defined as the inability to continue smooth functioning in either state of positive or negative inertia having encountered a discontinuity (stuck point, glitch) in experience.

In a problem solving model of learning, it is assumed that people prefer a state of balance (homeostasis) to imbalance. When the balance is markedly upset, a need is generated for redressing the grievance (process of adaptation). Provided a person has access to thinking through a problem, there will be an attempt to assimilate an answer, searching for relevant past experience to be used as a model for current problem solving. This is equivalent to pouring new wine into old bottles (taking the substance of the present problem and fitting it into a familiar structure for the purposes of applying what was learned from the past to solve the present problem).

When assimilation fails to work, as when the present presents a unique challenge to the person in question, there then is a need for a creative solution (an accommodation). New wine is put into a new bottle (taking the substance of the present problem and fitting it into a new structure—a creative solution.)

In this light it is interesting to examine the consciousness of presynchronicity prone individuals.

Note: The following examples of synchronicities and the contexts in which they are embedded are culled from detailed session notes of some patients receiving psychoanalytic psychotherapy.

Contextual Analyses of Meaningful Coincidences

The quality of the psychological stuckness or gridlock is dependent upon the attained level of the psychological development of a given individual. If the gridlock occurs in a person who is stuck in a preoedipal developmental stage (years one and two), the experience of dead lock will be one of fundamental physical/psychological survival (preservation of being). If the point of stuckness is experienced by an individual at a higher level of psychological development, the stuckness will be characterized by issues of intentionality, focusing, initiating, executing, and following through—giving ideas substance (issues of doing).

Here is a representative example of presynchronicity consciousness of a patient stuck in the preoedipal stage of psychic development.

In her present state of consciousness C feels as if she is in touch with what is real but is unable to sustain it. Thus she often finds himself shifting from clarity to confusion, turning 180 degrees in an instant. "It is one thing to have the courage of my conviction when I am in my right mind; but what do I do when I experience myself as mindless?" When in a state of mindlessness, she feels as if there is nothing, she is nothing. At such points, unable to access her own will, her frustration turns to rage, which is turned back onto herself, eventually converting to panic anxiety, creating unbearable tension, and culminating in explosive hysteria.

(Note the sense of desperation, feeling utterly stuck in the psychic state of the moment, unable to utilize any of her powers to free herself of overwhelming "negative" ego states. She feels as if she is in the grips of external and internal forces that are beyond her control.)

C details vivid memories of childhood when she was subjected to extreme physical and psychological abuse. Whatever she did resulted in stinging criticism. To survive she had to deny her own sense of reality, pretending that decidedly abnormal conditions were normal. "All roads led to bad, mad, sad, ineffectualness."

All she wanted to do was to curl up in a ball and go to sleep, but that was dangerous as well. Eventually this nonstop suppression of her natural self eroded her spirit causing wide splits in her sense of self and a devitalization of spirit at her core. (I noted that at this time she was beginning to experience that of which heretofore she had only been partially aware.)

It was now clearly established that it was difficult for C to confront distasteful external realities. Thus, when feeling put upon, disappointed or angry at some other person's attitude or behavior toward her, she denied their part, instead feeling as if she is somehow to be blamed for creating a conflict. To survive she blocks out, denies, dissociates her ever present horror story, coupled with a confusion of perpetual uncertainty as to what she is responsible for, from that which is independent of herself.

In this context, it should come as no surprise that she has had a learning deficit all of her life, selectively unable to concentrate. "If I am lucky I will get caught up in the magic of the day by erasing 'the horror' until that time comes back again."

At a point during the session the researcher mentioned the fact that when Jung was three years old, his mother was committed to an asylum which left his father bitter. (Thus the founder of synchronicities has an intimate, traumatic connection with the years 2 and 3.)

C's Synchronicity

As soon as I mentioned the numbers 2 and 3, C immediately related a dream of the previous night. She is in a room. Someone comes in and gives her the numbers 238 or 328. One of these combinations is supposed to be G's room—227-268 (G is her therapist).

C tries to get to G's room despite encountering many obstacles. She says she feels like a small girl and has to reach up high and touch them to figure out which number is which. She has a clear mission to get to G. But on the way, she encounters many difficulties (these are both real and of her own construction for the purposes of the dream). I associate to myself that she is talking about always feeling in between: one half in and one half out. C is wedged between being born and dying; to be or not to be; dead and/or alive; between her mother/father; between her parents/and herself; between the unconscious wish to be dependent and her dread and self hatred of it; between her wish to be autonomous and her fears she will be discovered as a fraud and so on in all areas of her life. She seems caught in a psychological cleft stick of seemingly unsolvable binary black/white, all or nothing dead locks. She easily gets short circuited, drained of all of her libido, feeling utterly stuck, trapped, zero pointed, devitalized at the core; nothing solid, either external or internal to hang on to; stuck between preoedipal consciousness and oedipal consciousness.

In the dream her friend is taking her around a mall. C drifts into a shop and sees an intricate little mechanical pig. It is amazing but frightening. It comes alive, opens up and splits apart. She wants to send it to a child, so she hands the salesperson $20.00 expecting change. Instead of the change she gets back a book of coupons worth $50.00. She is outraged wanting her money not the coupons. Once again C is frustrated beyond belief. Then she realizes she is late for her appointment with G. It is now 1:30 and the session was scheduled for 10:00. She panics. She goes to an office and asks for help to locate G.

This is when they give her the numbers 238 or 328. Her friend wants to go down the escalator, but C needs to go to see G in a different direction. She is stymied, but instead of feeling hopelessly caught in the horns of a dilemma, she uncharacteristically chooses to take a position, spontaneously saying to herself, "to hell with her, I'll meet up with her later." She then goes down a long tunnel confronting additional obstacles along the way to finally get to G.

Postscript to C's Synchronicity

I wonder if she is talking about her experience of rapprochement at 2 1/2? Something always went wrong. She is cheated, or dismissed, or brushed off or ignored. All of this makes her feel crazy and stirs up hysteria. She grew to hate normal conflict and would easily short circuit at even the hint of it. What would and should be a relatively innocuous problem for most people has turned out for C to be a matter of life and death stirring up seemingly unsolvable internal and external conflicts. In an instant her whole physical and psychological systems can freeze up, which she experiences as a no choice, no exit, "terrorizing" state of affairs. In such states (frequently stirred up) she feels "trapped for life."

At the very instant she chose to go her own way, leaving her friend on the escalator, C believed that all might be lost because of her choice to go her own way. But uncharacteristically, C let her desire to see G override her intense separation anxiety and fear of abandonment.

C appeared to make a true autonomous choice despite anticipated dangers. This uncharacteristic action was interpreted to be a significant development. It is known that a novel act in a dream usually means that the person is capable of doing the same act when conscious, but awareness of the fact is initially in a preconscious state. When awakened from the dream, the change in attitude had yet to be experienced consciously.

C associated more to the dream: “Obstacles every step of the way . . . [always] experiencing ultimate frustration.” Perhaps here is a key: To survive, C has had to endure whatever frustrations she encounters or else she dies. “No way out,” “I have nowhere to go . . . no other purpose—I don’t know where I came from or where I am to go.”

It truly seemed to C that she was not born of this earth, rather, that she was a deposited alien who has no earthly history nor shares in any of its rewards and purposes. Living in a foreign world her existence is almost completely devoid of meaningful connectedness and pleasurable significance. (This is how she felt as a child, and by force of negative aversive conditioning this same feeling of estrangement has persisted until this day.)

C feels that what is left is nothing and concludes that “it’s all my fault.” I indicated that her “nothing” is filled with terror, guilt, rage and the like. “I have no mind—and all is lost.”

This statement is the quintessence of despair, one short step from suicide. As all attempts to find herself were thwarted at every turn—totally blocked—all she could anticipate for certain was predictable frustration. As a result of suppression and then repression of her natural self she gave up expecting to have any faith, trust, hope, love, significance, libido, meaningful connections.

Thus a life devoid of meaningful connectedness has culminated in a sense of utter futility and cynicism that is dramatically expressed in the form of a repetitive organizing question she often asks herself: “Why hope, why get out of bed?”

Her experience that both her inside reality and external reality are “nothing” (no-thing-ness—without substance) being the major symptom of her central problem, the cure then, is to fill the insignificant nothing with a significant something. In this light she suffers from an impoverishment of spirit needing an effective “spiritual psychology” equivalent to cure her.

In a paper called “The Psychodynamics of Spirituality,” Williams the researcher locates the psychological origins of spirituality in the year one experience of the newborn child. This is the area that is central for the baby to either obtain or fail to obtain a cathexis with basic trust, faith, hope, love, the capacity to persist, and the beginnings of making meaningful connections with the object world.[19]

A child begins to cathect these vital experiences to the degree to which he/she is unconditionally accepted, i.e., loved without strings attached. Thus the “job” of the baby is essentially passive—that is, to be loved. If the child experiences enough love he/she will spontaneously grow a cohesive self structure (solid identity). Failure to experience enough love obviates the natural growth and development of a cohesive self.

C concluded the session saying: "I can't pursue my own mind—my own goals [an autonomous self], one who can take pleasure in his own choices." G replied: "Yes, and there you have why you came into treatment, why you stay, and what you want to accomplish."

C notes: "If cumulous clouds of terror weren't bad enough, there is also intense guilt for being late." She associates to the dream. "I am older now. Three years old then jumps to 15 or 16 years old—a variation on the same theme. I feel unequal to everyone. I can't see the numbers up high. If I feel them I will know what they are. I feel caught in a mysterious maze. The familiar becomes unfamiliar. I couldn't find you. I had to ask for directions to find your room. I became lost and frightened."

The researcher concluded that C is now more conscious of the intricate process that happens in her internal reality, intimately affecting her outside reality by blocking the expression of her natural self. This blocking prevents her from initiating and sustaining meaningful connections with herself and others.

Note: In retrospect, it is seen that what at first was thought to be a true autonomous choice may have been in fact less. So, as she was also frightened to show up late to see G, nevertheless—with respect to the analysis of synchronistic happenings—this session marked a major shift in this patient's consciousness as she was finally able to get outside her material by cathecting experientially that which she is really up against. (Soldiers in battle may be killed if exposed, but while still alive they are better off knowing the size, position, and other salient details of the enemy than being blanketed by an omnipresent fog.)

A Second Example: Presynchronicity Consciousness of a Patient Struggling to Maintain a Cohesive Sense of Himself The Case of D

D's present situational context has to do with his heretofore experienced attitudes about disappointing others versus himself As his identity has been based on others' opinion of him, the idea, let alone the act, of disappointing important people has been a potential threat to his self-esteem.

This has been so because D has equated disappointment with withdrawal of love. And withdrawal of love, by a love object, has been experienced as a loss of his own identity. It is as if he has felt that without a continuing experience of at-one-ment with the love object of the moment he would quite literally die of a broken heart. Therefore, whenever disappointment has entered the picture, D has tried to avoid directly dealing with it at all costs. At such "danger points" he has tended to break connections literally by leaving the scene or by cutting off his feelings.

D's disappointment allergy is a symptom of an inability to regulate his self-esteem—that is, it is virtually impossible for him at the present time to experience himself as his own final authority. To grow a cohesive self he must first experience himself as worthy to have one. D, aware of his problem, describes his therapeutic task in the following way. "To have self-worth, I have to trust myself or I choose on the basis of avoiding a lesser fear than a greater fear—the fear of abandonment or fear of hurting someone I love."

Everything is now up for grabs as the first assumptions about his core attitudes have been successfully challenged in his therapy resulting in his facing those feelings he automatically avoided. But, in squarely facing them at present, he feels trapped between untenable alternatives.

D reacts to these feelings of entrapment with intense frustration. The frustration stirs anger which in turn is turned back on himself culminating in feelings of depression, depletion, futility, and low self-esteem. It is as if he is surrounded by a psychological wall that bars him from moving in any direction: forward, backwards, sideways, or even remaining in idle.

This fundamental stuckness may be thought of as psychological gridlock equivalent to Jung's concept of debasement. For D, to stay or to leave threatens him with a loss of identity. Thus perched midway between the untenable past and a fear of the unknown future, D is in the midst of what might be referred to as a BB experience (the midpoint of a creative process of psychological transformation). (See Table 9.3.)

D's Synchronicity

"Now comes a situation where I am forced to be disappointing."

D's Reaction to This Synchronicity

D is impressed how life conspires to present material that is absolutely on mark with respect to the psychological issue at hand, "as if fate were constantly presenting tests in the great laboratory of real life. . . . Life seems to arrange for pertinent events to occur. Last session I could have had potentially disappointing news. The difference is that instead of us talking about it in the abstract it now becomes a very real vital event."

I asked him about his reaction to this and other synchronous events. He said it was acknowledgment of some of the messiness of life. He is interested not so much in how they arrive but in what can be learned from them. In this case he feels he has to make a choice. Why now? He answered: "we create in our own lives what we need . . . I needed to understand this more and come to terms with it—and will continue to until I face it and move through it or I won't progress."

Discussion: Parallels in the Presynchronicity Consciousness of the Two Examples

Contextual analysis of the presynchronicity consciousness of the two examples C and D reveals parallel contexts. Both C and D found themselves caught on the horns of an unsolvable dilemma—irretrievably stuck in the middle of a binary lock, causing each of them intense personal distress.

These conflicts are experienced as deadlocks (existential facts of life) because each and every conceived-of alternative solution feels inadequate to resolve the problem of the moment. Thus C and D both felt squeezed between the vice of what appeared to be two mutually exclusive attitudes, ideas, fantasies, actions. It is as if each person was a hero in a movie serial who suddenly finds himself in a steel chamber with no visible way out. Bad enough he is trapped. Worse is when the walls start to implode, threatening the hero with death by crushing.

Both C and D initially experience the deadlock with a sense of helplessness and hopelessness. In preoedipal consciousness this feeling is one of despair, perhaps best thought of as a zero point. What in inner space is referred to as a stuck point or psychological zero point might in speculating about the nature of outer space be parallel to the concept of a black hole. It is not unusual for people experiencing the zero point (such as C and D) to imagine they are going to implode, leading to catastrophic annihilation.

The Stuck Point: Psychological Gridlock

There are essentially two different and opposing attitudes people have with respect to being stuck between two apparently mutually exclusive feelings, ideas, principles, etc. One is despairing—and giving up—waiting to be rescued; the other is hope affirming—holding firm—proactively wishing to find some creative way out of the apparent deadlock.

The fact of a passive or active attitude to the perceived zero point has important ramifications with respect to the production of meaningful coincidences. While psychological gridlock is a necessary condition for the production of meaningful coincidences, it is this researcher's observation that it is not a sufficient condition.

For a meaningful condition to arise out of psychological gridlock there must at some point in the process be a proactive attitude to find some novel solution to the seemingly unresolvable stuck point. This means that while the subject may initially—and for a long time after—be in the grips of despair, believing he is a victim of crushing forces beyond his control (passive attitude), only if and when there is an active wish to initiate a process to change the deadlock will a synchronicity occur.

Summary

While all synchronicities examined by the researcher are embedded in contexts in which the subject experiences him/herself as hopelessly trapped in the middle of two seemingly mutually exclusive binaries, there are two fundamental attitudes to this state of affairs. The first attitudinal reaction is usually one of depression and passivity. The second attitudinal reaction is a combination of depression and passivity shifting sooner or later into an active wish to find a way out of the deadlock at all costs. This combined response to a state of psychic imbalance is to initiate a process whereby balance can be restored. This process is characterized by a proactive attempt to problem solve. I believe that this mixture of basic stuckness experienced as depression combined with a proactive wish to find an adequate freeing solution is the psychological soil from which synchronicities flower.

The Psychodynamics of Synchronistic Phenomena

My findings indicate that all examined presynchronistic contexts are similar in that they reflect a person who has a felt sense of imbalance seeking an elusively rebalancing resolution. It is proposed that this need for redress of imbalance initiates a process whereby failure at assimilating a solution changes to accommodating a creative solution.

It is further proposed that the central psychodynamics of this creative solution consists of an overlapping of two distinct forms of consciousness, preoedipal/primary process/durational and oedipal/secondary process/linear. The combination of these two different forms of consciousness takes the form of a synthetic or tertiary consciousness that is able to find an alternative solution to the seemingly opaque problem. Analogously, this is like the trapped person in the steel room either finding or creating a door to escape. Other names for this dialectic of experience might be psychodynamic consciousness, synthetic consciousness, and/or instinctual consciousness.

The negative vs. positive set of attitudes with respect to the stuck point occurs on two levels of experience (being and doing) and may be illustrated in Table 9.3 outlining the process of psychological transformation.

TABLE 9.3
Diagram of the Creative Process Implied in the Psychodynamics of Synchronistic Phenomena

A	*Nexus (B)*	*A´ = (C)*
Subjective Matrix	Some form of causality/acausality Intervening variables yet to be specified	Parallel Objective Event
AB	B	BC
	ABBC	
	b	
	b	

BB is the midpoint of a transformative experience. At this point it feels to the initiate as if all (his whole life) is up for grabs. There is an altered state(s) due to the fluidity and newness of significant changes going on. This is also a time when there is an overlapping of two states of consciousness:

(1) durational consciousness

Durational consciousness is dominated by the fantasy of at-one-ment—perfusion (perfect ease)—all harmony—no conflict (frustration free) perfection.

(2) linear consciousness

Linear consciousness dominated by a rational or mental feeling that all has its certain place—all is understandable in the form of abstract concepts.

The blending of the two states of consciousness forms a tertiary, synthetic consciousness in which the person is in touch with a mix of often contradictory feelings and mixed thoughts—the whole mix being experienced as complexity with all of its attendant uncertainties and ambiguities and unknowns.

The B, BB, b, b, points

The B point is the area of transition midway between A (the subjective event) connecting with A´ (the parallel event).

The bb point is the exact crossover point between A and A´ (where A´ = AB – BC).

It is at the bb point where the person experiences both an overlap of intense frustration felt as a triad of helplessness/hopelessness/along with a burst of creative energy taking the form of the partial birth of a synchronistic event. (This double experience of extreme negativity straddling positive creative energy is referred to in common, ordinary experience as despair just at the point of lifting.)

It finds expression in the phrase "it is darkest before the dawn." Reality may appear to be hopelessly bleak one moment, yet at the moment of significant change, opaque bleakness can turn into numinous release. Analogous experiences of this doubling phenomena are found in expressions such as "a phoenix rises out of its ashes" or "under certain conditions something seemingly appearing out of nothing."

Dr. R. Wittenberg (a personal communication, 1984), speaking about making meaning, said to the researcher: "human beings can make meaning (find patterns) in any selected raw data that is seemingly neutral."[20] (It might be a fruitful undertaking to review the origins of projective testing, starting with the so-called occult sciences: Kabala, I Ching, numerology, astrology, Tarot, and moving on to Rorschach's attempt to divine a test that could adequately differentiate obsessive compulsive personality types from schizophrenics utilizing ink blots that came about as the result [smearing ink on half folded paper].)

In this light, once a person is psychologically ready, that is, able to objectify that which previously has been a mystery, an objective parallel event is likely to occur which mirrors and confirms that which is now preconscious. This implies that, once a person is in a state of psychological readiness, if a meaningful event doesn't happen today, one would surely occur tomorrow.

The concept of readiness enables researchers to understand the process that leads to the production of a synchronistic occurrence from a naturalistic perspective (utilizing the filters of psychodynamics outlined above). This attitude is in marked contrast to that of Jung and his followers (who have about a ninety percent lock on the synchronicity theory market).

Jung and his followers conclude that utilizing psychodynamics only explains the subjective side of the synchronicity equation but does not and cannot explain the mysterious parallel objective, external event. Thus, they reason, since these events apparently happen a-causally, it is evidence that the universe is spiritualized (equated with Plato's concept of nous).

Thus, with respect to the stuck point, they have no other option than to treat it as if it is intractably existential. Thus there is nothing else to do but passively surrender, hoping that a connection can be made to a higher power which will somehow transmit knowledge into the passively receptive self seeking divine guidance.

By contrast, utilizing the concept of readiness, the psychodynamics of projection, and the process of accommodation (creative problem solving), this researcher believes it possible to understand the production of synchronistic phenomena from a naturalistic perspective. To achieve this objective, the first task is to shift one's attitude to the stuck point, from one of passive existential intractability, to one that views them as an active problem to be resolved.

A Crucial Pre-Condition for the Emergence of Synchronistic Phenomena: A State of Active Readiness

Static Inertia to Kinetic Energy

While it appears true that all synchronicities are associated with a given subject's experience of feeling psychologically deadlocked, it is equally true (in this researcher's experience) that the attitude toward the deadlock of the moment is crucial to the timing of the appearance of a given meaning and coincidence. Specifically, for a synchronicity to actually be experienced it is necessary for the subject to shift his attitude about the deadlock from passive to proactive. That is, as long as the deadlock is thought of as hopeless the person spins around in place so to speak like a snake biting his own tail. What must occur to generate a meaningful coincidence is that the subject has to move from judging his condition as hopelessly existential to hopefully problematic to proactively desiring significant psychological change.

Thus, for many sessions, previous to her synchronicity described above, C had been wrestling with attempts to experience autonomy with no particular progress either in "real" life or even in her dreams. The synchronicity associated with autonomy occurred at a point when and where C affirmed a proactive decision to risk the worst fantasies of potential and actual threat to her being. Along with the proactive decision to act despite the perceived threat she also asked herself the organizing question: what would be the worst thing that would happen to her if she in fact did upset her friend? This allowed C to attempt to objectify her intense feelings by reality testing instead of just over- or underreacting as a result of giving into a hypersubjective emotional state.

The same observation holds true for the timing of the appearance of the researcher's synchronicity referred to as "Saved at the Eleventh Hour." For many months he had been in the grips of despair previous to the appearance of this synchronicity. Try as he might to free himself from psychological bonds, all roads led to inactivity and negative inertia. This state of affairs continued until he generated a "head of steam" and proactively committed himself to proactively changing his reality come hell or high water. In this light, I believe it no coincidence that he had a meaningful coincidence the next day validating the observation that when he was ready to really act and not just pay lip service to changing, the conditions were finally ripe for a synchronicity to occur. (The organizing question accompanying his readiness to act was, does he have the power to persevere despite major setbacks?)

The fact of active readiness associated with the appearance of a meaningful coincidence cited in the two examples above may be generalized to the production of all meaningful coincidences. Thus, in this view, readiness has to traverse its own process ranging from passive readiness (a wish to attain something desired that is conflictualized but energized only to the point of "its a good idea") to a state of active readiness wherein the passive idea is now convened into the initiation of an active process potentially leading to significant change so that what was originally only passively wished for is convened into proactively seeking a creative solution.

Further, it is noted that soon following a proactive wish to find a solution to the seemingly intractable binary will be the creation of an organizing question. This organizing question will be suffused with libido (libidinized) or "magnetized," enabling it to both identify and to draw into its domain resonant material (information) derived from the flow of seemingly random events (the raw data of personal experience). This magnetizing or libidinizing process may be referred to as proactive meaning making.

Iron Filings Experiment in General Science

Proactive meaning is operationally defined as a process which combines contents from the creative unconscious and consciousness of a given human being and filters them through the form of a defined structure. The structure in each case is equivalent to an organizing concept which captures and synthesizes relevant raw data of experience. Capturing and synthesizing relevant raw data of experience takes the form of perceiving meaningful patterns in seemingly random bits of experience. Note the iron filing experiment in an eighth grade science lesson. The teacher takes a piece of plain white 8×10 paper and pours iron filings on top of it. Then she lifts the paper to chest level. Next she places a strong magnet underneath the paper containing the iron filings and moves it around. As the magnet is moving, one can observe the iron filings correspondingly moving on top of the paper arranging themselves into swirling patterns. The point of the experiment is to demonstrate the reality and power of electromagnetism. I believe this process has application to understanding the psychodynamics of synchronistic phenomena.

The white paper equals the state of psychological deadlock. The magnet equals the derived combination of the essence of the particular deadlock in question which generates a magnetizing organizing concept. The iron filings equal the raw data of experience out of which meaningful patterns will be derived.

Summary of the Psychological Conditions Leading to the Production of Meaningful Coincidences

Assuming the conditions surrounding the production of synchronistic phenomena are (1) a perception that one is caught in what feels to be an unsolvable existential deadlock (trapped between two mutually exclusive [untenable] positions, states of mind, alternative choices, etc.) and (2) a person in such a state of existential stuckness moves from a state of resignation to a felt desire to proactively find a way out of the trap, initiating a creative process whereby what is first experienced as hopelessly existential is now perceived as hopefully problematic ("As I am hopelessly trapped I might as well die" to "I refuse to give up, there must be a way out of this maze.") Formula: psychological deadlock + a desire for a creative solution = magnetizing an organizing concept wherein the particular organizing concept to be magnetized is derived from the essence of the psychological deadlock in question. (In a well-defined statement of a problem lies an embedded solution.) Another name for this process is proactive meaning. Analyzing this synchronicity it might be said that the subject, once having cathected his conscious desires plus activating his will and determination to do something about actualizing his desires into fact, was in a state associated with the production of meaningful coincidences. Now that the goal was clear it had the effect of being like a magnet drawing together any and all resonant material (information, ideas, leads, etc.) toward the production of a creative solution to his seemingly intractable problem.

In the process of psychoanalytic psychotherapy it is clear that synchronicities occur at the end of a three-step process. This process begins with a patient indicating they have reached a point of deadlock with respect to their despair about ever being able to either start some action which will lead them to a desired goal or stopping some action which causes them great distress. Whether a sought after change be either starting something or ending something, the patient subjectively feels stuck—spinning around in a psychological dishwasher—like a snake biting its own tail. The process which must occur and which is associated with the production of meaningful coincidences is that what is first considered by the patient to be hopelessly existential must shift to hopeful and problematical. He then has to commit himself to some proactive choice in which he demonstrates a willingness to struggle with struggle. Once committing himself to action, an organizing question will be generated which will be used in the service of a "magnet" attracting resonant material into its space. Once the deadlock is thought of as problematic instead of intractably existential, the solution, then, is found in resolving the issue at hand.

An Example of a Magnetizing, Libidinizing, and/or Organizing Concept

Once a commitment is made to actively struggle to change what seems to be an intractable dilemma, it takes the form of generating an organizing question. This organizing question in turn becomes libidinized or magnetized (cathected). The magnetized organizing concept acts to draw into its orbit resonant raw data of experience. What determines resonance is the degree to which a piece of raw data helps to further a solution to the dilemma at hand. An example of magnetizing or libidinizing the organizing concept follows.

Comments about the Synchronicity "Saved by the Rabbi at the 11th Hour"

This synchronicity was the second of nineteen major synchronicities recorded by the researcher. It occurred some three years after the "Lazarus Rising From the Dead" synchronicity.

The Situational Context

G is impacted seeing Munch's paintings, particularly identifying with a man shrieking on a bridge. He is feeling hopelessly stuck at a dead-end civil service job—vocationally trapped and psychologically paralyzed. He desperately wants to leave, but despite a master's degree in psychology feels underqualified to look for a more challenging job. However, despite his stuckness he feels as if he is reaching a breaking point.

The Immediate Context

A conscious decision is made to go back to graduate school to get a Ph.D. in psychology, but as money is needed he reluctantly asks his family for help. This request leads to a critical meeting with his brother-in-law, who assumes the role of the family spokesman. The brother-in-law tells G that the family thinks he is profligate and "expecting too much from others" and therefore his request is denied. The brother-in-law, also disparaging G's apartment, says to him: "How can you stand to live in this s—hole?" This remark (the straw that breaks the camel's back) induces a powerful internal reaction of rage in G, but because he is too insecure, he is uncertain as to whom it is directed—the family or himself. Thus while longing to lash out, paralyzed by crippling self-doubt, all he does, in fact, is to remain head bowed and mute.

The Psychological Context

Although G initially identified with the aggressor (joining forces with the attackers) he also felt that he had been abandoned, coupled with a powerful reaction of resentment which took the form of a wish to avenge himself. Thus despite feeling lost and confused in both love and work he was determined that he would exert every effort to find a more suitable job and to find the money to go to graduate school no matter what the cost and do it soon. Thus, now ready to commit, he shifted from passive inert resignation to proactive kinetic action. This shift from passive to active generated an organizing concept which he became conscious of in the middle of the restless night following the encounter with his brother-in-law.

At some point while mulling his options, G had a creative flash. He thought: stay where he was to maintain financial security but begin to look for a possible part-time job as a psychologist. This idea represented a compromise—"bridge" position—between suffocating at the job he hated versus risking financial insecurity to look for a dubious full-time job as a psychologist.

The Synchronicity: Saved by the Rabbi at the Eleventh Hour

With that idea in mind, the next day he turned to a coworker/friend and said that if she were ever to get a position as a part-time psychological tester, please tell him right away. Remarkably, only five hours later, the coworker said to G: "You will never believe what just happened." She then said that a rabbi, a friend of hers who also happens to run a drug addiction center, called her, asking if she knew of anyone who could give psychological tests part time.

Reactions to This Meaningful Coincidence

Though feeling deserted, there was also the feeling of being at the right place at the right time. Once again G experienced an eleventh-hour reprieve in the form of a stroke of good fortune. He noted a connection between his troubled state of mind, his feeling deadlocked, his wish to be saved coupled with a conscious willingness to change and the experience of a particularly meaningful coincidence. The synchronicity was experienced as if it was an answer to his prayers. Years later, G would view his good fortune from a more naturalistic perspective. For, at the time of the "amazing" synchronicity, he never considered the possibility (probability) that the source of his good fortune had been a combination of his asking for specific help from his coworker/friend and her likely good turn in soliciting a job for him from her rabbi friend, never revealing her good-natured secret to him.

Commentary

From a naturalistic perspective, the production of synchronicities (meaningful coincidences) may be explained by substituting synthetic causality in the place of conventional "scientific" causality as the link connecting the intra-psychic event A with the parallel external event A .

To repeat, synthetic causality is a hybrid concept composed of conventional causality plus psychodynamics. If this substitution is accepted, then linear logic (of the mind) is transcended by experiential logic (of thoughts, feelings, intuitions, and physical sensations). This more complex logic would be akin to Hegelian dialectic plus the unconscious. The basic assumption of experiential logic is that the world is held together not because of linear causality alone, but by linear causality and durational causality working in concert. This view of a hybrid causality shifts the origins of meaningful connections from the dry mind only, to creations of sentient, passionate whole selves attempting to forge meaningful connections with themselves and with the object world.

Synthetic causality takes as its starting points individuals mired in the "real" world, struggling to order their own chaos but often feeling intractably stuck between a seemingly endless progression of mutually exclusive positions. Once the struggle with struggle results in springing the deadlock of the moment, sooner rather than later many individuals predictably find themselves "trapped" in another seemingly intractable dilemma.

In this light, it seems valid to state that every man's existence is composed of moving from one problem to another. Or in the words of the instructive children's song: "A bear went over the mountain, a bear went over the mountain, a bear went over the mountain to see what he could see. He saw another mountain. . . ." To effectively negotiate scaling mountains—mastering problems—requires individuals to become increasingly adept in adapting, both with respect to assimilation (pouring new wine into old bottles) and accommodating (pouring new wine into new bottles).

Bearing the above in mind, it is this researcher's opinion that the key to understanding the nature of the process that leads to the production of synchronicities from a naturalistic perspective entails treating them as byproducts of human beings' need to accommodate creative solutions to seemingly intractable dilemmas. Additional names for accommodation are effective problem solving and/or creative problem solving.

The Creative Process as an Evolving Series of Additive Links of Expanding Consciousness of Links of Cause and Effect Chains

Viewing the production of meaningful coincidences from the vantage point of a science of psychodynamics indicates that it is centrally associated with attempts to induce significant change. Change in this connection refers to the perception that present "stuckness" (an experience of existential entrapment with no hope of release) is only illusory, and if so inclined, generates a proactive process whereby a failure to assimilate an adequate solution to a problem is converted into a cathexis of accommodation (creative process) producing alternative choices both in attitudes and in behavior. In short, static energy is converted into kinetic energy. Or, in other terms, negative reverberation oscillation is converted into positive reverberation oscillation. In the language of depth psychology, synchronicities are intimately related to the working through process. The working through process refers to the time spent by therapist and patient in thoroughly understanding the nature of a given problem complex so that once understood, informed choice replaces automatic impulsive or compulsive or frozen behavior.

Further, if, as hypothesized, synchronicities are correlated with the working through process of objectifying the subjective (either as an outcome of a life of natural self-reflection, or the outcome of an accelerated process of systematically working on the self—e.g., being in psychotherapy), then a string (a run) of synchronicities for a given individual would signify that a significant degree of problem resolution was taking place. If this is so, then the examination of a cluster or string or run of synchronicities for a given individual should evidence a progression of graduated consciousness (consciousness expansion).

(With respect to the process of psychoanalysis or psychoanalytic psychotherapy, an operational definition of consciousness is to verbalize previously unspoken thoughts and feelings. Hence the unconscious stands for unspoken words and feelings.) Thus one would expect with each additional synchronicity in a string of meaningful coincidences that each one reflects a common theme but that each additional coincidence adds its own more complex perspective of the matter at hand.

Thus runs of synchronicities (particularly occurring over a relatively compressed amount of time [hours, days, weeks]) serve the function of providing additional clues in a psychological scavenger hunt whose combined task is to provide the combination for springing the idiosyncratic lock of the moment, initially experienced as hopelessly entrapping.

It also appears that consciousness does indeed expand on a moment-to-moment basis. Witness the amazement of sensitive parents as they attune themselves to the remarkably fast changes their newborn makes as he/she adapts to internal and external reality.

Consciousness expansion may, of course, be readily seen over the course of many days, months, and years. The shift from a fetal position to standing upright unsupported is an enormous developmental leap to make in the space of only 365 days, more or less.

Piaget acknowledges the expansion of consciousness with his concepts of psychic organizers. Conscious expansion may evolve as in maturational steps such as moving from the oral to the anal period. Or, it can occur as the result of revolutionary responses to trauma (crisis). The expansion of consciousness can also be accelerated by engaging in systematic work on the self, as for example in a dedication to psychoanalysis three times a week over a ten-year period.

In this light, consciousness expansion occurs in incremental steps wherein one becomes gradually aware of individual pieces of what will eventually turn out to be a synthesized complex jigsaw puzzle. Synchronicities in this view may at one and the same time be regarded as a synthesized puzzle in its own right and are also the awareness of the first piece of a new puzzle.

Each box equals an individual synchronicity; box *a* is connected to box *b* and so on in an ascending order, which equals all synchronicities in a thread of synchronicities similar in reflecting a common theme and different in that each additional synchronicity reflects an increasing complexity of variation of the theme. The line throughout all of the synchronicities pictorially describes ascending states of consciousness in the process of expanding.

To illustrate the above, consider the following notes on D, a 38 year old male patient suffering from Avoidant Personality Disorder. This material summarizes his experience of key marker experiences motivating him to seek out professional help.

During the summer of 1991, D experienced himself hopelessly stuck. "I wasn't going anywhere and I felt empty." A major problem for him was his interpretation of this unpleasant state of affairs as existential; that is, it's the way it was. Seeing no other options, the patient sank into a deepening depression. Once in treatment he transformed his closed-ended, just-so "existential attitude" to one which viewed his depressed state as the surface symptom of some deeper set of unresolved psychological conflicts yet to be identified, hence unconscious.

During his treatment, at this time, D began reporting a number of meaningful coincidences. The essence of one of these has been previously noted in this paper.

Synchronicity 1: D Is Forced to Disappoint

The net effect of this synchronicity was that D now experienced (became consciously aware of) the core reason why he sought out treatment. This awareness enabled him to focus on present and past and anticipated future events which were in any way associated with the potential for disappointing others.

Up to relatively recently, D had automatically avoided any direct encounter with disappointing others. This was so, as his sense of self depended on the perception of approving authority figures. Therefore, he couldn't take the chance of alienating important people. (He dared not risk biting the emotional hand of people he depended upon.) So he would either acquiesce, or act out his diagnosis (avoiding conflict by either leaving the scene, or by detaching himself internally). His problem in recent days is that he is aware that to avoid or to acquiesce results, not in relieving him for the moment, but creating additional psychic pain. For to acquiesce now makes him feel as if he is a hypocrite and sellout; to avoid makes him feel isolated, depressed, filling him with an empty dead feeling.

D summed up his therapy experience to date as "initially needing crisis management but now I am now looking to improve the quality of my life." In that connection, he spontaneously began speaking about the correlation between being psychologically ready and the appearance of meaningful coincidences. D speculated about "unseen forces that we don't understand but clearly influence our lives, [adding] perhaps we don't really need to understand them. [Perhaps it is enough that we] just have the realization that there are other unseen dimensions—like radio waves and electricity. What is important is to harness the power and the energy so it can be focused and utilized." (He is, I believe, talking about cathecting his personal unconscious.)

In this light D has experienced his treatment as growing a structure (the self) to be able to harness his heretofore aimless energy. The method is of course him and me, session by session, identifying, exploring, and systematically working through his major problems. We are like Plato and Socrates walking in the woods of his interior reality. We dialogue together, always trying to objectify his subjective with me doing the same with myself as well. We gradually gain knowledge of his particular cause and effect connections which collectively detail the soul and substance of his experiential logic. To repeat: experiential logic is operationally defined as a combination of feelings, thoughts, and judgments, action plus transference positive and negative plus an overlapping of durational and linear logic plus what one uniquely brings to bear in generating creative meanings.

Up until the last few days D's conscious attitude to disappointing was let it ride—patching the difficulty at best. Now it is get underneath it. He now talks about himself as having been a great disappointment to himself. But having learned to better tolerate his imperfections he now wishes to get underneath the material. He is now aware that he is responsible for his choices and decisions. To patch means to expend little effort in trying to solve the problem of the moment. He can no longer shrink from the fact that if he avoids disappointing others then he will inevitably disappoint himself. Thus "while it hurts to face disappointment, it hurts worse not to."

Another Synchronicity in a Run of Synchronicities

In the next session, D reported that once again he randomly turned to a page in the book he had been reading and found a striking attunement between that which had been a problem in his mind and that which was being reflected back to him on the page. It struck D that he has been using the book, and indeed the whole world, as a reflecting mirror. He concluded that he must take more responsibility for mirroring himself. Once again this synchronicity is a marker that he is becoming increasingly more conscious of himself now having greater access to his own powers.

Runs of Meaningful Coincidences Associated with Childhood Traumas

Analyses of runs of meaningful coincidences indicate that what is being worked through may likely be a trauma, confluence of traumas, and/or a climate of trauma having its origin in childhood.

For example: D's coincidences are embedded in psychological and situational contexts which originate with the sudden disappearance of a loved relative (who actually died but D didn't know that fact for a long while) leaving him utterly confused, bereft, and overwhelmed with unexpressed and un-understood mixed feelings. In order to keep himself intact, D developed a style of muting internal or external conflict culminating in his diagnosis of avoidant personality disorder.

Synchronicity Prone Patients Associated with a Multi-Perspectival Point of View

It is noted that patients like C and D (synchronicity prone and synchronicity aware) order their internal and external chaos utilizing a multi-perspectival process. This process accesses a variety of streams of information (ideas, feelings, intuitions, and sensations) filtering them from a variety of perspectives (philosophical, psychological, psychodynamic, physiological, scientific, artistic, spiritual [esoteric occult], and political). This means that these people attempt to organize the raw data of their experience holistically rather than in parts.

In other words, these people have the capacity of viewing any piece of reality (internal and/or external) from a multiplicity of points of view utilizing various streams of information and often experiencing it as if it was all happening, in them or to them, simultaneously. However, what should be experienced by them as a treasured gift is, instead, experienced as an overwhelming burden, particularly so at the start of their treatment.

In this light, synchronicities (meaningful coincidences) are the externalized concretization (synthesis) of idiosyncratic processes working through the priority psychological problem of the moment. The most current synchronicity, then, is a marker that the problem of the moment has attained an adequate resolution although it is still in coded form (preconscious). Being coded, it needs to be decoded. (B. Honneger suggests that synchronicities be treated as though they were waking dreams, decoding them in the same way that dreams are analyzed, i.e., assessing the situational, psychological, and historical contexts in which they are embedded and associating individual elements of the coincidence to them.)

Predictions

An analysis of relevant contexts in which a synchronicity is embedded will reveal a psychological dilemma which initially is experienced as if it is unsolvable.

Synchronicities will not occur until and unless there is a shift from passive helplessness and hopelessness with respect to the attitude of entrapment to one that is proactively dedicated to initiating a process whose aim is to discover or create an adequate resolution of the problem at hand.

A run of meaningful coincidences should likely reveal "a golden thread" in which each synchronicity is like a clue in an elaborate psychological scavenger hunt, each one providing significant understanding to collectively work through a major psychological problem (trauma, traumas, or climate of trauma originating in childhood).

Conclusions

Synchronicities grow out of the soil of psychic conflict. In this view they are the end result of a psychological process which has as its aim the creation of a constructive resolution to what previously seems to have been an unsolvable stuck point. Thus synchronicities are intimately involved with a felt need for significant psychological change and transformation.

But, for synchronicities to be born, the attitude about the stuckness has to shift from passive to active. Once this is done, it is hypothesized, the energy used in the service of depressing the subject is now freed up to be available for "creative" purposes.

Analytically, it seems reasonably clear that synchronicities are intimately associated with creative decision making which is initially experienced as unsolvable dilemmas seeking resolutions. In this light, the psychoanalytic psychotherapy (and the psychoanalytic process) actively encourages these phenomena to occur as it both arranges the atmosphere to be that which is most conducive for synchronistic phenomena to appear, and implicitly and explicitly concentrates on identifying, exploring, and working through a given patient's stuck points, which is—in this researcher's opinion—the essential fact of meaningful coincidences.

Synchronicities are associated with the "working through process" indicating that a synthesis of various streams of information (cognitions, feelings, sensations, intuitions), filtered through a variety of perspectives (philosophical, psychological, physiological, scientific, spiritual, occult, political), has been attained and is crystallized in the form of the most current meaningful coincidence.

The resolution to the problem, initiating a process leading to the production of a synchronicity, is one which reflects the whole person's best answer to the problem at hand. In this connection, a quotation from C. Rycroft commenting on the nature and function of dream states parallels a similar conjecture about the nature and function of meaningful coincidences.

Rycroft states: "the existence of some mental activity which is more preoccupied with the individual's life span and destiny than is the conscious ego with its day-to-day involvement with immediate contingencies."[21]

Decoded meaningful coincidences indicate that there has been a notable expansion of consciousness. This expansion of consciousness is noted in a release of neutral energy (libido) which may be used for creative purposes. Indicators of expanded consciousness include a subjective experience of shifting from fragmented to cohesive; fusion to separated; projected authority to experiencing oneself as their own final authority; passive to active; diffuse to concentrated; black-white thinking to complexity; an overreliance on linear logic to synthetic (instinctual) logic; subjective to objective; relatively imprisoned to relatively free; relatively inadequate to relatively confident.

Viewed in the light of this paper, meaningful coincidences are naturalistic by-products of human beings' utilizing the totality of available informational streams filtered through multiple perspectives to arrive at the "best" resolution possible at a given time to free themselves from what initially seems like a never-ending entrapment in the horns of a psychological dilemma.

From this perspective, there is nothing mystical or divine about the origins of these anomalous events. While this analysis does rob the "magic" associated with only observing the surface, it nevertheless affirms a wondrous appreciation for the creative capacities of each person to order his own internal and external chaos.

IV

PRACTICAL APPLICATION

10

Synchronicity and Psychotherapy

One reason content is all-important in therapy is that the content of a human being's experience constitutes a good deal of what makes him a unique individual. Uniqueness in turn is a quintessential aspect of what constitutes a creation, because to be one of a kind is to be truly new with respect to the world of events and objects. One can be new in relation to a particular context, or in relation to what one was before, but something unique is new in relation to the known universe. Consequently, content of therapy and of a particular human being's experience is inextricably involved in the creative process.

—Albert Rothenberg, M.D.[1]

Still what Jung labeled as Freud's concretistic terminology and personalistic view of the unconscious manifests Freud's awareness that authentic transcendental experiences and insights ["spirituality"] are anchored in the individuals' personal life history and its instinctual roots. Psychoanalysis, I believe, shares with modern existentialism the tenet that superpersonal and transcendental aspects of human existence and unconscious and instinctual life [so much stressed by Jung] can be experienced and integrated convincingly—without escapist embellishments, otherworldly consolations and going off into the clouds—only in the concreteness of one's own personal life, including the ugliness, trivialities, and sham that go with it. It would seem that Jungian psychology and psychotherapy jump all too readily from the here-and-now of individual life, from concrete personal experience, to the collective unconscious myth, archetypes, religiosity, and "spirituality"—as refuge and healing visions to cling to, leading easily to evasions and hypocrisy instead of to genuine transcendence or in psychoanalytic terminology, to sublimation and true ego expansion.

—Hans W. Loewald, M.D.[2]

Overview

THE PHILOSOPHER WILLIAM JAMES, a pragmatist through and through, believed that ideas are a dime a dozen. For him, what makes one idea (theory) better than another is its "cash value" or practical usefulness.[3] Implied in the term "cash value" is the assumption that while all ideas (theories) work for some persons, the selection of what theory to use at any specified time with a particular patient is which theory works best. The criterion for "which works best" is derived from the particular goal of treatment.

As a sample of one, this author has no doubt about the practical usefulness of his naturalistic theory of synchronicities applied to understanding the nature of and uses of some synchronicity "material" spontaneously reported by some patients. However, to generalize these positive results to all of humanity is a grandiose leap. Thus, in the service of objectivity this chapter will apply Williams' synchronicity theory in the course of his working with three synchronicity prone patients.

Before discussing my work with some synchronicity prone patients I think it valuable to outline some notable differences between the Jungian supernatural perspective and my own naturalistic perspective. See Table 10.1.

TABLE 10.1

	Jung	*Williams*
Source of knowledge ("messages")	Archetypal knowledge	Self-generated
Location	Transcendent	Immanent
Method of transmission	Revealed—unmediated Intuited, "channeled"	Realized—interpreted Experienced
Change	Instant and permanent	Result of working through
Changing	Spontaneous	Struggle with struggle
Meaning	Absolute	Relative to the observer
Primary consciousness	Collective unconsciousness	Personal consciousness Collective consciousness
Self	Preformed before birth	To be formed
Role of the therapist	Co-creator	Encourage creativity

A Summary of Williams's Major Findings

Some Observations about Synchronicities

- Synchronicities are markers of significant psychological change.
- Synchronicities are markers of problem resolution in coded form.
- Synchronicities indicate a significant shift in attitude toward the problem that was previously experienced as unsolvable.
- The change associated with synchronicities results in an increasing cohesion of the self structure, and expansion of consciousness, a greater tolerance for ambivalence and complexity, and a strengthening of the autonomous ego function of synthesis resulting in notable signs of integration of a person's powers.
- The "message" embedded in the coded synchronicity is a self-generated communication for the purposes of furthering one's self development in the areas of being and doing.
- Synchronicities illuminate how a person generates his or her own meaningful connections as a byproduct of their developing awareness and utilization of what I refer to as "experiential" or "instinctual" logic.

Fertile Conditions for Synchronicities to Arise

- Most significantly my findings demonstrate that at least the synchronicities described in this book are seen to occur in the midst of highly specific and knowable conditions, thus fulfilling the criterion Taylor (1903) set forth for validating the presence of causation. Says Taylor: "Causation means sequence under definitely known conditions."[4]
- What initially appears to be like a shooting star or a firefly's spark when subjected to contextual analysis indicates that meaningful coincidences (synchronicities) (at least the ones described in this book) all happen in a highly specific and potentially knowable set of conditions. Fertile conditions for the birth of a synchronicity is when a person perceives that they are experiencing psychological "gridlock" in their frustrated abilities to resolve a seemingly unsolvable problem. This stuck point is typically described as the patient feeling trapped, weighted down, in a state of crisis. This finding largely supports Jung's observations. However there are major differences in what to make of these odd events and working with patients who present them.

Characteristics of Synchronicity Prone Patients

- Of course I am only limited to my own personal and professional experience so that there is every reason to believe that my sample is biased. (I estimate that I have heard approximately twenty patients report at least one synchronicity during the course of their treatment.) This of course would be a potentially noteworthy piece of research to see if what I have observed about my "population" of synchronicity aware patients can be generalized. The following can be said about virtually all of the patients I have worked with who spontaneously reported a strong interest in their meaningful coincidences.

- These patients are notably "truth" seekers who are greatly interested in the subject matter of speculative philosophy. Thus they are preoccupied with their frustrated desires to obtain satisfactory answers to their ultimate questions. The core question they present is a desire to know who they really are and what they really want. Typically they are highly articulate and are multitalented, but because they lack self confidence they tend to lack the capacity for taking themselves and their potentially "creative" pursuits seriously. They have notable problems in regulating their self-esteem. They initially suffer from intense negative affect intolerance. They hate and are intimidated by "normal" everyday feelings including frustration, confusion, ambivalence, not knowing, ambiguity, and the like. They tend to oscillate between being highly intuitive on the one hand to overrelying on utilizing lawyer-like linear logic on the other. They tend to be confused about "messy" feelings. Scratch the surface and it is commonplace to observe intense feelings of dissociation, surrealism, depersonalization, and derealization. A major defense appears to be identification with the aggressor so that they initially suffer from an overattention to pleasing others (or assiduously avoiding displeasing), resulting in feeling "lost" when it comes to knowing what is best for them at any given time.
- They tend to be "spiritually" preoccupied but not in the conventional sense of this term. Spiritual in the way I understand it has to do with primarily feelings thought to be the normal feelings associated with year one consciousness: love, trust, hope, faith, and persistence. It is no coincidence these people are synchronicity aware as they have a determined drive to make meaningful connections with themselves and the object world. Whereas they appear to have it "all" on the surface, they feel as if something is fundamentally wrong at their core, perhaps best described as having a "hole" in their soul. Initially they feel unable to experience themselves as whole people with basic rights to determine for themselves what the components are for living "the good life" irrespective of what anyone around them happens to think. In short all of these synchronistic patients are suffering from a lack of a clear definition of themselves. This means that while they yearn to take themselves seriously they intuitively know that they don't have a solid self to take seriously.

The Attitude of the Therapist in Working with Synchronicity Prone Patients

- A serious attitude about these anomalous phenomena obligates the therapist (investigator, researcher) to be aware of his or her primary speculative philosophical assumptions and attitudes. These include such questions as who am I, what do I really want, how do I access vital information, what is real and how do I know it, what is truly meaningful to me and what is my meaning of meaning. . . . There must also be an awareness about one's personal process—that is, how are meaningful connections made? Further there is an explicit or implicit set of attitudes concerning the issue of "spirituality"—a concern for ultimate essences and values.
- Here is where differences in basic assumptions about the nature of reality, knowledge of reality, and the means by which knowledge is accessed make a major difference in the way a given therapist is likely going to work with synchronicity prone patients. If you believe that the "messages" associated with synchronicities are vital information channeled directly from an assumed realm of archetypal knowledge hence no need to interpret it, then you as patient or therapist will respond to the material in a Jungian way. If however you view synchronicities as self-generated messages from one's self, you, the patient or therapist, should be encouraged to make as many meaningful associations with the material as possible. There are a few therapists who advocate working with synchronicities as if they were "waking dreams."[5] This is so because these occurrences appear to be creative by-products of a great deal of working through that has started with a seed, so to speak, and is now—in the form of a synchronicity—a visible flower.
- The vital information associated with synchronicities is relevant to the self of the individual both in a state of being (ranging from fragmented to whole) and becoming (ranging from scattered to focused and directed).
- Synchronicities can be used like reflecting mirrors, i.e., "psychological GPS" (global positioning reflectors) enabling the experience to locate and ground themselves in present time and space. For example: responding to a particularly meaningful experience D had in throwing the I Ching, I asked him what the answer to his question meant to him. He answered: "[It is] mirroring back to me—I know where I am—This is who I am—It is correct for me to be here—I take it as a kind of cosmic 'right on.'" (I am exactly at the point where I am located . . . aware of myself and my risks. . . .) Thus the "message" from the I Ching was used to reorient him. I understood D to be at a midway point between projecting his final authority versus accepting himself (and his personal unconscious) as the source of his final authority.[6]

- In this connection my findings strongly suggest that synchronicities are markers that the patient has made a significant synthesis and integration of previously dissociated data. If I am right, then what is being witnessed both by the therapist and the patient is nothing less than the visible emergence of their primary core creative self.
- In addition to synchronicities sometimes marking regressions to idealized states of infancy, the more weighted emphasis is a notable progression of the person toward increasing ego synthesis, integration, cohesion of the self, and accessing utilizing one's idiosyncratic creative process in the pursuit of generating meaningful connections with oneself and the object world.
- The synchronistic alert therapist enables him or her to view the overlapping contexts from which synchronicities spring: how they are markers of significant psychological change, how they reveal the life-central psychological theme of a given patient.

Person Specific Information

- When synchronicities are viewed in the framework of contextual analysis they are always seen to be intimately associated with the current preoccupation of the patient. Thus the decoded "messages" may be expected to yield "person specific information." In my personal and professional experience the embedded "message" is rarely symbolic of an archetype although if that happens to be the concern of a given patient then it might conceivably be so.
- The Jungian penchant for looking for predicted symbolism supposedly associated with a connection with archetypal knowledge seems forced and generalized when compared to the patient's own personal and specific associations to what he or she is experiencing.
- Synchronicities mark significant shifts in consciousness, the result of a person having accessed, synthesized, and integrated "vital" person specific information concerning their natures. The cathexis of this vital information and processing it is an application of experiential logic in the service of resolving the inevitable problems of daily living.
- Synchronicities indicate that the experiencer is engaged in a process of actively grasping and synthesizing seemingly disparate concepts derived from selected knowledge bases (i.e., speculative philosophy, depth psychology, spirituality, science, and the esoteric occult). Further, these concepts are in turn experienced through the prisms of a person's stream of informational sources including their ideas, feelings, intuitions, and bodily sensations. All of this is in a mix which when processed enables a

person to distill person specific vital knowledge for the purposes of effective problem solving.

Transference Issues

- It is relatively common these days to view the process of psychotherapy and psychoanalysis, and psychoanalytic psychotherapy, as an interactive "inter-subjective" collaboration. Thus there is a mixture of both the real therapist and the "transference(s)" therapist as well as the real patient and the "counter transference(s)" patient. And of course what makes this therapeutic mixture even more complex is the fact that the effect of whom on what material is often unconscious to either patient or therapist. However, when it comes to synchronicities here I believe is a time in the therapy when the patient really appears to be exercising true independence, autonomy, creativity, and originality. This is, of course, one of the key objectives that all schools of therapy agree upon.

Synchronicity Consciousness

- I have worked with patients who appear to have periods of time in which it appears to them as if they are having meaningful coincidences on a regular basis. In each and every case I have observed, the patient's material indicates that their previously dissociated selves are beginning to "come alive." It is as if previously split off "parts," "voices," "selves," "the me," "not me," were starting to "connect." Streams of information, bodily sensations, feelings, thoughts, intuitions, that initially appeared to be compartmentalized now appear to be ever so slightly but noticeably "converging." Reality that had been perceived as "blurry" and "surrealistic" begins to look more "clear," "sharper," and "richer." A reliance on linear logic begins to shift to what I refer to as "experiential" or "psychodynamic" or "synthetic" logic.
- In this view synchronicity consciousness is an important transition marking a patient's progress in having begun a notable growth curve toward a process of heretofore stalled ego synthesis, development of the self, integration of the personality, and a cathexis of their idiosyncratic creative core.

Runs of Coincidences and What They Reveal

- There is no question that runs of coincidences over time will identify the central theme of a given patient. In so doing they identify major turning

points in the treatment which signal not only evidence of synthesis and integration of previously disparate "material" but also noteworthy shifts in basic attitudes resulting in an expansion of the patient's consciousness.
- Watching a new patient experience a run of synchronicities is like witnessing the growth and development of a building under construction. There is first a whole that must be filled, followed by a succession of floors, until the roof is reached. Another apt analogy is a seed that is planted that once nurtured lays down a root system that eventually flowers.

To give the interested reader a slice of how I work with my synchronicity prone patients I will highlight some of the session material previous to, during, and after their experience of synchronicities. The material will also reflect some of the points made above.

The Case of D

Reflections

Synchronicities occur at transition points where the "me" and the "not me" collide and form an expanded view of the self resulting in an expansion of consciousness. Synchronicities indicate that there is an ongoing struggle (process) to reconcile the splits in oneself either in the area of being or doing.

Synchronicities indicate a revision of patterning like gestalts where in previously figure becomes ground. Synchronicities appear mysterious. . . . The key to interpretation begins with one's attitude to the mysterious. . . . is experienced essentially as entertainment, as in being a "numinosity junkie." Wanting to be a collector of such happenings and using them as evidence of the marvelous powers of the mystical universe. . . . Or one can use it as a starting point for identifying the idiosyncratic creative process of each individual looking for specificity of detail as to what constitutes the unique personal machinery of each. What makes the personal "watch" tick?

D understands that his issue is not so much knowing how the story will turn out—it is the same ending for everyone. We will die. The issue is that if one believes that this life is the only one we know for certain, how best to live it? The problem is that no one can answer that question satisfactorily for anyone else. We are all lost or found—aware or unaware—about the same mystery. No one can enter into the bloodstream of another and know what is or is not important to them. To accept responsibility for these facts moves one closer to accepting final responsibility for one's life. This, I believe, is the key to a naturalistic interpretation of meaningful coincidences—synchronicities.

Introduction and Overview of a Run of Synchronicities in D's Psychotherapy

The following details are culled from session notes.

Presenting Complaint

D came into treatment at a point where he felt himself to be quintessentially trapped, unable to choose between two potential partners. Feeling trapped meant there was nothing he could do on his own to motivate hope that he could resolve his dilemma. He was at a zero point. Associations to this dreaded state of affairs were entrapment, hopelessness, helplessness, powerlessness, and despair. He appreciated the fact that he was repeating a familiar pattern, but he could only see himself moving around in circles going nowhere fast. He said he needed to have a different point of view to be able to find a potential pathway out of the circle (his reason for coming into treatment), thus he was highly motivated to change, but was all jammed up—short circuited.

D's Reaction to the First Session

His reaction to the first session was that he felt helped. Hope was generated with the possibility of rescue—that is, perhaps, he thought, that information he would get could be used to find a way out of his circle of entrapment. He was glad to feel he had an ally so that he was not totally alone with his troubles. D also felt it helped him to define his specific issues (a large part of the reason why Freud refers to the psychoanalytic process as "the talking cure").

Identification of Core Themes

D expressed a clear desire to be rescued. Since he initially had a pan distrust of other human beings, "rescue" had "spiritual" implications. The concept of rescue implies for many—as it initially did for D—that there is an absolute reality that is the location of absolute knowledge, further implying absolute answers to essential questions, such as the nature of reality, the source of meaning, purpose, etc. Further is the fervent hope that this knowledge is contactable, might be experienced passively, and hopefully is potentially transforming, instantaneous, and has positive effects that will last forever.

D wants to be able to be in charge of himself—so treatment for him is helping him change from a person who experiences himself as ego weak, in need of rescue with an uncertain sense of who he is and what he is capable of doing, to a person who is strong enough to be able.

For D to accomplish this difficult task means that he has to be able to accept himself as his best source of knowledge to potentially free himself from his sense of entrapment. The knowledge he seeks has to be gleaned from the real experience of himself. It means feeling and thinking out of the box and daring to experience possibilities outside his usual categories of experience. His "me" has to get acquainted with his "not me." The not me has to be given an opportunity to be heard.

At this point D's "inadequacy paralysis" evoked a rescue fantasy. He is uncomfortable with his being, which leads to a decrement of self-esteem—a lowering of confidence—a return of overall inadequacy—a sense of fraudulence. He hopes for a revelation—a quick rapid transformation. He wants an "aha" experience of something substantial to hang onto. This illumination would be a clear sense of purpose that he hopes would inform his inadequate state of being. (This won't work—as he puts the clothes of the king on before he feels like the king.)

Conditions of Treatment

What D previously experienced as existential—it just is—a just-so story—is getting converted into a problem to be resolved. Existential chaos is made to reveal its unique logic. The process by which this is carried out is that the therapist holds up an objective mirror so D is able to objectively see the essential elements of his drama played out. The mirror has to be clear and objective as other mirrors may distort the issue and make matters worse.

The clarity of the reflection is experienced via words that equal special words delivered in a particular climate of genuine care and attention to detail. Concepts of attunement, specificity of detail, degrees of understanding, converge in generating hope and positive momentum.

The Core Issue

D wishes (as I suppose many do) for the therapist to hand him his own personal golden scarab that presumably will evoke a wholesale and permanent transformation in him. (Interesting that Jung reinforces this idea in his patient instead of interpreting the rather obvious positive father transference to her. It is also noteworthy there is no apparent detailed follow up re her treatment. Nor is it clear exactly what she wanted out of treatment in the first place.)

D feels it is difficult to exercise power on the outside. If something is experienced as too dense (like the book) he tends to get anxious, feels helpless, hopeless, and inadequate. With no positive resonance he experiences himself as lacking. This is only made worse by his "tuning fork sensibility," meaning he is aware of this process—he hates it, but once begun it has a life of its own. All he can do at such times is to watch this repetitive process unfold once again wishing he could control it. It is virtually impossible for him to remain OK within himself. The criterion for OK is D feeling he is good enough—adequate enough.

D feels he is stuck with something he can't get rid of. His associations concern his "hopeless" brother and the feeling that nothing could be done about it. He experiences this feeling as if it is a dark hole of chaos. It is easier to give into this feeling than to face up to the "black hole of external chaos."

He has a major problem in regulating his self-esteem. We need to create a cohesive self by helping him learn how to tolerate so-called negative feelings such as frustration, anxiety, depression, confusion, ambivalence, weakness, feeling overwhelmed, helplessness, and hopelessness.

On changing: It can and does occur but it necessitates struggle through resistance much like a root struggling to come up through the ground. The process is like trench warfare: fifteen steps ahead, eight back . . . We explored his attitudes toward his detachment.

D identified a gap between his standard of omniscience and a sometimes failure to attain it. It is hard to remain neutral as there is complexity he can't master at the moment. Instead is an anxiety of incompetence. He then either backs off or cuts off (a defensive isolation of affect and, worse, a decathexis of self libido—taking the form of a lack of confidence that he can eventually master the material if he perseveres).

The Immediate Context Preceding His First Reported Synchronicity

D feels caught up in internal and external forces beyond his control. No exit. No way out. Associated to these feelings is the traumatic experience of the blackouts and a memory of himself as a child waking up in a hospital disoriented and alone. This is further associated with his feeling insecure about his identity. Something to do with awareness of not fitting in and being trapped by his uninvited nature about which he is conflicted.

I did not know at this time that D was what I refer to as "synchronicity prone." But looking back it is clear that his therapeutic issues are parallel with every one of my synchronicity prone patients. Primarily he and they are preoccupied with the questions of final authority, the nature of reality, what is really real and how is that known, questions of value, and of what is essential. Additional questions of how one changes and transforms particularly in the face of strong internal and external resistances. Additional issues of dependency and autonomy, aggression, unity as merger or as convergence, meaning as plugging into absolute meaning or in creating personal meanings, expanding the self via struggling with struggle, getting acquainted with the not me and incorporating it into the me, reconciling divisions in the self by applying the lessons learned in personal experience. In short these issues are those associated with speculative philosophy.

He and they are hyperaware of what they refer to as "forks in the road" in which they experience inadequacy, frustration, helplessness, hopelessness, immobilizing passivity. There is often an appeal to the experiences of luck, chance, destiny, fate, synchronicity. Detachment is a characteristic defense used to block out feeling states that otherwise would be experienced as overwhelming. There is an aversion for feelings such as uncertainty, realistic fears, and anxiety. The field of vision narrows expressed as hyperconcern for small details at the expense of not being able to see the bigger picture. D needs to expand his perspective.

He complains of having a "learning block." He feels more like his retarded brother than he had previously ever considered. Has an attitude of black-white either/or thinking rather than the possibility of a creative "and." He wants knowledge of his ultimate purpose and believes more that the answer will have to come from him, not outside of him, but he doesn't know how to access this information. He is aware that for him meaninglessness is connected to hopelessness. The hopelessness is born and reinforced from his frustration in not being able to master whatever he is hopeless about. Therefore he needs to be able to pick a project and keep at it until he masters it. He has to have an experience of successful struggling with struggle.

Some Progress in Treatment

D's conscious attitude to growing a cohesive self is moving from a wish for passive rescue to active participation in growing his own self. In doing there is a cathexis of purpose and goal seeking. Plugging in what Jung refers to as the transcendent function, I call it a cathexis of meaningful connectedness with something in his self that is experienced as something that has meaning for him. I think he is cathecting the concept and the experience of meaningful connections.

A Few Months Later

D feels more and more quintessentially trapped re this particular issue. This is the soil in which synchronicities breed. [It appears that those who are most enthralled to the experience of synchronicities are indeed preoccupied with wanting to be able to have an experience of meaningful connectedness. They wish to convert (transform) meaningless disconnectedness into a vibrant sense of meaningful connectedness.]

Presynchronicity Consciousness of a Patient Struggling to Maintain a Cohesive Self

D's present situational context has to do with his heretofore experienced attitudes about disappointing others versus himself. As his identity has been based on others' opinion of him, the idea, let alone the act, of disappointing important people has been a potential threat to his self-esteem. This has been so because D has equated disappointment with withdrawal of love. And withdrawal of love, by a love object, has been experienced as a loss of his identity. It is as if he has felt that without a continuing experience of at-one-ment with the love object of the moment he would quite literally die of a broken heart. Therefore, whenever disappointment has entered the picture, D has tried to avoid directly dealing with it at all costs. At such "danger points" D has tended to break off connections literally by leaving the scene or by cutting off his feelings (detaching in one way or another).

D's "disappointment allergy" is a symptom of an inability to regulate his self-esteem—that is, it is virtually impossible for him at the present time to experience himself as his own final authority. To be able to do that he would have to take himself seriously. But it has become clear that he has no cohesive self to take. He has to grow a cohesive self. To grow a cohesive self he must first experience himself as worthy to have one. Aware of his problem, he described his therapeutic task in the following way. "To have self-worth, I have to trust myself or I choose on the basis of avoiding a lesser fear than a greater fear—the fear of abandonment or fear of hurting someone I love."

Everything is now up for grabs as the first assumptions about his core attitudes have been successfully challenged in his therapy resulting in his facing those feelings he automatically avoided. But, in squarely facing them at present, he feels trapped between untenable alternatives.

D reacts to these feelings of entrapment with intense frustration. The frustration stirs anger which in turn is turned back on himself culminating in feelings of depression, depletion, futility, and low self-esteem. It is as if he is surrounded by a psychological wall that bars him from moving in any direction: forward, backwards, sideways, or even remaining in idle.

This fundamental stuckness may be thought of as psychological gridlock. For D, to stay or to leave threatens him with a loss of identity. Thus perched midway between the untenable past and a fear of the unknown future, D is in the midst of what might be referred to as a BB experience (the midpoint of a creative process of psychological transformation). It is in this context of a felt sense of entrapment that D reports having had a meaningful coincidence.

Synchronicity #1

"Now comes a situation where I am forced to be disappointing."

Comments

On the surface one might understandably say this was no remarkable coincidence. However we aren't interested in what anyone else feels about this event—only D. What I think was remarkable for him was his experience of cathecting to cathexis. This was his first experience of being analytically aware of being analytically aware.

It is one thing to experience anything in the abstract including being a therapy patient. It is quite another to really experience being a patient. D was initially frightened to "lose control" and simply be. He took great pride in being able to use his analytic abilities to "figure things out" unless what he had to figure out are conflicts often involving "messy" emotions.

Post Synchronicity

D was thrilled that he had found a method to make potential sense out of the often seeming nonsense of his confusing experience. He eagerly takes the concepts I "feed" him session by session using them as psychological tools to search for pieces of his complicated psychological jigsaw puzzle and begin to put the pieces into meaningful patterns.

D had approximately 10 "major" synchronicities during the course of his lengthy treatment. Each one occurred at pivotal points in his struggle to grow a cohesive self. Each appeared to be the culmination of a great deal of "working through" until he could find his own way to synthesize the material. Each synchronicity clearly marked his notable progress in his valiant struggles with struggle to become the person he wished to be.

A Few Years Later

I asked him what was his first meaningful synchronicity. He associated to a time in grade school when he was singled out by the headmaster as having a good voice and told to join the choir. The timing was good. He was discovered. This passively being discovered transcended the risk in pushing himself out. This important memory was recovered in the context of D feeling an increasing amount of confidence and self-esteem.

At this point D hit a point where he felt that if he was climbing a mountain he had come to a plateau. In the past he would have felt his familiar sense of inadequacy and would likely have "detached" in one form or another. However, he had learned that his tendency to detach at such points didn't just happen but that the detaching was motivated. He was not clear that he used detachment defensively.

Picking up on the concept of "regression in the service of the ego" D said he understood how one sometimes has to go back (regress) to understand something in his past history in a new way for him to progress in the present. "I have to reverse in order to go forward." He was aware that he could stop treatment now and also stop making "trouble" for himself. He also felt that he had made too much progress to stop now.

His choice to continue at a point when in the past he would have been long gone indicated a significant shift in his attitude about who is, what he wants, and his willingness to struggle with struggle to attain what he wants and use it in ways which are meaningful to him. In short, I believe he had made a meaningful connection (cathexis) with his creative process.

We identified a fear of aggression. Pursuing this theme he had a screen memory of reaching out to play the piano at school when he was about six when his teacher rebuked him. He had multiple associations to this "traumatic" memory. Among the associations was his awareness of "don't stick your neck out" anxiety. Further to feel disoriented and confused made him feel unwhole and disoriented. Since this was never identified, he came to dread situations wherein he might feel this way. Obviously this became one of the major reasons for his motivated detachment.

Passage of Six Months

D was now clear that when he hits a place that is experienced as real but unacceptable he detaches and leaves the scene or detaches in some other way. The detachment prevents him from feeling disoriented and anxious but creates discontinuities in his own personal flow of experience which make him feel inert and wooden. He needs to hold his ground.

Additional synchronicities were experienced by him that appeared to function in Faber's concept of them being regressions to the best moments of infancy. In this connection synchronicities are important as providing feelings which are healing, soothing, and comforting. Unity outside the self is easy. He can merge with the absolute knowledge that all is OK. The merciful good mother atmosphere is induced with the explicit association of "here, lean on me." He can be soothed with external support. He can get good information from an informed father. He can transcend the self as split, defective, inadequate, confused. No doubt these were partially positive transference reactions to the nurturing and informative and caring therapist.

We learned together that his purposeful detachment was a substitute for solid ego boundaries. He has tended to merge with whatever has been present as if he were water to assume whatever structure there was at any time and place. So he could assume a pseudoidentity at any time by being at one with whoever he merged with. But he couldn't shake his awareness that this was all pretense.

The key to success was his learning to stand his ground at "forks in the road" and fully learn to experience all of the negative feelings and thoughts that accompany these daunting times. We further learned that synchronicities would occur when at these stuck points he would adopt a positive attitude of struggling with struggle to find a creative solution rather than to "detach."

As he became progressively more cohesive, D had a major synchronicity I refer to as his "Blue Rug" synchronicity.

Pre Synchronicity

D became increasingly more direct and tuned in to his various streams of information: intuitions, ideas, feelings, and bodily sensations. He was notably more spontaneous in his sessions. He laughed a lot and was thrilled about having read the *Story of Philosophy* by Will Durant.[7]

A lot of attention was paid to his wanting to outfit his dream house. Among the articles he most wanted was a special blue rug. Part of the difficulty in finding it was the fact that he couldn't seem to get clear as to what he really wanted. The issue of clarity of desires became his major preoccupation.

There were many associations as to why he seemed to be blocked in this area. The material seemed to indicate that if he really wants something badly enough he can be certain either he won't get it or it will be taken away. He found this matter to be intensely frustrating.

D took a week off to go on a vacation. Among his thoughts were his continuing attempts to specify the details of his much desired blue rug. In the midst of his mulling this over he unexpectedly had a vision of exactly what he desired. The vision clicked.

Walking through a town the next day he became aware of a small nondescript store that somehow drew his attention. Listening to his intuition he doubled back and following his nose—so to speak—went inside the shop, instantly seeing his "dream rug" on the wall.

His interpretation of the exquisitely "good timing" of this coincidence is that as he became more concrete in his intentions he serendipitously found the perfect resonance in a store. The lesson for him to learn was: when the details are clear as to the object of desire which is desired—a laser-like focus plus magnetized atmosphere—when the corresponding "pattern" is found: Voila. Sometimes, as in the search for the perfect rug, it is conscious; the perfect match is on the surface. Other times the process appears to be unconscious and at such times the resonating external event will take the form of a synchronicity. I believe that if he had not found his perfect rug that particular day, he would have come across it sooner rather than later.

D went on to achieve his initial goal in treatment to organically assume final authority of his life. In the course of his successful treatment notable milestones were punctuated with meaningful coincidences.

A Notable Change in a Patient Who for Years Had Only Bitter Struggles with Her Difficult Mother: Case of G—Case 2

Runs of synchronicities demonstrate working through the patient's central issue. In the case of G her core issue was how to separate and individuate from an engulfing mother figure. Each of her synchronicities marked evidence of an expansion of herself, a greater sense of cohesion, vitality, basic rights clearly reflected in her increasing ability and confidence to stand firm with her engulfing mother without losing her sense of self. Each synchronicity indicated an increasing sense of integration and cohesion.

G said that she has been feeling as if she is on the other side of a time tunnel. She feels different and better. She made the startling observation that perhaps she should try to forgive her mother. (This a clear shift in consciousness: a reversal of a multiyear attitude. Her experience was like seeing the same dots but connecting them differently resulting in two or more different patterns. Note reversible images such as the vase that turns into two women facing each other [rashomoning experience].[8])

G spoke about her synchronicity experiences. They began with her having "dared" give her doctor "spiritual" advice. She felt he would be angry at her for overstepping boundaries. Much to her surprise he wasn't upset with her. This allowed her to associate to an old friend who had functioned as a spiritual teacher for her many years ago. He said he was forming a Jewish spiritual group. That was perfect timing as she had been actively considering a new group experience as well as to participate in something Jewish. This idea combined the two needs for her.

This group was in contrast to another group possibility that wasn't Jewish. Thus she has cathected the experience of positive and negative resonance. This implies she has a more cohesive identity. This theme of reunion applies to both interpersonal and intrapsychic connections.

G's major theme has been her intense ambivalence conflict with an engulfing, well-meaning but pushy mother who is seemingly uncontainable. Even though G is 40 years old and understands the dynamics of her situation very well she has been emotionally tied. So she finds herself locked in a relationship where she can't tolerate being with her mother yet at the same time can't leave her. She has tried for years to get her mother to change.

Pre Synchronicity

G is aware of the larger sweep of her therapy as having come in detached and cut off from herself and the object world. She initially retreated into "an inner cave to heal. Now she is coming out and rejoining the world as it is." She has been in the grips of a seemingly unresolvable ambivalence conflict with both herself and herself, and herself and the object world. Plugging in object and self constancy is a major concern and focus of her treatment. It is no coincidence that we spoke of her being colicky as a newborn and believing her mother was overwhelmed by it. Now she says that she can try to be more optimistic. She has been considering the fact that try as she might to change her mother, she is almost resigned to the fact that this wish is never going to come to pass. She had a novel thought when she was about to leave her last session: "Maybe I should try to change myself," referring to coming to terms with her understandable ambivalence she has always felt toward her difficult mother. She seemed to be hinting at the fact that she might give up her guilt for feeling so understandably hateful.

G's Doo Wop Synchronicity

While walking into Grand Central Station on the way to visit her mother, she saw and heard a group of guys singing doo wop. She experienced them doing four-point harmony and took it as a sign that she was doing well. The four-point harmony was a projection of a newfound harmonization in herself. The civil war and the revolution are coming to a peaceful conclusion.

Post Synchronicity

G went on to effect a major shift in attitude with her cantankerous mother. Thus the change signaled by the synchronicity resulted in a lasting change marked by a significant expansion of her consciousness. I think the harmony she heard in the station was a resonance of her starting to come to terms with her understandable ambivalent feelings about her frustrating mother without condemning herself for feeling so intensely negative. In finally accepting her dissonant feeling she could quiet her punitive superego and let her ego begin to harmonize her core self.

The following case of C is a detailed account of the importance of synchronicities in this complicated patient's therapy experience.

The Case of C: Three Synchronicities Spanning the Course of Ten Years of Her Therapy

Overview

My findings strongly indicate that meaningful coincidences (synchronicities) are indicators of significant change. Subjectively they are felt to be highly important in and of themselves to patients who report them. Objectively they are undoubtedly markers of a confluence of previous uncathected or "scattered" powers of the patient having integrated. Further, accompanying this integration of powers is an expansion of the patient's consciousness. After the synchronicity they report feeling significantly different about themselves—more vital, more purposeful, and more integrated.

The material which follows, culled from session notes, is a prime example of the importance of synchronistic experiences with respect to C gradually cathecting her evolving self, her personal unconscious, and her creative process.

The two synchronicities to be highlighted and discussed will first be viewed as embedded in situational and psychological contexts. Her core problem—a frustrated desire to be a dedicated, productive person and poet—spans ten years of clock time.

Distant Psychological Context: "C" Session Notes as of 01/20/01

"Pressure if I am with someone else" [even my daughter]. "I can't relax." [C is defined by reactions to or against the object world.] "I can accommodate others but I can't be natural. I am awkward, empty, something or someone else takes over and I lose myself. I feel tedious, slightly angry. I can't connect. I'm suspended. I can't ignore someone else's presence. Can this habit be broken? . . . "

[A familiar theme] "I don't like going to work. I have to pretend to be someone I'm not." [I indicated that she didn't always feel this way—When did her attitude to work change?] "Just before I came to see you," she answered. "I used to work seven days a week. I had to do something else to escape the children. I could lose myself pretending I was doing something. . . . I was desperate not to fail. . . . I had an identity—a structure—something to go to—get out of . . ."

What interfered? "I was so at odds with myself then as I am now. Always trying to quell a raging fury—hating most every moment of my existence—rarely finding inner peace—an absence of ease . . . No place to be easy and comfortable . . . Everything is a painful effort. . . ."

And here with me, I asked? C answered: "If I find a synergy with others—then I can lose myself—and all the anxiety disappears. . . . But when it ends it is devastating as now I am back floundering trying to find myself again. The only place I can work is in total isolation." Then why not be a hermit, I asked? "What if I wake up and see I made an error?" [C is deathly afraid to make errors, which for her represent quintessential failure.]

"I have to keep all forces at bay . . . a stalemate . . . a compromise all the time to keep myself functional. To be totally natural here [or anywhere] could weaken me. I would be too vulnerable. To feel needy is to feel powerless. My power is in not needing. If I expose a need I could be hurt—they could destroy or weaken me. If I were to admit my neediness it would weaken my façade" [of actual or supposed to be self sufficiency] "it would open up a wound so great that I would pay dearly to make it well: a precarious balance."

[I felt unusually speechless—nothing to say—nothing new—nothing helpful. So I remained silent. Then, just as it seemed we would be unable to go beyond this point C came up with an idea.] "I was thinking what my life would be like if I could harness my forces and direct them in a focused way?"

[With me C takes the lead in reversing herself as negatively defined by a resented object world to defining herself by organizing her own chaos. She gives herself a prescription for a potential creative way out of her fundamental troubles.]

I noted that for a brief time I felt truly stuck in C's presence. I agreed with her that we can't mess with the precarious balance she mentioned. We can't force an entrance past the pseudo self nor does she seem able to tolerate much longer her life of falseness. Then in the midst of the stuckness, she herself came up with a creative formula. What if she defines herself not by what she lacks but by what forces she has that need to be named, taken seriously, harnessed, and directed to chosen goals. In other words what if she shifts her libido from despairing over what should have been or shouldn't have been but, instead, directs it to what is and what might possibly be?

Despite her frustrations C keeps persisting in her writing class which she discovered on her own.

1/22/01

C spoke of feeling estranged most of her life. I understand it as estrangement from estrangement. She is clearly changing. . . . While the writing is good she feels driven by it. "Is my writing," she asks, "an excuse for sanity? Or is it an excuse not to deal with the world? In the midst of it seems purposeful but I have to feel somewhat successful. It requires a lot of directed libido. Pleasure stirs its own anxieties. . . . When I finally posted my story I felt a moment of release and I was proud of myself" [a rare admission]. "But I worry about whether it is delusional. Can I sustain it? Do I really have something to say?"

C's writing seems to be a unifying structure, concept, and experience for her, as I think the exploration of synchronicities is for me. Maybe C reflected the guilt I feel in forsaking practicality, obligations, and socialization.

C told me about an Internet "kindred spirit—a writer from SA" who validates and shares with her. Made her realize that it is no wonder she writes the way she does—having felt like an orphan who has had a bleak existence. The essence of bleak? I asked. C said "bleak is empty, gray, hollow, tedious, horrific, hysteria, painful, screaming, irrationality, and hostility." [I am certain this is a verbal picture of the psychological atmosphere she breathed for seventeen years of her life.]

What, I asked her, would be her experience of herself if she could really commit to affirming herself as truly authentic—and her writing as well? She associated to her reactions to frustration—to be able to turn the switches on or off at will—except that sometimes the fuses short circuit. C, I believe, is talking about her difficulty in regulating her self-esteem, particularly so as it relates to her natural self. What her natural self is completely eludes her. I said to her that I don't think her problem is her being out of touch with reality but being very much in touch with a past and present reality that she detests but often feels powerless to do anything about.

So I see her using the writing as a transitional experience to negotiate in Winnicott's terms indeterminate space but still vulnerable to some feared attack or at least noxious influence of her parents.[9] Is it projected sadism? Is it that she threatens to cut whatever vestige of a thread of hope they will love her right because she still doesn't have a solid enough to fall back on if they don't?

Segue to two years later . . .

Commentary

Significant psychological change is possible but very hard to come by and is always dogged by strong conscious and unconscious resistance. Progress is often measured in small increments. Further it is like the trench warfare of World War One—14 trenches ahead, eight back. The trip up the mountain of success is never straight up. The obstacles that inevitably have to be overcome necessitate the potentially successful patient to commit to a tedious and troublesome struggle with struggle with no guarantee of ultimate victory.

However if the commitment is made to undertake the trip into one's inner space and the laborious, often unscintillating scut work of generating meaningful connections in each therapy session is accepted, eventual success will most probably result.

Along the way to eventual success are, in some cases, one or more synchronicities, indicating unmistakable progress in accommodating a creative resolution with respect to the frustratingly seemingly unsolvable core preoccupying issue. C was still preoccupied with the same issue but the conditions were building which were conducive to producing a major synchronicity.

Situational and Psychological Contexts: 05/10/03

Two weeks before the next coincidence, C was berating herself for not having stuck with something and mastered it. She has gotten to this point many times in her past and tends to give up. Eventually she gets sufficiently motivated to begin again but she "feels there is an invisible barrier that keeps her from starting." This near paralysis is viewed in the larger context of questioning the meaning of her existence asking such questions as: "Who am I really? And what do I really want to do?"

Material followed of a traumatic nature that explained how it is that C has found that being natural is experienced as if it is a potential threat to her very existence. Thus she has found it nearly impossible to express the most creative part of her in a sustained authentic manner.

It became clear to me that from birth she has been imprinted with a filter of shame having nothing to do with her. She appears to have been consistently rejected, belittled, and unnourished. She has internalized this as "never good enough" whether she is in a state of being or doing. She longs to be "straight forward, easy, with no embarrassment" but feels constricted and restricted.

She can't shake the impossible standard for herself that she is either perfect or imperfect, all or nothing. And since she can never be good enough she believes herself to be a quintessential failure.

She is increasingly more aware that in order to preserve whatever cohesive self she has been able to muster she has to keep her natural self in hiding. Thus it is clearer to both of us that what she originally experienced as being originally isolated was later defended against by herself, self-imposing isolation in the form of compartmentalizing the best part of her. In other words the multiple splits in herself that she has for most of her conscious life believed were a just-so story (her existential fate) are now understood to be an unconscious defensive measure to protect herself from feeling totally worthless. In effect she has an allergy to her natural self. This explains why she is forever frustrated from making a connection with her creative process—that part of her which is most unique and original.

The Current Context

Beginning to realize that she is her own worst enemy, C has dared to take risks extending her boundaries. At this time—precoincidence—C has once again taken a course in creative writing and has been dutifully struggling to complete all of her assignments. She has found the most current assignment very difficult to master but she was able to turn in something she was uncharacteristically proud of.

Thus C was shocked to receive what she initially believed to be a total rejection by her teacher, who she has esteemed as "the best teacher I have ever had." What shocked her was not the comments she felt were negative, but the fact that she had thought she had done so well only to be told that she missed the mark. This totally unexpected event reinforced her extreme belief that no one could be trusted—including herself.

C's immediate reaction was to plummet. C experienced an automatic psychic meltdown—her self-esteem short-circuiting, totally spinning out of control. This was not a new experience for her. But in the midst of this traumatic repetition of certain psychological disaster something happened that was completely new.

As she was falling apart, C, vividly aware of what was happening, surprisingly found a way to intervene in such a way that she was able to put a brake on her fall. Putting this painful occurrence into perspective (testing reality) enabled C to reverse the spin, calm herself down, thus preventing herself from having a "nervous breakdown." This intervention was a unique major event for her—a true therapeutic breakthrough.

After calming down—and rereading the instructor's e-mail—C was shocked once again as it turned out that she misinterpreted his remarks. While there was a certain degree of criticism, in the main, her instructor's comments were quite laudatory and encouraging. C was amazed she could have so distorted what she had initially read as crushingly negative. It was in this context that two weeks later C experienced another "major" synchronicity.

A Major Coincidence: "The Short Story/Friend Coincidence" 05/22/03

C tells me that at the beginning of her treatment she surfed the Internet looking for sites that would enable her to figure out her diagnosis. She indicated that her therapist (me) kept putting her off with statements like "you are suffering from acute confusion." She never indicated at the time that she preferred a more precise label such as "schizoid personality disorder."

As she was surfing she came across a paper on women, abuse, and trauma written by a friend of hers in college who had apparently become a psychotherapist. C sent her an e-mail to which J sent back no response.

That was ten years ago. Now ten years later C coincidentally ran across her friend's name once again on the Internet. The occasion this time was in conjunction with C turning in a writing assignment on a long-distance writing course. C came upon J's name in the capacity of a writing instructor. Again C sent an e-mail to J to no avail.

This time, C wrote to J again indicating she was "befuddled" by her lack of response. Pressing the point, C said that they had once been good friends, and therefore she was at a loss as to why J had not bothered to acknowledge receiving her attempts to contact her. A few days later when C turned in a story for an assignment that included J as one of the principal characters she coincidentally got an e-mail from J, who apologized for her lack of responsiveness bringing her history up to date.

C was surprised by the timing of J's response coming as it did with her having just submitted a story with her prominently mentioned in it. Her immediate reaction was to feel "dumbfounded." "She finally responded after ten years of tracking her down."

Commentary

The final coincidence of the timing of the submitted story and the long awaited e-mail was the last of a "run" of coincidences. The run began with finding J on the Internet as a psychotherapist specializing in problems with which C was intimately involved.

The second was again running across J's name as a writing instructor just as C had made a commitment to taking writing seriously. It was as if her "friend" and she had parallel lives, of a sort.

C's Experience of the Synchronicity

C compares the present and the past viewing both herself and her friend as naïve and having no worldly knowledge. She felt they were both "raised in a vacuum." She felt as if she simply reacted having no sense of a substantial self. "Everything was surface," nothing inside.

Post Synchronicity—The Following Week

During the week following this coincidence, C struggled with the fact that she couldn't quite find the "hook" to satisfy the appropriate demands of her writing instructor. She went through her predictable litany of inadequacy, pessimism, and shame. But unlike any other time I have worked with her she was determined to press on. She explained that completing this assignment felt as if her whole life is on the line. But it is a purposeful choice, not a fallback position.

C recalled a traumatic time in her life when she had felt abandoned by her mother and her husband to fend for herself and her two babies. Complicating matters was the fact that she was recovering from a painful hysterectomy. C felt overwhelmed but believed she had no choice but to rise to the occasion and take care of her children. Soon after this realization C had to climb three flights of stairs to come to the assistance of one of her children who had gotten caught in the wheels of her bicycle while playing on the front lawn and was taken to their apartment badly hurt.

C experienced this event as an impossible ordeal—a quintessential zero point. She felt entirely alone, overresponsible, in desperate need of help that was not forthcoming. This memory (a screen memory) was both a real occurrence and a symbol for countless times in her life when she felt overwhelmed but totally responsible for others. She felt then as now that her life is always between a rock and a hard place. Making matters worse has been the feeling that she can never do enough or do it right. With these burdensome feelings at the core of her foundation C valiantly struggled through her life feeling there were no other alternatives open to her.

C was able to reflect on the fact that it has been at these "forks in the road" when she has tended to implode, explode, compartmentalize, panic, become depressed, short circuit, fall apart, fragment, and the like—automatically. Now, finally, she experienced a newfound capability to remain relatively neutral accepting the fact that to master the material—successfully solve the problem of the moment—create a viable path for herself, she would have to willingly struggle with struggle to accommodate a creative solution.

After wrestling with four or five revisions of her story she finally was able to "find a hook" and experience a rare sense of well-earned pride in her accomplishment.

Commentary

Once again the naturalistic theory of synchronicities appears loud and clear in adequately explaining the conditions under which (1) meaningful coincidences arise (a major psychological impasse in which all potential "answers" seem to be mutually exclusive); (2) a point reached where the experiencer refuses to implode, meaning that it holds the frustrated aggression in neutral instead of turning it on the self and "imploding"; (3) stimulating their idiosyncratic creative process; (4) coming to new realizations about themselves which have the net effect of successfully challenging and eventually overcoming distorted "pathogenic" ideas and fantasies about oneself and the object world; (5) resulting in a revolutionary way to view oneself and one's powers that results in a notable synthesis and integration of previously split off (dissociated) attributes, powers, abilities, capacities, and the like; (6) punctuated by a synchronicity marking this notable psychological progression—and with its presence (7) a notable expansion of consciousness.

Segue—to approximately nine years later . . .

Another Major Synchronicity: "The Greek Synchronicity" 05/22/09

While reading the Poetry Daily on the Internet, C was attracted to an ad for a two-week workshop on the Greek island of Spetses. C was familiar with the work of the leader. C felt unusually excited, which was an important fact as she had felt dispirited and dull for weeks. She said to herself: "I wish I could do that—but I can't do it. But wouldn't it be great if I could. But the timing is bad. I'm in the middle of starting a new business and . . ." C then instructed herself to sleep on it. She woke up the next morning and without any hesitation signed herself up on the Internet, saying to herself, "I have to go."

C associated back to a time forty years ago when she went on her first trip to Greece. At that point in time C felt her life was stalled. She felt her poetry like herself was going nowhere. "I'm just stuck." Now back in the present she experienced herself getting excited. "Nirvana! Imagine being on a Greek island for two weeks, back to Greece after forty years, writing and talking about poetry, being with people who enjoy what I enjoy. No more online classes. I couldn't have asked for a better present and have it come to me out of the blue."

After applying for the class on Easter Sunday, she realized that her best friend S had lived on a Greek island for awhile. She called S who told her that Spetses was famous for its beautiful fir trees. When C said she was going to go to a poetry workshop in an institute, S asked her what the name of the woman was who was in charge. Upon hearing the name, S said, "I know her very well. We are like sisters. She saved my life. We are best friends, sisters at heart. She literally got me to a hospital for an emergency."

C was shocked. "Of all the places in the world I could have gone to and you know the woman who runs the place." S said: "And she will take good care of you." "You know X very well so I will have an entree. How odd that is. I choose someplace out of the blue and S knows it well. This was meant to be. All of these things are coming together."

The Situational Context

The choice was out of the blue. (A cathexis of spontaneity—C gave into an essential need and want.) "If my parents knew they would be upset. But so what? Before I would have felt guilty—now I don't care. Who is in charge of my life anyway?" [Time equals libido]. "I make my time, I choose my priorities. I have been caught in a circle. I haven't stepped out. When I die all I can say I did was be a dutiful worker—responsible—but I won't feel I made any meaningful connections." [C—free associating] "Like the past—on a trip with my friend J—it's mainly a blur. Back to Athens. The last time I was there we got caught in a coup. I didn't understand the seriousness of it. Shooting—stores closed—a real adventure—ran out of money. I had to use my wits to get a man to buy me a train ticket. From suicide to survival—the life force versus the death instinct. During that time a lot was compressed. I nearly committed suicide—then a great adventure in Greece—but then my father forced me to go home. My mother is a textbook: why bother about my psyche and my soul?"

C's Experience of the Synchronicity

How impressively far she has "traveled" in her forty years from projecting her final authority onto her parents to beginning to accept herself as her own final authority. After six decades she is finally cutting her psychological umbilical cord.

What did this experience mean to you? I asked. "I couldn't believe that after saying all day No, No, No! That I would wake up the next morning and without skipping a beat I allowed myself to sign up. I kept telling myself to be rational and responsible." You dared to defy logic? "I had the feeling that if I told my parents what I was going to do they would try to make me feel guilty for not going to Detroit to see them. But I kept saying to myself: too bad. It's my life—I'm allowed to go wherever I want to.

"I wanted to be in the workshop—I like Greece—I needed to get away—many more things were just right. The idea spoke to me. I wasn't doing something aimless." You mean it was an escape with a purpose? "I was excited." [C's excitement has been in the context of nearly six months of neutral at best.] "When I knew that S figured out where I was staying I realized this is simpatico all around." This is instinctual "tuning fork sensibility" as another patient, D, used to call it. "I hadn't read about it," said C, "it just spoke to me. I had no thought about actually going away. Here I am with no money, my family is in crisis, and I have an Internet startup to attend to."

So, C, now that you ran the "experiment," what is your conclusion? "It's the best thing I ever did in my life." My conclusion is to go with your gut . . . take chances. Spetses seems like a magnet that attracted all of her needs together. But to let the process unfold she has had to connect with and to accept herself as worthy of being herself. C has clearly turned a corner in her treatment and it has been punctuated with this Greek synchronicity.

"Greece was a moment of synthesis—everything came together. I had no expectations and everything was easy. The special moment that happened—a total surprise—I experienced a strong connection—it was all so right. It's new and strange."

Post Synchronicity—Two Weeks Later

There have been a few occasions since C has been back home that she has had to make important decisions and has done so using her instincts to good effect. She feels as if she is truly a changed person for the better. "I feel free to make choices. Maybe I will go back to Spetses next year. Maybe I will live in Spetses. When I die I don't want to say that all I did was work and be responsible. I want to feel I had great experiences. I had the feeling in Greece that one of the Gods gave me a gift . . ."

Commentary

Whether or not there are transcendent conscious forces which intervene in the lives of human beings—in this case C—it is evident, in reading the material of ten years of concentrated effort on her part, that her struggling with struggle to grow a valued self that can also take herself seriously has been clearly demonstrated with synchronicities marking her moments of significant change.

C, like D and also G, began her therapy feeling broken, devitalized at her core, hoping for a miracle cure. They each elected to take an extended trip into their inner space, choosing me to be their guide. Along the way by means of session by session in which they made meaningful connection after meaningful connection they forged solid self structures with accompanying strong egos and strong autonomous ego functions.

Clinically I believe that synchronicities mark the autonomous ego function of synthesis being highlighted and gradually plugged in, so to speak. As this occurs, the patient for the first time in their life has a clear path way to making a felt connection to their idiosyncratic creative self.

I believe the most significant difference in my attitude to synchronicities compared or contrasted with Jung is his enthrallment with the numinosity and my appreciation for the slow steady process that has to go on—at least with patients—to burst forth with the flower.

I can now finally appreciate what my psychoanalyst—Dr. R. Wittenberg—meant when he kept trying to get me to understand the following. He repeatedly said that the first bars of Beethoven's much admired Fifth Symphony that begins with the blaring sounds of *da da da daa* are not what makes that symphony the powerful force it is. It is the filigree that supplies the context from which the loud sounds make their impact felt.[10]

For me, a commentary by an extraordinary therapist in his book *Letters to Simon* captures the essence of what I am trying to convey as to the nature and importance of synchronicities. He calls such events Analytic Moments. I.H. Paul (1973) states:

> Now, occasionally—repeat, occasionally—something special happens during the process. It may, but need not, be accompanied by a change in your state of consciousness, perhaps by a reverie or deeply contemplative state of mind. In any, now you are talking "from the gut" and with feelings that are rare and different. It may be an altogether new feeling for you, or it may be a long unexperienced old feeling, but it feels rare and profound—even shaking. You may be having a new insight into yourself or into what you were talking about when it came on: but it's the sense of revelation that really counts—the sense of something deeply valid and authentic for you. It doesn't have to be so new or so startling; but it does feel rare and revelatory. It's an Analytic Experience. . . . Analytic Experiences, then, despite their relative infrequency, are events of critical importance and impact. Some therapists refer to them as Peak Experiences; I prefer Analytic because that emphasizes the fact that they are heightened experiences in Knowing. In my opinion, they are acts of acute Understanding, and therefore likely to have a profound effect. Such experiences are memorable and moving, but also traumatic. They are probably the stuff out of which basic change is and against which major defense are applied.[11]

The parallel between Paul's description of Analytic Experiences and synchronicities is strikingly similar. I would only add the following suggestion. When it comes to identifying the effects of a synchronicity, what Paul would refer to as an Analytic Experience I prefer to call a Synthetic Experience. The reason for this is that the profound experience of "knowing" that Paul associates with an Analytic Experience is additionally broadened and deepened with those patients who experience a synchronicity. The types of synchronicities I have identified in this book have marked the presence of a notable process of synthesis, integration, and expansion of consciousness accompanying their synchronicities.

For those who wish to decode your own or others' synchronicities, try the following.

On Decoding Your Own Synchronicities

It bears repeating that a person does not have to be a patient in analytic treatment for an extended amount of time to be able to benefit from the self-generated messages sent to you from your creative core. The following are some guidelines to effective decoding.

- Decoding implies a process that is for the purpose of illuminating the assumed "hidden" or embedded information. Relevant questions are: what is the nature of this information, from where is it generated, how is it best utilized once decoded. Alternative answers to these questions will obviously determine the attitude of the therapist in working with a given patient who spontaneously presents synchronicities as material for his or her sessions.
- By all means keep a journal of those experiences you feel are noteworthy for any reason. A journal is not a diary, so you may enter anything you wish at any time. It might be that months go by without a single entry. Or you might fill up half the book talking about only the last two days of your life. Make sure you date each entry.
- When a synchronicity occurs, describe it in detail and insert it into the journal material you have amassed.
- Before you consider the synchronicity, ask yourself if you can identify a problem with which you have been preoccupied that has seemed virtually impossible to resolve. If you can do so, according to my theory, your synchronicity indicates you have a preconscious solution that needs to be decoded so you can take the new path you thought would never be available to you.
- Now look at the details of your synchronicity.
- Identify the two halves of the synchronicity which will be equivalent in meaning.
- Then "free associate" to either one or the other or both halves of the synchronicity. Bear in mind that if I am correct the details of the synchronicity will have an intimate and inevitable link to what you identified as your pressing unsolvable problem.
- Keep at it as sometimes the meanings and the "message" are elusive.

A Personal Synchronicity

In my struggle to do justice to the contents of this book I had a number of timely coincidences. One of the most significant one was when I was reading over the notes I made concerning D's treatment. I noted that the date of one of his synchronicities was July 4th, which symbolized an increasing feeling of inner freedom for him. At the time I was reading these notes I was aware that I had been struggling to let myself write more spontaneously in completing this book versus my usually highly structured "safe" approach. At the moment I noted that D had felt unusually liberated reinforced by the symbolic timing, I felt deep within me a loosening which I interpreted was giving myself permission to be as spontaneous as I wished to be. It was at this time when I noted that it was, not very significantly, a few minutes after 12 midnight. But a great deal more significant to me was the fact that the date of the new dawning was July 4th, 2009.

Time to Finish

This book has truly been a labor of love. I hope I have done justice to the material. It is difficult to leave off as I literally have about three hundred or so additional pages with what I believe to be relatively fresh commentary on this challenging material. So I will choose to call it a work in progress. But before I end I must share a couple more synchronicities with you.

In Closing:

A Really Remarkable Synchronicity

The Coincidences Keep Piling Up

In an article I wrote, "The TIGER'S TALE—THE GAME OF GOLF and the GAME OF LIFE"—an article that has so far had zero readers[12]—I had a remarkable synchronicity as I was writing it.

The Context in Which My Synchronicity Was Embedded

So you understand the context in which this synchronicity occurred, a brief summary of the article above is necessary.

After Tiger Woods's superlative performance at the British Open, I was in awe about his superlative performance winning the British Open to say nothing about his overall performance in general. I have tried in my article to spell out my interpretation of his formula for success.

To this end I view his success from the perspective of a formula my psychoanalyst periodically said to me over the period of an eleven-year psychoanalysis, 3 sessions per week. His formula is time equals libido.

It is assumed that linear time does not exist in reality but is a necessary and convenient construction for aiding human beings to have some order to existence.

Libido is simply basic energy which is consciously or unconsciously directed to some end. I applied the time equals libido formula to what I believe is Tiger Woods's formula for success. No one alive appears to have more focus and determination than Tiger Woods. He is totally committed to be the very best golfer in the world. Besides having a clear-cut goal he also struggles with struggle to perfect every part of his game on a daily basis. When you add talent, plus determination and practice, it is no coincidence that he has obtained his objective and is able to sustain it.

The Synchronicity

As I was writing this article I had another one of those amazing synchronicities. Just as I was relating my analyst's formula time equals libido to understanding Tiger Woods's formula for success I heard on a National Public Radio program the following statement: "Wittenberg's device [utilized] as a diagnostic tool." Amazing? Probably not to any of you who are reading this unless you are informed that the name of my psychoanalyst was Rudolf Wittenberg.

Still stranger is the coincidence of the enormous importance of Tiger Woods's father for him—no less the importance of my psychoanalyst's (my spiritual father's) significance for me.

My Interpretation

The steps in interpreting synchronicities from a naturalistic perspective are:

Step I. Identify both halves of the synchronicity.

(A) In this case the subjective event going on in me at the time of the synchronicity was my consciously mulling over the formula time equals libido often mentioned by my analyst.

(A) The objective "external" event is the voice on the radio saying, "Wittenberg's device [utilized] as a diagnostic tool."

This event satisfies the definition of a synchronicity. The two halves are not causally related in the conventional sense of the term but they are linked together by an equivalence of meaning.

Step II. Identify the specific contexts in which the synchronicity is embedded. These contexts are (1) the current surface practical concern, (2) the current psychological issue, and (3) the historical psychological issue.

In the present case: I was aware that I had a wealth of information amassed over the forty years of my investigating the perplexities of meaningful coincidences. I was also aware of the need and desire to stop researching and share the information in a book. But the thought of actually committing myself to writing a book was daunting, that is, it stirred painful anxiety. My habitual way to cope with the intensity of the anxiety was to employ a defensive attitude of mañana. That is, I will get to it tomorrow—today I do more research.

My mind was aware that I was fudging as tomorrow stretched into another tomorrow and that tomorrow stretched into another tomorrow. In the background of my rationalization I heard the voice of my deceased analyst saying his often repeated phrase to me, "Time equals libido." Whereas the few short words sounded profound to me, I could never quite capture their significance on the level of really feeling their meanings.

I had a run of free associations. A number of questions came to mind. What was the anxiety all about that I was obviously trying to avoid? Wasn't it obvious that I would never begin to write the book if I didn't figure out what my anxiety was about and face it head on?

In the midst of mulling these questions I had a strong feeling of missing my dead analyst. I loved seeing him and being with him. I often hated the material I brought in but I loved—for the most part—dialoguing with him.

Ulysses by James Joyce came to mind with me identifying with Stephen Dedalus searching for his "spiritual" father, Bloom.[13] There was no question my analyst was my "spiritual" father. I also thought back to my real father, who was not very fatherly. He put me down all the time, undercutting my assets. "You think too much." It was only recently that I began to understand that he was competing with me and was afraid I would steal his thunder.

At the same time I realized that my analyst—my spiritual father—was forever encouraging me to take my ideas about synchronicities seriously. He offered to read my journal, but I was too frightened to show him so I never did. But I know now he would have approved.

As these and other associations came to mind I was once again aware of the three-word formula in the synchronicity: Time equals Libido. Now I began finally to realize the significance of the formula for me. There is in fact no time. Time is an illusion. There is only the energy—some of which is my own unique amount. Further I have the power to choose how much and in what direction to channel and direct my available energy. I can choose to direct it toward writing a book about my ideas and observations concerning the nature and uses of synchronicities or not. I can start one this very moment or never start it at all. The choice is strictly up to me. With that awareness crystal clear in my consciousness, I understood the meaning of my synchronicity. I need no permission from my father to begin to write my book on synchronicities. And although I appreciated my analyst's unflagging support and encouragement to take myself and my ideas seriously, I realized that my job is for me to be my own good father and give myself permission to write my book if that is what I really want to do.

Mulling over my thoughts and feelings in this way led to the realization that I have no obligation to either please or fear displeasing various father figures. I first need to please myself and let the chips fall. I realized my libido was itching to start my book. The time was now. . . .

I heard the message that was frequently delivered from my psychoanalyst. But I had the final responsibility to understand what the words meant for me.

Step III. If my theory was right, then the synchronicity indicated that I had already found an adequate creative solution to free me from my blockage. In this case the solution was to simply assume the responsibility of making a clear choice to either write or not to write the fantasized book on synchronicities and stop the infernal obsessing.

Step IV. If it is accurate that a synchronicity is a marker of significant psychological change, then concrete evidence of that fact should be obvious in relatively short order. In my case, I heard the suggestion of my wife that I should seriously consider writing the book I had for years talked about but never got around to starting. Within a matter of days I wrote a proposal, sent it to a number of publishers, and secured a contract to write this book in a relatively small amount of time.

I recollected that I entered my analysis a slave to linear time. I came to appreciate in the sessions that at least I could breathe free transcending space and time, allowing, if I so desired, to just be. Part of the benefits of allowing myself to have that experience enabled me to make a genuine connection with tradition—a concept I had all but completely rejected. The tradition of which I am speaking is the sense of being connected to a long line of sensitive, caring, true professionals who have dedicated their lives to helping others reconcile their internal divisions with their primary tools being the consistent delivery of straight, real, authentic, powerful therapeutic words.

Conclusions

- The key to understanding the process that leads to the production of synchronicities from a naturalistic perspective entails treating them as by-products of human beings' needing to accommodate creative solutions to seemingly intractable dilemmas.
- My approach to synchronicities only refers to the earth plane on which we live and struggle for surviving and thriving. Along every person's personal trip through life there are inevitable "forks in the road." The attitude toward these stuck points is essential for a salutary outcome. In all cases there is a problem to be resolved that is initially experienced as unsolvable. There are essentially two attitudes to the perception of

quintessential "stuckness": passive surrender or an active willingness to struggle with struggle to continue to search for an accommodating solution. The choice to struggle with struggle—no matter what—stimulates a person's idiosyncratic creative process. This process enlists a person's various streams of information: thoughts, feelings, intuitions, and bodily sensations in the service of finding relevant "clues" in a psychological scavenger hunt. Each clue is like identifying and grasping a piece of a complex, multileveled psychological jigsaw puzzle. When enough pieces (clues) are gathered together which reveal a recognizable pattern, this indicates that the problem that sparked this search is well on the way to being resolved. Much of this work in generating meaningful connections happens unconsciously—and is thought to be the province of the personal not the collective unconscious. In place of the idea of a search for revealed absolute meaning instead is the idea of realized meanings as the by-product of a person's search for meaningful connections with himself and the object world.

- Viewing the production of meaningful coincidences from the vantage point of a science of psychodynamics indicates that they are associated with significant psychological change and transformation of the self. Change begins with the experience of the experience as encountering a "fork in the road," which is experienced as psychological "gridlock." The initial attitude to the experience of quintessential stuckness is existential entrapment. If the person can be induced to struggle with struggle their proactive attitude to the perception of being hopelessly pinned will stimulate their idiosyncratic creative process. Thus static energy is converted into kinetic energy, or in other terms negative reverberation is converted into positive reverberation oscillation. If the patient persists in their attitude of struggling with struggle, the desired outcome of a creative solution to their seemingly unsolvable problem is greatly enhanced. If and when a solution is "found" it will be announced in the form of a synchronicity which—because it is in the preconscious—has to further be decoded.

Finally, bearing in mind that researching this most challenging topic continues, it is apt to conclude my current efforts quoting the Ralph Waldo Emerson poem: "Do not follow where the path may lead. Go instead where there is no path and leave a trail."[14]

Notes

Preface

1. C. G. Jung and W. Pauli, *The Interpretation of Nature and the Psyche* (New York: Pantheon, 1955).

2. C. G. Jung, "The Structure and Dynamics of the Psyche," *Collected Works*, vol. 8, trans. R. F. C. Hull (Princeton, N.J.: Princeton University Press, 1960), 159.

3. C. G. Jung, *Memories, Dreams, and Reflections*, recorded and edited by Aniela Jaffe, trans. Richard Winston and Clara Winston (New York: Vintage, 1965).

4. Jung, *Memories, Dreams*, 155.

5. H. Ellenberger, *The Discovery of the Unconscious* (New York: Basic Books, 1970), 670–3.

6. S. Freud, "Dreams and the Occult," in *Psychoanalysis and the Occult*, ed. G. Devereux (New York: International Universities Press, 1953), 94.

7. New Testament Bible, John 4:48–50.

8. D. Bair, *Jung: A Biography* (New York: Little, Brown, 2003), x.

9. T. Kuhn, *The Structure of Scientific Revolutions* (Chicago: Chicago University Press, 1996), 52–3.

10. H. Guntrip and D. Winnicott, in *Freud and Beyond*, ed. S. A. Mitchell and M. J. Black (New York: Basic Books, 1996.), 124–38.

11. Jung and Pauli, *Interpretation of Nature*, 24–29.

12. E. Jacobson, *The Self and the Object World* (New York: International Universities Press, 1964), 14.

13. G. Devereux, ed., *Psychoanalysis and the Occult* (New York: International Universities Press, 1953), 31–32.

Chapter 1

1. A. Schopenhauer, "Transcendent Speculation on the Apparent Deliberateness in the Fate of the Individual." in *The Roots of Coincidence* (New York: Vintage, 1972), 107–8.
2. M. Sadhu, *The Tarot* (London: Allen and Unwin, 1962), 2.
3. The Emerald Tablet, www.themystica.com/mystica/articles/e/emerald_tablet_the.html.
4. Jung, *Memories, Dreams*, 150.
5. A. Koestler, *The Roots of Coincidence* (New York: Vintage, 1973), 120.
6. C. G. Jung, "Synchronicity: An Acausal Connecting Principle," in Jung and Pauli, *Interpretation of Nature*, 143.
7. Jung, "Synchronicity: An Acausal Connecting," 36.
8. Jung, "The Structure and Dynamics of the Psyche," 159.
9. Jung, "Synchronicity: An Acausal Connecting," 51.
10. Jung, "Synchronicity: An Acausal Connecting," 143.
11. I. Progoff, *Jung, Synchronicity, and Human Destiny* (New York: Julian, 1973), 108.
12. Jung, "Synchronicity: An Acausal Connecting," 118.
13. A. Bailey, *A Treatise on White Magic* (New York: Lucis, 1934), vi–vii.
14. F. Joseph, *Synchronicity and You* (Boston: Element, 1999), 180.
15. Lexicon of Jungian Terms, www.nyaap.org/index.php/id/7/subid/40.
16. C. G. Jung, *Two Essay on Analytical Psychology* (New York: Meridian, 1965), 235–40.
17. Progoff, *Jung*, 20.
18. Kuhn, *The Structure of Scientific Revolutions*, 52–53.
19. *Rashomon* (1950), www.imdb.com/title/tt0042876/.
20. Progoff, *Jung, Synchronicity*, 167.
21. Progoff, *Jung, Synchronicity*, 167.
22. Progoff, *Jung, Synchronicity*, 166.
23. R. Aziz, *C. G. Jung's Psychology of Religion and Synchronicity* (New York: State University of New York Press, 1990), 3.
24. J. S. Bolen, *The Tao of Psychology: Synchronicity and the Self* (San Francisco: Harper and Row, 1979), 80.
25. *Star Dust*, Nova Science Television Series, January 30, 2001.
26. C. I. Lewis, *Mind and the World Order* (New York: Dover, 1929), 424.

Chapter 2

1. Jung, *Memories, Dreams.*
2. Jung: *Two Essays*, 235.
3. Aziz, *C. G. Jung's Psychology*, 168.
4. Jung, "Synchronicity: An Acausal Connecting," 493.

5. A. Jaffe, *The Myth of Meaning in the Work of C. G. Jung* (Zurich: Daimon Verlag, 1983), 151.

6. Jung, "Synchronicity: An Acausal Connecting," 118.

7. Aziz, *C. G. Jung's Psychology*, 24.

8. R. D. Stolorow and George E. Atwood, *Faces in a Cloud: Subjectivity in Personality Theory* (Northvale, N.J.: Jason Aronson, 1979), 103.

9. Stolorow and Atwood, *Faces*, 107.

10. Stolorow and Atwood, *Faces*, 107.

11. C. G. Jung, "Modern Man in Search of a Soul," in *The Creative Process*, ed. B Ghiselin (New York: New American Library, 1952), 209.

12. Jung, "Modern Man," 214.

13. Stolorow and Atwood, *Faces*, 18.

14. Jaffe, *The Myth*, 119.

15. Stolorow and Atwood, *Faces*, 179.

16. Ellenberger, *The Discovery*, 680.

17. Jung, *Memories, Dreams.*

18. Jung, *Memories, Dreams*, 72.

19. Ellenberger, *The Discovery*, 680.

20. Jung, *Memories, Dreams*, 63.

21. Jung, *Memories, Dreams*, 168.

22. Jung, *Memories, Dreams*, 100.

23. Jung, *Memories, Dreams*, 100.

24. Ellenberger, *The Discovery*, 687.

25. Ellenberger, *The Discovery*, 688.

26. Ellenberger, *The Discovery*, 689.

27. Ellenberger, *The Discovery*, 697.

28. Jung, *Memories, Dreams*, 115

29. Jung, *Memories, Dreams*, 117.

30. Jung, *Memories, Dreams*, 119.

31. Ellenberger, *The Discovery*, 695.

32. Stolorow and Atwood, *Faces*, 87.

33. Jung, *Memories, Dreams*, 149.

34. Jung, *Memories, Dreams*, 149.

35. Jung, *Memories, Dreams*, 149.

36. Jung, *Memories, Dreams*, 149.

37. Jung, *Memories, Dreams*, 155.

38. Jung, *Memories, Dreams*, 158–69.

39. Jung, *Memories, Dreams*, 362.

40. Freud, in Jung, *Memories, Dreams*, 363.

41. Freud, in Jung, *Memories, Dreams*, 362.

42. Freud, in Jung, *Memories, Dreams*, 363.

43. Freud, in Jung, *Memories, Dreams*, 363.

44. Freud, in Jung, *Memories, Dreams*, 361.

45. Freud, in Jung, *Memories, Dreams*, 150.

46. Freud, in Jung, *Memories, Dreams*, 150.
47. Jung, *Memories, Dreams*, 364.
48. S. Freud, *Letters of Sigmund Freud 1873–1939*, ed. Ernst L. Freud, trans. Tania Stern and James Stern (London: Hogarth, 1961), 364.
49. Freud, *Letters*, 339–40.
50. Freud, *Letters*.
51. Jung, *Memories, Dreams*, 163.
52. Jung, *Memories, Dreams*, 165.
53. Jung, *Memories, Dreams*, 168.
54. Jaffe, *The Myth*, 153.
55. Ellenberger, *The Discovery*, 170.
56. Jung, *Memories, Dreams*, 170.
57. Jung, *Memories, Dreams*, 178.
58. Ellenberger, *The Discovery*, 447–8.
59. Jung, *Memories, Dreams*, 347.
60. Jung, *Memories, Dreams*, 184.
61. Jung, *Memories, Dreams*, 183.
62. Jung, *Memories, Dreams*, 184.
63. Jung, *Memories, Dreams*, 190.
64. Jung, *Memories, Dreams*, 191.
65. Jung, *Memories, Dreams*, 188.
66. Jung, *Memories, Dreams*, 311.
67. C. G. Jung, "On Synchronicity," *Collected Works* (London: Routledge and Kegan Paul, 1965), vol. 8, par. 982, 525–6.
68. Jung, Synchronicity, 33.
69. Jung and Pauli, *Interpretation of Nature*, 33.
70. C. G. Jung, "On the Nature of the Psyche," *Collected Works*, vol. 8, par. 405, 205–6.
71. Aziz, *C. G. Jung's Psychology*, 80.
72. J. W. Jones, *Contemporary Psychoanalysis* (Binghamton, N.Y.: Vail-Ballou, 1991), 115.
73. Aziz, *C. G. Jung's Psychology*, 84.
74. C. G. Jung, "Mysterium Coniunctionis," *Collected Works*, vol. 14. par.745, 524.
75. Jung, "On Synchronicity," 525–6.
76. Dierdre Bair, personal communication.
77. Freud, "Dreams and the Occult," 93.
78. E. Fromm, *Escape from Freedom* (New York: Holt, Oral Book Edition, 1994).
79. S. Freud, "Psychoanalysis and Telepathy," in Devereux, *Psychoanalysis and the Occult*, 59.
80. R. D. Laing, "The Range," http://thinkexist.com/quotation/the_range_of_what_we_think_and_do_is_limited by/223818.html.

Chapter 3

1. Jung and Pauli, *Interpretation of Nature*, 44.
2. G. Johnson, *Fire in the Mind* (New York: Vintage, 1996), 288.

3. Freud, "Dreams and the Occult," 94.
4. Freud, "Dreams and the Occult," 93.
5. A. Kaplan, *The New World of Philosophy* (New York: Vintage, 1963), 15.
6. Kaplan, *The New World,* 19.
7. Kaplan, *The New World,* 19.
8. Kaplan, *The New World,* 20.
9. S. Freud, "The Uncanny" (1919), http://people.emich.edu/acoykenda/uncanny1.htm.
10. Devereux, *Psychoanalysis and the Occult,* 25.
11. H. Deutsch, "Occult Processes Occurring during Psychoanalysis," in Devereux, *Psychoanalysis and the Occult,* 134.
12. Deutsch, "Occult Processes," 134.
13. R. Greenson, *The Technique and Practice of Psychoanalysis* (New York: International Universities Press, 2000), 3–6.
14. Greenson, *The Technique,* 23.
15. Greenson, *The Technique,* 2.
16. Greenson, *The Technique,* 2.
17. Greenson, *The Technique,* 2.
18. Greenson, *The Technique,* 2.
19. C. G. Jung, "Psychology and Literature," in *The Creative Process* (New York: New American Library, 1952), 219.
20. Stolorow and Atwood, *Faces,* 179.
21. Jung, *Memories, Dreams,* 8.
22. Jung, *Memories, Dreams,* 52.
23. Stolorow and Atwood, *Faces,* 93.
24. Stolorow and Atwood, *Faces,* 101.
25. Stolorow and Atwood, *Faces,* 106.
26. Stolorow and Atwood, *Faces,* 107.
27. Stolorow and Atwood, *Faces,* 106.
28. Jung, *Memories, Dreams,* 194.
29. Stolorow and Atwood, *Faces,* 107.
30. E. M. Forster, *Aspects of the Novel* (New York: Harvest, 1956), 1.
31. C. G. Jung, "Synchronicity: An Acausal Connecting," 514.
32. Jung and Pauli, *Interpretation of Nature,* 43.
33. Aziz, *C. G. Jung's Psychology,* 112.
34. M. von Franz, "Meaning and Order: Concerning Meeting Points and Differences between Depth Psychology and Physics," in *Jung in Modern Perspective,* ed. R. K. Papadopoulos and G. S. Saayman (Hounslow, Middlesex: Wildwood House, 1984), 272.
35. C. I. Lewis, *The Mind and the World Order* (New York: Scribner's, 1927), 227.
36. Devereux, *Psychoanalysis and the Occult,* 21.
37. Devereux, *Psychoanalysis and the Occult,* 25.
38. Devereux, *Psychoanalysis and the Occult,* 33.
39. Johnson, *Fire in the Mind,* 314.
40. C. E. M. Joad, *Guide to Philosophy* (New York: Dover, 1957), 227.
41. Devereux, *Psychoanalysis and the Occult,* 38.
42. Devereux, *Psychoanalysis and the Occult,* 44–45.

43. Devereux, *Psychoanalysis and the Occult*, 45.
44. Devereux, *Psychoanalysis and the Occult*, 32.
45. Devereux, *Psychoanalysis and the Occult*, 394.
46. A. E. Taylor, *Elements of Metaphysics* (New York: Methuen, 1961), 182–3.
47. Taylor, *Elements*, 170.
48. Lewis, *Mind*, 24.
49. Jung, *The Interpretation of Nature*, 118.
50. Lewis, *Mind*, 231.
51. Lewis, *Mind*, 118.
52. Lewis, *Mind*, 196.
53. Lewis, *Mind*, 119.
54. Lewis, *Mind*, 119.
55. Kaplan, *The New World*, 152.
56. Rudolf Wittenberg, psychoanalyst, personal communication, 1978.
57. Jung, *The Interpretation of Nature*, 118.
58. S. Braude, *ESP and Psychokinesis* (2002), www.BrownWalker.com/books/Braude.htm, 179.
59. Braude, *ESP*, 186.
60. Braude, *ESP*, 187.
61. Braude, *ESP*, 188.
62. Braude, *ESP*, 188.
63. K. R. Rao, "On the Nature of Psi: An Examination of Some Attempts to Explain ESP and PK," in Aziz, *C. G. Jung's Psychology*, 75.
64. Rao, "On the Nature of Psi," 75.
65. Rao, "On the Nature of Psi," 75.
66. W. James, *The Principles of Psychology* (Cambridge, Mass.: Harvard University Press, 1981), 5.
67. Lewis, *Mind*, 30.
68. Lewis, *Mind*, 248.
69. P. H. Phenix, *Realms of Meaning* (New York: McGraw Hill, 1964), 5.
70. Phenix, *Realms*, 248
71. Phenix, *Realms*, 6.
72. Phenix, *Realms*, 6.
73. Phenix, *Realms*, 194.
74. Phenix, *Realms*, 211.
75. Devereux, *Psychoanalysis and the Occult*, 394.
76. Jung, *The Interpretation of Nature*, 42.
77. Progoff, *Jung, Synchronicity*, 83.
78. Jung, "On the Nature of the Psyche," 205–6.
79. Aziz, *C. G. Jung's Psychology*, 64.
80. Jung, "Synchronicity: An Acausal Connecting," 435.
81. S. Bach, "Narcissism, Continuity, and the Uncanny," *International Journal of Psychoanalysis* 56 (1975): 78.
82. Jung, "Mysterium Coniunctionis," 537–8.
83. Jung and Pauli, *Interpretation of Nature*, 82.

84. T. McFarlane, "Physics, Depth Psychology, and Beyond" (2002), www.integralscience.org/psyche-physis.html, 2.

85. McFarlane, "Physics," 6.

86. McFarlane, "Physics," 6.

87. McFarlane, "Physics," 7.

88. Jung, "Mysterium," 537.

89. McFarlane, "Physics," 8.

90. McFarlane, "Physics," 8.

91. McFarlane, "Physics," 8.

92. V. Mansfield, *Science, Synchronicity, and Soul-Making* (New York: Open Court, 1995).

93. McFarlane, "Physics," 17.

94. Aziz, *C. G. Jung's Psychology*, 188.

95. E. Whitmont, "The Magic Level of the Unconscious," *Spring* 94 (1956): 58.

Chapter 4

1. Lewis, *Mind*, 235.

2. E. Kant, in *Guide to Philosophy* (New York: Dover, 1957), 149.

3. C. G. Jung, "Modern Man in Search of a Soul," in *The Creative Process*, ed. B. Ghiselin (New York: New American Library, 1952), 218.

4. C. Wilson, *Beyond the Occult* (New York: Carroll and Graf, 1988), 216.

5. Freud, "Psychoanalysis and Telepathy," 59.

6. Freud, "Dreams and the Occult," 93.

7. Johnson, *Fire in the Mind*.

8. Lewis, *Mind*, 271.

9. Lewis, *Mind*, 230.

10. M. D. Faber, *Synchronicity: C. G. Jung, Psychoanalysis, and Religion* (New York: Praeger, 1998).

11. Faber, *Synchronicity*, 2.

12. Faber, *Synchronicity*, 33.

13. Faber, *Synchronicity*, 12.

14. R. Schafer, *Aspects of Internalizations* (New York: International Universities Press, 1968.

15. Faber, *Synchronicity*, 12.

16. Faber, *Synchronicity*, 49.

17. Faber, *Synchronicity*, 123.

18. Faber, *Synchronicity*, 30.

19. Bolby, in Faber, *Synchronicity*, 5.

20. Mahler, in Faber, *Synchronicity*, 5.

21. Bolas, in Faber, *Synchronicity*, 57.

22. Klein, in Faber, *Synchronicity*, 5.

23. Winnicott, in Faber, *Synchronicity*, 5.

24. C. G. Jung, in James Olney, *The Rhizome and the Flower* (Berkeley: University of California Press, 1980), 45–46.
25. Faber, *Synchronicity*, 63.
26. Faber, *Synchronicity*, 25.
27. Spitz, in Faber, *Synchronicity*, 27.
28. Stern, in Faber, *Synchronicity*, 27.
29. Winnicott, in Faber, *Synchronicity*, 57.
30. Winnicott, in Faber, *Synchronicity*, 59.
31. Faber, *Synchronicity*, 109.
32. Faber, *Synchronicity*, 57.
33. Faber, *Synchronicity*, 37.
34. Faber, *Synchronicity*, 84.
35. Faber, *Synchronicity*, 62.
36. Faber, *Synchronicity*, 125.

Chapter 5

1. Wilson, *Beyond the Occult.*
2. R. W. Emerson, "Do Not Follow," in *The Essential Writings of Ralph Waldo Emerson* (New York: Modern Library Classics), 2000.
3. L. Van der Post, *Jung and the Story of Our Time* (New York: Vintage, 1976).
4. R. Wittenberg, personal communication.
5. Van der Post, *Jung and the Story of Our Time.*
6. S. Freud, *The Uncanny* (New York: Penguin Classics, 2003).
7. B. Honegger, personal communication.
8. J. Redfield, *The Celestine Prophecy* (New York: Warner, 1997).
9. C. Wilson, *The Outsider* (New York: Orion, 2001).
10. J. Campbell, *The Hero with a Thousand Faces* (Princeton, N.J.: Princeton University Press, 1972).
11. H. Zimmer, *The King and the Corpse: Tales of the Souls' Quest of Evil*, ed. J. Campbell (Princeton, N.J.: Princeton University Press, 1971).
12. H. Hesse and B. Creighton, *The Steppenwolf: A Novel by Herman Hesse* (New York: Picador, 2002).

Chapter 6

1. Taylor, *Elements of Metaphysics.*
2. W. Blake, "For Everything That Lives Is Holy," in *The Complete Poetry and Prose of William Blake* (New York: Anchor, 1997).
3. C. G. Jung, "Problems of Modern Psychology," in *The Basic Writings of C. G. Jung* (New York: Modern Library, 1993).
4. Sadhu, *The Tarot.*

5. Clifford Bias, personal communication.
6. Clifford Bias, personal communication.
7. S. Freud, "Psychology and Faith," in *The Future of an Illusion* (New York: Norton, 1989.)
8. Don Conte, personal communication.
9. R. B. Perry, *The Thought and Character of William James* (New York: Vanderbilt Library of American Philosophy, 1935).
10. A. Kaplan, *The New World.*
11. D. Suzuki, *Introduction to Zen Buddhism,* foreword by C. G. Jung (New York: Grove, 1994).
12. Suzuki, *Introduction to Zen.*
13. W. B. Yeats, *The Collected Poems of W. B. Yeats* (New York: Scribner's, 1996).

Chapter 7

1. W. Loewald, *Papers on Psychoanalysis* (New Haven, Conn.: Yale University Press, 1980).
2. S. Freud, "Instincts and Their Vicissitudes," in *The Freud Reader* (New York: Norton, 1985).
3. R. D. Laing, "The Range."
4. Wilson, *Beyond the Occult.*
5. H. Guntrip, *Schizoid Phenomena, Object Relations, and the Self* (New York: Basic Books, 1999).
6. P. L. Giovachinni, "The Frozen Introject," *International Journal of Psychoanalysis* 48 (1967): 61–67; and Giovachinni, "Frustration and Externalization," *Psychoanalytic Quarterly* 36 (1967): 571–83.
7. Guntrip, *Schizoid Phenomena.*
8. B. S. Pantanjali, *Aphorisms of Yoga* (London: Faber and Faber, 1938.
9. M. Nicoll, *Living Time and the Integration of Life* (London: Stuart and Watkins, 1952).
10. Pantanjali, *Aphorisms of Yoga.*
11. Frank Lachmann, personal communication.
12. D. Winnicott, in Guntrip, *Schizoid Phenomena.*
13. Guntrip, *Schizoid Phenomena.*
14. Pantanjali, *Aphorisms of Yoga.*
15. S. Arieti, *Interpretation of Schizophrenia* (New York: Basic Books, 1974).
16. B. Spinoza, *The Ethics* (New York: Hafner, 1954).
17. M. E. Jones, *Guide to Horoscope Interpretation* (New York: Quest, 1981).
18. A. Leo, *Esoteric Astrology* (New York: Destiny, 1978).
19. J. Lilly, *The Center of the Cyclone* (New York: Ronin, 2007).
20. C. Wilson, *New Pathways in Psychology* (London: Little Hampton, 1972).
21. Yeats, *Collected Poems.*
22. Giovachinni, "The Frozen Introject."

23. R. Waelder, "The Principle of Multiple Function," in *The Psychoanalytic Theory of Neurosis* (New York: Norton, 1945).

Chapter 8

1. G. A. Williams, personal communication.
2. Waelder, "The Principle of Multiple Function," *Psychoanalytic Quarterly* 5 (1936): 45–62.
3. Spinoza, *Ethics.*
4. Frank Lachmann, personal communication.
5. S. E. White, *The Unobstructed Universe* (New York: Ariel, 1988).
6. H. Greenacre, "The Family Romance of the Artist," *Psychoanalytic Study of the Child* 13 (1970): 9–36.
7. Guntrip, *Schizoid Phenomena.*
8. Bailey, *A Treatise on White Magic.*
9. A. Vaughn, *Patterns of Prophecy* (New York: Hawthorn, 1973).
10. Greenacre, "The Family Romance."
11. C. Wilson, *The Occult* (New York: Watkins, 2006).
12. W. James, "A Suggestion about Mysticism," *Journal of Philosophy, Psychology, and Scientific Methods* 7, no. 4 (1910): 85–92.
13. I. A. Paul, *Letters to Simon: On the Conduct of Psychotherapy* (New York: International Universities Press, 1973), 108–9.
14. N. Roberts, "Apocalypticism," *New York Times*, 30 March 2009, A1.
15. H. Nagera, "Children's Reaction to the Death of Important Objects," in *Psychoanalytic Study of the Child* 25 (1970): 360–401.
16. A. J. Heschel, Certain Dawn, www.certain dawn.org.
17. J. Dewey, *The Quest for Certainty* (New York: Capricorn, 1929), 312.
18. J. Piaget, *The Child's Conception of Physical Causality* (Totowa, N.J.: Littlefield, Adams, 1930).
19. Sadhu, *The Tarot.*
20. Freud, "Dreams and the Occult," 97.
21. L. Le Shan, *The Medium, the Mystic, and the Physicist: Toward a General Theory of the Paranormal* (New York: Allworth, 2003).
22. R. Wilhelm, *The I Ching*, trans. C. F. Baynes (Princeton, N.J.: Princeton University Press, 1967).
23. Wilhelm, *The I Ching.*
24. *Rashomon*, http://en.wikipedia.org/wiki/Rashomon_(film).
25. Rudolf Wittenberg, personal communication.
26. Ghiselin, *The Creative Process*, 13, 29.
27. R. A. Spitz, *The First Year of Life* (New York: New York University Press, 1965).
28. J. Joyce, *Ulysses* (New York: First Vintage International Edition, 1990).
29. Academic Press Dictionary of Science and Technology, www.gly.uga.edu/railsback/1122sciencedefns.html.

30. W. Penre, "The Great White Brotherhood," posted at Illuminati News, 8 June 2004, www.illuminati-news.com/great-white-brotherhood.htm.

31. S. Freud, "Those Wrecked by Success," Standard Edition of the Complete Works, vol. 14, 316–31.

32. J. Swift, *Gulliver's Travels*, rev. ed. (New York: Penguin Classics, 2003).

33. M. Tolpin, "The Infantile Neurosis," in *Psychoanalytic Study of the Child* 25 (1970), 273–308.

34. S. Freud, "The Schreber Case," in *Three Case Histories* (New York: Touchstone, 1996).

35. *The Prisoner* Television Series (1967), www.imdb.com/title/tt0061287/.

Chapter 9

1. Waelder, "The Principle of Multiple Function," 43–62.

2. P. Noy "A Revision of the Psychoanalytic Theory of the Primary Process," *International Journal of Psychoanalysis* 50 (1969): 155–77.

3. D. W. Winnicott "Transitional Objects and Transitional Phenomena," in *Collected Papers* (New York: Basic Books, 1958), 229–42.

4. Rudolf Wittenberg, personal communication.

5. S. Freud, "The Uncanny," Standard Edition of the Complete Works, vol. 17, 191, 217–52.

6. R. Jahn, "On the Quantum Mechanics of Consciousness, with Appendix to Anomalous Phenomena," *Foundations of Physics* 16, no. 8 (1986): 721–72.

7. H. Kohut, *The Analysis of the Self* (New York: International Universities Press, 1971).

8. Spitz, *The First Year of Life*

9. E. Erickson and J. M. Erikson, *The Life Cycle Completed* (New York: Norton, 1998).

10. Freud, "The Uncanny."

11. Spitz, *The First Year of Life.*

12. M. Mahler, *The Psychological Birth of the Human Infant: Symbiosis and Individuation* (New York: Basic Books, 2000).

13. Piaget, *The Child's Conception of Physical Causality.*

14. L. Kohlberg, *Lawrence Kohlberg's Approach to Moral Education*, Critical Assessments of Contemporary Psychology (New York: Columbia University Press, 1991).

15. James, *The Principles of Psychology.*

16. Spitz, *The First Year of Life.*

17. Kohut, *The Analysis of the Self.*

18. L. Silverman, F. Lachmann, and R. Milich, *The Search for Oneness* (New York: International Universities Press, 1982).

19. G. Williams, "The Psychodynamics of Spirituality: The Higher Power and the Personal Unconscious," 1999, www.gibbsonline.com/spirit.html.

20. Rudolf Wittenberg, personal communication.

21. C. Rycroft, "Symbolism and Its Relationship to the Primary and Secondary Processes," *International Journal of Psychoanalysis* 37 (1956): 137–46.

Chapter 10

1. A. Rothenberg, *The Creative Process of Psychotherapy* (New York: Norton, 1988), 181.
2. H. W. Loewald, *Papers on Psychoanalysis* (New Haven, Conn.: Yale University Press, 1980), 416.
3. W. James, *Pragmatism* (New York: Dover, 1995).
4. Taylor, *Elements of Metaphysics.*
5. B. Honneger, *Spontaneous Waking State Psi as Interhemispheric Verbal Communication* (San Francisco: Washington Research Center, 1979).
6. Wilhelm, *The I Ching.*
7. W. Durant, *The Story of Philosophy* (New York: Washington Square, 1970).
8. *Rashomon.*
9. Winnicott, "Transitional Objects."
10. Rudolf Wittenberg, personal communication.
11. Paul, *Letters to Simon*, 108–9.
12. G. Williams, *A Tiger's Tale.*
13. Joyce, *Ulysses.*
14. R. W. Emerson, *Collected Poems and Translations* (New York: Library of America, 1994).

Bibliography

Arlow, A. E. "Psychoanalysis and Scientific Method." In *Freudian Paradigms*, ed. H. Rahman. Chicago: Nelson Hall, 1977, 345–53.

Aziz, Robert. *C. G. Jung's Psychology of Religion and Synchronicity*. New York: State University of New York Press, 1990.

Bach, S. "Narcissism, Continuity, and the Uncanny." *International Journal of Psychoanalysis* 56 (1975): 77–86.

Bailey, Alice. *A Treatise on White Magic*. New York: Lucis, 1951.

Bair, Deirdre. *Jung: A Biography*. New York: Little. Brown, 2003.

Baker, A. *Modern Physics and Anti-Physics*. Reading, Mass.: Addison Wesley, 1970.

Balint, M. "Notes on Parapsychology and Parapsychological Healing." *International Journal of Psychoanalysis* 36 (1955): 3–35.

Beloff, J. "Psi Phenomena Causal vs. Acausal Interpretations." *Journal of the Society for Psychical Research* 49 (1977): 573–82.

Bennett, J. G. *A Spiritual Psychology*. London: Hodden and Stoughton, 1964.

Bettelheim, B. *Freud and Men's Soul*. New York: Vintage, 1983.

Blanck, G., and R. Blanck. *Ego Psychology*. New York: Columbia University Press, 1974.

Bolen, Jean Shinoda. *The Tao of Psychology: Synchronicity and the Self*. New York: Harper and Row, 1979.

Braude, S. E. *ESP and Psychokinesis: A Philosophical Examination*. Parkland, Fla.: Brown Walker, 2002.

Brenner, C. "Facts, Coincidences, and the Psi Hypothesis." *International Journal of Psychoanalysis* 38, pt. 1 (1957): 6.

Brunton, P. *The Quest of the Overself*. London: Rider, 1970.

Combs, Allan, and M. Holland. *Synchronicity: Science, Myth, and the Trickster*. New York: Marlowe, 1996.

Coppolillo, H. P. "Maturational Aspects of the Transitional Phenomenon." *International Journal of Psychoanalysis* 48 (1967): 237–46.

Deutsch, H. "Occult Processes Occurring during Psychoanalysis." In Devereux, *Psychoanalysis and the Occult.*

Devereux, George, ed. *Psychoanalysis and the Occult.* New York: International Universities Press, 1953.

Dewey, J. *The Quest for Certainty.* New York: Capricorn, 1929.

Durant, W. *The Story of Philosophy.* New York: Washington Square, 1970.

Eisenbud, J. *Parapsychology and the Unconscious Date.* New York: North Atlantic, 1993.

———. "Seduction by Synchronicity." *Letter to Psychic* 49 (1997): 573–82.

Ellenberger, Henri F. *The Discovery of the Unconscious.* New York: Basic Books, 1970.

Faber, M. D. *Synchronicity: C. G. Jung, Psychoanalysis, and Religion.* New York: Praeger, 1998.

Federn, P. *Ego Psychology and the Psychosis.* London: Imago, 1953.

Fenichel, O. *The Psychoanalytic Theory of Neurosis.* New York: Norton, 1945.

Fraiberg, S. *The Magic Years: Understanding and Handling the Problems of Early Childhood.* New York: Scribner's, 1959.

Freud, S. "Determinism, Belief in Chance, and Superstition: Some Points of View" (1901). Standard Edition, vol. 6, 239–79.

———. *On Creativity and the Unconscious.* New York: Harper and Brothers, 1958.

———. Standard Edition of the Complete Works of Sigmund Freud. Various papers including: Premonitions and Chance; Psychoanalysis and Telepathy; Dreams and Telepathy; The Occult Significance of Dreams; and Telepathy. 24 vols. Ed. James Strachey et al. London: Hogarth Press and Institute of Psychoanalysis, 1953–1974.

———. "The Uncanny" (1901). Standard Edition, vol. 17, 191, 217–52.

Ghiselin, Brewster, ed. *The Creative Process.* New York: New American Library, 1952.

Giovacchini, P. "The Symbiotic Phase." In *Psychoanalysis of Character Disorders.* New York: Jacob Aronson, 1975.

Grattan-Guinness, I. "What Are Coincidences?" *Journal of the Society for Psychical Research* 49, no. 778 (1978): 949–55.

Greenson, Ralph. *The Technique and Practice of Psychoanalysis.* New York: International Universities Press, 2000.

Griffin, D. R. *Parapsychology, Philosophy, and Spirituality.* New York: State University of New York Press, 1997.

Guntrip, H. *Schizoid Phenomena, Object Relations, and the Self.* New York: Basic Books, 1999.

Hardy, A., R. Harvie, and A. Koestler. *The Challenge of Chance.* New York: Random House, 1974.

Holms, A. C. *The Facts of Psychic Science.* New Hyde Park, N.Y.: University Books, 1969.

Jacobson, Edith. *The Self and the Object World.* New York: International Universities Press, 1964.

Jaffe, Aniela. *The Myth of Meaning in the Work of C. G. Jung.* Zurich: Daimon, 1970.

James, William. *The Will to Believe.* New York: Dover, 1956.

Joad, C. E. M. *Guide to Philosophy*. New York: Dover, 1958.
———. *The Recovery of Belief*. London: Faber and Faber, 1951.
Johnson, George. *Fire in the Mind*. New York: Vintage, 1996.
Jones, James W. *Contemporary Psychoanalysis*. Binghamton, N.Y.: Vail-Ballou, 1991.
Joseph, Frank. *Synchronicity and You*. Boston: Element, 1999.
Jung, C. G. *Memories, Dreams, and Reflections*. New York: Pantheon, 1961.
———. *Modern Man in Search of a Soul*. Trans. Cary F. Baynes and W. S. Dell. New York: Harcourt, Brace and World, 1968.
———. "Mysterium Coniunctionis." In *Collected Works of C. G. Jung*, vol. 14. London: Routledge and Kegan Paul, 1965.
———. "On the Nature of the Psyche." *Collected Works*, vol. 8.
———. "The Psychological Foundations of Belief in Spirits." In Jung, *Psychology and the Occult*. New York: Routledge, 1987.
———. "Psychology and Religion West and East." In *Collected Works*, vol. 2.
———. "Synchronicity: An Acausal Connecting Principle." In Jung and Pauli, *The Interpretation of Nature and the Psyche*.
———. *Two Essays on Analytical Psychology*. New York: Meridian, 1965.
Jung, C. G., and W. Pauli. *The Interpretation of Nature and the Psyche*. New York: Pantheon, 1955.
Lachmann, F. M., and R. D. Stolorow. "Idealization and Grandiosity: Developmental Consideration and Treatment Implications." *Psychiatric Quarterly* 45, no. 4 (1976): 569–87.
Lewis, Clarence Irving. *Mind and the World-Order*. New York: Dover, 1929.
Kaplan, A. *The New World of Philosophy*. New York: Vintage, 1963.
Kaplan, L. J. *Oneness and Separateness: From Infant to Individual*. New York: Simon and Schuster, 1998.
Koestler, Arthur. *The Roots of Coincidence*. New York: Vintage, 1973.
Kohut, H. *The Analysis of the Self*. New York: International Universities Press, 1971.
Kris, E. "Art and Regression." *Academy of Sciences* 6 (1944): 236–50.
Kuhn. Thomas S. *The Structure of Scientific Revolutions*. Chicago: University of Chicago Press, 1996.
Lacan, J. "The Mirror Stage." In *Ecritis*. New York: Norton, 2007.
Loewald, Hans W. *Papers on Psychoanalysis*. New Haven, Conn.: Yale University Press, 1980.
Maslow, A. H. "Towards a Psychology of Being." New York: Von Nostrand. Cited in W. H. Blanchard, "Psychodynamic Aspects of the Peak Experience," *Psychoanalytic Review* 56, no. l (1969): 87.
May, Rollo. *The Courage to Create*. New York: Norton, 1975.
Mitchell, E. *Psychic Explorations*. Toronto: Capricorn, 1978.
Modell, A. H. *Object Love and Reality*. New York: International Universities Press, 1968.
Noy, P. "A Revision of the Psychoanalytic Theory of the Primary Process." *International Journal of Psychoanalysis* 50 (1969): 155–77.
Ogden, C. K., and Richards, I. A. *The Meaning of Meaning*. New York: Harcourt Brace and World, 1923.

Paul, I. H. *Letters to Simon: On the Conduct of Psychotherapy.* New York: International Universities Press, 1973.

Peat, F. David. *Synchronicity: The Bridge between Matter and Mind.* New York: Bantam, 1987.

Phenix, Philip H. *Realms of Meaning.* New York: McGraw Hill, 1964.

Piaget, J. *The Child's Conception of Physical Causality.* Totowa, N.J.: Littlefield, Adams, 1930.

Pierce, C. S. "Pragmatism." In *The Encyclopedia of Philosophy*, vol. 16. New York: Macmillan, 1967.

Progoff, I. *Jung, Synchronicity, and Human Destiny.* New York: Julian, 1973.

Rothenberg, Albert. *The Creative Process of Psychotherapy.* New York: Norton, 1988.

Sadhu, Mouni. *The Tarot.* London: Allen and Unwin, 1962.

Schmeidler, G. "ESP Breakthroughs: Paranormal Effects in Real Life." *Journal of the American Society for Psychical Research* 61 (1967): 306–25.

Silverman, L. H., F. M. Lachmann, and R. H. Milich. *The Search for Oneness.* New York: International Universities Press, 1982.

Solomon, J. C. "The Fixed Idea as an Internalized Transitional Object." *American Journal of Psychotherapy* 16, no. 4 (1962): 632–44.

Spitz, R. A. "Bridges: On Anticipation, Duration, and Meaning." *Journal of the American Psychoanalytic Association* 20 (1972): 721–35.

———. *The First Year of Life.* New York: New York University Press, 1965.

Steiner, R. *Esoteric Development.* New York: Anthroposophic, 1982.

Stolorow, Robert D., and George E. Atwood. *Faces in a Cloud: Subjectivity in Personality Theory.* Northvale, N.J.: Jason Aronson, 1979.

Taves, Ann. *Fits, Trances, and Visions.* Princeton, N.J.: Princeton University Press, 1999.

Taylor, A. E. *Elements of Metaphysics.* New York: University Paperbacks, 1961.

Ullman, M. "Psi and Psychiatry." In *Psychic Explorations*, ed. E. Mitchell. New York: Capricorn, 1976.

Vanover, R., ed. *Extrasensory Perception.* New York: Norton, 1945.

Vaughn, A. *Patterns of Prophecy.* New York: Hawthorn, 1973.

———. "Synchronicity, Causality, and Consciousness as Creator." In *Program and Presented Papers of the Parapsychology Association*, 22nd Annual Convention, 1979.

Von Franz, M. "Time and Synchronicity." In *The Voices of Time*, ed. J. Fraser. New York: George Braziller, 1966.

Waelder, R. "The Principle of Multiple Function: Observations on Over Determination." *Psychoanalytic Quarterly* 5 (1936): 43–62.

Whitmont, Edward. "The Magic Level of the Unconscious." *Spring* 94 (1956): 58.

Whitmont, E. C. *The Symbolic Quest.* New York: G. P. Putnam's Sons, 1969.

Williams, G. "The Psychodynamics of Meaningful Coincidences." Paper presented at the First International Paranormal Convention, Fort Collins, Colo., 1979.

———. "A Theory and Use of Meaningful Coincidences." Unpublished paper, 2000.

Wilson, C. *Beyond the Occult.* New York: Carroll and Graf, 1988.

Winnicott, D. W. "Transitional Objects and Transitional Phenomena." *Collected Papers.* New York: Basic Books, 1958.

Index

About the Author

Gibbs A. Williams, PhD, is a psychoanalyst and supervisor in private practice in New York.

Breinigsville, PA USA
28 January 2010
231535BV00002B/2/P